Talking to Strangers

A Motorcycle Journey through the 50 States &
State Capital Cities of the United States of America

NICHOLAS S GILROY

© Nicholas S Gilroy, 2013

Published by N S Gilroy

A CIP catalogue record for this book is available from the British Library.

ISBN 978-0-9575792-0-0

Cover design by Nick Gilroy
Cover photo credits: Mike Hume, York, England

Prepared and printed by:

York Publishing Services Ltd
64 Hallfield Road
Layerthorpe
York YO31 7ZQ

Tel: 01904 431213

Website: www.yps-publishing.co.uk

This book is dedicated to the independent and unsupported traveller, adventurer and explorer.

Follow your dreams

Until one is committed, there is hesitancy, the chance to draw back, always ineffectiveness. Concerning all acts of initiative and creation, there is one elementary truth, the ignorance of which kills countless ideas and splendid plans; that the moment that one commits oneself, then Providence moves too. All sorts of things occur to help one that would never otherwise have occurred. A whole stream of events issues from the decision, raising in one's favour all manner of unforeseen incidents and meetings and material assistance, which no man could have dreamed would have come his way.

Whatever you can do,
Or dream you can, begin it.
Boldness has genius,
Power and magic in it.

"Talking to Strangers" – The big picture

Original planning map with pins in state capitals and optimised route connected by rubber bands. With selected scenic deviations, it was the route I took.

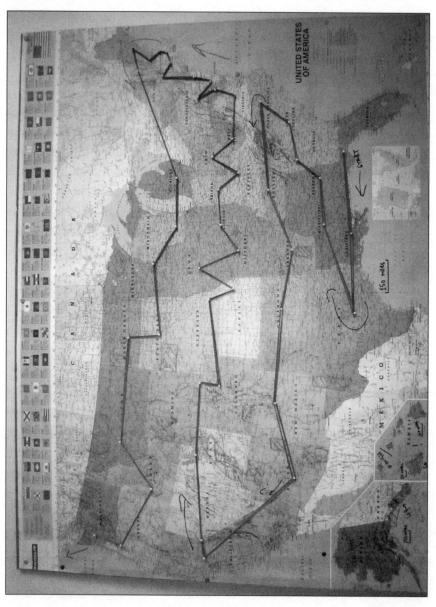

Contents

Introduction

The seeds of this journey were sown over ten years ago. I was chatting with some travelling friends. We were all over the globe in this conversation and eventually got to the USA. We compared how many states we had visited over our travels and I recall we all hit the late teens or early twenties. I remarked that an interesting journey would be to do the lot in one go. You could use the state capitals as navigational points and design a route around them. It would work. I didn't get a lot of enthusiasm from my companions. However, I never let go of the idea and immediately got hold of a large map of the USA. I placed a pin in each state capital and over the following months and years, I would connect each pin with rubber bands in an attempt to optimise the best route. The map followed me from home to home. Weather and seasons were the main factors to consider, as well as trying to make the route the simplest. Six months would be a good timeframe. It could be done. At the time of concept, I was not a biker. Now quite an experienced biker with significant international coverage, the journey just had to be done on two wheels.

Theme Talk

Following a long journey, every adventurer's objective is to produce a book. Maybe transform that rough written journal into a manuscript and then join the minefield of wannabe authors in an attempt to get your gem published. I am no different. A journal has to be done and requires much discipline at the end of each day. At the end of a long day, sometimes after several hundred miles in a variety of weather conditions, the last thing you feel like is parking yourself in front of a laptop and writing. I was advised by a well known adventure travel writer that it has to be done, so things are fresh in your mind and recollections are accurate. That turned out to be excellent advice. But the book will not stand alone as a travel log. There has to be a theme. I thought long and hard about my theme and even considered the history of the state capitals. Would this work? I was passing through them, after all. It could, but I am no historian and the time required to research each capital city would steal precious time when I should be on the road and exploring this immense country. Maybe a little history. I kept an open mind and kept rolling on, writing a few words in the evening. Then it hit me. Use a tool that I have. What am I good at? Without knowing it, I was doing this every day, sometimes several times. I was talking to strangers! I have always been told by friends and past colleagues that I can talk the hind legs off a donkey. I am never backward at coming forward. Use this personal attribute, do it! For the next 25,000 miles, I would have a captive audience. My accent alone attracts people to me. No appointments necessary, on-the-road contacts from waitresses to senators, with a lot of interesting folk in the middle. That was it; my theme is the people I have met on this diverse geographical journey. *Talking to Strangers*.

Looking at the map

The USA is a vast country covering several time zones with many climatic variations. My main research over the years involved the route. This provided the foundation or infrastructure for the journey and everything else hung on this. A six-month trip, let's say February to July, over such a huge area, required the planning to be just right. I couldn't start in the north in February. That would be no fun. I had to start in the south, but how would I progress from the south? I couldn't charge north then south. That would mean leaving the sunny south and ending up in the wintry north in short time. No, there was only one sensible option and that was to describe several east-west and west-east sectors, gradually progressing north through the country in layers, as the seasons improved. At the same time, and in order to satisfy my journey objectives, these big geographical slices had to pass through all the state capitals. All 49 of them. I shall talk about Hawaii later. Much later on! So, I divided the country into months for ease of planning and each sector was allocated a bit of the calendar. Flexibility was essential, as I soon discovered. The weather caused some delays here and there and I deviated from the main route to take in several National Parks. It sounds quite straightforward and my planning and organised mind made it so. Keep it simple is a great adage of mine. Essential during such a large project. I named each sector, which corresponds to a part of the book. The route I planned and the order of capital cities I visited, proved to be the most favourable – and is exactly how I did it.

Arrival

The selection of the bike was easy: the BMW R1200GS Adventure, which is the longer range version of my bike in the England. A bike with attitude!After a full year of planning and preparation in 2007, I decided to do the journey, as my planned route, from February to July 2008, with a contingency to run over into August. So, it was serious now; I was committed.

After several emails and telephone calls, the BMW dealers in Fort Myers Florida got my dollars. I had decided to start on a new machine. The bike would require running in, but that was all part of the process. It would have been nice to show off a GB licence plate around the 49 states of the USA, but I soon learnt that a Florida plate outside Florida generated a lot of interest.

It was February 1st 2008. The dealers were ready for me and the bike was in a central location in the showroom. My shark's mouth had already been fitted which pleased me, but most important, the GPS was all wired in and sitting there ready to go. Very soon, I discovered this would be my most useful tool. The sales manager had my route map draped over the front of the bike and quite a lot of folk were milling around awaiting my arrival. Having owned a version of this bike in England, my familiarity only required a short handover. What really surprised me in my first couple of hours in the show room, was there were a lot of doubters throwing comments my way. 'You're going to do what?' 'Do you know how big the USA is?' 'Have you really thought this through?' Even the owner chipped in and remarked, 'This is a very ambitious project.' Having spent a considerable sum of money here, I was not really appreciating these comments. Humans can be very cruel and a lot of folk go to a football match not just to see the winners. I remained positive and convinced myself that I would be a winner. It was as simple as that. Good preparation is the hard work. The doing is the easy bit. I was about to start the doing. Consequently, I shut off the barrage of unsavoury remarks, completed the paperwork, had a hamburger at the weekend BBQ function and returned to my motel. I would collect the bike in the morning after I had shrugged off the jetlag.

Running In

The dealers were empty the next morning when I collected the bike. It was Sunday after all. Returning to my motel, I fussed over the machine, walked around it several times, did a bit of low-speed car park manoeuvring and then was ready for a ride. It was just a quick run, more to familiarise myself with the roads and signage than anything else. The bike handled fine and no different from my slightly lighter version in England. The GS Adventure looks a bit broader around the shoulders and has a much larger fuel tank. That's the big advantage for this trip. Fully laden with panniers and fuel the bike is very stable, and not greatly different from the standard GS. Caution is required at low speed when a few extras of RPM on standby will save embarrassment.

I decided to ride down to Key West to do the running in and get some mileage on the bike prior to the first service. Departing Fort Myers first thing on a Monday morning was not ideal. The commuter traffic was heavy and this was my first real experience of the American motorist. It was quite alarming to say the least and drivers were more concerned about eating, drinking and using their cell phone rather than driving. I even saw one lady driver (driver? that's the wrong word) who was reading a book! What have I let myself in for? And this was day one. I did notice that the overhead traffic lights are a great advantage for the biker; you can really see well ahead and plan accordingly. So at least I had found one plus point from my early experiences on the American Highways. Once clear of Fort Myers, Bonita Springs and Naples, it was a straight run through the Everglades. The interesting bit came when joining Highway 1 south of Homestead, where the road suddenly followed narrow concrete bridges over Florida Bay and the ocean. It's called the Ocean Highway, where you really got a feel of being at sea, especially when crossing Seven Mile Bridge further south west. Many small settlements or Keys are dotted around the route, where resort cafes, marinas and air boat stations are plentiful.

Closer to Key West, I had my first experience of a large group of Harley Davidson riders. The infamous HD fraternity were thrust upon me, or rather I thrust myself upon their rather pedestrian progress. A mass of chrome and leather, they were cruising along, or rather thudding along in no rush whatsoever. They seemed a friendly bunch and threw the odd nod and wave my way. The biking fraternity around the globe mostly wave at fellow bikers and so far, it seemed to be the same over here. The HD rider wave is like nothing I have seen. They drop their arm to the side – no deviation and nothing like raising the arm as I do. Even by following my restricted run in RPM, I easily weaved through them, to be simultaneously over-flown by a formation of military jets from the local naval air station. A far more pleasing noise from the jets than the thud thud from the HDs. Should I have chosen a motorcycle that is an iconic piece of Americana to do this trip? This subject would be brought up frequently in the future.

Key West is certainly an interesting place and the most southern point of the USA. An apt location to throw a marker down for this journey. The town is centred on a grid of streets, full of art galleries, bars, clubs and restaurants. I think they call the place bohemian. Over dinner, I experienced my first good contact and networking opportunity. An elderly couple were keen to hear about my journey and thrust their son's business card in my face. 'Look him up, he is the manager of an exclusive hotel in Marlborough, Massachusetts, he will give you a good rate.' I took the card, but couldn't think that far ahead. When would I be up there? June time I think; it seemed an age away. I hadn't got to my first state capital yet.

Key West held my attraction for only one night. I was keen to have a closer look at the Ocean Highway. It is quite a unique route for a biker. It's a ribbon-like structure, curving and climbing into quite elevated sections, rather like a child's slot car track. It was an enjoyable experience with the backdrop of a clear blue sky and turquoise ocean. For a moment, a formation of pelicans joined me on my right shoulder. They held station for just a couple of seconds and then banked over towards the ocean.

I stayed in the small town of Key Largo the following night. Only about a hundred miles north of Key West and quite close to the Florida peninsula. It was whilst arriving here that I had my first experience of road rage. Slowing to turn left, a small car zoomed past on my right with all the occupants hanging out of the windows. They were kids, baseball caps on backwards and trousers half way down there backside. Those sort of people: 'You're in the wrong lane dude, this is the fast lane.' I gave them a wave and swore into my helmet. This actually turned out to be the only example of road rage that I experienced throughout my whole journey. Everything was much cheaper here in comparison with overpriced Key West. I found a delightful motel location, with accommodation in beach huts overlooking Backwater Sound. My bike attracted the attention from a group of sun seekers from Washington State in an adjoining hut. They suggested six months was more than enough time for my journey and three months would do it. I explained I wanted to see the country and not just charge through it. It wasn't a race. Further advice followed. No later than September in Alaska and watch out for wildlife in Idaho and Oregon. They were all experts on England; they had been to London once. I gleaned that they had travelled a bit in the USA and across the Atlantic once. The most vocal from the group, with quite an arrogant persona, took great pleasure in informing me that the food in Britain is awful. Apparently we even make a mess of a hamburger. He should know; he is an expert traveller with much global coverage to base such a comment! I didn't start hostilities, but simply stored this experience away. The subject would reoccur.

My brief Keys experience ended the following day as I rode the Ocean Road northbound for Homestead and back up towards Fort

Myers. Homestead was nice in the middle, but the outlying areas were not pretty. Just mile after mile of tired looking motels and fast food joints. Car parks lined with trucks, just like you see at the cinema, it reminded me of scenes from *In the Valley of Elah* I saw recently. I may be encountering some of these motels as I progress. Then it was back through the Everglades. This time I was on the waterside of the road and they were not logs or trees in the water I could see. They were alligators, hundreds of them. That's what all the people were gaping at. There was nothing stopping them venturing onto the road. Apparently that is rare as they prefer to stay in the water. Nonetheless, a gator strike with the new bike was not on my agenda. At a roadside diner, a waitress gave me a vivid account of a giant python wrestling with a 12 foot gator for several hours, before eventually swallowing it. 'It was right outside my porch, you have to be so careful, folks just throw away those snakes when they get over big to handle.' This ended in disaster for this python and it literally burst.

Further north, there was much road resurfacing in progress. They call it construction in the USA and boy would this become a common theme throughout my journey. I was intrigued to see signs saying 'State Prisoners in Work Force'. There they were, in straw hats and orange tabards over their work clothes. All smiling and waving as I passed. I like this idea, they should get Brit offenders over to help. That would be a laugh, what with the 80F temperatures and gators at their ankles – there would be a health and safety furore. So that was my brief experience of the much talked-about Key West and the impressive Ocean Road. For me, it was more important to have been to the most southern point in the USA where Cuba is only 90 miles away. I could now concentrate on starting the real journey.

It was a relief to leave Fort Myers after the first service to the bike. That should do me for 6,000 miles and get me well out to the west. I have the comfort of the roadside warranty, all I need now is an insurance policy to stay alive. A lot of that is in my hands, but the traffic northbound through Punta Gorda, Tampa, Clearwater and St Petersburg was very heavy. Stop start stop start. When there's traffic, there's traffic. When there isn't, there's a lot of sky. I had not seen much sky yet and was

7

really looking forward to the big states later on. Early days. Crossing the Sunshine Skyway Bridge near St Petersburg, I experienced my first toll. $1. I am sure I would encounter a lot of these. North of the St Petersburg-Tampa urban sprawl, I got into the countryside and less-populated areas. This part of Florida is probably the least well-known to the tourist. Probably because there's not a great deal to see. It's pretty average scenery up here. Further north, I dropped into the small town of Homosassa to say hello to Coralee and Nick who had very kindly let me register the bike at their address. That was another hurdle I had to attend to. I think that ended the formalities and I could now really concentrate on getting to my first state capital. It was the end of the day and I stayed in the small town of Crystal River. Motel prices were half here as they were further south.

The next day was clear and warm. The humidity had gone, which made for comfortable riding. As expected the bike was performing very well and I was becoming a bit more liberal with RPM and acceleration. It was a straight run through to Tallahassee the state capital.

I checked into a central motel in Tallahassee and was eager to explore. The warm sunshine, tree-lined streets and floral smells percolating around, gave a nice feel to the place. The Capitol Buildings, both old and new, were quite impressive and provided good tours. One guy in the visitors' centre heard about my journey and loaded me down with gifts. T-shirts and Florida this and that. I had to be selective what to keep considering my space available. It was the paperweight of the Great Seal of the State of Florida that caught my eye. That would be my lucky charm for the trip. Along with a copy of Jack Kerouac's 1950s novel *On the Road*, they would see every state. The visitor centre guy was a kind man, unlike the old boy wearing a Mooney aircraft baseball cap bent over a book. He just couldn't comprehend the immensity of my journey and casted much doubt on successful completion. *'How many times are you gonna cross the country?'* I dislike negative people. I limited my explanation to him, reminded him I was British and made off to explore the rest of the city. I was in a great position and the preliminaries in Florida had taken no time at all. I had allocated all of February to complete early formalities, which had only taken a few days. That included the run down to Key West, the bike service and other bits and pieces. I had not anticipated being in Tallahassee until March 1st. I was there in early February, putting me nearly a month ahead of schedule and in an excellent position to start the first geographical bit of this journey – 'The Saw Tooth Sector'.

Part One – The Saw Tooth Sector

Tallahassee-Florida to Raleigh-North Carolina

2,909 miles

The Saw Tooth Sector -
Tallahassee FL to Raleigh NC

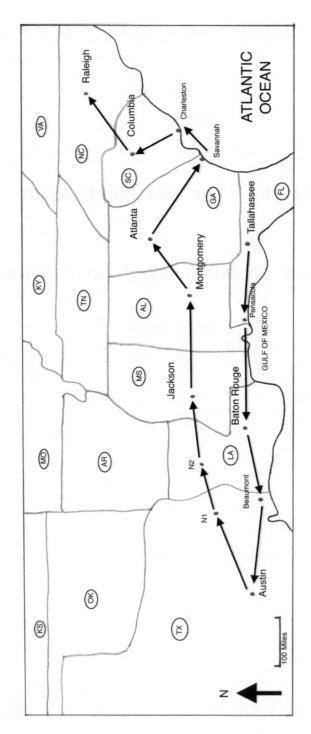

KEY:

N1 - Nacodoches
N2 - Natchitoches

(FL) Florida - complete state decode at end of book

12

DATE	START	FINISH	MILEAGE	CUMULATIVE	COMMENTS
10 Feb	Crystal River FL	**Tallahassee FL (1)**	164	992	
11 Feb	Tallahassee FL	Tallahassee FL	29	1021	Local City Ride
12 Feb	Tallahassee FL	Pensacola FL	192	1213	I-10
12 Feb	Pensacola FL	Pensacola FL	40	1253	Naval Aviation Museum at Pensacola NAS
13 Feb	Pensacola FL	**Baton Rouge LA (2)**	247	1500	I-10
15 Feb	Baton Rouge LA	Beaumont TX	190	1690	I-10
17 Feb	Beaumont TX	**Austin TX (3)**	247	1937	Interstate & USA 290
19 Feb	Austin TX	Nacogdoches TX	247	2184	USA 79 & 7
20 Feb	Nacogdoches TX	**Jackson MS (4)**	355	2539	USA 21/87/I-55
23 Feb	Jackson MS	**Montgomery AL (5)**	255	2794	I-20 & US80
24 Feb	Montgomery AL	Montgomery AL	30	2824	City & local-Day
24 Feb	Montgomery AL	Montgomery AL	8	2832	Social-Night
25 Feb	Montgomery AL	Stone Mountain GA	174	3006	Stone Mountain for **Atlanta GA (6)**
25 Feb	Stone Mountain GA	Stone Mountain GA	5	3011	Local & Fuel
29 Feb	Stone Mountain GA	Savannah GA	260	3271	I-16
29 Feb	Savannah GA	Savannah GA	19	3290	Local
February Total				**3290**	
01 Mar	Savannah GA	Savannah GA	50	3340	Toynbee Island
02 Mar	Savannah GA	Charleston SC	119	3459	I95/US17
05 Mar	Charleston SC	**Columbia SC (7)**	119	3578	I-26
05 Mar	Columbia SC	Columbia SC	35	3613	Columbia City & local
06 Mar	Columbia SC	Concord NC	112	3725	Interstate network
06 Mar	Concord NC	Concord NC	11	3736	Local recce Speedway Blvd
07 Mar	Concord NC	**Raleigh NC (8)**	165	3901	I-85/I-40/US1

Chapter 1

Florida Panhandle

As the name of this first geographical bit of my real journey suggests, it has a huge cut back on it. Heading west as far as Austin, Texas, I will then be doubling back on myself on the way up to the Carolinas. This is really the only section where I found it necessary to do this. There are a lot of states and capitals to capture in the south east of the country. The 'saw tooth' is the geographical compromise that I made. It would be beneficial later on when my sections are in relatively straight lines.

I had a considerable feeling of purpose when preparing to leave Tallahassee. I was starting the first part of the real journey. I had done the preliminaries and things were now getting serious. Other factors started to pour into my mind and it was the first time I had really considered and taken seriously the weather. So far, I had been graced with typical Florida conditions of blue sky and hot sunshine. Leaving Tallahassee, it was grey and very cool and the forecast for the next couple of days was mentioning things like torrential rain, wind and the likelihood of tornados in the gulf region. My initial and rather ambitious intentions were to go direct to Baton Rouge. A distance of 450 miles. Possible, but I was very concerned about the weather and decided to go about half way and stop at Pensacola. I just wanted to make some progress on my map and decided to take the Interstate rather than hug the coast via Panama City. It was just like a European dual carriageway, two lanes all the way and lots of commercial vehicles. It is worth pointing out that in America, a truck is a recreational vehicle used considerably by young men as their run around and to show off to the girls. It can be used as a macho thing – hey, look at my shiny truck! More serious use of this vehicle is by contract workers and similar, where it is common to see a big aluminium tool box on the back. The large stuff with sleeping unit in the cab, sometimes almost as big as an apartment, hauling freight trailers around are known as 'semis'. Slightly confusing.

In no time at all, I arrived in Pensacola and moved onto Central Time and gained an hour. I was still in Florida, which was a slight negative psychological factor. When would I eventually get out of this state? The pan handle extends considerably to the west. In Pensacola there was a gap in the weather systems and the sky was clear, although I had lost that humid and warm feel from further south. Pensacola has a significant US Navy contingent including a very impressive air museum. The majority of the guides in the museum are retired naval aviators, attired in smart khaki trousers and blue blazers. I met several, including a former Cutlass, Vigilante, F4 and Tomcat carrier pilot. He was full of carrier and flying tales and we could have talked all week. What really makes this museum unique is that amongst the World War 2 exhibits, at weekends, real actors play scenes, which injects a feel of real-time authenticity. With a bit of imagination, you could almost be at action stations! It was quite a special place. I arrived back at my motel just in time. The weather had deteriorated considerably and the sky was full of thunderstorms. Turning the TV Weather Channel on, revealed a metrological mess in the Gulf area. Outside the sky turned from grey to nearly black and it was only 4 pm. The trees were rustling and shaking in a very eerie manner and everything seemed to go quiet. It was another film set. I couldn't even hear the traffic from the nearby Interstate. Then there was a most alarming siren type noise, like a cat being strangled and at first I could not identify its origin. I quickly discovered it was a local warning and a side tone to the TV. The Weather Channel commentary reported tornado activity close to my location supported by very red-looking doppler radar images. It turned out to be a good decision to stop here. I could have been in the middle of this on the way to Baton Rouge.

The tornado passed 10 miles to the north. I was more concerned about my bike than anything else and kept a constant watch through the rain spattered window. It was a close call and for the remainder of the trip, I paid particular attention to the weather.

The following day, the chunk of bad weather had moved rapidly east and was attacking the Florida peninsula. The morning was cool and windy with much dampness still in the air. It was still a rude awakening after the tropical conditions I had experienced in south and west Florida. I choose to put my thermals on under my riding kit, wear winter gloves and put the heated hand grips on maximum. I needed to. The morning provided a bit of state hopping, crossing through the coastal stubs of Alabama and Mississippi before passing in to Louisiana. The terrain here, as expected, was very flat and marshy. I could see the ocean and fingers of land south east of New Orleans stretching out in the water. Today was another Interstate route, however. I was quickly gaining familiarity with the road infrastructure and Interstates would soon become my least popular route selection. The Biloxi tunnel provided some shelter from the icy wind which was charging in from the gulf. It was damn cold. 20 miles west of Biloxi, the clouds cleared, leaving a brilliant blue sky and warm relief from the chill.

A coffee stop in a roadside diner in Diamondhead provided some respite from the chilly morning. I parked the bike next to a couple of patrol cars and quickly entered the café. It was like one of those scenes from a movie. The place went quiet and everyone looked around and stared at me, including the four police officers. Blimey, do I have two heads or something? No, I am not from Mars folks, just over the water. We speak the same language don't we? The waitress whispered that it was my accent that probably surprised everyone. Petite and very attractive with a lovely smile, she reminded me that this was rural Mississippi and it's not very often they get strangers through here. She became focused on me, very talkative and was not seeing other customers at the counter. 'Who are you, where are you from, where are you going?' I felt a little embarrassed, but I noticed that others were listening to my travel plans through the country with interest. The waitress was absolutely astonished. I thought she was going to faint. I didn't fancy leaping over the counter and checking her pulse with my frigid hands. The police over here have shooters! It turns out that she was a single mum and worked here to make ends meet. She could not recall the last time she left the county, never mind the state of Mississippi and my juggernaut of a trip was not comprehendible. As I left, she insisted that I return one day and tell her about my adventure. Even some of the locals that had frowned over their coffee and bagels as I arrived bade me a friendly farewell. It was quite a sobering experience and confirmed to me how fortunate I was to be doing this. I soon crossed the border into Louisiana and on to Baton Rouge, my second state capital.

Chapter 2

TV Premiere in Louisiana

I didn't fancy wrestling with the Baton Rouge downtown traffic and checked into a motel close to the Interstate. America seems to be built for the traveller and groups of motels and restaurants line the roads around the cities. Obviously there are good neighbourhoods and not so good neighbourhoods. Later in my trip, I would drop all concerns of where to stay and more often than not cruise into the heart of a city. I shed my biking kit and put on some casual clothes. I was about to make a phone call and receive a phone call that would spice up my trip considerably. First it was a quick visit to the unique State Capitol Building in this southern city. It's worth mentioning French explorers here. They discovered wooden poles topped with red dye or it could even have been blood. These red-topped poles were on the original site of the city. They were marking hunting grounds for the local tribes. They provoked the name Baton Rouge – red sticks. The name survives today. Completed in 1932, the new State Capitol Building is the tallest in the USA and unlike any domed Capitol that are the norm. It's an impressive and unique art deco high-rise that dominates the Baton Rouge skyline. Panoramic views of the city and the mighty Mississippi River are seen from the cupola 450 feet up. The interior is richly decorated, with much marble and ornate adornment. It is possible to view the corridor where the controversial Governor of Louisiana, Huey Long, was assassinated in 1935.

I met English classical pianist Jack Gibbons and his American partner Mary in Kettlewell in the Yorkshire Dales in England last summer. I was on my motorcycle and had pulled over for a pub lunch. I sat down on the same table as Jack and Mary and enjoyed the Morris dancing that was in progress across the road. It was a Morris dancing contest, with many bells, sticks and fancy costumes on show. It could only be England. It was Mary's American accent that gave me the cue to introduce myself and tell them of my future trip. I soon discovered that they lived in Baton Rouge and they offered me a social invitation. That is extremely dangerous thing to do to Nick Gilroy. Any invitation received is always followed up. A surprised Mary answered the phone and I reminded her of our meeting last summer. Although we had exchanged limited communication, they had not expected my arrival so soon. But I explained that Baton Rouge was early on in my route. Needless to say we all met for an enjoyable dinner, where I was able to sample some good gumbo cuisine. The term 'gumbo' can be misused in this region. It is not a generic term for Louisiana cuisine. It is in fact a Louisiana soup or stew, reflecting the blend of rich cuisines of Indian, French, Spanish and African cultures. So it's a real mix – just like the food down here – and there is no hard and fast recipe for a gumbo. We had a gumbo for starters, followed by alligator, with a bit of lemon fish. All local, including the ale to wash it all down. Good stuff. Mary and Jack gave me a lift back to my motel and were a little concerned about the area I had chosen to stay. It seemed okay to me and my bike was still there. They were extremely surprised with the limited space I had to carry things in my bike panniers for a six-month trip. One pannier for clothes, one for laptop and documents and one for tools and bits and pieces. I had to be strict with what I carried and hence was again put in a dilemma when showered with more gifts. Where would I put everything?

The following day, I received a surprise phone call from Randy, Mary's father. Randy is the president of a local biker's chapter, which has representation across the country. He was keen to meet me and also connect me with the local media. That was fine, anything for a bit of a laugh. Following that chat, TV producer Bob called me. He sounded so laid back in his southern drawl, I thought he was going to fall off the phone. His programme wanted to do a story on me and the following morning, I met him and fellow producer, an attractive blonde called 'TW'. TW arrived in red leathers on her pearl white Harley 1800cc cruiser, complete with lots of big red lip kisses all over it. Bob was on a BMW – the camera platform. TW did the talking and gave me an informal interview as we poured over my route map. I was departing Baton Rouge that morning and the TV team followed me out of town, filming as we went. Simultaneous, I was escorted by a couple of HD riders from the local chapter. Quite a departure over the Mississippi Bridge westbound towards Texas. They filmed me for 35 miles or so west, before we made a pit stop in a local roadside visitors centre. I think we took the place by surprise making a lot of noise on arrival and parking in the wrong place. An angry-looking security guy approached and pointed to where we should park. My new American friends pacified the irate guard and when he found out I was a Brit, he was extremely embarrassed. As an apologetic gesture, he gave me a free map. Maps, I don't use maps, I'm totally electronic! The TV team headed back east to Baton Rouge and I continued west. Apparently, I made their programme the following week.

With all the extra distractions that morning, I had completely forgotten the basics. The weather forecast was again not on my side, with rain, wind and tornados heading east. I made it as far as the Texas border and stayed in Beaumont in the south east corner of this huge state. But who has heard of Beaumont, Texas other than the inhabitants? I awoke Mary Ann, the motel receptionist, from her reading. I had to speak very slowly for her to understand me. We got there in the end and in sympathy, she gave me the best discount in the world for my room. I would play on this accent thing in the future and along with the veteran charities I am supporting, it was giving great ammunition for accommodation discount. My communication dilemmas, or rather humorous events, continued that day. In a nearby diner, a waitress was stunned when she heard me speak. She had heard nothing like it before and actually pinched my arm to check if I was real.

The weather rolled in later that day. It was grey, black, wet and windy. Not realising it, I was having my first anxious moment. What have I taken on? The immense distances still to cover. I had only been on the road a week or so. I felt the first and disgustingly horrible feeling of doubt and failure in my ability to do the journey. It was too wet to get to the closest restaurant for dinner and I made do with a delivery pizza and a four pack of beer for my dinner spot. The rest of the evening I meticulously planned a rural route through the Texas countryside to get me to Austin the next day. I had heard good things about Austin and the thoughts of a vibrant state capital helped dilute the blues I was feeling right now. South East Blues.

Chapter 3

Into Texas

It rained all that night, leaving a rather damp feel to the place in the morning. Water was dripping off my bike as I prepared to leave. The motel parking lot had developed several small swimming pools. A couple of Texan businessmen sidled my way and we chewed the fat for a couple of minutes. They were both tall, dressed very smartly, including expensive-looking Stetsons. In that unmistakable and impressive Texan accent, they advised caution about using rural routes today. There was a lot of standing water and some of the roads were flooded after yesterday's storms. They suggested I take the Interstate to Houston and then cut across to Austin on the 290. I couldn't really ignore advice from locals and decided to do that. After a quick buffet breakfast, I said farewell to Mary Ann at the front desk. She was reading the same book and enthusiastically wished me safe travels. The morning sun was heating the damp surfaces quite quickly, causing a steaming effect. It was rather impressive and the sweet smell of vegetation was evident. I felt much better this morning. This journey was not going to be a physical challenge; I was fit and prepared. My bones were ready for this. It was undoubtedly going to be a mental challenge. To combat the potential spooks percolating around in my mind was essential. Essential early on as well, in order to maintain a clear mental picture with no doubts. Doubts lead to under-confidence, which could damage everything. It was to be a mind game that I had to win. After all, I was taking on the USA alone.

I recall from a past trip that the Houston skyline looked particularly impressive at night. It was even better in the bright morning sunshine against a clear blue sky. A myriad of multi-coloured reflections from the close group of glass-sided, very tall skyscrapers. I didn't get close to the downtown, just whizzed around the east and north east on the orbital. Surprisingly, I found myself weaving around to avoid potholes. Some of them looked quite deep. Potholes on an orbital motorway around one of the country's major cities! I was a little surprised. I think this was my first experience of poor road conditions. This aspect was to become a major observation of my motorcycle trip – everywhere. My last visit to the city was to watch the Houston Oilers versus the Cleveland Browns in an NFL play-off, nearly 20 years ago. Alas, the former no longer exist. What happened to the Oilers and that explosive quarterback? Time advances, memory fades.

Merely the excuse for a leg stretch and not for a lack of go forward juice, I stopped at a fuel station just off the highway at Brenham. Whilst inhaling the delightful smell of a strong coffee, I was alarmed to see a small group of bikers running towards me. There were three of them, two guys and one gal, all dressed in leathers with badges all over the place. They had seen me some miles back and without knowing it, had followed me here and were keen to have a look at my rig. My rig, not what I was wearing, the bike, the luggage, the set-up – yes, that's what they call it here. 'That's a damn fine rig you have there.' They were out for a Sunday ride; what else do bikers do on Sundays? We talked for a while and they even invited me to join them on a huge loop route they had planned that day, including a monster burger at a famous biker's grill. It was difficult to decline, as it sounded fun, but I was on my daily mission and was keen to get to Austin. They had seen few BMW bikes and certainly not my model and all of them, including the gal, spent a good ten minutes walking around, poking and prodding. 'What's this, what CC? What speed do you cruise at? Do the bags come off? Where next?' They were harmless and very friendly Harley people. I liked them. I would meet hundreds of this type over the next six months. But remarkably, I would meet very few BMW riders in this vast country.

There were no other real highlights on the rest of the way to Austin. I was in the country and the agricultural territory of eastern Texas is a barren and featureless landscape. Some trees and a lot of cattle. Some stylish-looking farms and some shabby-looking holdings with rusty tin roofs and mailboxes on crooked roadside poles. I am looking forward to the mountains. The Appalachians will be my first experience of North American hills later on in this sector. Arrival in Austin was quite challenging to say the least. It was Sunday and the traffic was still manic. My confidence was growing and this time I just went for the jugular and made for a motel in the middle of down town. It looked a nice place, hopefully there would be no security dramas being so central. I could see the dome of the State Capitol building from my room. 6th street beckons.

The Capitol Building has Italian renaissance features with a central drum tower and dome. There are few deviations from the domed Capitol Buildings throughout the country. It was a blue afternoon and the gardens and marble building looked particularly impressive. A keen breeze was flying the Stars and Stripes and the Texan state flag to their full extent. The flags were generating that distinct *thunk thunk* noise as they stretched in the strong breeze. The national flag was on top of course. However, I am sure Texans would prefer it if their state flag was flying on top. General chit-chat here reveals that there should be the Republic of Texas and then the USA. A bit of banter thrown in here, but I heard this so often. As I am finding so far, the interior of the Capitols are richly decorated. Austin was no exception. The lower dome has a collection of portraits of past governors. George Bush was there and hence I had the opportunity to point my finger at the then President of the USA and say, 'Good Afternoon...!' It may be interesting to share a moment with this Texan, if ever I got the chance, which is extremely unlikely. Close by were Texan battle paintings and a fine example of the Alamo attracted my attention for some time. The gardens enticed me out of the cool marble arena and a small gathering at the main gates caught my eye. A beautiful bride, or rather bride-to-be, was under close attention from her photographer. It was a pre-wedding photo shoot and after I introduced myself, my photographic participation was invited. That was a nice touch from some delightful Texans. I moved on from my Austin capital bride to the rest of the city.

Austin is known as 'the Live Music Capital of the World'. I am sure there will be strong objection to this title not just from places like Nashville, but from other places around the globe. Americans must know best as after all they have the Baseball World Series, with only home participation. So, I didn't let this title cloud my judgement and took a look at 6th street where it all happens. It was early in the season and for my visit, it wasn't all happening. Few venues had music on the go and the bars and restaurants were meagrely populated. There were more down-and-outs on the streets than well-heeled clientele soaking in the reputation of the place. However, I must revisit in the summer.

Chapter 4

Don't Mess With Texas

Aaaaaaarrrrrrrrrrrrrrrggggggggggggggghhhhhhhhhhh.

I awoke with a hell of a start, sweating and shaking. In an instant I leapt out of bed and punched the wall as if to expel the memories of my awful dream. Next door got an unrequested early wake up call. It had been an appalling nightmare. The dream happened at the end of my sleep cycle, close to dawn, and everything was so vivid. I was riding my motorcycle through the desert, but the desert was an old yellow parchment map of the USA. The edges of the map were on fire and getting closer and closer to me in the middle, until I was consumed in the flames and ashes. What was left was the poster of Uncle Sam, the one of the serious-looking elderly man. He was dressed in top hat with big stars around the rim and white shirt with big red bow tie and a blue jacket. He was pointing at me, with the caption underneath, 'Do you know how big the USA is and have you thought this through?' It was unreal and just like some of the comments I had received, it was so dramatic. I was shaken, but not disturbed. The immensity of the trip was obviously rattling around my unconscious and attacking at my weakest moments. Good, I was talking this through to myself and equipped with my confident persona, I reckoned I could think of a mental plan to combat this intrusion. Sooner rather than later would be better. Early trip nerves that during this dream had gone too far. I was going to sort this out quickly.

After the rude awakening to my day, I left Austin in quite an upbeat mood. It was an easier departure than arrival from this city that I must visit again. For 10 minutes or so I was weaving on the busy urban Interstate and then off into the countryside on routes 79 and 7. Very quickly I had the road to myself and passed again the flat and featureless agricultural land of eastern Texas. The fields were full of cattle, longhorns, Herefords etc., plus paddocks full of horses and newborn foals.

It was the same as the other day; the countryside revealed some expensive-looking ranches where horses were frolicking in neat paddocks bounded by white-railed fences. The yards of these places were full of shiny-looking vehicles. But there seemed to be more run-down properties. Wooden houses with tired-looking windows with poor-fitting blinds and drapes. Empty rocking chairs sat on wooden slatted decking. Some had abandoned trucks out front left to rust away. Some had old-looking vehicles that were obviously still in use. The traditional square shaped Chevy and Ford of the 60s and 70s; cars from well before the arrival of the modern shape of today. There was mile after mile of places like this. It was a lot to take in and my mind was working overtime, which was quite scary after my bad dream last night. It was another movie scene. What I was seeing could be twenty years ago. This could be a film set from the recent movie *No Country for Old Men*. I recall that was set in southern Texas and it was as plain as day this morning as I guided my bike through the sweeping roads.

It was not the glitzy Texas depicted in TV dramas *Dallas* and *Dynasty*. Although I saw the occasional oil donkey, this was big cattle land, broken up by the towns of Hearne, Marquez, Crocket and Centreville. These towns are equipped for the surrounding agricultural requirements. Vehicles, tractors, equipment and huge stores dominated the urban footprint. I pulled into a large fuel station in Marquez for coffee. It was busy with locals in and out for fuel and provisions. They were all dressed in jeans and checked shirts. Some were wearing Stetsons, some weren't. I got no words from the locals, just the nod of the head and a touch of the cap. They were busy with their day and I was a stranger in town. Thankfully

I regained conversation in Nacogdoches, said to be the oldest town in Texas with much Indian history. Today, Nacogdoches retains much of a historic image centred on a quaint market square. Like everywhere else, the local arterial road is cluttered with fuel stations, fast food joints and motels. I choose to stay in town for the night which put me about halfway to Jackson, Mississippi. It was only mid-afternoon and I had plenty of time to have a quick look around. Given the opportunity, a nosey in the visitors centre is always useful, which I did here. I quickly learned the local history from a couple of well-informed staff. A legend here tells the story of an old Indian Chief with twin sons Nacogdoches and Natchitoches that lived near the Sabine River. When the sons grew up, the Chief sent them on their way to make their own settlements. One went for three days towards the sunset and the other three days towards the sunrise. Nacogdoches settled three days towards the setting sun and that's where I had just arrived. Natchitoches settled three days towards the rising sun, over the border in Louisiana. The two brothers remained friendly and the road between the two similar sounding settlements was well travelled and became a recognised trade route. I would have a look at this route and sister, rather brother, town of Natchitoches tomorrow.

I engaged in conversation with the only other visitor in the centre. She was a well-built, middle-aged lady, dressed in blue jeans and a green jacket. With reading glasses perched on the end of her nose and a bundle of tourist leaflets under her arm, she looked on a mission. Interested in my travels, it turned out she was a truck driver and had spent much of her life on the road. I couldn't get a word in edgeways after this and was given a verbal machine gun account of the best routes, best diners, best truck stops, where to get a shower and even where to get a woman. Blimey! The ladies behind the desk had a giggle at her commentary. I tried to remember the highlights, especially the diners. She must know having been a truckie for over 20 years. I made a few jottings in my notebook which I had started to carry with me for such events. Sometimes invaluable information would come my way. 'Speak to the locals' is one of my mottos. Later on that afternoon, I was sitting comfortably in a patio café watching the world go by. It was next to a ladies hairdressing salon and the girls were outside having a cigarette and enjoying the warm Texan afternoon. We chatted for a while; it was my accent as usual that started things off. They thought I was Australian. Hmm, interesting. I wonder if this international misidentification would continue? The husband of one of the hairdressers was a keen biker and kept in touch with me throughout my journey from time to time.

I was recounting my dream that morning and thinking how I could successfully combat the monster that was obviously in there. Physically, I was as fit as a butcher's dog, so that was something I didn't have concerns about. But I had never experienced anything like this mental challenge and I was determined to defy it. I was just about to leave the café and return to my bike when a small delivery truck went past. It was loaded with small boxes. It struck me instantly. It suddenly occurred to me that I could use something I had seen as my mental model to extinguish any further anxieties of my long journey ahead. It was the box! How often have you heard your boss say, 'we must think outside the box', or 'how better can we do this and make more money, we must think outside the box'? I could do the opposite here. I could 'stay inside my box'. My box could be a day's plan of 200-400 miles or whatever and I would slide this box along my route as I progressed. I would maybe look ahead a week, or perhaps two weeks at the most, but certainly no more. It was pointless getting excited about months ahead. That was it; this would be my mental plan. I would stay inside this box, my box for a small segment of the journey and move it along the route. It could work and keep Uncle Sam nicely contained.

Today, I started the north east line of this 'saw tooth' sector. Almost doubling back on myself, but I will benefit from this once westbound from Raleigh. Yes, I am still in Texas. It is a big parish down here, so '*don't mess with Texas!*' I felt much better with my new mental plan and returned to my motel, looking forward to seeing twin brother Natchitoches in the morning.

Chapter 5

South East State Hopping

I was too early for the September Meat Pie Festival in the attractive town of Natchitoches. It was quite similar to the twin town I had just left. Cobbled streets in the centre, lined with neat red-brick buildings decorated with southern-style balconies and terraces. It had been a grey and cool run through eastern Texas, crossing into Louisiana once east of the Toledo Bend Reservoir. The keen wind was creating quite a chop on the surface, whilst morning fisherman, with water up to their waist, cast their lines. It was good to pass through the twin towns, both very attractive and still very quiet so early in the year. Continuing east, I had a feeling of very warm confidence. Maybe it was the injection of caffeine, or maybe a spell from Indian Natchitoches. The sweeping road was quiet with no traffic in my way. I was progressing well and had an almost bullish feeling, with fingertip contact on the bars, as I guided the bike through Louisiana. I was paying no attention to my speed, but enjoying the countryside pass by. It wasn't green – it was brown bush land, with a lot of very isolated farms and houses. Passing a new town bypass and over a large spanned bridge, I noticed the bike symbol on my GPS was in the river! Slightly amusing. Obviously this road was too new to be captured on map data. Talking of which, it is absolutely amazing that the whole of North America, in detail, apart from this bridge, is copied on a small card no larger than a postage stamp, that is inserted into my GPS and simply reads over the existing European maps. What a tool. The GPS also shows speed and I noticed a slight discrepancy of about five mph between bike speedo and GPS readout. I wasn't looking at either. A white car went in the opposite direction and glancing to my left as it passed, I noticed it was a state patrol car. White with a big blue stripe down the side and lights everywhere. Each state and even county has different coloured patrol cars over here. On a journey like this passing through so many boundaries, it was just impossible to anticipate what to look out for. There is only one answer and that is to keep to the speed limit. This morning I wasn't. I noticed I was doing 70 mph, which is over the limit. But what was the limit on this road? 50, 55 or 60? It can be confusing and full attention to road signage is required. The patrol car illuminated and did a U-turn in pursuit. He was after me! I thought I had got away with it. I pulled over and mentally prepared for the meeting with the law. My first of the journey. I would try and play it cool. The patrol car pulled in behind me, the lights dazzling to say the least. The officer was on the radio, maybe checking my plate, and by the time he got out, I had my documents ready. Dressed in a light blue uniform with a multitude of badges and attachments including a side arm, his approach was polite and then he made no confusion why I was pulled over. 'Reason for stopping you, ya doin' 70 in a 50.' He didn't examine my licences, didn't even open them, but merely visually scanned them whilst asking a few more questions. 'Is this your bike? Where are you from? Where are you goin'?' I think a Brit on a German bike with a Florida plate may have been too much for him. Although he had the look all over his face which said, 'Mr Gilroy, I would love to give you a ticket, but I wouldn't know how to do it.' When I said I was going to Juneau, Alaska – but today only as far as Jackson, Mississippi, he stepped back with a blank gaze. I could almost read his mind. He was full of more questions, but that was enough for him. He gave me a few directions, issued a 'be careful' and was off, rather in a hurry. That was decent and I guess he had bigger fish to fry, or maybe he was heading back to the station for morning coffee. Who knows.

I tempered my confidence after my brush with the law that morning and continued east. The bike was purring or rather growling through the Louisiana countryside. Crossing into Mississippi at Natchez, I stopped for a quiet lunch and then passed over the Mississippi River for the second time on this journey. I was only a hundred miles north of Baton Rouge where I had been only a couple of days ago.

I had done 300 miles already that day and was getting ready for a beer. I jumped on the Interstate at Brookhaven which would take me directly to Jackson. To amuse myself, I was comparing my route today as if flying a military fast jet. I had just experienced a big low-level section, seat of the pants stuff, following the nape of the earth. Low level complete, I had pulled up for the easy route home, as if in the terminal radar pattern under directions of air traffic control. I was on the Interstate, simply following the needles on the GPS all the way to destination. 50 miles to go. Feet up and relax and cigar on the go. 40 miles to go. Auto pilot on. 30 miles to go. Boring, but I was finding that the Interstate was unavoidable in certain places when you wanted to get somewhere directly. I'd had the fun in the countryside. 20 miles to go. Nothing much to see but truck wheels and fellow travellers cocooned in their metal containers. Some waves, some headlight flashing and of course some attractive travellers to ogle at. 10 miles to go. This is the point I would have a quick arrival brief and toggle through the GPS directions to my selected destination. Take Exit 92C, right onto I-20, exit 47A, north on I-55, exit 96B and follow High Street, right onto Greymont Street and the motel is on the corner. That should do it and another run-through at five miles to go, to try and mentally visualise it. It looked simple, but arrival into Jackson around rush hour was not the easiest, encountering freeways, underpasses and multiple flyovers. Trusting the GPS and hanging on took me directly to my first choice of motel where I could see the State Capitol Building. I was slightly alarmed that I had to speak to the receptionist through a voice grill. She was enclosed in a secured room with large glass panels. It was like an entrance to a prison. Hmm. I didn't like this one – there was no warm friendly lobby here with fruit bowl and glossy magazines, that was for sure. I moved across the road to my second choice. Here I was greeted in an extremely cool manner by a slightly disfigured lady in her mid-fifties. Her face was crooked, maybe the result of a stroke, and she walked with an awful stoop. My motorcycle or 'motor scooter' as she called it was the problem. 'I want it out of sight in your room.'

'Is there a problem?'

'You are in Jackson, Mississippi,' she hissed in her strong southern drawl. Undeterred by her less than friendly introduction, I explained my motorcycle was just too big to fit in my room. With a piercing stare, she uttered 'follow me'. It was a nice room and my bike would snugly fit under a nearby stairwell. No problems, what was all the fuss about?

Chapter 6

Everyone's Talking About Jackson

Night had fallen by the time I was ready to eat. The day's events had left me road-weary and I decided to pass on the thought of eating alone in a restaurant. A sandwich and a couple of beers would suffice and there were a couple of fuel stations with shops very close. Strolling across that way, I immediately noticed a police patrol car on the forecourt of both fuel stations. The officers were out of their cars and leaning against the entrances close by. They weren't here for a football game. Perhaps I had chosen to stay in the wrong part of town? This was confirmed when I engaged in conversation with two of the officers as I left the store with my purchases. One male, one female, they were in their thirties and dressed in a typical city dark blue police uniform, covered with metal badges, cloth badges and rows of multi-coloured medal ribbons. The lady officer, an attractive blonde, complete with deep red lipstick, had a chest or rather breast full of medal ribbons. Sergeant Lipstick started laughing at me, was it my accent, or my choice of place to stay. 'Do you like your motorcycle and is it insured? Where are you staying? Do you not read the newspapers? You are in Jackson, Mississippi. We have quite a crime rate here.' Her male colleague chastised her open humour and said she was having a laugh at my expense. 'But go careful – where you are staying is fine. If any one stops for a chat, just offer them a beer and your accent should confuse them. That's it. We're expecting some action later on, but that is normal here.'

Arriving back at the motel, the rooms near me had filled up and the majority of occupants were contract workers with trucks and huge tool boxes. I got talking to a couple and they were also aware of the crime rate in Jackson. 'We look after each other and if we hear any disturbances through the night, we will be up and at them. We carry more than tools.' I guess they were tooled up – literally! 'We shall keep a watch on your motor scooter.' That was nice of them and I retreated to my laptop and the Weather Channel.

By the time I took breakfast the next morning, the place was quiet and all the contractors had left for their day. The front desk lady with the stoop was not on duty and had been replaced by an Asian-Indian couple. Later I learnt that they were the managers. It is a trend throughout the USA that Indians manage motels, normally the mid-range or cheaper end. Sometimes, including here, they have family members working on the premises as well. So in England it's restaurants and corner shops and in the USA it's motels. Indians get everywhere, but they work damn hard. The manager insisted on giving me a ride in his limo to the Capitol Building, even though I could see it and it would have been little over a 10-minute walk. He took convincing that I was quite capable of walking back to the motel.

Jackson Mississippi turned out to be not the most vibrant place I have visited. A nice Capitol Building as normal, but as I have already found elsewhere, quite a dead city centre consisting of law courts, government buildings and offices, oh and a couple of tall, grey chain hotels. Older buildings have more character and it was nice to see that the original Greyhound bus station, complete with illuminated sprinting hound, had survived. It was now tastefully converted into a local business. The same cannot be said about the gargantuan 1923 King Edward Hotel and the Sun 'n' Surf 'Motor Hotel'. The Sun 'n' Surf must have been a forerunner to today's motel. Both appear to have been derelict for decades with much decay and detritus evident. With lunch on my mind and local knowledge needed, I asked the receptionist in the city newspaper building if there was a restaurant or diner downtown. She didn't know. I was astonished and she went for the Yellow Pages until I said don't worry, I will find somewhere. I found a sandwich bar eventually. Although with exceptions, Jackson is following a trend I have been finding. Shopping is in out-of-town malls, eating is in strips of fast food diners out of town and accommodation is in motels congregated around the road infrastructures approaching town. I suppose the latter makes sense, but some of these American towns and cities today just don't have any heart or atmosphere. Maybe when the King Edward Hotel was in its heyday and folks were staying in the Sun 'n' Surf, there was a buzz about the place. Who knows?

I made it back to the motel before the rain. Rain again and worse forecast for the evening. I think the Indian housekeeping team, brother and sister-in-law to the manager, took pity on me. They brought a curry to my room. That was appreciated and my first Asian meal since leaving England. It was delicious, although I didn't see all of it. A cataclysmic thunderstorm hit the area and a lightning strike momentarily took out the city's power. The whole city went down and came back on progressively in grid areas. It was curry by torchlight. The lightning illuminated the skyline, showing split-second images of the towers, domes and spires. The storm eventually passed and the power was eventually restored. I was looking forward to leaving Jackson.

The city had its final bite. The sky was blue the following morning, a contrast to the last couple of days in this very grey place. I was enthusiastic to leave and progress east into Alabama. Whilst preparing the bike, I had a quick circuit of the car park, only to find the wheels completely lock up. Both wheels were locked solid and refused to rotate. I was nearly thrown off, but managed to stop and make things safe. What had happened I do not know. I couldn't believe it, a new bike and I just wanted to get the hell out of here. Quickly calling an engineering contact at the original dealers did not shed any light on the problem. We scratched our heads and eventually decided it needed to be looked out by a specialist. I decided to use the BMW callout and get recovered to the nearest dealers. I had alerted the Indians of my problem and advised them I could be here longer than anticipated. They gathered around asking questions and wobbling their heads. A couple of African-American young guys were circling the car park watching the incident. They wanted a piece of the action and were trying to sell me cosmetics amongst other things. Their cars were full of merchandise if you can call it that. Simultaneously on cell phones and attempting conversation to me, they were jabbering away in a most incomprehensible drawl. My conversation their way was not polite. Baton Rouge was where I was to be recovered and I spoke to the engineering manager, Cory, who said he would stay open until I arrived. What a pain having to return to Baton Rouge and going off route. What could be the problem? Then it suddenly occurred to me – the bike had been under the stairwell for a couple of days. A lot of rain, no problem, but whilst manoeuvring out of the area this morning I may have moved the hand guard and the brake lever could be trapped. That is exactly what had happened. Moving the misplaced guard into its normal position and the brake lever became free and the wheels turned. Arrgghh! Why didn't I think of this before alerting the south east of the USA 30 minutes ago! Maybe it was too obvious to check the obvious! A quick robust road test with some aggressive braking revealed all was normal – thank God! After consultation with Cory in Baton Rouge, he agreed: I should continue and he had heard of similar incidents to this. By now the recovery truck had arrived and was making ready to hook up my bike. An explanation of the new circumstances and a few dollars pressed into the driver's oily hand for his troubles and he was on the way home. In a most incredible southern accent, he uttered that he had been looking forward to the trip south, but no problems anyway.

What a morning. I eventually left at 1 pm. I should have been tucking into lunch in Montgomery, Alabama by now. My thoughts were spinning with the events of the last couple of days. It wasn't the city of Jackson that was exciting, it was the other occurrences – what with the dialogue with the Jackson City Police followed by my alarming chat with the contractors at the motel about city crime. Oh and the shift change between some colourful waitresses who were arguing about rate of pay in the local waffle house was quite amusing. It's a strong accent down here. As if not enough, sitting in the dark through that earth-shattering thunderstorm last night certainly concentrated my mind for a few hours. This morning's mechanical and multi-cultured incident in the motel car park capped it all. Things would get better now. There are many places in the USA called Jackson and I am unsure if the 1963 Billy Ed Wheeler and Gaby Rogers song, covered by Johnny Cash, refers to where I am. What's for sure, I shall not be talking about this Jackson.

Chapter 7

Alabama Harleys

It was a grey and cold Saturday morning. Where to stay in a state capital city was a subject I must address to avoid some of the experiences of Jackson. I had been put in touch with a Harley Chapter in Montgomery and taken the advice of one of those guys on where to stay. I was checking into a motel in Montgomery before I knew it.

I was slightly out of the city centre and required a short ride to the downtown area the next day. The place was quiet, but had a refreshing feel on a bright and cool Sunday morning. It appeared so far to be a complete contrast to Jackson. I actually parked my bike right outside the Capitol Building and was the only visitor around by the looks of it. Whilst rummaging around in my bag for a camera, a state police car went past very slowly. He was having a good look at me. I must have looked suspicious and I expected at least a challenge for identification from the officer. I waved and he waved back and went on his way. Another attractive, domed Capitol Building. Apart from the odd exception, they are all sort of the same. Some are big, some are small. Montgomery's is an impressive building with columns and a dome. What was striking in the gardens, especially considering my journey, was that the other states of the USA were represented by a stone tablet complete with state motto and state flag flying overhead. All set in a crescent, you could actually walk the states of the USA in no time at all. I did that and would remember how easy it was as I would be tramping thousands of miles over the next few months. This city, with much Confederate and slavery history, has a quaint and clean old town. Wooden period homes, red brick industrial buildings and the Union Railway Station. Alas, it was Sunday and nothing was open. I had to return to my motel to get a coffee.

I met the 7 Bridges Motorcycle Chapter for a couple of drinks later that day. This chapter is part of the Iron Warriors group which has representation throughout the USA. Membership is restricted to serving or retired police officers and fire-fighters and they must ride an American bike. That doesn't leave much choice. Owning an assortment of HDs, including a Dyno Wide Glide, a Screamin' Eagle Road King, a Fat Boy and an Ultra Classic, I met Jethro, Breeze, Rooster and Drop. They all pulled up outside my motel and made a hell of a noise. I am not into all that Harley racket and could not imagine enduring such a cacophony on my journey. In comparison, my bike is as smooth as silk. Apparently they like to be heard and comment that other road users can hear them coming. Loud pipes may save lives. Well, okay. I followed them through the busy evening traffic to a bar grill. It was quite a classy joint and probably a frequent watering hole for the group. A table was immediately prepared. Over drinks, we compared words and accents for a while which generated much humour. *'Y'all 'avin' a good time and what y'all doin?'* The southern drawl is unmistakable. I hadn't been called Australian yet which was refreshing. What was apparent from my brief encounter is that the group is a brotherhood and the members are all very close. New guys have to endure a six-month probationary period prior to acceptance. What did surprise me was that they are quite happy to drink beers and then ride with no worries. I suppose they operate with the knowledge that most US domestic beers are not strong. They were surprised with my strict bottle and throttle regime of no drinking whilst riding. They were all content to drink a beer or two and then ride away. It's all part of the culture. One guy from the group mentioned that the alcohol has no effect on riding when moving: it's when you come to a stop that a wobble could be a problem! I shall stick to the coffee thank you!

The following morning, I was escorted out of town by State Law Enforcement Officer Jethro. I am not sure if his title was a formal name for a local policeman, but I didn't care as he insisted that he bought breakfast. We ate typical Alabama breakfast food consisting of bacon, eggs, biscuits, sausage gravy, hash brown casserole, grits and fried apple, all washed down with some decent black coffee. It was quite a plateful and should do me until Atlanta. Jethro rode with me for a few miles and then turned back towards Montgomery, making an awful noise with handfuls of RPM as he left the highway.

The Harley Davidson is undoubtedly a big cultural thing over here. Their attitude to riders of other bikes is simple in that you are recognised as riding a bike. What badge it has on it doesn't matter. This must be the reason why the HD riders enthusiastically acknowledge other riders as they pass them on the highway. It was refreshing and I have had no similar hosting from BMW riders so far. I know nothing about the HD range but remain satisfied that my BMW is the bike for this journey. Also an iconic piece of Americana, I didn't really appreciate how serious the owners of these motorcycles take things. Their bike, their riding attire, their chrome, their chapter. It's a serious part of American life with more HDs than any other bike in this huge country. The HD attracts owners from all spectrums of life and I would encounter thousands of riders throughout my journey through the USA over the next few months.

Chapter 8

Under Surveillance?

It was less than a month ago that I arrived in the USA at the congested Atlanta airport. I remember looking down on the busy network of roads, looping around the area almost serpent-like. Today, I was on that road system, passing by the airport and gazing at the busy sky. It was mid-morning and road traffic was light as I weaved around Atlanta towards Stone Mountain. I had chosen to stay in an eastern suburb of the city and access public transport to get to the downtown. It was an experiment. I wasn't keeping an eye on traffic behind, more on the traffic ahead. However, I did notice one car that had been at a safe distance tailing me for some considerable time. It followed me all the way to Stone Mountain and the motel. I thought nothing of it. Later that day, that same car was right there and the occupant, a gent in his mid-thirties, had checked in a couple of rooms down. Soon he was joined by another guy and they were exchanging notes and dialogue and making lots of cell phone calls whilst occasionally looking my way. They seemed to be operating in a shift. One would always be there. This continued for much of my stay in that motel. Maybe my mind was working overtime, or I had seen too many movies, but I had a feeling I was under surveillance. Could that be so? But why me, I have a credible background. But on the other side of the coin, the American security system these days is pretty sensitive and I was doing something I suppose some would consider quite strange. A

next door burst out laughing and said, 'No, no. Over here we pronounce that Rejeana to avoid any confusion with the word that rhymes with your pronunciation! Oh and by the way, with that accent you are not from these parts.' I quickly got in that I was not from Australia. My company at the bar was Jim Trovato, a businessman in the furniture world. A trade meeting had brought him to the Atlanta area. We talked for sometime on the usual subjects, including sport, religion and politics. When he got the urge, he would take a trip outside for a cigarette, returning to announce it was still very cold out there. 'Yes, Jim, its been brass monkey weather today. Look that one up on Google.' It was my first serious conversation about USA politics and Jim welcomed my view on the election campaign and the forthcoming Democrat and Republican contest. My views and knowledge on this subject would mature considerably. What else was on TV at the moment? It was also my first experience of American hospitality and Jim extended an invitation for me to his home, but I had to make a specific date. His partner, also in the furniture world, was shortly embarking on a business trip to China and Jim suggested I made it before then. He lived in Greensborough near Raleigh, North Carolina. It was on my route, however, I had to take in the coast and Columbia, South Carolina first. I now had more urgency to leave Stone Mountain and Georgia. Jim's urgency to leave the restaurant precluded him from paying his bill.

Chapter 9

Coastal Diversion

It was much milder the next day and the forecast was to be warmer down on the coast. I left early and well before my surveillance friend or friends had arisen. It was good to be back on the road. I was quickly clear of the Atlanta urban sprawl and heading south east towards Savannah. With plenty of time on my side, it was almost essential to have a look at the historic towns of Savannah and Charleston. They are very close together, allowing easy access, before picking up on my original track for Columbia and Raleigh. The route south east was through heavily wooded areas and quite a bit of swamp. There was almost a feeling of holiday and festival as I arrived in Savannah. It was already very warm and T-shirt weather. A big difference to trudging around Atlanta a couple of days ago when I was shivering with every breath. The place was so busy, with traffic here, there and everywhere. Shoppers, weekenders, business folk, tour buses, horse and traps, you name it. It was a different world. I couldn't seem to get away from aviation in this country and again I had noise from the air. Staying in the southern part of the city, I didn't realise I was on the flight path to Hunter Field. I could almost reach up and touch the airliners and military aircraft as they passed by on final approach.

The southern hospitality so widely publicised about this place met its reputation. Hip, historic, robust and refined. Quite an interesting place with impressive architecture, spooky cemeteries and deep history to explore. Savannah confidently boasts that it is the south's most beautiful historic city. Established in 1733, it was the first colonial and state capital of Georgia. Millions of visitors are attracted each year to crawl over the historic district and enjoy the fine architecture. I rode around the place for a few hours, experienced the many cobbled streets whilst dodging the tourist tram cars and horse and buggies.

A group of HDs attracted my attention in the historic district. I wonder what chapter they were from? They looked awkward about where they had all parked and sure enough an alert local soon asked them to move along – but only a couple of metres where bikes should park. They were all Brits touring portions of the southern states. They had shipped their bikes over and the large lettered GB license plates stood out and looked out of place. After only a short time, I had become accustomed to the USA small licence plate. We chatted for a few minutes and exchanged road tales. They were heading back to Florida tomorrow and were all concerned about the weather. This subject seemed to crop up most days. I confirmed for them that Florida was under assault from some heavy stuff and checking the daily forecast would be advisable.

Over dinner in a local Italian restaurant, I met Mark Jones and his wife. We chatted across the bar and took in the scene around the heavily populated dining room. Also a traveller, but more work-orientated, Mark was interested in my journey. I related to them my Jackson experience and that I had probably stayed in the wrong part of town. We had a good laugh about it, but then my new friends took it upon themselves to find out from their network of contacts the best places to stay in the cities I would next be hitting. Their connections extended through Columbia, Raleigh, Nashville, Little Rock, Oklahoma City and Santa Fe. They promised me emails of advice where to stay and even suggested I could ring the city police and ask for advice. Interesting, I never thought of that.

Located 18 miles east of Savannah is Tybee Island. I had a ride down the following day for breakfast. It was quiet and there was no sign of sun, surf and fun, befitting the motto of Savannah's beach resort. Heavily tanned from years in the sun, the lady in the visitor centre suggested a quick ride around would be enough to give me a feel for the place. The lighthouse dating from 1733 was worth a deviation from the town centre, oh and the new beachfront luxury condominiums I am sure would attract the high-dollar earners from the city. It was while looking at the condos from an empty beach view car park that I had to do some quick talking to avoid a ticket penalty. The ticket guy, an old boy and local resident, eventually relented and made off looking for alternative trade. 'I'll let you off because you are a biker.' That was nice of him.

Like anywhere really, it's only when you sit down and have a good look around that you can get a good feel for a place. I choose to do this over brunch. Brunch was okay. The town, well, it was okay too I suppose, but the rubbish bins were overflowing on the street and already the bars were full. It wasn't much past noon. It took the edge off this pretty little place and maybe it was just too laid back for my liking. Whilst talking to the tourist office lady, I did learn a bit of recent history that could have taken the edge off Tybee Island itself. It goes back to 1958 when a B47 bomber carrying a hydrogen bomb on a night exercise collided with an F86 fighter plane. The pilot ejected from the stricken F86 and the B47 was left damaged and barely able to maintain flying speed. In order for the B47 to become lighter and more controllable, permission was granted for the bomber to jettison the hydrogen bomb and down it went into the water close to Tybee. The B47 made an emergency landing back at Hunter Field, very close to my residence in Savannah. The bomb has never been found and is still lurking in the depths of water and mud somewhere out there. I wonder if this little gem of an incident was hushed up at the time?

Later that day, I gave Savannah my critical eye. It has a most delightful downtown and historic district, even equipped with a public transport system. Not to mention a variety of tourist carriages available. The parks were green and the azaleas were out and it was very warm. But even so early in the year, the town was busy and commercialism was growing, even though the quaint historic image is trying to be maintained. A waitress in a tea shop remarked that in the summer months, the masses of visitors and the excessive humidity make the place almost unbearable. I wonder what Oglethorpe, the British General and founder of Georgia, would think as Savannah creaks with these visiting hoards during the summer months. In fairness, you could spend a week in this place quite easily. I had a couple of days before heading up the coast to have a compare and contrast with Charleston.

Leaving Savannah was the same as arrival. Wall to wall traffic. Surprising considering it was a Sunday. However, after a quick ride north on I-95, highway 17 took me through the pretty coastal plain into South Carolina and onwards to Charleston. This route was flat all the way, but nonetheless quite interesting. There was almost a touch of the Everglades, with curving lagoons interspersed with many swamps and old trees bent over touching the water. I wonder if anything slippery and slimy was lurking down there in the depths and hidden vegetation. Maybe a cottonmouth looking for breakfast on this warm morning, or even a discarded python. It doesn't bear thinking about; I am happy on the road thank you. It was only a short hop up to Charleston and very soon I was crossing the impressive Ravenel Bridge that led onto Johnnie Dodds Boulevard and my motel. The bridge was one of those double span and multi-lane constructions with walkways across. It must have been some engineering feat to build this monster of a bridge spanning the wide Cooper River and Charleston Harbour. The water looked a long, long way below. Sunday morning joggers were out and about on the enclosed bridge sidewalk and there appeared to be more humans than vehicles for a short time. That was nice as it gave a better opportunity to take in the impressive Charleston Harbour over my right shoulder. I choose one of my 'usual suspect' chain motels and was having a great time negotiating a good rate with the amusing front desk lady. It was only midday and whilst my room was being prepared, I took lunch in the adjoining diner. It was here I met Noal Sharp.

Noal Sharp was a no-nonsense man in his early sixties with a bush of steel-grey hair and matching beard. Thickset, with a very firm handshake, I learnt that Noal was a former truck driver of some forty years experience. He was envious of my trip and still yearns for the road.

'I used to drive Kenworth and Freightliner trucks with powerful Caterpillar engines. We would do vast distances in the days before strict regulation of driver hours. Leaving the east coast with a full load,

I could be dispatching in LA within three days at a push. It was quite normal. Other than live cattle, I have hauled everything over the years, including aircraft and automobile parts, jet fuel, dump trucks, mobile homes, you name it! The trucks were good and food and fuel were cheap. Consumables are expensive today and a truck driver is just not used to paying $35 dollars for a decent lunch and what with a $4 dollar gallon of fuel on the way! That said, I do miss it. We were special road users and stuck together. Today there is no camaraderie and it's a new set of folks at the wheel.'

I related to Noal my impressions of the truck driver I have encountered during my 3,500 miles so far.

'I prefer not to take the Interstates, but when I do, the turbulence caused by the large trucks just makes you want to get past them quickly. Some of the truck drivers wave, some don't. Some stick rigidly to the speed limit, some don't. My main concern is the number of drivers I see using their cell phones and eating and drinking. Sometimes all three at once! I guess they think they are kings of the road and look out all. When passing a truck, sometimes I gaze up at the cab. I normally get a friendly wave or nod, but sometimes a look of disapproval. Accelerating past a large semi the other day, I got a surprise when at first I didn't see a driver. A second take revealed a petite young lady, complete with a lovely smile and ponytail bobbing along as she grasped the wheel, guiding the multi-axled behemoth along at a thunderous pace. She looked content in her job and maybe in a rush to get to Savannah and the weekend.'

Illness forced Noal to leave the cab and along with his wife Lisa, they own a couple of diners here in South Carolina.

'So Noal, this must be quite a change and less stressful in comparison to doing all those miles across the continent?'

'Hell no, this restaurant life is far more stressful. Look around and see all these waitresses we have to keep in line. They bring all their problems to work and give them to their Poppy to solve. Yer, that's what they call me, Poppy Huh. Give me the road any day!'

Noal was still very sharp.

Very much with a US Navy heritage, formerly Charles Towne and now Charleston, the place is full of superlatives like Savannah. 'Everything you have heard is true' and 'Where history lives' to give a couple of examples I remembered. The city has a low-rise cityscape and the prominence of many church spires is very evident. It was known as the Holy City because of the numerous churches that dot the skyline. On first view, it was very similar to Savannah. On the coast, a busy approach and a compact historic district. But there was a warmer feeling to Charleston. Although there were plenty of tourist carriages about and tours in progress, there did seem to be fewer people. The place was less cluttered and navigation on foot around the grid of streets in the historic district was a breeze. It was the large colonial style houses on Battery and Bay Streets that caught my attention. Whites, blues, pinks, columns, shutters, large small, quite a collection. Landscaped gardens lined with palm trees; this was millionaires' walk without a question. Chatting to a painter who was giving the exterior of one of these delightful homes close attention, I found out that most are holiday homes and that they very rarely come on the market for sale. I must work harder. Just in from this fine collection of homes, elegant bed and breakfast and restaurants are tucked into the neat surroundings and cobbled streets. To set the scene, a movie shoot of a civil war drill squad was taking place overlooking the harbour. My motorcycle would have been out of place here and I am glad I was on foot. Whilst contemplating the surroundings over a sandwich in the Noisy Shrimp, I think that Charleston just got my vote after my quick coastal diversion. Others may disagree and prefer the busier Savannah, but this morning I drifted into many historical thoughts here in South Carolina.

Chapter 10

Speedway Boulevard

I was back on to my original route and a quick ride up to Columbia, the capital city of South Carolina, was next. I passed the small towns of Harleyville and Orangeburg. Although surrounded by pretty countryside, the only thing I found exciting in Columbia was some sort of demonstration taking place outside the Capitol Building. I think it was by a disabled group demonstrating about financial benefits or something similar. The Capitol Buildings seem to be the place to have your demonstrations and they were making a lot of noise. Heywood Stuckley gave me a personal tour and commented on the history of the Italian renaissance styled Capitol building. Columbia is a purpose-built capital city: the street pattern is on a grid system for ease of navigation, it is central to the state and close to two rivers.

I did however meet my first BMW Adventure rider in town. I forget his name, but he was an air ambulance helo pilot in the local area. I arrived at the cafe first and watched him arrive soon after. His speech was slow, methodical and very deliberate. I only hope he wasn't like this when starting his helo on a medical scramble. We talked for a while and he kept on saying I hope I wasn't his next accident pick up and be careful out there. Once was enough but the times he mentioned this made me want to leave his company and go and find some fresh air. I did when he eventually finished his sandwich and I left into the fading light back to my motel. My helo friend went to work.

I had a dilemma to solve. There was some torrential rain forecast in the next couple of days. Shall I go directly to Raleigh and get ahead of a good soaking, or stop over at Speedway Boulevard near Charlotte? I had been contacted by another adventure rider, this time from Charlotte and he suggested a meeting. My inquisitive mind made the decision and I went to Speedway. At least I would get some NASCAR history in my veins on the way to Raleigh. Raleigh was the end of the first part of the journey. It was the end of the Saw Tooth Sector. That would be quite a significant geographical milestone.

I wondered why Speedway Boulevard got its name. It was obvious on arrival. The spur off the Interstate which is populated by the normal collection of motels and diners is dominated by the 180,000 capacity speedway circuit. It's NASCAR HQ, basically. I met ex-Marine Mike Acres later that day. We talked NASCAR for a couple of hours over dinner. I knew nothing about it really and hence Mike's chat was quite interesting. Enter the automobile, during the prohibition years of the 1920s, the undercover business of whiskey or 'moonshine' running began a boom undercover operation. It was the transportation of the moonshine that generated competition between the drivers or 'bootleggers' as they were known. These were the guys who illegally ran the whiskey from hidden stills to hundreds of markets around the southeast states. They drove at high speeds at night and it was normal to be pursued by police. If caught, penalties were high. As bootlegging became common, the drivers began to race amongst themselves on Sunday afternoons and then use the same car for their illegal operations at night. Inevitably, people came to see the races and such events became popular on the back roads. This racing developed in the 1940s and 1950s into stock car racing and the National Association for Stock Car Auto Racing (NASCAR) was founded. The rest is history. Daytona in Florida had an original beach circuit and Lowe's Motor Speedway here at Speedway Boulevard was one of the original venues. It's twice a year and a week-long event including car and truck classes. The Sprint Cup is the main stock car event where speeds of 200 mph are achieved around the circuit. It's a 36-race season from February through to November and 80% of NASCAR teams are based within 40 miles of

Charlotte. So over a couple of beers and a basket of chicken legs in a racing car-styled diner, I had quickly become a NASCAR expert. Shock absorber manufacturer and Suzuki rider Mike has ambitions to work for a NASCAR team. However, he did quickly mention that competition for jobs is fierce, even though there are several teams in the local area.

Meeting with Mike was worthwhile after all, when I consider the short lesson I got on a huge piece of Americana. Before arriving in North Carolina, I had certainly heard of stock car racing, but I was not familiar with NASCAR. With Mike, I had just met a person on my travelling way and immersed myself in a chunk of American history unfamiliar to me.

Chapter 11

North Carolina Deluge

It was a grey and cool morning. The banks of cloud were almost nudging into the undulating countryside, trailing curling tendrils in their wake. It wasn't raining yet, but I could smell and taste water. It wouldn't be long and the Weather Channel, albeit in their normal glamorous manner, had got it right. There was a huge area of low pressure over the Carolinas with torrential rain forecast all day. I speeded out of Speedway Boulevard and decided to get to Raleigh directly on the Interstate rather than larking around in the countryside as Mike had suggested. I wanted to make that invitation to Jim Trovato's place on Sunday. I got about halfway and then the heavens opened. Torrential rain and incredible spray from the busy traffic. My visibility was considerably reduced. The conditions did nothing to slow down other traffic. It was just like being at home – when it's wet, let's all go faster! Isn't that spray and rain pretty! I passed several accidents in the final 50 miles of the run into Raleigh, but contained my speed in accordance with the atrocious conditions. I saw lots of blue and red lights, with drenched policemen in their mackintoshes dealing with stationary traffic where incidents had happened in the slippery conditions. There were no other bikes to be seen, I wonder why! I got an awful lot more waves and flashes from other road users. Maybe they were a friendly acknowledgement or maybe a warning to get off the road – you are mad! Whatever, the bike handled like a dream and arrival in Raleigh for me was trouble-free.

It was quite an amusing scene when I had a look at my first choice motel, which was slightly out of downtown. Standing at the counter, a large pool of water quickly appeared at my feet and was causing a slip hazard. As if on standby, a member of the housekeeping team was there in an instant with a mop and bucket at my feet as I dripped, or rather flowed with the remnants of North Carolina rain. The desk clerk looked on with amusement as he munched his pizza and was thrusting the motel guide towards me. Next to me a lady was giving the manager a hard time. She was complaining about something that I didn't detect, but she was not happy. She was very angry. I think a bystander may have had a good laugh at the scene which had developed in seconds. A mobile swimming pool maker and a very irate guest! The pizza eater had my interests at heart and suggested I go to their new sister motel which was closer to downtown. After all, it was the weekend and I had heard that Raleigh was an entertaining place. The closer to the action the better! I took his advice, punched the new address into my GPS and after 15 minutes through the rain, I was there. They were expecting my arrival which was nice. Pizza eater must have phoned ahead. The construction in the motel was not quite finished and I exchanged chat with some of the workers in the lobby. My soggy appearance made them laugh. They were Polish. They get everywhere – not just in GB.

A blue, breezy and refreshing morning introduced the weekend in Raleigh North Carolina. The wind was playing eerie music as it surged through the small collection of skyscrapers. What a cool place with a beating heart to the city centre. A compact downtown with bars, restaurants, cafés and the sound of live music drifting around. So far, I have found crossing a road in the USA quite a test. Walking around a town is just not a common thing in this country. Pleasingly, not only does Raleigh have pedestrian crossing facilities, but also a good public transport system and you can actually get around town on a bus.

I treated myself to a first journey haircut in a very traditional barber shop. I am not long in the chair these days, but there was time enough for the owner James Smith or Smiddy and his Puerto Rican barber to make a big fuss of me. A Brit biker in Raleigh was rare. Smiddy even wanted to include me in the lunch order when an extremely busty young lady from the café next door popped in with pen and paper and big smile. There had been cell phone chat and she wanted to hear me talk. For a moment, I felt like some circus act, but it was all harmless or rather hairless fun. Around the corner, the desk clerk at the downtown high-rise hotel even let me explore the top floor restaurant which provided quite a nice city panorama, especially of the State Capitol Building. The Capitol Building is Greek revival in design, sitting in compact and well-manicured grounds. Named after Sir Walter Raleigh, Raleigh had to fight off competition from Salisbury, Hillsborough and Fayetteville to take the seat as the state capital. I was reliably informed by the ladies behind the visitor desk that there may have been some skullduggery during the selection process. I am sure there was more than skullduggery around in 1794. One of the ladies boasted that she had been to the 50 state capitals and was eager to hear about my trip. She and her husband had completed the full set over their lifetime and not in a gargantuan six-month tour. She was guarded with en-route information and advised I should take them as I find them. I was only in number eight with a lot of territory ahead. Raleigh got my vote, an invigorating place.

Including the miles down to Key West and back up to my start point, after 3,900 miles, I have completed the 'Saw Tooth Sector', and the first part of my journey. No real dramas and still in one piece. Well apart from having my bones shaken by a tornado in Pensacola and not forgetting an amusing brush with the law in rural Louisiana. The 'saw tooth' optimised my travelling through the eight south east states and capital cities. Some locals in Austin questioned why I didn't continue west from Austin into California. If I had done that, returning east later on, it would have left a lot of shuffling around to cover missed ground. I stuck with my plan. The map of my journey is beginning to unfold and I have covered quite a bit of ground already. If you stretched out this 3,900 mile dog leg west from the east coast, I would get my feet *and wheels* wet at the other end somewhere in the Pacific. Leaving Raleigh for Phoenix, the route is straight with only five capitals to pass through. This will allow more flexibility for diversion. So far, apart from the departure to the coast, I kept pretty much to my planned route. The weather was challenging to say the least. From glorious sunny and hot conditions in Florida during early February, I subsequently encountered several weather delays en-route. Thunderstorms and tornados in Pensacola-Florida, thunderstorms in Beaumont-Texas, freezing conditions in Atlanta-Georgia and more thunderstorms and rain in the Carolinas. They are brutes of thunderstorms over here – thunderstorms from hell would be an apt description. Further north was a different story and very much a wintry tale. There had been masses of snow causing chaos to most walks, roads and flights of life. If nothing else, it is confirming that my route selection so far is working. I shall be in the Northern States much later on in the year, although looking over my shoulder, all that snow is not that far north of me really. I hope it stays there.

Part Two – West for Phoenix

Raleigh-North Carolina to Phoenix-Arizona

2,962 miles

West for Phoenix

Raleigh NC to Phoenix AZ

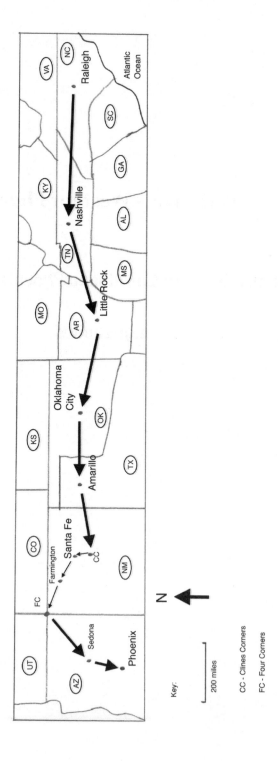

DATE	START	FINISH	MILEAGE	CUMULATIVE	COMMENTS
09 Mar	Raleigh NC	Summersfield NC	155	4056	US158
10 Mar	Summersfield NC	Summersfield NC	80	4136	Local & dog search
11 Mar	Summersfield NC	Asheville NC	174	4310	US158 & I-40
11 Mar	Asheville NC	Asheville NC	7	4317	
12 Mar	Ashville NC	**Nashville TN (9)**	319	4636	US19/US441/I-40
16 Mar	Nashville TN	**Little Rock AR (10)**	357	4993	I-40
20 Mar	Little Rock AR	**Oklahoma City OK (11)**	350	5343	I-40
22 Mar	Oklahoma City OK	Amarillo TX	250	5593	I-40
22 Mar	Amarillo TX	Amarillo TX	15	5608	Local & Route 66
24 Mar	Amarillo TX	Amarillo TX	130	5738	Palo Duro Canyon & local Amarillo
25 Mar	Amarillo TX	**Santa Fe NM (12)**	282	6020	I-40 & US 285
25 Mar	Santa Fe NM	Santa Fe NM	14	6034	Local City
27 Mar	Santa Fe NM	Farmington NM	224	6258	US 84/64
27 Mar	Farmington NM	Farmington NM	15	6273	Local City
28 Mar	Farmington NM	Sedona AZ	380	6653	US64/160/163/89
29 Mar	Sedona AZ	Sedona AZ	79	6732	Local area & Jerome
30 Mar	Sedona AZ	Chandler AZ	131	6863	I-17 & link road
31 Mar	Chandler AZ	Chandler AZ	97	6960	**Phoenix AZ (13)** & Chandler local area
March Total				**3670**	
1 April	Chandler AZ	Chandler AZ	12	6972	**Bike 6K service CHANDLER BMW & local**
2 April	Chandler AZ	Chandler AZ	17	6989	Chandler local
3 April	Chandler AZ	Chandler AZ	93	7082	Cave Creek
4 April	Chandler AZ	Chandler AZ	20	7102	Local & airfield

Chapter 12

7 Dogs

Sunday was a rude awakening. I got tangled up in the Raleigh nightlife
the night before. It had been robust rock music in one of the popular
bars; the band was very good, playing 1980s covers. A local ale had
caused the damage. Thankfully, or not so in this case, over the last 20
years or so, micro breweries have proliferated in the USA. Gone are
the days when it was only domestic beer such as Budweiser, Miller and
Schlitz and the like. Last night had been good ale and the taxi ride back
to my motel was late. The clocks had advanced one hour. It was officially
spring and the front desk was on the phone urging me to check out. I
was late!

It was a crisp, blue Sunday with not a cloud in the sky and a little
chilly around the gills. Today was the day for my arrival at Jim's place
somewhere in the North Carolina countryside. I was on my way west
to Nashville, so no concerns about losing route time, but I had a few
hours to kill before arriving. Raleigh was quiet as I departed; perhaps
everyone was still in slumber after their night on the town. The cool
air quickly wiped my cobwebs away and soon I was in beautiful green
rolling countryside. It was very European-like as I passed through the
small communities of Oxford, Roxboro, Yanceyville and Reidsville. The
roads were extremely quiet and the only accumulation of vehicles was
in church car parks. Everyone was at Sunday worship, or that's what it

seemed like. There was something missing from the countryside and it eventually occurred to me. There were no country pubs scattered around as you would find in England. The country pub is something you take for granted back home, from town to village to hamlet. Not so in North Carolina so far.

My GPS took me directly to Jim's address. He hadn't said much about his place when I first met him in Georgia and I didn't know what to expect. Would it be a small or large place, detached or semi-detached? I was unsure. My first sighting of the long, steep driveway made me do a quick circuit of the local area to re-check the address. The correct location was confirmed on my second pass and the huge Victorian style house on a hillside set in 32 acres of prime North Carolina countryside was indeed my destination. Arriving on the private gravel approach, I was met by seven very friendly dogs of various shapes and sizes. Jim's attractive blonde partner, Pam, welcomed me into their cavernous home. Cell phone close to her ear, she shared conversation with me simultaneous to her father in Maryland, as she gave me the choice of the green room or the pink room and mind the rugs, the floor is slippery beneath. After changing, I was introduced to the dogs and a mug of hot tea returned the warmth after a refreshingly cool ride. Jim and I chatted whilst Pam busied herself around the kitchen preparing dinner. He stressed that he had subsequently paid for his dinner back in Stone Mountain and would have hated it if Regina, sorry Rejeana, had missed some dollars from that evening. We had a laugh about that and made ready for dinner with no bill. I felt relaxed and at home and already I was receiving fantastic hospitality.

A group of Jim and Pam's friends joined us for dinner and it was quite a large gathering. They were all professionals and businesspeople from the local area. We all exchanged travellers' tales and discussed my route. Many questions were generated – the mileage, the weather, when do I expect to finish etc. – the type of questions I had now grown accustomed to and had answers primed and ready. My brain was picked about home, especially travel advice for the American traveller to Europe. A couple were planning a jaunt and were enthusiastic to plan how much time they should spend here and there. With the exception of one gent, none of the group had been to England. His experience of Blighty had been London only, where he did not have good recollections of the food. It was rather an arrogant statement, which inferred that only good food was available in the USA. This was disappointing when he confirmed over pool in the games room downstairs that his culinary sample did not venture out of chain restaurants and included some burger bars.

I was picking up a theme quite common with some of the population in the USA. Some folk think, and yes I agree it is generally the minority, that only the good and the best come from the USA. Not just food, everything. When this view is accompanied by an arrogant stance, it can be galling to say the least. It maybe a global naivety from a population that in general does not travel. A large percentage of the population do not even have a passport. I have so far put the American population in groups. The professionals and the workforce: they work so hard in such a workaholic manner that they never travel and are not encouraged to travel unless for work purposes. This group accounts for the majority of the population. Then there are the minority groups, the retired people who have time and money to do some travelling, and of course the military who have to travel. It was a bit of a shame I was having these thoughts whilst receiving excellent hospitality from my fine hosts Jim and Pam, who undoubtedly are quite unique and exceptionally polite and kind Americans.

At evening's end, the older and bolder hounds of the group stayed in the warmth. A couple of the younger ones joined us in the frost outside to bid farewell to the guests. A headcount at bedtime confirmed that one dog was missing. It was the exuberant young Labrador, Winston. Jim and I did a quick search of the area with no success. There was no sign of our young canine friend who may have got hopelessly lost in the dark and cold night. The following day, he had not returned and concern over his safety was growing. A new member to the group, he may not have tuned into his new surroundings. The next day I rode a big sweep of the local area, sometimes getting lost myself in the meandering, very rural neighbourhoods. There was no sign of Winston. It was encouraging that we had not seen any evidence that he may have been hit by a vehicle. He could be still out there somewhere, unless he had met his fate with a coyote or an aggressive stag. The afternoon spring sunshine peaked with just enough warmth to allow a seat in the garden for a couple of hours. It was quiet and peaceful and a million miles away from the busy towns, cities, Interstates and highways that I have encountered and would further encounter. My two days in the quite spectacular North Carolina countryside had almost been a mini holiday. This was an invitation that delivered and went beyond all expectations. A marvellous experience from hosts I would love to meet again. With batteries fully recharged, I was ready, if not slightly reluctant, to progress west for Nashville.

The following morning when I left, Winston still had not returned.

Chapter 13

Great Smoky Mountains

I reluctantly left Jim's place and headed west for Nashville. Let the journey roll on. It was a lovely blue morning and I decided to stop over in Asheville, about halfway to the city of music. The Great Smoky Mountains came into view as I cleared Winston-Salem and got closer to Hickory. This was quite an event on the journey. My first sighting of any mountains. Later on, especially on the west side of the country, I would be taking daily views of huge mountain ranges such as the Rockies and the Sierras for granted. But I remember it was quite a feeling of progress as I arrived in Asheville, with good views of the Smokies, with some peaks up to 6,000 feet. I felt quite upbeat and I was developing quite a routine. Route planning, weather planning, where to stay, what to do, what to write and most important what to eat! I strived to eat the healthy things and not fall into the fast food trap. Its got to be chicken, pasta and fish, with the occasional treat of something like a burger – as long as it was a decent one. My mental plan seemed to be working as well and I was keeping the geographical extent of the journey under control. It was a simple mental model and a mind game, but required concentration with no big geographical deviations. On a long and maybe boring ride, I had introduced some simple, smaller mind games into my day. I never went down the route of listening to music through my helmet as it takes away a lot of perception of the riding game and most importantly you cannot hear the engine note. I was happy to ride and listen to the sounds of the world outside my inner world. The traffic, my bike noise, people etc. The road sign had a good mind game function. It was name recognition. If I was in the mood I would look out for a sign that matched the name of a person I knew or had known. It was then a recap of him or her and where are they now. If it wasn't a favourite person, I would quickly move on until I found a road sign of someone nice. That could be distracting!

Asheville, renowned for the nearby Biltmore Estate, turned out to be a vibrant little town with a plethora of arts and crafts shops. It was a tasteful place with a smattering of bars and restaurants in a compact centre. The day was just warm enough to have an outdoor lunch and for a moment I thought I could be in an English market town. It had a nice and relaxed feel. I ate healthily in the evening and my cute little waitress turned out to be another single mum. I seemed to be making a habit of meeting single mums. Maybe I was going to the wrong places. I did have a fantasy of meeting an attractive Texan lady with a lot of oil. That would do nicely. Later on I would be passing through Texas again and would have one more shot at this fantasy. My waitress tonight was so young and didn't look old enough to hold the responsibility of being a mother. Her younger partner was holding the baby that night. She talked very well and surprisingly could comment on most things including the election campaign. I felt a little sorry for her and parted with a larger than normal tip. Leaving the restaurant, the sound of an electric guitar blasting out from a rough-looking building attracted my attention as I headed home. It turned out to be a music and watering hole for some real roughnecks. There were a few old bikes outside and inside the sparse population was made up of male and females with long hair, tattoos and earrings. The blaring music was my cover and no one noticed me and offered conversation. That was pleasing as talking in the place would have been impossible. It was cold outside and the chilled beer in the music bar didn't help. However, I could have been colder if I had chosen to stay in a cabin deep in the Smoky national park, but Asheville provided suitable entertainment.

I had to have a closer look at the Smokies and the route over the top of the range was the only sensible option. Not only to provide some good views on a clear morning, but to exercise the bike through some twisties. I wasn't disappointed with the morning – even the mountain approach through Dellwood and Maggie Valley was seat of the pants stuff. I unexpectedly climbed through 4,500 feet, passing collections of wooden cabins and smart restaurants in the foothills. At Ravensford the road and terrain got serious as it climbed over the spine of the Smokies. The North Carolina-Tennessee State Line marked the summit of the road around 5,500 feet. It was cold at this altitude and huge icicles were hanging off the rock faces. The viewing point was full of kids from nearby states on their spring break. They were all comparing notes of when and where they had been. I was the only biker present and felt just a little out of place in what was obviously a walker and campers' hangout. A hazy morning provided a moody vista of the Smokies, with the peaks of Mounts Kephart, Chapman and Hardison angling a dramatic background. I am sure many black bears and deer would be prowling in the thick forested cover below. What a contrast to Florida.

Descending into Tennessee, the north west flank of the Smokies still dominated the cool vista. Passing Gatlinburg, the scenery became much flatter, until really coming down to earth in Pigeon Forge. Famous for the nearby Dollywood estate, the Great Smoky Mountains Parkway runs through this extremely commercial town, where hundreds of motels and diners line the roadside. It was a culture shock to say the least after having been high in the mountains only an hour or so previously that morning with only few people around. It was only midday and the ugly thought of staying in such a commercial place was the catalyst I needed to continue west to Nashville. I am sure that would be an interesting place and stopping at midday in good riding conditions seemed a waste.

Whilst refuelling at Knoxville, a local with an incredible accent descended upon me and began interrogation. Still on the fuel station premises, his conversation followed me when I pulled aside for a quick sandwich. It soon became clear that he was a local delivery driver around Knoxville only. He had no idea where Nashville was and he bellowed, 'It's over there somewhere, it will take you hours.' It was only 150 miles or so and I anticipated being there for cocktail hour. But the alarming thing was, this guy was serious, he really didn't appreciate where Nashville was. Nashville of all places! This guy was obviously someone who travels from home to work and returns with the odd trip to the mall or a bar. That's it. As long as these types of people are happy, that's the main thing. Not all the world's population have the hunger of wanderlust. Throughout our conversation, I noticed in my peripheral vision a dark limo with one guy sitting behind the wheel reading a newspaper. I thought no more of it until I pulled away and he began to follow me. Here we go... was my mind working over time again? Should I do the road sign game now or what? The limo guy was definitely on my tail as I progressed west in now very warm conditions. The undulating hills of eastern Tennessee took my mind off him and I thought of a game to check him out. The road looked reasonably free flowing and I couldn't see any police cars – that would be impossible anyway, I was in a different state and who knows what colour they would be. I opened the bike up over the speed limit for several miles and pulled well clear of my pursuant. Five minutes later, he was right back on my tail, a safe distance behind, but yes that was him, white shirt and dark glasses. I tried this a couple of times and no sooner was I in clear traffic than he was right back there. Very interesting, especially after my observations back in Stone Mountain. I wonder, I really wonder if I was under surveillance? Surely the American Secret Service have bigger and better things to spend their money on. Unless this guy was just playing a game as well. I would now treat it as a game, but thought quickly of another test. I pulled off at a service station, twiddled my thumbs for 10 minutes and rejoined the Interstate. I checked my mirrors and there he was right back on my tale.

I lost my assailant in the busy confluence of Interstates in Nashville. I also lost functionality of my GPS. Damn! It just greyed out just when I needed it desperately. I was surrounded by trucks, with my shoulders at wheel level and minimum visibility in most directions. It was extremely busy around 5 pm and I couldn't recall exactly what exit and route I needed to find my motel. I learnt from this that a basic route written on my windscreen with a fibre pen may be a good back-up. Luckily I spotted the sign of the motel on the side of the Interstate and was able to navigate there with no further stress. Thankfully the majority of towns and cities have elevated signage for motels and diners. 'Come and stay here', or 'Come and eat here' or 'Best deals in town' etc. Sometimes I had thought they were overkill. Today I changed my mind. Getting that GPS fixed was a priority over everything before I continued en-route. In the meantime Nashville summoned.

Chapter 14

Music City

I was staying a little out of the centre, a location recommended by Mark the guy I had met in Savannah. I was beginning to find that any area that had an accumulation of motels and diners on the Interstate close to a city, are generally okay areas. Here you are surrounded by travellers who just want a bed and a meal. They are normally not in bad neighbourhoods. Maybe the area I stayed in Jackson was verging on a bad area, but it wasn't a war zone. In a gas station store close to my motel was the first time I had been asked to produce some ID. I had a small collection of stuff including some beers and the assistant would not accept my GB photo driver's licence. It must be my passport, which was back in my room over the street. Quite a line of shoppers, including a couple of police officers, was gathering behind me as the bespectacled assistant with nail-bitten and grubby fingers handled my ID. He just didn't recognise it and refused the sale. Keeping my cool, I just left the goods on his counter, uttered a few less than polite words and left. The police apologised on his behalf and I added, 'Good advert for a visitor eh!' I made do with a local restaurant and then once more the sound of loud music attracted my attention. Some bands have gigs that spill out of the city centre and this one was in a real locals' den. In the dark and smoky place, the band was rehearsing for tomorrow's performance. A couple of locals at the bar mentioned they would be worth a listen should I return tomorrow, although he suggested I would find more interest downtown. This guy was a truck driver and was keen to pass on tips from his driving experiences. In a short time, he got around most of the country after which I retreated to my room to have a look at the misbehaving GPS.

Nashville is a city renowned for music venues and very much has an emphasis on country and western. Any C&W fan from around the world may have made a pilgrimage to Nashville. Broadway is where it all happens which is bang in the city centre. I made it down there for lunch the next day and it was quiet. The evening would be different I am sure, as all the music bars are just lined up one after the other on both sides of the wide street. I was starting to get a bit blasé about my visits to the State Capitols, however, Nashville was an interesting exception. I tagged on with a group of bankers who were receiving close commentary from attentive guide Michael. *'It's the 9th oldest Capitol Building – it's 150 years old and has been continuously used.'* Modelled on Greek revival architecture and classically designed, it is classy. Nashville became known as the Athens of the south, with columns and statues in the Capitol Area portraying very much a Greek emotion. In the 1950s, nude statues were controversially removed from the Capitol Area and buried in the Tennessee countryside. Most were destroyed, but Michael mentioned that some are still intact and lay undetected. Quite surprisingly at the end of the tour, Michael introduced me to the group and asked me to give a quick talk about my journey. This caught me by surprise, but I managed to put a few words together which impressed the young Nashville bankers.

Nashville has a frequent bus service and I was able to get a bus back to my motel. The helpful and chatty driver dropped me off right at the entrance, even though it wasn't a formal stop on his route. He said no one would know and since this was his route all week, did I want picking up tomorrow? That was a nice touch and I took a note of the times he would be passing.

The next couple of days were wet and windy with thunderstorms. The spray completely engulfed the nearby Interstate, turning it into almost a maritime transport artery. Nashville was a pleasing place to have a slightly extended stay. It gave me the opportunity to play on the bus system and have several trips downtown to sample the vibrant Broadway music scene. As I anticipated, all the bars and music venues fire up mid-evening and vibrate until well after midnight. The cool thing to do was to eat in one of the many fine restaurants or grills and then stroll in and out of the music bars. It was a great people-watching street, populated by both the European tourist and Americans dressed in cowboy-style attire, topped with Stetsons. Although C&W is not my favourite music genre, it was easy to tell a good and not so good band. The bars with the good bands were bursting at the seams with drinkers and dancers. The bars with the not so good bands were not so full. The Nashville experience was unmissable and it's a shame I did not have such a memorable impression of Austin.

My unplanned downtime allowed me to catch up with some en-route arrangements. The GPS was a priority and on inspection, the SD card with all the North American mappage was out of its slot. Maybe the bumps and jolts of the roads had caused this. Some tape to hold it was the quick fix and I would monitor its success next time on the road. It was Little Rock next and I thought I would look into a method of identifying a good part of town to stay in. There isn't such a website that shows such information – it would be discriminatory apparently. I could call the city police as Mark had suggested, or plan to stay somewhere near a golf and country club. The latter could be a plan that would work, let's face it residential areas near such places are normally quite nice. Calling the police should be quite amusing, what with my accent, and so I decided to do just that. I would call the downtown police department in Little Rock and ask for advice. It turned out to be quite a laugh and making myself understood and my question clear was quite a challenge. I felt sorry for the poor desk sergeant who I am sure wondered who on earth he was talking with. We eventually communicated and he said for Little Rock, west is best! So, I planned with that advice in mind. I am not sure if I would go down this route again and a personal perception of a place to stay, as my country familiarity was growing, was maybe the best selection process.

I had had some fun in Nashville and although I had to make progress, I was rather reluctant to be heading west. Although it was dry, the storms of the last couple of days had left a very cool feel to the place. I kept forgetting it was still only mid-March and spring by no means had got hold. I passed a city called Jackson, which immediately provoked recollections of my stay in Jackson, Mississippi. Now they were amusing recollections. This was Jackson, Tennessee, I am sure a different place and maybe the place in the song? The sky was grey for 350 miles. Even the city of Memphis and the Mississippi, which I was crossing for the third time, looked dank and forlorn. My mood was brightened up considerably whilst chatting to a couple of attendants at a fuel stop. African-American young ladies, they were full of flowing southern words and I had to listen very carefully to understand them. They wanted to hear all about me and what I was doing passing by their territory on a cool grey Sunday morning. I think I made their day. The weather brightened up considerably arriving in Little Rock as I headed for the western side of town and the GPS was working all the way. My fix must have worked. The motel I selected looked okay and had a rather nice restaurant on the side. Another city to explore.

Chapter 15

Looking for Bill

I thought I would go in search of Bill Clinton in the city that was his headquarters for several years. The Capitol Building was the place to start. I was surprised to be in another pedestrian friendly city with a bus service. Taking a number 5 from outside my motel, the friendly driver dropped me off opposite the Capitol Building. Another domed building greeted me, this time a huge affair with massive columns and bronze doors, all set in delightful gardens where the cherry blossoms and magnolias were on the verge of blossom. The grounds contain an array of impressive statues and memorials, including a large soaring eagle in the USA medal of honour area, which is set aside from the main gardens. My first sighting of Bill was his portrait amongst other former Governors on the marble-galleried walls in the very quiet Capitol. Twice governor of Arkansas, the youthful gaze from Bill at his desk was almost unrecognizable from his figure today. The Capitol Police advised it would be a long walk to the downtown area and I would be sensible to get a taxi. This sort of advice from Americans was sometimes inaccurate and as mentioned earlier, they are just not a walking population and drive everywhere. It was only ten minutes later that I arrived, on foot, in the farmers' market area of the city. Here old industrial buildings have been converted into tasteful restaurants and lunchtime grazers were already creating a buzz. What was good advice from the Capitol was try the Flying Fish for lunch. It was busy which was a good sign and getting a seat in the canteen-like establishment was a challenge. It was a bit rustic, order and collect food at the counter, chequered tablecloths, much fish art on the walls, fishing nets on the ceilings and tinny jazz clattering around some old speakers. It was a fun place and the food was good.

Maintaining the Clinton theme, a short walk from the Flying Fish is the William J. Clinton Presidential Centre. Sometimes referred to as simply the Clinton Library, Bill has put together quite a collection of facts, figures, displays and global gifts from his eight years at the helm of the USA. The impressive exhibition is accommodated in a huge futuristic slab of a building on three floors, almost like a spacecraft from *Alien*. It is complete with a penthouse for the occasional Clinton homecoming. He was not at home today. On arrival I was greeted by a posse of friendly guides dressed in smart blue suits adorned with Presidential décor. From limo in the lobby, to mock up of a White House State room, it was a few dollars well spent and an interesting look-see at Presidential life. Well done Bill.

The bus ride back to my motel was not enjoyable. The central bus station was not at all far from the farmers' market and Bill's place. The passengers hanging around were all local city folk and I stood out like a sore thumb. I really did feel out of place with stares and much comment coming my way. It was daylight, so no problems, but if it had been at night, I would have jumped in a cab. It was only a quick hop on the bus and far cheaper than a cab ride. To compound matters the bus driver was just damn rude and refused to change a $5 bill. I had to go racing into the bus station, persuade the clerk to break her conversation with her co-worker and almost plead for some change. It was hard work and the message was quite clear. The driver was making his point: what are you doing on my bus! You should be in a cab! It was an obvious statement and none of his passengers even looked at me. Whilst on buses in other cities, I had got a similar feeling, but nowhere so far as strong as today. I am not in the slightest prejudiced against the colour or creed of the global population, I am simply transmitting my observations here and I was made to feel extremely uncomfortable.

I got off the bus a little earlier to explore a mall. It was whilst walking around the mall that I came across a gun shop and was drawn in to do some Brit investigatory chat. At first it was just like going into any store, 'Can I help you sir? Anything you need advice on today?' Everything was there from hand guns in glass cases, to rifles standing vertical in racks. Then the ammo, boxes and boxes of it – some of the bullets looked like they would take down a dinosaur. It's a cultural thing over here, gun laws are different to Europe and taken for granted. When I started talking, my accent sort of broke the ice, especially when I said I was just having a nosey around for a couple of moments. The store owners were both armed and although reluctant at first, they opened up with chat about the American and the gun. 'Have a feel of this one, it's a Smith and Weston, this is a Magnum, now how about a rifle for size?' Different states have different rules, but in general if I was a US citizen they could run a check on me right there in the store, check my future use for the weapon and if I didn't have any criminal record or black marks against me, I could walk out armed to the teeth. I was advised by many travellers that I should carry a gun to defend myself from bears. More of that later on. Leaving the gun store we all shared a laugh. I asked if guns would ever be banned to the public in the USA. The gun sellers both laughed and one said. 'If guns were outlawed, only outlaws would have guns!'

Jim from North Carolina had just made contact and passed on that a local farmer had returned the Labrador with wanderlust. Apparently he was welcomed back into the large canine group and Jim was accelerating to the vet to get the dog electronically tagged. That made for a small celebration over a couple of ales here in Little Rock on St Patrick's Day. The American population, including all and sundry in Little Rock, were in a boisterous mood and ready for a night of celebration. A lot of Americans of course claim heritage to the Emerald Isle. Today, I was called Irish as well as Australian; I am starting to get confused myself.

The next couple of days were a wash out and I stayed in Little Rock. I seemed to be struggling against the weather so far in March, with only small windows of opportunity to progress. It was certainly unsafe to ride in thunderstorms and when tornados were likely and forecast. I wanted to complete my journey in one piece and having a bit of patience was essential. Once west of Oklahoma, I would start to get into the red rock country of New Mexico and Arizona where more settled conditions are normal at this time of the year. That would hopefully be by the end of the month. For the moment I spent hours poring over the forecast, trying to pick an ideal opportunity to get to Oklahoma City, which would involve crossing the southern end of tornado alley.

Chapter 16

BUFF

For a typical day's ride, I normally plan two routes. A countryside meandering option and a boring direct option on the Interstate. Leaving Little Rock, my rural choice was 400 miles right out into the sticks and then diving into Oklahoma City at the end. Breakfast in Mt Ida, lunch at Talihina, afternoon tea in Seminole and then descend upon OC for beer and medals around six. That's what I wanted to do and I spent hours planning for it. However, the storms and torrential rain over the last couple of days had left rivers swollen and the ground waterlogged. I would have needed floats to attempt the rural route. Maybe one of those boats with a huge fan would have been useful. The type you see in the Everglades. How cool going from Little Rock to OC in a boat! Today that would have been two useful things coming out of Florida – my bike and the fan boat! On a serious note, the weather had been horrific with fatalities in Missouri, over 100 local roads closed and 700 flights cancelled in and out of Dallas. The place was a mess. Reluctantly I opted for the boring run west on the Interstate. Actually, it wasn't that bad and with bright and breezy conditions in pretty green countryside, the 350 miles roared by. There was much evidence of flood water here and there, with some fields looking like lakes. It's worth mentioning that an Interstate route is not always that boring, unless you are outrunning a tail, or weaving around big trucks. Outside cities, the Interstate, freeway or expressway – call them what you will – are only two lanes wide and although normally going in straight lines from major city to major city as was their design, they do follow the contours which can make for an interesting and undulating ride depending what mountain range they are taking on.

I pulled off Interstate 40 just inside the state of Oklahoma and found a local service area. It was Ed's Truck Stop and made for an interesting breather and consolation for not being in the country. As normal, the fuel station included a grocery store and diner. Both were absolutely immaculate with a fantastic buffet lunch available in the diner if you fancied it. I opted for an omelette at the bar and took in the rest of the population. There were few folks around, it was only 11 am-ish and the waitresses had lots of time to have small talk with the kitchen staff through the hatch and engage with me. This eating at the bar is a great thing in the USA and ideal for a solo traveller. Just plonking yourself down at the bar takes all the pressure off sitting alone at a table. I don't mind that, but the potential for chat and making contacts at the bar is immeasurable. We don't have the same culture in GB and dining alone is not the norm. That is not the case in the USA and my rich bar dining experiences added to the spice of my journey considerably. This diner had a large collection of kids' pedal cars on display on an elevated shelf. Old ones, new ones, antique ones, you name it. Almost a museum feel, dramatically contrasting to the stainless steel and turquoise-cushioned furniture. The waitresses neglected their duties whilst chatting to me; it was the accent again and they admitted to never having met an Englishman, never mind an Englishman on a motorcycle in Oklahoma.

Oklahoma City was settled in an area known as the 'unassigned lands' and after some attractive countryside earlier that morning, my approach to the city gave that feeling. Flat and quite boring with not a lot to see. In 1889, 10,000 homesteaders on the 'Oklahoma Land Run', settled in what is the now downtown. They formed a tented city overnight and today, the population of the metropolitan area numbers over a million. Of course, no tents around, but a modern city with many industries and recreational facilities. It's arriving in a city when the Interstates grow a few lanes and the traffic gets busy. Very busy when you reach a confluence of routes with many flyovers, bridges and underpasses. Like most Interstates, I-40 gets you right into the downtown, and OC was no different. That's what they are good at. In England it would be like looking down from your high-rise office window onto the M25, or M1. What was especially unique about arriving here is that there is a damn big Air Force base slap bang downtown. Well almost, it's a little to the east of centre. Tinker Air Force Base boasts some impressive statistics. With over 26,000 employees, it is the largest single-site employer in the state. The complete installation covers nine square miles and has over 770 buildings. Quite a place and it is the home to many types of aircraft including the B52 Stratofortress. I am glad I was at the journey's end, as the wind had risen considerably. It had turned out to be one of those bright, clear and very windy days which are typical of this region in spring. Tumbleweed would have been blowing in the days of the homesteaders. Approaching the city, the characteristic dirty exhaust trailing from a large black silhouette on the horizon was unmistakably a B52 bomber making an approach into Tinker. We were converging, at different speeds naturally, but as I got closer the gargantuan aircraft was crabbing considerably in the cross wind, almost flying sideways. It passed over me on I-40 and looking up, I could nearly count the rivets down the side of the fuselage. Developed as early as 1946, test pilot Tex Johnston took the prototype to the air in 1952 and could not have predicted what an iconic American aircraft he had introduced to the world. Originally designed for Cold War operations, the BUFF, as the B52 is known, has seen service in many theatres, right up to today. Threat of retirement was always reversed when some future use for its unique role cropped up. Its operational life has been extended to the 2020s – could there just be a glimmer of hope that it could be around 100 years after its birth? An amazing slice of aviation history for the Big Ugly Fat Fellow!

I stayed in the part of the city recommended by another confused city police desk sergeant. I had called ahead from Little Rock, but this would probably be the last time I would take advice. With confidence and familiarity of my journey increasing every day, I would now do my own neighbourhood assessment. It was an okay part of the city, cluttered with motels and diners and a bus service. Yes, another city bus service! The ride downtown the next day passed through old and gritty neighbourhoods and involved a change at a transit station. It had a similar feel to the bus station in Little Rock and I am glad my onward connection arrived quickly. The downtown area is so spread out, that once dropped at my destination which was the State Capitol, I was marooned and would need further transport to get elsewhere. I should have brought the bike down, but fancied a liquid lunch. So the State Capitol is another huge statehouse with the normal pillars and domes, but quite surprisingly the impressive dome was an addition in 2002, replacing the former saucer-shaped ceiling. Atop the dome is an impressive statue of a Native American named 'The Guardian'. It was Good Friday and quiet inside. The white Indiana limestone with pink and black granite certainly gave a cool feel in the airy and echoey interior. Plentiful and tasteful art and the exquisitely decorated dome interior, brightened up the cavernous guts of the Oklahoma State Capitol. Number 11 on my trail.

The taxi driver honked his horn loudly as approaching the Capitol and was looking for his fare to be wearing an orange jacket. It was me, but the midday warmth had persuaded removal of my jacket as I strained to photograph The Guardian. The driver was Iranian. When he found out where I from, he wouldn't stop talking about football. Manchester United this, Chelsea that, and Arsenal the other. Nothing similar in Tehran, he loved English football. His chit-chat was encouraging as he didn't look talkative when I got in his cab. When I managed to get a word in edgeways, I told him to lead on and take me where I should go with only a day left in town. That was an optimistic comment considering I had not checked the weather for tomorrow yet. He said I must visit the Murrah Building area and then have lunch in Bricktown. That's exactly what I did and his commentary suitably substituted for any city research that I had missed.

Oklahoma City made international news for the wrong reason in 1995. Timothy McVeigh set off a bomb in front of the Federal Government Murrah Building. The building was destroyed, killing 168 innocent people. McVeigh was executed in 2001 for his crime and his act was, at the time, the deadliest act of terrorism within the USA. Local residents were stunned, why could something like this happen in such a normal-regular-boring city, call it want you want, as Oklahoma City? The site is now home to the Oklahoma City National Memorial and Museum. It is a moving and sombre place with memorials for the victims in a garden area with a pool providing reflections. Many visit the grounds to have their own reflections. Whilst I was there a young girl was standing close beside one memorial stone whilst her companion, maybe her father, took her photograph. She was pretty and full of life and the stone obviously marked the resting place of a loved one. It was a very moving moment and I suddenly felt quite emotional. The little girl remained calm and maintained a smile, but it was a smile of yearning, yearning that the person whose memorial she was visiting was still with her. They left hand in hand, heads bowed, with occasional glancing looks at each other. This brief experience certainly concentrated my mind and put everything in focus. For that little girl, I would complete the journey. Uncle Sam was very much contained at the moment.

My visit to Oklahoma City ended in Bricktown, which is known as Oklahoma's entertainment district. With a railway and industrial heritage, the area eventually went under urban revitalisation, with its new title, Bricktown, as late as the 1970s. Today, river walks, bars, restaurants and the impressive ball park provide a beating heart to this traditional part of town. I ate a nouveau cuisine open sandwich on the elevated patio of Nonna's. Remarkably no fries and enough fresh fruit on the side to act as a dessert. What a treat. Nearby, the tall, red brick walls of former warehouses dominate the area. I am sure they could tell interesting stories. A tourist trolley bus took me back to the motel area, making that the third type of public transport in one day in one city. Things were certainly looking up.

All the Americans I'd met so far said give OC a miss, there's nothing really there. Well, I found the place appealing, what with the rail, oil and stockyard history. Not forgetting Route 66 and a bit of jazz. The first big city on the plains. Miles of nothing and then suddenly everything – nearly everything. Back into Texas next.

Chapter 17

The Big Texan

So Texas got a second pass, this time through the panhandle in the north of the state that is the size of France. Amarillo turned out to be a convenient and interesting stop. It was 250 miles in a oner on I-40 from OC and the bike's range was probably good for another 100 miles. My rump wasn't. The road just seemed to be straight forever and ever as far as the eye could see, with little deviation and no hills. The buildings of Elk City provided a small contrast to the nebulous terrain prior to entering northern Texas. Amarillo, the Yellow Rose of Texas, offers city facilities in a small town atmosphere. If you stayed on the Interstate, you would flash by it in no time. I stayed in a motel on the Interstate, but the city was in touching distance. Starr, the lady at check in, was tall, slim, blonde, talkative, charismatic and very attractive. I think I wanted to marry her on the spot. She was more interested in telling me about her HD biking partner and young son who rides pillion, than checking me in. I was more interested in her. They dressed their eight-year-old in all the riding kit, including leather chaps, and he sits on the back of a Fat Boy. Starr passed on all the top places to visit in the local area, including a good Mexican restaurant next door and a canyon I should look at not far south. The Mexican population and the Mexican restaurant were becoming a dominating theme. Maybe because I was still in the southern states, but so far everywhere I went there were plenty of Mexican restaurants and not a lot of others.

I had already ridden some of the original Route 66 and in Amarillo, the 'Mother of all Roads' or 'Main Street America', is where east meets west on this iconic old road that originally connected Los Angeles to Chicago. Officially removed from the highway system in the 80s, only portions remain. In Amarillo, evidence of the old road still exists around 6th Avenue. It was a quiet Saturday afternoon and the faded wall murals and quiet bikers' cafes did give the place a yesteryear feel. Closing my eyes for a moment, I could be in the 60s. There were some groups of bikers around and a lot were congregated around Clyde Ledbetter's leather shop. Clyde was hard at work plying his trade for the HD rider. Leather chaps made to measure, jackets made to measure, badges, gloves, you name it. He was hardly seen behind his pile of work and even had the time to run multiple conversations over the din from hammer and sewing machine. The HD crowd were full of weekend banter and in a raucous mood. I was accepted into their conversation and enjoyed some Texan chat before leaving Clyde's shop. Trawling the bric-a-brac stores I was in search of a piece of Route 66 memorabilia. Something with Route 66 written on it was what I was after, a bit of old brass or metal or something. Alas, nothing like that was left, all gone to the hardcore collectors and I made do with a replica vehicle licence plate. I did find a piece of metal later that day, in my rear tyre! It was a nail. Maybe Route 66 was having a final bite. Damn and the next day was Sunday, it would have to wait until Monday when I would have to search for a bike shop. It's so tempting to remove a nail from a tyre, but that could result in the tyre deflating. On the flipside, it's not advisable to leave a nail in for a long trip, as the increase in temperature and speed could 'fling' it out and you know what's next. So, it had to be dealt with and the worst case scenario was a new tyre. Maybe it was providence that I wasn't on the road the next day, as it turned out to be one of the coldest Easter Sundays on record. Texas is not the place you normally associate with the cold and after the storms I experienced in Beaumont, I was certainly getting a meteorological reality check in this huge state.

The Mexican next door to the motel was okay – the beer was cold anyway. The food, well, it's all the same on a Mexican restaurant menu. Taco this, tortilla that and crispy things to dip into a bland red sauce that needs heaps of Tabasco to pep it up a bit. You have to study the menu very carefully to drag out a decent piece of chicken or fish. Maybe I had seen enough Mexicans, but in this part of the country, there is not much else. This place had a decent bar which was quite a gathering place for the traveller. I strapped myself on to stool and whilst enjoying a couple of night caps I was joined by Danny Latham. He was in need of company and was quite impressed how cheap the whisky was at $2.50 a shot. I lost count how many he had. He was driving down to San Antonio in southern Texas to meet a brother and their 96-year-old father. He was boasting about his truck and fifth wheel he had outside and how self-sufficiently he travelled. 'I don't need motels or restaurants, everything is in the fifth wheel, all I need is a bar. Must walk the dog before I turn in.' I had to get Danny to explain what a fifth wheel was. It turns out it's the type of trailer that hitches directly onto the flat-bed of a truck by means of a fifth wheel – hence the name. Apparently that system is considered better than a standard tow bar. After the description, I saw nothing else but trucks towing a fifth wheel trailer around the highways. Danny went on to tell me that he rarely flew around in the USA. He didn't like flying anymore. A former military pilot, his flying career came abruptly to an end in the mid-60s in Vietnam. He used to fly the F4B with VMFA 513 out of Da Nang. For someone in their late-sixties, he looked in good shape. Tall, well built, shaven head, I could almost picture him now in a flight suit, giving the rookie pilots on the squadron a hard time in his western drawl. Fuzzy Buffalo, as was his r/t call sign, was on his fifth mission of the day at the peak of the conflict. 'Fully fuelled up, armed to the teeth, rolling down the runway in full burner, you're kind er committed.' He recalled it all. 'Intel told us there were no spooks around, but I got a glimpse of a bright flash to my right in the woods and the missile hit the nose cone. I had recollections of my feet dangling in fresh air and that was it. Darkness. Next thing I knew was waking up in a hospital bed quite broken up. My back-seater also survived and was next to me. We both never flew again.' Danny was happy to talk about this and even commented that as young men, they never thought of why they were there. They were serving their country and didn't question international politics. He added it would be different today; going through that conflict had given him a more questioning culture. He wanted to talk about Iraq and Afghanistan, but it was late and we both left the bar slightly worse for wear.

I found a back street place where a helpful Kevin at A&M Cycles removed the offending nail with almost dentistry skill. It was tiny and had not penetrated fully, so the tyre lived. Feeling upbeat about this outcome and with the heat returning, I took Starr's advice and went in search of this canyon she mentioned. Palo Duro Canyon sits about 20 miles south of Amarillo and is locally known as the Grand Canyon of Texas. Once east of the town of Canyon, the road to the park was signposted, but some of the roads were not on my GPS. It was quite an isolated place. I had expected a gravel road, but was surprised to discover a 16-mile asphalt loop road on the basin of the multi-coloured geographic spectacle. The area could be Texas' best kept secret – after all who has heard of the Palo Duro canyon unless you are a geologist? I found out about it by chance, as my normal research of the local area did not reveal its existence. I wonder how many other gems like this are hidden around this vast country? It was still early in the season and even on such a fine blue day, there were hardly any folk about. Even the well-equipped RV parking areas were uncluttered. I am sure that would change in a couple of months. But today, Easter Monday, there were probably more hibernating rattlers than humans in the park.

Not to be missed before leaving the pan handle was a visit to the Big Texan restaurant. It was my last night and Starr had arranged for the restaurant limo, complete with bull's horns on the front, to pick me up. Rattlesnake was not on the menu, apparently it's seasonal and they were all still asleep at this time of the year. I was happy about that, as canyon country where I had been earlier that day was prime rattler territory. I made do with a steak and a couple of ales and took in the cowboy-like scenes around me. A blur of waiting staff dressed in jeans and check shirts were attending to the busy dining room. The large room, also with gallery seating, was aptly decorated with bison and stag heads. Western music clattered in the background and the smell of cooking steak from the large open kitchen filled the air. There was a lot of action. The thought of taking on the restaurant challenge didn't even enter my mind. It's something which is really only fit for the constitution of a hungry Anaconda. The challenge is attempted frequently by the foolhardy and for those whose eyes are bigger than their bellies. Few succeed in an attempt to get the $72 meal free. The meal, which has to be consumed in one hour, is a 72-ounce steak. That's quite a chunk of cow. Then there's all the trimmings including potatoes, veg, salad, bread and shrimp cocktail. The contest is strictly timed and failure results in you parting with dollar. In fact, so confident is the restaurant that participants will not succeed, you pay first. The reasoning behind this is simple. After the meal, experience has shown that after consuming that amount of food, diners feel so ill, they cannot reach for their wallets. It's quite a ghastly affair, where contestants are positioned on a table on an elevated platform with puke bins close by, all in full view of the restaurant. I was rather glad that no competition was in progress whilst I was dining.

Leaving Amarillo, I had lost the opportunity to meet my Texan lady with a lot of oil. However, I did fall in love with an extremely iconic piece of Americana. I was able to run my hands over the fabulous contours of a brand spanking new Ford Mustang. The sales lady at the dealers across the road from my motel gave me the full story of the muscle car and even suggested I shipped one back to the England. She would mention that of course, anything is possible in the land of opportunity.

Chapter 18

Clines Corners

Thankfully the Easter chill had left the Texas pan handle as I left Amarillo and continued west. Crossing into New Mexico, the air actually smelt warmer and the scenery started to change quite quickly. I was now entering a red and brown landscape. If it wasn't for the long straight road populated with the usual traffic, I could be on another planet. Talking of the road, it was more impressive than the other day approaching Amarillo. It was undulating just a little, but straight as a die towards the horizon. It was a clear morning and I reckon I could see in excess of twenty miles – straight. The roadside power electric pylons, with drooping cables, framed the road and it looked like one of those road trip scenes from the movies. I needed some road signs to start one of my mind games – and quickly! What was quite scary was the complete barren landscape either side of the road. There was absolutely nothing but scrub and sage bush vegetation. No cattle, no buildings, few side roads, nothing. Talking to some locals in the comfort of a Santa Fe bar later that evening, a road user said you just pray you never break down on that road and never think about travelling at night. It was so isolated. Arriving at Clines Corners, I pulled into a service station and was a little perturbed that the wind was rocking me as I got off the bike and refuelled. It was clear and blue and the strong wind that had blown up was creating sand devils. The sand was even getting into my coffee. It was a different world here and quite hard to grasp the dramatic changes in the landscape. It was only a couple of weeks ago that I was way out east in the Carolinas and Tennessee where it was very green and I felt in a different country over here. Entering New Mexico that morning I was mulling over the different states and their characteristics and you could almost describe each as different countries. They are certainly big enough to warrant geographical segregation and all have their unique defining character. Different cultures, different people, different accents, different food – well apart from the plethora of the Mexican menus that clutter the tables. What was slightly alarming and it only just occurred to me, was that apart from small local trips around my stop-overs, I had used Interstate 40 all the way across the country from Raleigh, North Carolina to Clines Corner, New Mexico. That was over 2,000 miles. That would have to change quickly. I think the weather had been a factor here and when I got the window of opportunity to progress, the simplest way was jumping on the Interstate, which had got me to where I was.

The final run into Santa Fe was off the Interstate and on highway 285 for a hundred miles or so. It was a quiet run, in equally isolated looking terrain that I had experienced earlier that morning. Getting closer to Santa Fe, I was waiting to see the typical collection of high-rise buildings characteristically marking the business downtown area. Still nothing as I got very close and it became apparent why. There isn't a high-rise. Santa Fe is 'The City Different'. With much Spanish heritage, Santa Fe is today a centre for arts which very much reflects the multi-cultural character of the city. It has a unique style which is based on a central plaza, with a radiating grid of streets. The imposing buildings are based on a Spanish Pueblo Revival look. Local rules passed that new and rebuilt buildings, especially those in the historic district, must have a Spanish style, with flat roofs and other features defining New Mexico's adobe construction. What this has produced is a city full of character, with a strong Spanish feel. Sitting in the plaza, in the shadow of St Francis Cathedral, it was easy to imagine being somewhere in Mediterranean Europe.

Like the city, the State Capitol is very unique. The latest Capitol is the second the city has had. Today's Capitol was completed as late as 1966 and remarkably has no dome or pillars, as has been the distinguishing features of most State Houses so far. That would go against the architectural grain in this city and what you see is unique to say the least. It's flat-topped and built like a great American Indian roundhouse, or Kiva. Neoterritorial to be exact. It was refreshing to discover something unconventional and I am glad the lady in Raleigh had not given away any information on what to expect in Santa Fe. Locals seemed to be proud of their unique Capitol and the ladies in reception offered a warm welcome. It had its collection of art, but not to the extent of elsewhere. The interior was more like a museum. The compact adobe city centre is very close to the Capitol and many art galleries are dotted around the streets. Their theme concentrates on wildlife and western scenes, befitting to the area. I got talking to one art shop owner as I was admiring an incredible bronze statue. It was a cowboy carriage being pulled by four horses over rough terrain. It was the price of the statue that would buy a couple of houses in New Mexico that generated my expletives. I was quickly advised it was a limited edition by a well-known American sculptor and would sell in quick time. That's why she probably could afford a second home in Montana. She highly recommended Montana and even suggested a viewing point in Glacier National Park that I should find. I stored that away for the future. Montana? I think that was in July.

An American traveller in 1849 wrote about Santa Fe with much critique. 'I can hardly imagine how Santa Fe is supported. The country around is barren. At the north stands a snow-capped mountain while the valley in which the town is situated is drab and sandy. The streets are narrow and a Mexican will walk about town all day to sell a bundle of grass for a dime. They are the poorest people I ever saw, subsisting on muttons, onions and red pepper.' Walking around the place, I could picture some of his description. Dried red peppers and chillies are still sold all over the place in market stalls. But how the city has transformed its image over 150 years. Today, it holds the reputation of being a destination for the discerning and quite wealthy traveller. I guess it is the art that attracts those sort of visitors, who have that sort of money.

My next capital city was Phoenix, Arizona. However, what lay between should not be missed and required diversion. I wanted to see Monument Valley and the Four Corners area, prior to heading for Phoenix. There was a lot of territory to cover, which required quite a lot of planning. I was feeling extremely tired and quite drained and only hoped it wasn't the lurgy hovering around. It was while researching my departure for the next day that I discovered, by accident, that the elevation in Santa Fe is 7,000 feet. What with the elevation, heat and clear air, I think I was suffering from a combination of journey fatigue and altitude sickness. Not to mention that my body is continually subjected to different weathers as I am moving rapidly over large distances. Quite a challenging cocktail all round really. It was a strange feeling that I had not encountered before. Every part of my body just wanted to rest, which was quite annoying when I had so much to do. I felt as if I was walking around in mud and my speech was slurred as if I had been partying for a week. Maybe a good meal, light refreshment and a good night's sleep would do the trick. But I think this altitude acclimatisation can take a few days, so I eagerly awaited my status in the morning. I had planned to head due north out of Santa Fe and run west along the Colorado border towards the Four Corners. That meant more elevation. An interesting few days ahead I think.

Chapter 19

Lone Wolf

Everything felt in the right place the next morning; I think my body had made a quick recovery. The Weather Channel was getting excited about very strong winds in the Four Corners area later in the day and rather reluctantly, I shook my bones vigorously, made the bike ready quickly and was on the road by 7 am. Getting ahead of the strong wind was my aim. It was clear and bright, with only light commuter traffic around in Santa Fe at that time of the morning. Over the years I have always been quite an early riser; once I am up and about, it's a great feeling. But, it's the extraction from a warm bed and comfortable slumber that takes the effort. Once the oxygen is bubbling around my arteries, my body energises and is ready for action. Rather like a lizard gaining heat from the sun to go and catch that fly. Quickly clearing to the north of the city, I had route 84 very much to myself. A start point of 7,000 feet elevation in Santa Fe was etched in my mind and with the GPS altitude function selected on, I watched with interest as I was quickly climbing. Suddenly the landscape transformed into spectacular reds, oranges and browns, revealing ravines, gorges and canyons along the roadside. The early morning sun was casting amazing hues and shadows across northern New Mexico. It was very good advice from Joe in the Santa Fe Tourism Department to take this route. Joe was an amazing character and his booming and modulating American tones gave the impression he was permanently reciting some words for a comedy play. He had the looks for a comedy; an African-American, Joe looks if he has seen too much sun over the years and with a shock of grey fuzzy hair and white flashing teeth, he certainly was an engaging character. We ate some of his homemade cookies whilst poring over a map of New Mexico yesterday. It had to be this route he said; you will see the Rockies not far north and then make a stopover in Farmington. I was recalling his words and matching his description to that morning's live picture. Once north of Espanola and after about 80 miles, the red rock escarpments gave way to a plateau area with a lot of snow in the fields. From warm red rock into forest and snow fields, it was like going from one season into another. I passed through many small settlements, including Cebolla, Tierre Amarilla and Los Ojos, all with a rustic and isolated feel to them. Stretched along the roadside, they all looked similar, with a good selection of fuel stations, small diners and grocery stores. Piles of fire wood outside the small houses, some with snow still on their roofs, gave a wintry feel. Approaching the town of Charma, a large wolf ran straight across in front of me. I made out his distinctive thickset black, grey and white physique and thin pointed muzzle. I didn't have to brake, but he was quite close. He gave a quick glance my way and then quickly made it to the snow fields and disappeared into the cover of the pine forests to my right. I wonder what he thought of my shark's mouth on the front of the bike?

I took brief refuge in the small town of Charma which sits quite close to the Colorado border and with an elevation of 8,000 feet, was the highest point that morning. It felt quite cool and my breath and coffee steam were heavy on the morning thin air. Shattering the stillness and perhaps struggling with the altitude, I watched a helo make an approach to a local pad, with a hell of a rotorblade clatter. I had only been on the road a couple of hours and this cool air was certainly a contrast to the relatively warm spring day yesterday in Santa Fe. It was a different world up here and it so easily could be northern Canada or somewhere in Scandinavia. Not far to the north of Charma, the southern range of the Rockies was right there. I had lost the orange and red morning canyons to be replaced by what Colorado is best known for. Someone had mentioned

I would see the Rockies on this route, but I had not anticipated I would be this close to the mountainous snow and ice landscape. The lady in the visitor centre urgently advised me not to progress any further north as the road was closed after overnight snowfall. Thanking her, I mentioned I was heading west, but she again stressed no route into Colorado was possible from Charma.

The 100 miles that morning had been the most scenic and impressive of my journey so far. It had only taken me 6,000 miles to get excited about the terrain! It would set a personal theme and my comment so far on the USA is that west is best folks! The Land of Enchantment here in New Mexico suitably endorsed my feelings. West from Charma and rather too soon, I descended rapidly and was quickly below the snow line. Thankfully there was no snow on the good road and I was surrounded by a rocky landscape. It was rather like a miniature version of what I had seen so far. On this route, the towns were replaced by industrial sites that support the very active oil and gas industry. The undulating road became heavily populated with works traffic. They all carried a tall antenna with a small flag on top. I later learnt that this was not for show, but had a dual function. The flag flying on the antennae enables road users to see works traffic in the very undulating terrain and different coloured flags had different functions within the industrial sites. On arrival, Farmington was like an 'antennae and flag vehicle' city. This place was obviously the hangout for the workforce, as evidenced by masses of their trucks, a collection of motels and hotels and a line of eateries. With an almost frontier feel, Farmington, in the heart of America's south west, is an ideal location to explore the delights of the states that join to make the Four Corners.

With a combination of thriving local industry and a hub to the spectacular four-state geology, I was confidently informed by the motel check-in lady that the local property market is booming. Apparently, even Californians were swooping in to scoop up a second home. I found this quite surprising considering the nationwide slump in real estate that was broadcast daily on the national news channels. I didn't offer my comment on this, which was surprising for me; I was keen to unload and start planning for the next day. These small towns I stayed in were always great fun and perhaps illustrated the real America. Clear of mainstream tourist areas, clear of tourists and only locals and the workforce. My room had two king size beds in it and when given this opportunity, I would typically spread all my kit out on the second bed to check it over. I had my laptop up and running on the net, kit laid out, sandwich on the go and felt quite content after a good 230-mile run this morning from Santa Fe through fabulous countryside. I was standing at my open door looking at how dirty my bike was getting when an RV pulled up next door. The driver wasn't that careful how he occupied his parking space and ended up quite close to my bike. It was okay, I nodded at the well-dressed driver and thought nothing more of it. I did notice this guy was perhaps not part of the local workforce, but maybe a business traveller, but what I did notice was that his vehicle had a collection of small antennae scattered around the place. That can be normal these days what with drivers' on-board toys, but they looked more than normal on this vehicle. I returned to my kit and decided I desperately needed to do some laundry and scoured around for some quarters. The quarter is the only useful American coin quite honestly and I had run out. Reception I am sure would help and I made my way there. The guy from the truck was in conversation with the front desk lady and I distinctively heard him say 'Brit' and 'biker' and my name. Interesting. I had taken the panniers off the bike, which have some GB coverage and nothing was showing my nationality. During my brief visual encounter with him, I had not spoken, but if I had, my Australian accent would have thrown him! Very interesting. I got some change and at the same time asked advice for a decent restaurant for dinner. Returning to my room, the guy next door invited himself in and confidently announced he was my 'roommate next door' and could offer any local advice. I was sitting at my laptop and engrossed in Monument Valley, however, and simply passed on a hello and thanks. As he left, he stopped and purposefully observed all my kit laid out on the bed. Cameras, recording devices, tool kit, you name it, he was doing an inventory check. His precise movements gave the impression he was taking mental photographs. His behaviour continued outside, where he spent an age looking at my bike. Very strange, he was either genuine, a thief or something else. He didn't take anything out of his vehicle and an hour later he was gone and I never saw him again. My suspicious mind was working overtime and I was thinking I should talk to someone about this. I had now experienced a few similar incidents that I couldn't explain. It was 50-50, maybe I was creating some security interest, or maybe not. But what was interesting about this guy was that he didn't ask me any questions about what I was doing and how I was doing as the majority of Americans had done so far. If he was a spook, he was the first one that had spoken to me. A very different approach. I was staying with some American friends in Phoenix at the end of this journey sector and I would talk to them. In the meantime, I continued with my planning to depart New Mexico tomorrow, have a quick look at Monument Valley in southern Utah and then get back on track into Arizona. I was still up at over 5,000 feet in Farmington and although my head was perfectly clear and not fuzzy like yesterday, my limbs were heavy and I was dragging myself around rather Neanderthal-like. I knew that after an early dinner, I would be unconscious for at least eight hours. I felt rather bullish about my encounter today and was treating it like a big game. Whatever, I was ready for more. Bring 'em on!

Chapter 20

Marlboro Country

It was overcast and cool first thing the next morning with a thin layer of ice over the bike. By the time the engine was running for a while and I had loaded up, the ice was gone and glimpses of the early morning sun were straining through the high cloud. The local workers emerging from their rooms were all dressed for the cold in thick jackets and woolly hats. The coolness that greeted me that morning did nothing to deter my spirits as I knew today I would be amongst some stunning scenery. Clearing Farmington on route 64 quickly got me out towards Shiprock and then further west into the north east corner of Arizona. At the small town of Teec Nos Pos, it was a quick diversion to the north to get to the Four Corners site. I have mentioned this before, so a bit about this unique geographical place deep in Navajo Indian territory. The Weather Channel frequently refer to 'strong winds forecast' and 'sizzling temperatures expected' in the Four Corners area, so I had to have a look at this place that is so often mentioned from the comfort of a forecasting studio in some metropolitan monster at the other side of the country. Four Corners is the only place in the USA where four states come together at one place forming a natural corner. Arizona, New Mexico, Utah and Colorado are bolted together here and you can stand, lie stretched out, jump up and down, or whatever turns you on, in all four of these fantastic states at the same time. I made do with standing; it was daylight and a few visitors were already on the site. The monument was refurbished in 1992 with a bronze disk embedded in granite. It's quite a lump of bronze and you would need a big truck to take it to the pawn shop. Each of the state boundaries radiate from the disk and each state's seal rests within the state's boundary. It was very tasteful and an enjoyable stopover and where a young Australian couple – real Australians – gave me some excellent advice. They were keen to pass on that there was no need to drive into Monument Valley National Park and mix it with the tourist buses. Great views of the buttes are available from the roadside. That turned out to be good advice and gave me the opportunity to cover a lot of miles that day.

Having been in four states already, I could park up, put my feet up and consider a day's work done. But no, it was only 10 am and I had oodles of time to make progress. Leaving Four Corners, it was already getting warm and I really felt established now in desert and red rock country. The roadside vistas were just acres of yellow and red sand, interspersed with few grassy areas. Huge rock escarpments and buttes stood out dramatically against the warming morning blue sky. I got to the small Navajo town of Kayenta, which sits in north east Arizona, and with a few motels around it looked the sort of place that serves tourist needs for trips to Monument Valley. Straddling Arizona and Utah, the scenes for the next few miles up to the valley area were straight from movie sets and cigarette advertising posters. Still early in the year, traffic was light and I could easily imagine no road and just a track through the desert where Navajo Indians would tramp between reservations years ago. Their backdrop were the stunning buttes and rock formations of Monument Valley including West Mitten Butte, East Mitten Butte, Stagecoach, King-on-his-throne and Eagle Rock, to mention but a few. The Indians from that era would not be impressed to see today's hoards of visitors in this once sacred area. Every form of transport, from balloon to bus, provides the paying tourist with some of the world's best views. My view was from the roadside and away from the crowds. There was not a sound and the shimmer from the morning's increasing heat added to the spectacle of this quite special area. That was sound Australian advice.

Leaving Monument Valley, I was now carving a south-westerly track deeper into Arizona. Tuba City was an option for a night stop, or I could progress as far as Sedona, which would ideally place me for arrival in Phoenix. Phoenix was the end of this journey sector. It was now hot, but not yet uncomfortable. The Navajo Trail, now route 160, took me into Tuba City. For part of the route, a rail track parallels the road and I overtook a couple of long freight trains. My speed was not excessive, but the locos were obviously struggling with an enormous weight of rock from local mining facilities. A wave towards the driver gave me a blast on the horn; that characteristic wailing sound of American trains. Canyon and desert landscapes continued all the way to Tuba City. In the far distance, an impressive snow-peaked mountain range dramatically stood out. Looking at the map later, I discovered that I was over a hundred miles from these mountains when I first saw them. Tuba City is the largest Navajo Indian Reservation and most residents are Navajo. The name means Tangled Water which probably refers to the many springs below the surface which are the source of several reservoirs. It was hard to imagine a lot of water just under the surface in this very dry and arid climate. It was a topic of conversation I would address with my Phoenix hosts in the near future – just where does the metropolitan monster of Phoenix and all its surrounding satellite cities get water to serve a modern thirsty population? Tuba City was in a jumble with road construction and I found only one motel and a couple of dusty streets. Shall I stay here or shall I go on another 100 miles into the Sedona area? Local advice and refreshment was needed and I also needed to extract my thermal lining from my riding kit. It had been cold leaving Farmington, New Mexico that morning with ice on bike and cool breath on the air. Now it was in the 70s and I was sweating like a pig. Locals at a fuel station laughed at me when I suggested an overnight stay here. 'One motel, one Navajo visitor centre to look at and that's it. The roads are a mess; continue on if I was you.' That general feeling was confirmed by a local HD rider who had pulled up and was examining my bike. He was a Navajo guy on quite an old machine; his faded black leather jacket was adorned with loads of chapter badges and frills on the sleeves. I took the dual advice I had received and decided to press on. With a wave and smile from his creased brown face, the Navajo HD rider gurgled off into the dusty high street. It was one of those decisions that I would maybe later find out was worthwhile, or I had missed out on an interesting place. Whatever, it was only the one night I was considering and I continued towards those big mountains I had seen earlier. I cleared south of Tuba City, and for a short time the Grand Canyon lay only 40 miles to my west. I continued south and was soon amongst those mountains forming part of the San Francisco Volcanic Field – dominated by Mount Humphreys, Agassiz and Fremont. They provide a dramatic northern shield to Flagstaff, but they just didn't look as impressive close up. The visual perception from a considerable distance, as I had seen from north of Tuba City, was far more pleasing to the eye.

After a day and 350 miles in desert and red rock, surrounded by huge buttes, rugged canyons and mountain ranges, I was brought down to earth with a real slam in Flagstaff. Not literally thankfully. I just had to get through the place quickly and find Sedona. But I arrived around commuting hour and the place was wall-to-wall traffic. I just had to find route 89A. I found it and was soon back into the comfort of the countryside and impressive canyon country. The road to Sedona is probably one of the most scenic routes in the USA. It's like Monument Valley, but all the rockscapes are squashed together, forming dramatic canyons. Sedona is in the middle of this lot and the local geographical spectacle has turned the town into a commercial and congested cocktail. It's a shame but I guess businesses have to survive. I continued on the road through and only a few miles south found the delightful village community of Oak Creek. I had been on the road 400 miles, started with ice in New Mexico and finished with sweat in Arizona and was extremely grateful to find a first-class motel overlooking tremendous red rock canyons. This would definitely do for a couple of nights prior to completing this sector down in Phoenix. My varied route and considerable distance today may have thrown off any tail. I had seen nothing suspicious, unless the Navajo HD rider was undercover. I wonder what the remainder of Arizona would have in store?

Chapter 21

Sunday Morning Pie Cafe

Sedona is a photographer's paradise if you are careful not to get people and tourist shops in the frame. The main attraction is the stunning collection of red sandstone formations. The best time to get the camera out is dawn and dusk, when the rising and setting sun generate brilliant orange and red glows. Away from the busy town of Sedona is the contrasting and historic Jerome. Perched at over 5,000 feet elevation and on a 30-degree incline on top of Cleopatra Hill, Jerome is locally known as America's most vertical city. It's quite a twisting climb to get to the elevated centre which provides long views east towards Sedona. It's an old copper mining town that sits on what were the largest mineral deposits in Arizona. Today the mines are silent and Jerome has become the largest ghost town in America. With a population of less than 500, Jerome relies upon the tourists that are visiting Sedona to drop by. It was a hot Saturday morning when I arrived in the narrow streets and there were more of the HD community around than locals. They had their machines all lined up and undoubtedly were showing off their chrome and leather, whilst arriving and departing machines made as much noise as possible.

From an external view, appearances haven't changed in nearly a century. Many of the buildings used by present-day businesses are those built after the fires of 1899. Due to the vertigo-generating incline, gravity has pulled a number of the buildings down the slope. One that collapsed was the town's jail. A notable section is the Cribs District, where in a back alley 'prostitution row', was a busy part of town at the height of the copper mining era. That industry seems to get everywhere. The last mine closed in 1953 and the town was designated a National Historic District. In complete contrast and with limited historical background, Sedona grew up as a farming settlement and became well known for the quality of its fruit, especially the abundant apple orchards. Soon the attractive red rock and rugged beauty was no longer a secret and Sedona became a tourist location. Today, it is overflowing with art shops, galleries, boutiques, restaurants and lodgings. Jerome makes for a splendidly gritty alternative.

Oak Creek was a quiet little hideaway, and with a fuel station and a couple of watering holes provided all the facilities I needed away from its busier big brother. The Bell Rock scenic area adjoins the north end of the village and huge rock formations sit literally on the roadside. Next was Phoenix and the only route south was on Freeway 17. It was a quick run down in excellent riding conditions, although a keen wind was quite testing around some of the sweeping bends. Completely by chance, I stumbled upon a coffee shop of local repute for my morning leg stretch. It looked a normal diner, large car park and only one or two bikes about, all HDs of course. It was Rock Springs Café, very famous for fruit pies and perfect pastries for over 20 years. I later discovered that most bikers plan their route around a stopover at Rock Springs Cafe. If I could squash one in my luggage, a Rock Springs pie would make an excellent peace offering to my hosts down in Phoenix – or Chandler to be exact. The coffee was good, as was the chat with the servers. They were all quite senior ladies, who obviously enjoyed working in an establishment with such notoriety. From inside the busy café, I heard one or two bikes arrive, but thought nothing else of it. Refreshed and ready to leave, I was astonished to find the car park bursting at the seams with HDs and a busy crowd. It was a bikers' week apparently and this gathering accounted for a high percentage of Phoenix's leather and chrome brigade. My bike was surrounded and so was I very quickly. Thankfully it was a friendly mob and we exchanged road talk. Some even took my photo. I was the only non-HD owner amongst maybe 200 bikes. I engaged in conversation with one guy who turned out to be a former Air Force fighter pilot and latterly an airline driver. Today he was dressed in the normal HD attire of jeans, leather chaps, leather jacket with much decoration, all topped with a coloured handkerchief over his head and dark shades. It just goes to show that looks can be deceiving. Whilst flying from British bases, he amusingly recalled that he got the best gin and tonics ever in the Officers Mess. So there you go, terrible food in Britain, but damn good gin and tonic! That made me laugh all the way to Phoenix.

It was refreshing to find such a unique café with a varied sweet and savoury menu. It is a commonly known fact that America has its fair share of overweight people, not helped by the nation having an overabundance of fast food eating places. But let's not forget that my country has a similar problem. It is so easy to eat the wrong things and neglect exercise. I have lost count of the fast food and drive-through restaurants I have encountered. I saw a food outlet the other day where you punched some numbers into a keyboard, spoke a few words into a speaker and a young lady on roller skates brought your order out to the car. A bit difficult to sample this piece of Americana on a motorcycle, but cool nonetheless. The diners and the like in the cities have tall advertising signs guiding you to the calories – 'come and eat here.' I am sure they compete with each other as to who can have the tallest, largest and most colourful sign. The food is fast, and the portions are huge – which you can make huger – but normally it tastes good. Balanced and nutritious... hmm, I'm not sure. It is actually possible to hunt out the chicken, pasta and fish dishes hiding from the burgers and wings that normally get the menu headlines. Most places are now aware that it is prudent to cater for the health-conscious. Mind you, finding what I would call a normal sandwich is a challenge. A 'regular' sandwich choice in America could feed a family. I have been amused and slightly disappointed on a few occasions now to receive derogatory comments about food in England. Not only do we make a mess of a hamburger, but what is that green gunge that comes with fish and chips? Of course these type of comments are normally coming from American tourists who really never venture out of tourist-style eateries. If only some of them would hunt out a decent pub and that good restaurant, because there are hundreds. Already, I have sniffed out some excellent restaurants in America. It's not normally the easiest thing to do in biker's kit, but on the odd occasion and normally assisted with local recommendations, I treat myself to a swanky restaurant and have a swanky meal. I would eat well in Phoenix.

Chapter 22

Sentimental Journey at Chandler

After Rock Springs, it was only a couple of blinks of the eye and I was back into USA gridlock. That's quite a trend over here, miles and miles of open space and then an urban monster towering from the ground, cluttered with all the associated human trappings. This urban monster was Phoenix, but almost hub-like, Phoenix is central to the surrounding satellite cities of Chandler, Mesa, Tempe, Glendale and Scottsdale. Altogether this Arizona megatropolis ranks as the fifth largest conurbation in the USA. There was massive road construction on arrival from the north and I was re-routed through the affluent area of Scottsdale. After an unscheduled tour of Paradise Valley and a close inspection of Superstition Freeway, I eventually found Chandler where I was hosted by the Sepulveda family. Sheree and Natalie greeted me on a hot and still Sunday morning, not a cloud in the sky. It was only late March and already very hot. The summer in Arizona is uncomfortably sizzling. At that time of the year, it is painful to be outside and locals move from air-conditioned home to air-conditioned office to air-conditioned shopping malls and only sit outside if they are next to a swimming pool and covered in chilled cans of beer. I was disappointed to discover that both Martin and his son Mark were out of town on business trips. It was a great shame that I would not see them to share my travel tales. However, it was apparent that Sheree had an itinerary for me, as much I insisted on a quiet week after 7,000 miles on the road. No sooner had I arrived, I was whisked around the block and moved into one of the family homes. It was a large house with big rooms and tall ceilings. It reminded me of some of the places I had seen in Santa Fe. This was my abode for the week, where I occasionally saw a fellow lodger who seemed to be on permanent night shift at the fire station. When I did have the chance to talk to him, it turns out he had just left the Marines after three tours of duty in Iraq and had recently relocated to Arizona from the Bay Area of San Francisco. It was a woman that dragged him down here and after the relationship had failed, he decided to stay put and try a different state. I forget his name, but he was as wide as he was tall and his daily work-out schedule in this heat would have produced stamina fit for a professional boxing match. His mental stamina however could not accept my journey and he thought I was mad and offered little conversation on the geography on the USA.

My week in Chandler was a blur of heat, busy roads and busy shopping malls. I quickly gained familiarity with the grid of streets and freeways, assisted by my faithful GPS which here was essential. My first expedition was down into the Capitol area of Phoenix, where the original Capitol is now a museum. The business end of politics is discussed in 1960s-style buildings that flank the copper-domed neoclassical Spanish style original State House. I soon discovered that I was not alone that morning. Walking from my bike to Capitol Buildings and the gardens, I was being followed everywhere by a tall thin gent in casual attire. When I sat down, he sat down close by. When I walked off he followed, when I read the inscriptions at the war memorials, he was nearby. Enough and I decided to make conversation. Alas, it was near impossible and all I got out of him was, 'It's a nice day isn't it.' Game on again! The impressive anchor from USS Arizona quickly diverted my thoughts from this Monday morning encounter. I would see more of this huge ship in the waters close to state 50.

Throughout the week and over dinner at BJs, Zipps, The Keg, Geudos and Rula Bulas, this security thing came up in conversation with Sheree and her friends. They were open-minded about my observations and suggested it could be happening, or it may be my imagination. All were non-committal. Maybe I should try and take some photographs of these guys that are supposedly following me around. I was now in state number 13 and my observations so far are providing reasonable evidence that I am being tailed. I could ask to speak to someone in a police station, but that would gain nothing and they wouldn't tell me anything. Whilst giving an informal journey presentation over a pizza lunch at Sheree's work later in the week, the audience almost went silent when I commented on the security issue. Everyone clammed up.

It was a fitting end to my stay that a B17 wartime bomber should make a visit to Chandler municipal airport. One of 14 or so still airworthy around the globe, this particular aircraft has striking nose art of Betty Grable posing in blue swim suit. Betty's shapely legs were legendary and at one point of her career were insured for over one million dollars. That was a lot of dollar then. This shot of Betty peeking over her shoulder was a favourite amongst American soldiers in World War 2. Nose art pin-ups were always photograph-based and at the time of this shot, Betty was apparently pregnant and hence her pose is with her back to the camera. A strange but true story. The aircraft was named after the 1944 song 'Sentimental Journey' sung by Doris Day. Sentimental Journey was built by the Douglas Aircraft Corporation in Los Angeles. She was prepared for the invasion of Japan, but never saw action and only got as far as the Philippines. Her presence at the airport created quite a spectacle. Also delighted to see Sentimental Journey was former Air Force pilot and local resident Gordon Clark. Gordon was full of flying stories from his Voodoo jet fighter days. I couldn't get a word in. He fondly recalled being stationed in England in the early 60s where after a busy week's flying, they would hit London in search of entertainment. 'Those were good days in Europe and we didn't have a care in the world!'

Standing at the tail of the B17 and projecting my gaze forward, the aircraft looked primed for flight. The brilliant blue Arizona sky was contrasting sharply with the machine's silver skin. It was a fitting view. My thoughts were now focused on departure from the area and heading west towards the distant blue horizon of the Pacific Ocean and California.

Part Three – In California

Phoenix-Arizona to Las Vegas-Nevada

2,603 miles

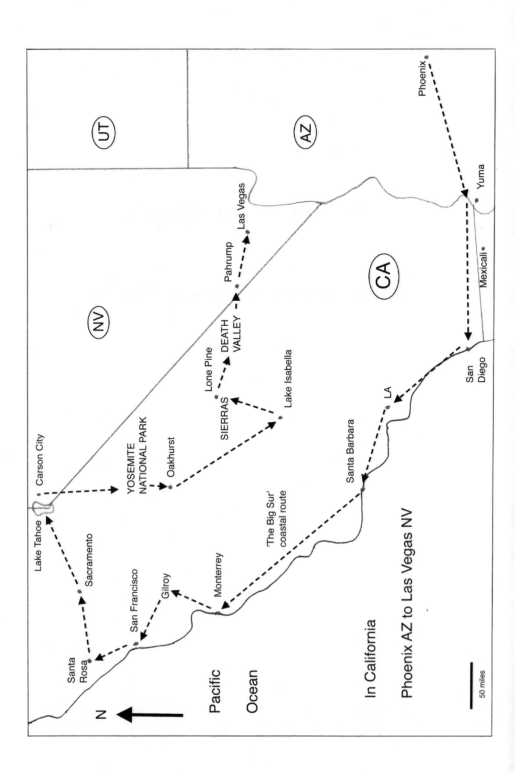

In California
Phoenix AZ to Las Vegas NV

DATE	START	FINISH	MILEAGE	CUMULATIVE	COMMENTS
5 April	Chandler AZ	San Diego CA	353	7455	US237/I-8
6 April	San Diego CA	San Diego CA	33	7488	City & Beach local
7 April	San Diego CA	Santa Barbara CA	215	7703	I-5/PCH
8 April	Santa Barbara CA	Santa Barbara CA	38	7741	Mountains & local
9 April	Santa Barbara CA	Monterey CA	250	7991	Route 1 & The Big Sur
10 April	Monterey CA	Monterey CA	142	8133	Carmel Valley-Carmel/Monterey
11 April	Monterey CA	Half Moon Bay CA	137	8270	Via **GILROY** & Santa Cruz-via US 1
12 April	Half Moon Bay CA	Mill Valley CA	46	8316	US 1 coastal. Golden Gate Bridge
12 April	Mill Valley CA	Mill Valley CA	26	8342	Local & coastal route 1
13 April	Mill Valley CA	Mill Valley CA	39	8381	San Francisco & Golden Gate Bridge areas.
14 April	Mill Valley CA	Santa Rosa CA	46	8427	US101 north
15 April	Santa Rosa CA	**Sacramento CA (14)**	90	8517	Nappa Valley
16 April	Sacramento CA	Tahoe City CA	131	8648	US50 & 89
16 April	Tahoe City CA	Tahoe City	33	8681	Lake Tahoe scenic ride
17 April	Tahoe City CA	**Carson City NV (15)**	40	8721	US27 & 50
18 April	Carson City NV	Oakhurst CA	267	8988	US88 & Yosemite National Park
20 April	Oakhurst CA	Oakhurst CA	87	9075	Local south Yosemite area
21 April	Oakhurst CA	Lone Pine CA	320	9395	41/178/14/395
22 April	Lone Pine CA	Lone Pine CA	90	9485	Sierra Nevada Mountains
23 April	Lone Pine CA	Las Vegas NV	220	9705	Via Death Valley
24 April	Las Vegas NV	Las Vegas NV	27	9732	**New tyres @ Las Vegas BMW**

Chapter 23

A Deathly Gust

The next state capital on my journey was Sacramento, California. I could cut in a straight line from Phoenix in a north-westerly direction to the Californian capital. However, that would be extremely boring and I would miss out an awful lot of the Golden State. I was ahead of schedule and with time on my hands, I decided to introduce a huge diversion. From Phoenix, I would take the southern Interstate, hugging the Mexican border, due west to the Pacific Coast. San Diego would be a good aiming point. From there, I just had to hold the coast as much as I could, maybe as far north as San Francisco, which would take in the Pacific Coast Highway and the Big Sur. From Frisco, I could cut into Sacramento and then jump across the border to Carson City, the capital of Nevada. Those two capitals are very close together. There was still much to see in California, so after a very brief Nevada border incursion, I could re-enter California and run down the east side of the state to have a look at Yosemite, the Sierra Nevada Mountains and Death Valley. That would put me in a good position to have a brief pit stop – literally – in Las Vegas for some new tyres. Onwards from Vegas it would be north through Utah, with a pencil deadline of making Salt Lake City by May 1st. This bit of map shuffling gave me two weeks in California and two weeks in Utah. That should do it.

I had thought about an early start from Chandler to avoid the heat of the day. That was a futile idea and it was hot enough to fry an egg on my bike at 9 am. These excessive temperatures were something I would have to get used to. It was the water intake that was the important thing that stopped dehydration and prevented my brains frying through my helmet. I drank like a fish and felt continually waterlogged and could hear the water sloshing around inside my guts as I went around corners. This water thing worked, no matter how hot it was. In a previous life, I learnt a good tip to check if the body was working properly in overheating conditions. If you are peeing frequently and it is clear, all is well down below and you are hydrated. If your pee becomes discoloured, you are becoming dehydrated and the darker the colour, the shorter of water your body is. Not the best medical renal analysis, but a hell of a good benchmark. Pee clear and stay healthy was my aim! I was peeing like a racehorse and it was as clear as water, so no worries in the plumbing department at the moment. I was unable to say goodbye to my ex-Marine house mate. He was rarely about and was either polishing a fire engine or running around the Arizona state boundary. That left my fine hosts and after my farewells to Sheree and Natalie, I was very soon clear to the south of the Phoenix urban monster and in the desert. Route 347 took me through a flat and rather featureless landscape of sand, sand and more sand. It was barren and if you parked up, left the road on foot and walked for 10 or 15 minutes, disorientation would takeover, probably followed by heat stroke – and then if you were not prepared, death would spoil your day. Sobering thoughts. Maricopa brought a sense of normality back to my thoughts and appeared to be a busy little town going about its business like any other town on a Saturday morning. Stationary in morning shopping traffic, a generous family must have seen my veteran charity signs on my bike luggage and flagged me down waving dollar bills out of their car window. I didn't get close enough to read what value the greenbacks were, but close enough to shout to them, 'use my website to contribute!' Maybe I should have taken the money and treated myself to a charity lunch, but my integrity took over. Route 347 gave way to Interstate 8 that would take me all the way to San Diego. The day was becoming hotter now and my idle thoughts of heat survival again filled my mind as passing through the Sonoran desert. I would have to pace the 350 miles to the coast and have plenty of breaks.

Gila Bend was first on my agenda where I had arranged to meet Ed and Michelle from the Phoenix Iron Warriors riding chapter. They wanted to meet at 8 am and I suggested 10 am was far more civilised. I was to look out for a café decorated like a spaceship, probably populated by a lot of bikers. Was that insinuating bikers were travellers or aliens? I found the 'starship' and arrived before Ed and Michelle. Yes, the place was heavily populated with the HD crowd of varying shapes and sizes. I guess they were all out for their weekend ride and quite remarkably I heard a couple of them say they must get home before it gets too hot. This heat thing was why an early morning meeting time was suggested. Retired Police Officer, Ed Schoolcraft mentioned that the riding season down here can be quite short because of the excessive heat. It was only early April and the local bikers were already concerned about the Arizona heat. Thankfully I am not down here in July.

Back on the road the desert landscape continued as far as Yuma. The temperature had risen to 90F and inside my jacket was a flowing river of sweat. After refuelling the bike, I think I must have drunk three litres of water. It was now the hottest part of the day and I was reciting that old saying that 'only mad dogs and Englishman go out in the midday sun!' Very apt, but at about halfway to San Diego, I decided to press on. Quite a large city on the Mexican and Californian border, Yuma is known for a couple of things, a big Marine Corps Base and extremely big sand dunes. I saw evidence of both. Military helos were flying around making a lot of noise and obviously forgetting it was the weekend. A little to the west of Yuma, the sand dunes filled my roadside view and the increasing wind was blowing sand off their rippled contours. Heat and now wind, not the best combination, but it was bearable at the moment. Crossing the state line into California, the freeway passes very adjacent to the Mexican border. I got a glimpse of the Mexican city of Mexicali through the heat shimmer to the south. Along this portion of the route, I counted at least four border patrol checkpoints. Most cars were pulled over for a document check. Luckily I wasn't. Obviously my security notoriety had not reached these parts, or more likely, in view of the heat, the guards were sympathetic to my cooling needs that required constant motion. At Coyote Wells, the desert ahead gave way to a mountain range and passing through here is where I very nearly had an unscheduled stop. The first signs of any danger were in fact road signs warning of severe cross winds for the next 60 miles. The road continually climbed through the mountain range and peaked at 5,000 feet. At certain points the road climbed and snaked through several passes and there was absolutely no protection from any wind that was out there. The ride was now elevated and open and very quickly I felt extremely vulnerable. The wind had now increased so much that I could not hear the note of the bike's engine or even passing traffic. All I could hear was the snarl of the wind which followed me through every contour I was describing. So far so good and the ride was a bit buffeted but not dangerous. I was giving myself a real rollicking not only for not checking in detail the wind forecast today in this area, but also that I would be passing through a high mountain pass area. Or was it always windy in these parts? Whatever, I had neglected a thorough route brief of this section in my enthusiasm to get back on the road after a week off. It's something my Phoenix hosts did not mention, but sitting in the relative safety of a car, a mountain pass and a bit of wind is not something to worry about unless you have a spinnaker attached to the roof. The temperature had plummeted to 55F and that egg wouldn't fry right now. The bike was well balanced and behaving well and I thought I had it hacked, until my confidence took another hit when I passed another 'high winds for 60 miles' warning sign. San Diego couldn't come quick enough. The road was extremely quiet and I had not seen another bike since Yuma. Maybe bikers stay off this piece of Interstate? It was while cranking around a big sweeping left hand climbing bend, with a vertical rock face close to my right when my day was so nearly spoilt. I was hit by a huge gust from the left. It all happened so quickly and in that short space of time, my mind was recycling a lot of damn rubbish instead of reacting as maybe I should. My bike, my bones, I am only just in California, my camera, my laptop, you name it. It was crisis time. Before the gust hit me, I was in a bank to the left following the curve nicely and everything was under control. When the gust hit, it actually moved my whole riding attitude and pushed the front wheel sideways off the course I was following. From banking over to the left, in a split second, I became upright and my world was full of the rock face.

I remember it vividly. Maybe I was reacting as I should, as an almost instinctive correction got me back on line where I had been. There had been no time to consider changing anything and I left brakes, gears and throttle alone. It was a snap lean over to regain safety. I think bodily analysis at that moment may have proved adrenaline is brown. That was the most terrifying moment on a motorcycle I have experienced. If there was more of that to come, I felt like getting off now and hitching a ride to the coast. After that rather rude intrusion into a Saturday afternoon, I am pleased that the remainder of the ride was uneventful. Descending from the mountain pass, the temperature recovered a little to 65F, but nowhere near the sizzling 90F of the Arizona desert. I was in another country again, although the delights of being back on the road after nearly a week off had so nearly ended in an early check-out. Descending down to the coast, it was grey and overcast with no bright blues of sky and ocean to greet me. There was a thick layer of marine cloud shielding the sun from this subtropical part of California. The locals have a saying that is thrown around, 'May grey and June gloom', when making excuses for the overcast weather. The grey had come a little early this year – it was only April.

I revelled in surprise phone calls to old friends. It's more interesting than a boring and impersonal email and that surprised but familiar voice on the other end of the line tells a thousand stories. I was coming here anyway, so if Randy Elkins was not at home, so be it. I think I had mentioned my long range USA road trip to him over 10 years ago. Eureka, he was in and invited me around for coffee. Things can change over 10 years and I reckon I heard the gurgling of children in the background. Could a professional bachelor have changed his colours? It was still grey and cool when I navigated around the quiet freeways in a sleepy San Diego and my dilemmas of yesterday seemed a million miles away. I found Randy's place nestled nicely in the middle of quite an interesting part of town. Wooden-style houses, with small front drives and gardens, dominated the neighbourhood. Corner grocery stores, hairdressing salons and the odd bar complemented the neat neighbourhood. It was mid-morning and still quiet. The only residents up and about were washing their cars and watering garden plants.

Humans have the same routine and do similar tasks around the globe, even on the same day! My thoughts after the earlier telephone call were confirmed. Randy was now a father of two young boys. He dual-tasked their safety management with my coffee requirements, as his Australian wife started the geographical quiz. Had I been there, am I going there, what did you think of there? etc. Both global travellers, now with two small children, their immediate travel ambitions had been curtailed. After a catch-up from the last decade, I left their friendly and exceedingly tidy abode after a couple of hours. I think they thought I was quite mad taking on the whole USA, but all things considered, and after surviving 7,500 miles and quite a few eye-watering incidents, I was beginning to have a bullish confidence about the whole journey. Albeit I continually reminded myself of an old maxim I frequently used in younger days. When you have that warm feeling of over-confidence, stand back and re-examine the situation. Look for the 'gotchas'. Thankfully I was doing this all the time without knowing it. The weather would continue to be my biggest challenge – everywhere.

I found a laid-back beach area of town and had a laid-back afternoon. The grey sky was giving way to blue and there was even the threat of some sunshine. This beach area, one of several dotted around the city's footprint, had a real cosmopolitan feel. With a blend of surf shops, art galleries, boutiques, small grocery stores and attractive beach frontage homes, I felt relaxed and at ease. Street music, dog walkers, couples walking, lovers holding hands, joggers dressed in not a lot and skate boarders tricking, all provided rich people watching snippets. I took the scene in from a street-side café and watched a couple examine my bike. In the end they joined me for a coffee and told me they were on a long weekend break from Indiana. I ended up picking the lady up from the street. Her chair collapsed and she went from Sunday stroller to the most embarrassed Sunday café dweller, in very very quick time. By the time her partner returned with a coffee and cake, she was back to normal and to hide her embarrassment, she insisted that their home of Indiana was the best state remaining on my journey. Surprising, I have never heard any accolades about Indiana. 'I must get to Indianapolis well before or after the 500 race which is at the end of May.' I never thought anything more of that remark.

Chapter 24

LA Rider

At the beginning of this trip, one of my main objectives was to ride the Pacific Coast highway here in California. I wanted to hug the coast all the way up to San Francisco and keep the ocean in sight. San Diego was the start point for this exercise and the colossus of Los Angeles lay in my way. It would be pointless and time consuming to route around the east and north of LA and get mixed up in the delights of unknown neighbourhoods. The logical option which I mentally prepared myself for was to simply keep on route 1 through the guts of LA and be spat out to the north west around Santa Monica. Mr Google said it looked quite simple – it was route 1 all the way – although the road gets a few different names through the city. I just had to find route 1.

To avoid any peak traffic northbound from San Diego, I planned a leisurely departure of around 10 am. It was another gloomy morning, but thankfully it was dry. My only way north initially was on Interstate 5 as far as San Clemente where I should pick up route 1. Traffic was very heavy on 5 with 'it's Monday morning let's all go very fast' type drivers. This route carries a lot of traffic between two of California's major cities and I was being sucked into their wake. It was impossible to keep to the speed limit. The truck drivers I am sure had a mentality of racing and everyone seemed in a rush. Good morning Monday. To make matters worse, the road surface was appalling and that's being polite – it was awful. I couldn't believe I was on a major Interstate in California. North of San Diego, the surface quickly became grooved, rutted and just to concentrate the mind, potholed. I was changing lanes frequently to avoid my bones being rattled around. Attempting to put into context the roads surface versus my bike, I reminded myself I was riding the biggest and most robust enduro styled bike in the world, but it was still a dreadful ride. It would have been better to be off road completely. Once past Camp Pendleton, San Clemente came into view, my cue to leave the Interstate and find route 1. As well as using my GPS, I had got into the habit of writing on my windscreen, names of small towns I would pass on the route. It was a useful cross reference and if I saw a sign for a place I was expecting to pass through, it calmed any navigational anxieties through busy areas. Today, I had programmed a motel in Santa Barbara as my final destination and written down San Clemente, Newport Beach, Sunset Beach, Long Beach, Redondo Beach, LAX, Santa Monica and Malibu. I would follow the towns and ignore the GPS until clear of LA when it would settle down on the coastal route. Glancing at it from time to time, it was always suggesting a different route to Santa Barbara. My Heath Robinson navigational methods worked a treat and I was very quickly easing through the LA traffic. Soon route 1 was consistently signed as the Pacific Coast Highway or simply PCH all the way. Big green signs with white writing, 'Pacific Coast Highway' – that will do very nicely thank you. This is where I wanted to be and in short time I was passing by, or rather under the airport and clearing LA to the north west at Santa Monica. It had been a relative breeze and the traffic was moving all the time. So that was LA. I could have got under the skin of the urban monster for a couple of days and explored exotic areas such as Hollywood, but that was never on my agenda. The city of Malibu was far more an appealing place and I made it there for lunch. It has quite a stretch of beach on the ocean and the community is famous for a warm climate where movie stars and entertainment people hang out. Alas, I didn't meet anyone rich whilst taking a sandwich. Apparently all the rich and famous live in salubrious pads either propped up on stilts in the mountains, or close to the beachfront. It's a nice place and a popular licence plate reads 'Malibu: a Way of Life'. Although the beach front spreads for several miles, it amused me why it is designated a city. I am sure there are strict criteria before a place is nominated city status, but everywhere in the USA seems to be a city. 'You are now entering the city of Gobbledygook population 278.' It is rare to encounter a town or a village. LA is a city. San Diego is a city. Malibu?

As expected, great views of the Pacific continued and I called it a day in Santa Barbara. Santa Barbara could be and is a city. More of a city in my perception than the very attractive but much smaller Malibu. It has a big downtown, a big airport and a university. Component parts of a city perhaps. It was the magnificent setting of ocean views with palm tree-lined marinas, and the backdrop of the Santa Ynez Mountains that was appealing. I certainly would not have any problem about picking the wrong neighbourhood to stay here. My motel was on Shoreline Drive, only a short walk to the sea front and a little longer into downtown. I could plainly see that this would make a nice place to live if you could afford a house. Generally an expensive place, it was in a fuel station opposite my motel that I encountered my first $4 gallon of petrol. I mentioned with amusement to the Asian-Indian manager that this was the most expensive fuel I had bought so far during 8,000 miles on the road. This was like red rag to a bull and he got himself in a real tizzy explaining in a most animated way why he was forced to increase prices. 'It's the damn taxes, I have no option, this is California.' His amateur dramatics created a few laughs with the locals. I wonder if I would encounter a $5 gallon of fuel anywhere in my trip?

The title of the 'American Riviera' or 'California's South Coast' is most appropriate for the beautiful Santa Barbara. The downtown area has many trendy boutiques and a collection of eateries to tempt most palates. Alternatively, and hidden away, are a couple of sea food delights on a pier next to the glitzy yacht club. I found a great restaurant right here, which was obviously the hangout for the yachtie brigade. It was verging on pretentious, but the fantastic food put the establishment in the very bearable category. The dining room was atop a small bar and tastefully furnished with wooden chairs and tables. The smells from seafood cooking in the open kitchen to the rear were percolating around, creating havoc with my taste buds. Outside a fresh breeze had sprung up and the sounds from swaying palm trees and the crashing surf was heard inside. All the ingredients for a pure Santa Barbara Riviera experience.

The Santa Ynez mountains, a west-east mountain range, rise dramatically behind Santa Barbara, with several peaks above 4,000 feet. Early the next morning, I picked out a circular route through the mountains. Low cloud hung over the coast. However, after a few minutes, I was in blue sky looking down at the snaking shore. The hillside is full of expensive homes, accessible by roads that get progressively narrower and less maintained. I took a short cut on Painted Cave Road and although further residences were ahead, it suddenly deteriorated dramatically with acute hairpins and astonishingly steep gradients. I had to turn around and backtrack to the main road. Nothing was captured on my GPS up here. I got back onto the main forest route that looped around and eventually brought me back into Santa Barbara via Rattlesnake Canyon. For 40 miles and a couple of hours, I was away from the modern trappings of a city and in complete isolation with very little traffic seen. This time it was forest and mountains. In Arizona the other day it was desert.

If riding the Pacific Coast Highway was a meal, LA, Malibu and around Santa Barbara made a good appetiser. Some city, some coastline and mountains. Small samples but not a lot of everything. I had got a taster for bigger things. Tomorrow, the most famous bit of the route, The Big Sur, would undoubtedly be the main course. This section is held with high status for road trips, especially for bikers. Further up the coast towards Monterrey and San Francisco, I am sure would make an enjoyable dessert. I was ready for the main course.

Chapter 25

The Big Sur

Departing Santa Barbara, I lost the coast for a couple of hours and found myself in undulating green agricultural land. Approaching San Luis Obispo, the agricultural theme gave way to fruit orchards and I regained the coast at Morro Bay. North of here is where the main course was served and it was pretty much as on the menu. The most famous and certainly most talked about section lay before me. It's The Big Sur, a forested area on the coast that forms part of the Pacific Coast Highway. Very soon I was in spectacular scenery of huge fir trees in the valleys and gorges spilling down to the ocean. The forest greens contrasted to the dazzling blues and turquoises of the ocean below. The coastal contours changed from soft cliff curves with pasture and gorse bushes, to jagged, aggressive rocky fissures. At sea level where the ocean smell penetrated my helmet, all changed dramatically in a moment when the curvaceous beauty of a road suddenly elevated me hundreds of feet up looking down on the shimmering blue. At windy sections, the surf crashing into the rocky shore was easily heard. An exhilarating biker's route, although in some parts quite testing especially with a strong coastal breeze never far away. The terrain is striking for over a hundred miles. The Santa Lucia Mountain range appears to rise out of the Pacific. Refreshing smells of pines fill the air contrasting with the salty ocean. You need to be a passenger rather than a rider to appreciate the tremendous vistas. It was mid-week and the route was clear of traffic. Few bikers were around, although at a photo stop I got talking to a couple riding a large HD. They were on a weekend break from NYC and riding the coast for a few days before flying back to the east coast. I had been following them for some time and had noticed their bike wasn't the ideal machine for tackling the twisting road. They were cornering rather cumbersomely, unlike my bike which was tackling the contours like a national hunt racehorse at its peak. Between big gulps of fresh Pacific air, the NYC couple made this observation and contrast which was unprovoked. They commented 'I looked as if I was enjoying myself'. An accurate observation. Maybe the HD is only good for going in straight lines? I kept that view to myself, but riding the GSA around the Big Sur was about as good as it can get in a riding experience. It was all over too soon and clearing the thickly forested area, route 1 runs into Carmel and Monterrey.

Was it to be Carmel or Monterrey for a night stop? I had heard of both from my general knowledge of California, but hadn't really done any serious mind shuffling about where to stay that night. They are very close together, although as I quickly found out, extremely different. Carmel oozes a pretentious atmosphere, where the compact town is centred on a small grid of streets with expensive-looking shops equipped for the high-dollar locals. I was alarmed and slightly amused when my access to the 17-mile scenic road was denied. With a firm and impolite statement, the lady at the entrance kiosk unequivocally ordered me to turn around, venting forth, 'motorcycles are not allowed down here.' So be it, it saved me $10 and Monterrey got my vote. Clint Eastwood was probably unavailable for a beer anyway. However, that lady certainly needed some lessons on human relations. Maybe stuck in her little kiosk, she was suffering from Carmel Cabin Fever. In complete contrast a quick recce of Monterrey revealed a place with much more character. Larger than Carmel, Monterrey offers a blend of unpretentious normality with a collection of shops, busy bars and good restaurants. Some of the bars are based on an English pub and hence for a couple of days I felt quite at home. Within walking distance of the town centre and I think I am confident in stating Monterrey is a town, I stayed in a delightful motel run by an Asian-Indian family. The owners didn't have a great command of English and they did look concerned every time I saw them. Whilst messing around with my bike on the second morning, it all came out when I was confronted by the lady of the partnership. It turned out that they had a simple tax enquiry and hope I didn't mind them asking me for advice as I spoke good English. I used my growing network of American contacts and quickly got an answer from Jim in North Carolina. The Indians were pleased with the news which answered their tax question and quickly full of smiles. We all got on with the day ahead. My day was a scenic 50-mile looping ride through the Carmel Valley. The almost European-like countryside was surprising and beautiful. At only 20 miles from the coast at the start of the valley, the route started with expensive golf courses and pretty villages, giving way to acres and acres of vegetable growing land.

Ever since I had thought about this journey, I had held a fascination for one town. I had even decided to re-route there if necessary to have a quick look. It wasn't necessary as the town of GILROY was only just up the road from Monterrey. Gilroy is known as the garlic capital of California which was quite an interesting association with my name. We cannot forget artichokes and grapes that are also grown locally. I recall several years ago sampling a fruity Grenache called 'Clos de Gilroy'. That's a better association with my name. It was a hot morning as I arrived in the busy little town. Huge watering machines lined the finely manicured fields, flourishing with greenery. I found the town's sign of 'Welcome to Gilroy'. That's the photo I wanted and then I could be away back to the coast. I had a lunch invitation somewhere near Santa Cruz, which I could access via the Hecker Pass, close to Mount Madonna County Park. Prior to departing Gilroy, I caught a glimpse of the offices of the *Gilroy Dispatch* – the local newspaper. Shall I drop in? I was easily convinced, after all when would I be back in this place. Entering the building I announced to the receptionist, 'Good morning, my name is Gilroy,' after which the ladies in the open office behind all burst out laughing. I told one and all what I was doing and in short time, I was introduced to the editor who dispatched a reporter and photographer my way. *'Gilroy in Gilroy'* made for an interesting article for them and I think I hit the next edition. Prior to leaving, I had another look over the gorgeous Ford Mustang at the town's Ford dealership. An apt piece of Americana in my town.

The Hecker Pass was not for the faint-hearted and after a leisurely morning in the flat growing lands around Gilroy, I was quite surprised to encounter such testing terrain. A contact in Phoenix had put me in touch with Dan Shea. I found his 1920s Monterey-style house set in five acres of finely manicured gardens just north of Santa Cruz. Dan, a retired Silicon Valley entrepreneur was interested in my journey and the veteran charities I was supporting. It was the hottest day of the year and we had lunch in the garden. Dan had beers lined up in the cooler ready for my attack, however, I declined considering I was heading further north to San Francisco later that day. It took a bit of persuading that I was quite content to drink water. It was evident that Dan was surrounded with all the trappings that were the result of a successful business career. A huge, finely furnished house, beautiful gardens and an extremely relaxed attitude to life. I am working on that myself, but Dan added that he had experienced years of stress whilst working in the city. It was now catch-up time with grandchildren and garden. His wife, an interior designer, was still a workaholic and in the city that day. We talked for ages on the geography of the USA and lots of advice came my way. Utah dominated Dan's commentary and he has become instrumental in an art foundation that operates in an exclusive location in the southern part of the state. He invited me to that establishment and would communicate with his business partners and inform them that I would be heading their way. That should work – another week or so in California, briefly in Las Vegas, which would put me in a good position for southern Utah. Our conversation had eaten into much of the afternoon and Dan strongly advised getting through San Francisco at this time of day would not be a good idea. Make the bridge by 3 pm or suffer in the traffic, even on a bike. It was already 2 pm and Half Moon Bay just south of Frisco would make an interesting stop. It was Friday and with the reputation of the best fish and chips on the coast, it sounded a good place to stay. Leaving Dan's place, it was hot, but not Arizona-style. There was a nice cooling breeze from the Pacific that followed me all the way up the Cabrillo Highway to Half Moon Bay. My thoughts for the remaining 60 miles or so were all about the hospitality of Americans. I was becoming very relaxed about my journey and able to analyse events. I had not met Dan before and yet I was treated like family. This came about by receiving a short text message from a previous contact. 'Go to this address for a good lunch.' The kindness of strangers was becoming quite a theme.

Chapter 26

A Classic City

I found the fish and chip restaurant in Half Moon Bay and it lived up to its reputation. It was quite hard to appreciate that this little town was close to the sprawling urban areas of the Bay Area within 30 minutes' drive. Like so many other coastal retreats on the Pacific Coast, campers and trailer tourists populated the seashore and a selection of eateries in a tasteful main street catered for evening needs. In a local bar, I met a couple of young guys who were enjoying dinner. When we got chatting, it turns out they had lived in the town all their lives. They both worked in a local hotel and very rarely went anywhere else. This was their regular hangout on a Friday night and the thought of a trip up the coast to San Francisco never appealed to them. They had everything they wanted in this small town, girlfriends, work, shops, recreation and homes. My thoughts again went back to the young mother I met in a diner on that cold February morning back in Louisiana. I could appreciate why she was geographically restrained, but these young guys? They both had sports cars outside and you would think they would be charging about throwing their testosterone around.

The next morning was quite special. It was a short trip I would enjoy boasting about for years. How often do you say that you went for a quick ride to San Francisco and across the Golden Gate Bridge on a Saturday morning?! It would make for interesting biker's talk back at some of my North Yorkshire haunts. I followed the coast all the way and soon was in the Sunset District and then followed the signs for the bridge. It was a clear blue morning with no characteristic low cloud hanging around the bay and the skyline of San Francisco over my right shoulder looked impressive. Traffic was heavy, but flowing quickly, which would have been different yesterday afternoon. It was good advice to delay my arrival. The chic neighbourhood of Sausalito was my first stop. I had been recommended this place to stay which would be extremely handy for the city. With yachts lined up in the blue waters and a blend of boutiques and posh-fronted restaurants populating the main street, I immediately got the impression that it's where the affluent locals live. I wasn't wrong. Nice if you have the dollars to afford an apartment with a view looking towards your yacht. I shall have to work harder. I couldn't find a motel in Sausalito, maybe it wasn't the sort of town to have motels for the traveller. It's an expensive hotel or nothing. Mill Valley only a short distance further on was my second choice and I found a motel there no problems. North of Frisco, the Pacific Coast Highway becomes the Shoreline and Coastal highway and snakes all the way up into Oregon and beyond. I just had to sample a stretch of this to the north without getting carried away. Alas, I encountered weekend traffic leaving the city and it was gridlock for miles. I made do with some photographs of the coast from the roadside, where I got talking to a rider on a racing bike. He was in a multi-coloured full leather suit and when he had finished his cell phone chit-chat, engaged with me for a while. My journey was of interest to him and we both shared comments on the American rider and the HD. It was the first cautionary conversation I have had about American bikers. He urgently advised me to stay clear of gangs of bikers who have their own patch. Don't even speak to them. He didn't actually mention Hell's Angels, but I knew where he was coming from. Apparently, my bike would make a nice target for a heist, after which it would be broken down and sold and become untraceable overnight. Charming! I asked him if such gangs were only around the Bay Area, but he confidently advised they were all over the USA. Well, so far I had not encountered any gangs as described and all the HD riders had been very friendly. If I kept out of the guts of huge metropolitan areas, where gangs maybe had strict territories, I should be okay. I was grateful for this information and at least the afternoon had proved sort of useful. I recall the conversation with one of the HD guys I had met in Alabama. He was a retired special police officer with a professional network around the country. He insisted if I got into any trouble, I had to call him ASAP. I should check if I still had his card ASAP! I should also ask my Alabama contact for his thoughts on my under surveillance suspicions. But maybe not, he probably wouldn't give me an answer. I was certainly not deterred about riding around the city of San Francisco tomorrow as planned.

Crossing the Golden Gate Bridge the next morning, I was following an original 1960s Ford Mustang. Soft roof folded back, the driver was enjoying the warm April morning. Although moving very sedately, I stuck behind him and took in the view. An interesting American iconic duo. The bridge-the car. It would be easy to roll back the years and reminisce about the Mustang in Bond's *Goldfinger* or more appropriate and probably best-remembered, the Mustang in the police thriller *Bullitt*, set here in San Francisco. Glancing in my mirror, I noticed I was being followed by a new model Mustang convertible, an appropriate coincidence! Clearing the bridge, I headed for Marina Boulevard and parked up. I wanted to see the bridge from here and take in the views over a coffee. Many people had the same idea and the morning was full of joggers, walkers, photographers and dog walkers, all enjoying an unseasonably hot day. Some folk even had their laptops out and were surfing the www simultaneous to people watching. It was that sort of place. After an hour or so of brain soothing, it was time to get lost in the city. I had no route, I wasn't even going to follow any GPS prompts, I would leave that to getting back to Mill Valley. All I wanted to do was ride around the hills and probably get lost, but experience this classic city from the best seat in town. I had no luggage on the bike and it felt gutsy and nimble. Broadway, China Town, Geary Boulevard, Pacific Heights and Market Street were just some of the districts I covered in a couple of hours. I was dodging Chinese waiters carrying full pig carcasses over their shoulders, chasing trams, accelerating past cabs, braking to avoid tourists and racing through traffic lights. I was a boy on a toy! I even found San Francisco Street on top of one of the many hills, where the bridge provided a great backdrop from between the skyscrapers. Yes, San Francisco is full of character, the bay, the bridge, the ocean, the hills and of course the multi-cultured districts highlighted by a frenetic China Town. San Francisco is one of the few classic cities remaining around the planet. Only the likes of Hong Kong, Rio de Janeiro and Sydney can claim to rub shoulders with this Californian beauty. I was a happy biker going back over the bridge to Mill Valley. In celebration of my successful morning, I dropped into Sausalito for a late lunch in one of those waterside restaurants. I chose a seat outside and looking across the bay, over Alcatraz, the city stood proud on the skyline. It was almost surreal, almost a postcard shot with no cloud, and only a smudge of haze to restrict visibility. Returning to my bike, I noticed it had a twin – same colour, same everything. It looked like a BMW advert. The owner of the twin and his pretty girlfriend complete with pink riding helmet quickly appeared and we exchanged BMW stories. He hadn't been out of California! I think my 8,500 miles through 14 states so far was somewhat embarrassing for him. This guy gave me some fantastic local advice which made up quickly for his geographical deficiencies. He gave me directions to the best viewing areas for the Golden Gate Bridge and San Francisco. Conzelman Road was the place and he wasn't wrong.

Tomorrow was Monday and I would be back on the capital trail cutting inland to Sacramento. Whilst checking route and weathers, I noticed I had an email from a perfect stranger. John McLarty from Santa Rosa had heard about my journey and offered hospitality. Santa Rosa was just up the road and nestled in prime wine growing country, would make for a good stop prior to Sacramento. I swiftly replied to John and booked myself in for coffee tomorrow morning.

Chapter 27

Wine Country

It was a quick run up the 101 to Santa Rosa and I simply sat back and let my GPS direct me to John Mclarty's home. John lived in a nice part of town, big detached houses with driveways and adjoining garages. I had arrived around 10 am and the place was so quiet and in complete contrast to the hectic San Francisco of yesterday. John greeted me at the door and ushered me inside. Tall, medium built, with a shock of grey hair, he immediately mentioned his hearing aid and gave me advanced warning I may have to be loud with my conversation. That was no problem for me. He sat me down and started the questions, who, where, why, what, when! Almost a mini interrogation and all this before I had taken my jacket off. After 15 minutes or so, I hinted for a coffee and whilst John was manoeuvring in the kitchen, I returned the questioning. It turned out that he had seen a newspaper article about my trip and as a Korea War veteran, had decided to make contact. After his military service, he had a long career as a Police Officer, most lately as a Captain with the California Highway Patrol. Now retired, he lived alone after losing his wife a couple of years ago. My mind was quickly working overtime and I thought at the right moment, I should ask John for his comments on my suspicions of being under surveillance. As a retired police officer, he should be able to provide a decent answer. Could John be part of the surveillance operation and was being tasked to check me out at close quarters? I hardly think so, but anything is possible. When I introduced the subject and told him of my observations in several states, he was extremely non-committal and wanted to change the subject. This didn't really help me, however it was worth a try. Once our preliminaries were complete, he insisted I put the bike in the garage, after which he would give me a tour of the nearby wine area. I recall he had a couple of cars and the one on the drive, a Cadillac, was what we headed off in. It was a typical American saloon-sedan type car to me, but it was the multi-coloured Cadillac badge that was the hallmark of a once highly reputed brand. Today a traditional Cadillac is a big heavy gas guzzler and they have maybe lost that once-special niche in the American automobile inventory, to be replaced by more economic brands from Europe and Japan. We passed a Corvette roadster and unlike the Cadillac, this marque of Chevrolet still holds a special place in vehicular Americana. From that drop dead gorgeous 1958 double head-lighted roadster, the Corvette has held production all through the years to the very sporty version with stealthy streamlined contours of today. In every word, the Corvette is a muscle car, a poser's car and a high-dollar car. It's in a different league to the Mustang which has caught my eye so far. John had one major ambition remaining and that was to own a Corvette. Not necessarily a new model, but a roadster with a bit of attitude. For the remainder of our meeting, I urged him to buy one. If you've got it, flaunt it.

The remainder of the day, we cruised around several wineries in the Santa Rosa area. It was a couple of hours in fine buildings, set in neatly manicured gardens, whilst enjoying wine samples. It did a lot to elevate the California viniculture into my most frequently drank league. Until now my wine drinking habits have been stolen by Australia, South Africa and Chile. A decent Californian red is now in contention. Our wine drinking continued over dinner in the evening when I was introduced to John's partner Susan, *'Five-Buck Chuck'* and an excellent steak. *'Five-Buck Chuck'* is a very drinkable and juicy red that has gained notoriety in California and successfully competes with expensive labels at only $5 a bottle. With 'Charles' somewhere on the label and with teeth and lip-staining qualities and very pleasant to the palate, 'Five-Buck

Chuck' certainly gets my vote. We put the world to rights with verbose conversations enhanced with a lot of *'Five-Buck Chuck'*. With John's interesting background, I urged him to write a book. I also urged him to follow his dream and buy that Corvette.

The next morning, John tried to load me up with a couple of bottles of *'Five-Buck Chuck'*. I just didn't have the room as is normal and thinking of wine at 9 am after seeing a lot of it the night before was just not appealing to my constitution. I felt okay, but was rather glad Sacramento was quite close. It turned out to be a nice spur of the moment visit to John's place and the wine area. If I had seen his email a day later, it would have been too late and I would have been clear to the east. A most opportune visit and departing Santa Rosa, the route took me through more neat and tidy vineyards, before picking up Interstate 80 into the guts of Sacramento. I settled for one of my regular motels, nice and central and walkable to the downtown. An HD guy I met way back in Louisiana had given me a biking contact in Sacramento to look up if I had the time. I gave him a call. Remarkably I was expected and he said he would be around in 10 minutes and would give me a ride downtown. He was laughing and said I had to look out for a big black truck at the front of the motel. I hadn't a clue what to expect and sure enough a short while later, Lt Michael Rinelli of the Sheriff's Department of Sacramento County Police Department, pulled up at the lobby in that big black truck. Slightly rotund and with a shaven head, he was in the uniform of a typical American cop. Dark suit covered with big badges and lots of gadgets and guns on his waist. Mike was still laughing when he shook hands and immediately said I was not staying in the best part of town and I would find out why in a moment. Inside his car was like a roomy version of a fighter aircraft. Lots of digital displays and a couple of big screens. In the background was his control, chirping away on the radio with typical police things that you normally associate with a TV series. '55 yur location, okay we have a report of an assault at Lang Avenue off 47th. 29, can you assist.' Mike turned the volume down and added, 'usual shit.' A mile or so from the motel, Mike pointed out quite a lot of homeless folk around the roadside and he added they tend to wander a bit at night, so be careful. I wasn't over-fussed, it was only for one night and there were a couple of restaurants within walking distance of the motel before I got to the homeless camp. It should be okay. Dropping me off at the State Capitol Building, Mike confirmed there was nothing really to hold me in town more than one night and I should head out towards Lake Tahoe in the morning. Set in beautiful gardens, the Californian State Capitol Building is said to the most impressive in the country. The white domes and columns certainly looked good against the blue sky and the colourful flowers and refreshing fountains were dazzling in the bright spring sunshine. The Governor or *'Governator'* of this state however does hold some celebrity status and I was enthusiastic to find out if Arnold Schwarzenegger was in his office today. The big airy and cool building was relatively quiet and after walking past a portrait of former President and Governor Ronald Reagan, I found the present Governors office without getting lost. Not surprising, this was the first Governor's Office I had found with a security team outside. I was politely informed by a State Capitol Policeman that Arnie wasn't in today. The security guard gave me Arnie's card which is the closest I got to him. It was mid-afternoon and I decided to do what Mike Rinelli the Police Officer said I shouldn't. Walk everywhere. A cab at this time of day was not on my radar. I wanted to find the restored old town down by the riverside, then it would be a 15-minute walk back to my motel, maybe dodging a few of the homeless posse. I found the comfort of the old town eventually which was eerily quiet. I could have ridden a horse down the street without any conflict from resident cowboys. This was the place for an evening's playtime, where quite a few bars and eateries in restored buildings are set back from the wooden boardwalk providing a yesterday feel. After an hour or so looking at Huntington & Hopkins Hardware and the Pony Express monument, avoiding the offer of a tattoo or body piercing at River City, and slurping a beer in Fanny Ann's Saloon, all ended with a walk past the Wells Fargo Supreme Court leading me back to the river and a gentle stroll home.

Chapter 28

The Secrets of Lake Tahoe

Sacramento was okay. I had a few laughs here and there, but a brief stay was all that was required to tick off state capital number 14. Number 15 was very close and I could easily go directly to Carson City in Nevada, before cutting back into California as planned. However, I was following Mike Rinelli's advice and heading for Lake Tahoe which sits high up in the mountains on the way to Nevada. It was good advice, as the quick 130 miles turned out to be one of the most scenic runs of my journey so far. Highway 50 took me out of the sprawl of Sacramento into the countryside towards Placerville. Once east of Pollock Pines, I was in the thick forest of the Eldorado National Forest. The road started a steep climb through this very dramatic alpine looking area of fir trees and very rocky mountains. I noticed that my GPS topped out at 7,348 feet as the road twisted and turned to the summit. Either side of the road, impressive snow-covered mountains and huge slabbed ledges dominated the view. It had got extremely cool and rarefied at this altitude and I was experiencing another one of those incredible temperature gradients. If I had stayed in the lowlands around Sacramento today, I would be in shorts and T shirt enjoying a hot spring day. Up here, thermal clothing was very much the order of the day. Highway 50 became a rapidly descending Highway 89 all the way down towards the lake which was standing out dramatically against the rugged mountains and snow fields below. Reaching the level of the lake, I was still at 6,200 feet and the temperature had not recovered to anything like tennis weather. It was very cold and the air was very thin. I had heard quite a few stories about the ghoulish secrets of Lake Tahoe. My inquisitive mind figured a night stop in appropriately named Tahoe City would be a good place to do some snooping.

I had arrived at the quietest time of the year. The ski season had been and gone and the summer walking groups and canoeists had not arrived. So, it was heaven. Heaven in a beautiful setting of a deep blue lake surrounded by snow-capped mountains. Californian tranquillity personified. I wonder if I would be this short of breath in heaven? This altitude thing had turned me into mobile sluggishness again. I thought my body may have got used to playing at altitude by now, but not so. Perhaps my continual changes in geography were not enough for full acclimatisation. I felt as if my real body was detached and I was dragging it behind. I had two bodies today. Thankfully they tended to merge into one when I got astride the bike when I had to concentrate my mind. Adrenaline! The 'city' had a nice mix of motels and log cabins, blended with an assortment of restaurants and bars decorated with animals' heads and fish in glass cases. I briefly met a Brit biking trio on hire bikes out of Los Angeles. They were cramming as much of the state into a two-week fly-ride mini adventure. A short distance up the lake shore and California becomes Nevada and the small lakeside towns take on a slightly different image. In accordance with the reputation of Nevada, Incline Village for example has a casino. It looks a little unusual in the lake and mountainous resort setting.

A ride around the Lake from California into Nevada and then back into California was refreshing to say the least. It was one of those cool spring afternoons, where you had to stare at the sun with closed eyes to feel any warmth. Out of the sun, the chill was right there and with the backdrop of snowy mountains peaking at over 10,000 feet against the deep blue lake, it made for quite a wintry scene. Lake Tahoe at 1,645 feet deep is the second deepest lake in the USA. The deepest is Crater Lake in Oregon which I would visit later in my journey. The mysteries in the depths of Lake Tahoe intrigued me and what better than a chat with a boat hand at the marina to ask some questions. The young man was guarded at first and then became more open as my questioning continued. He was busy scrubbing the jetty, simultaneous to answering the office telephone several times. He relaxed and set the scene. It is rumoured but not confirmed that the famous ocean explorer Jacques Cousteau and team made several dives into the dark and cool depths in the mid-70s. He was allowed to do this, as long as his findings were not published. What was published was the dramatic statement Cousteau made, which simply said 'the world isn't ready for what was down there'. It's the depth and extremely cold temperatures that hold the secrets. Rumours are that the lake has been the dumping ground for bodies associated with gang-land killings. Fisherman even call one part of the lake 'the grave'. The cool temperatures do not allow gases to form in bodies and hence they remain preserved for centuries and not bloat and float to the surface. A grisly thought.

My chat with the boat hand at the marina made for an interesting 20 minutes or so. It was obvious from his body language that the locals perhaps know more about the secrets of the lake than they are willing to tell. Today, permission has to be granted for any diving and certain parts of the lake are out of bounds to divers. Maybe the secrets of the lake are best kept in its depths.

Chapter 29

Descent into Carson City

It was a cold morning. With a clear blue sky, the early morning sun was creating deep blues in the lake and with the snow-capped mountains not far away, it was a refreshing scene. Whilst checking out at the motel, the owners were giving their proud commentary why they were here. Formerly from rural Montana, they had given up the 'big sky state' to be here in what was quite a tourist location, although this was the quiet time of the year. In jeans and checked shirt, the owner was still dressed for Montana and he was enthusiastic to give me a guided tour of their new annex to be opened soon. It formed a tower and balconies provided more impressive views of the lake. My route out of town followed the lake shore into Nevada, through the Nevada State Park, before picking up highway 50 for the short descent into Carson City. It was a snaking descent from 6,200 feet at the lake's shore down to 4,700 feet into the dusty streets of the Nevada State Capital. With California close by, Carson City is unique in that it is one of two state capital cities that borders another state. The other is Trenton, New Jersey, which borders Pennsylvania. It was only a 40-mile trip and I was installed into a downtown motel by coffee time, giving the rest of the day to explore the small city with much history.

Named after famous frontiersman Christopher 'Kit' Carson, Carson City was founded in the early boom days of silver and gold mining and has a rich and colourful frontier past. Following the discovery of gold and silver in the local area, the city became a thriving commercial centre. It soon became a freight and staging post and a collection point for the timber originating from the Tahoe basin. At the peak of development, trains passed through Carson en route Silver City and Reno. The city had a frontier feel and the local workforce roamed the streets in gangs. Shootings, stabbings and street brawls were common. However, and unlike the remainder of the state, assailants were effectively contained in the state prison located in Carson. At the end of the mining and rail boom, the city returned to normality and the population fell dramatically. For a period in history, it was the smallest state capital, but population levels have now returned to over 50,000. Today the city still has a unique and compact feel, with only one main drag in the middle of a grid of side streets containing a smattering of hotels, motels and casinos. Hidden amongst the side streets are bars and clubs where prostitution is legal and regulated.

Sitting in a bowl and with mountains in most directions, it was still hard to remember that I was walking around streets that were over 4,000 feet above sea level. The air was thin at the city level which had rather a desert feel to it, which was in contrast to the sturdy surrounding terrain. Other than the security guard, the State Capitol Building was empty. It was one of those occasions when I was realistic in saying I had the whole place to myself. Alas, other than its impressive Alaskan marble walls and French crystal windows, the small Capitol Building held little to engage. The surrounding gardens, resplendent with spring blossoms and a rambling statue of Kit Carson, were far more photogenic. A couple of museums, including the old mint building, provided some interest and dinner in the once famous and now restored St Charles Hotel and adjoining Firkin and Fox saloon, made for an interesting evening diversion. A day in the Nevada State Capital city was enough and it's not a destination for a full-blown vacation unless you have a fetish for casinos, bars and prostitutes– oh and a little slice of history that put the place on the map. My incursion into Nevada would be brief for the moment and the mountains of eastern California were beckoning.

Chapter 30

South to Yosemite

South-bound the next morning, I felt I had not given Nevada the justice it really deserved. My attention had been restricted to the compact state capital city, almost a glancing blow. I would give the state another glancing blow in the near future when dropping into Las Vegas for a mechanical pit stop – literally – for some new tyres for the bike at the BMW dealers. My mileage calculations and tread wear pointed to this plan. From Carson, I could have charged across Nevada on Interstate 80, taken in the Bonneville Salt Flats in western Utah and ended up in Salt Lake City well ahead of schedule to start my 'Big East' sector across the country. It was tempting and maybe a challenging prospect, as like a few other stretches of roads in the USA, route 80 across the Sagebrush state is reputed to be the loneliest road in the USA. No, I stuck to my original game plan and decided to take in eastern California, drop into Vegas and then ride through most of Utah south to north and end up in the Mormon capital around the end of the month. Geographically, it was a decision I did not regret.

Clearing the desert scrub like countryside around Carson City, I was quickly crossing back into California and surrounded by rich and green agricultural land. Ranches were big and plentiful around the towns of Paynesville and Woodlands, where large herds of healthy cattle were busy grazing on the spring grass. These farms were almost perched on the foothills of the Eldorado Range National Forest Mountains. I would be getting very adjacent to these mountains in short time. Joining route 88, I left the fertile plains behind and was very quickly climbing the Carson Pass, which surprisingly peaked at 8,500 feet. I wasn't expecting to be that high on this route. It became cold very quickly and it was the start of another one of those most diverse rides through quickly changing terrain. I was soon above the snow line and in a wintry world of jagged peaks, snow fields, frozen lakes and lines of mountains as far as the eye could see. I briefly recall a few words from a biking couple a few states back. They uttered with much enthusiasm that if I chose to take 88, I would be in for a real treat. They were not wrong, apart from the extreme chill even with heated grips on maximum. It was a marvellous experience. It all ended very quickly, when another geographical chunk of the day came before me. It was the rapid and twisting descent down the other side of the pass, quickly through the snow line and suddenly engulfed in very thick coniferous forests. So thick that the smell of pine was oppressive and conjured thoughts of yuletide. It was a great relief to get down again as the temperatures suddenly warmed my cool parts somewhat better than the feeble attempt made by a coffee earlier in the morning. Suddenly it was very warm again and I was in rolling green countryside. Passing through the small towns of West Point, Angels City and Jamestown, the locals were out and about dressed in shorts and T-shirts. It was whilst roaring through the beautiful rolling and curvaceous road heading south towards Yosemite that a roadside scene made me take a second glance. Beside a parked car, one guy was looking on, whilst another guy was beating something viciously with a large heavy tool. Slowing as I passed them by, it was a large snake, about as thick as my forearm that was getting the clubbing. Bar talk late that day informed me that rattlers are abundant in the verdant pastures of eastern Californian and this poor serpent, maybe awoken early by the mid-April warmth was getting the treatment. I saw several dead snakes on the road for the next 20 miles or so. They obviously liked this county. Maybe the snake-killing duo had been out on the cull all morning.

After the twisties of the morning through a cool and wintry wilderness, my next ascent close to Yosemite was almost climatically the opposite. At the town of Mocassin, I picked up route 120 and the

New Priest Grade Road was a hairpin admirer's delight. I was able to quickly zip past slower traffic whilst simultaneously glancing over left and right shoulders at the tremendous views down the precipice slopes back towards Moccasin Reservoir. It was quite some view and the concentration to tackle this darling of a road had turned me into a sweating and grunting rider. Awesome. At the top of the climb, I was particularly conscious of my dwindling fuel reserves and had heard much about the extortionate fuel prices at the few service facilities in Yosemite Park itself. I needed to refuel before I got there and my first stop at Big Oak could only yield a low octane grade that would make the bike grunt. I got what I wanted a little further on, which would do for the rest of the day. My fuel consumption today was hugely high and uncharacteristically less than normal, considerably affected by the rapidly changing terrain I had encountered. With both bike and body refuelled, it was onwards to the entrance to the National Park. The Rangers, complete in their green fatigues and smart fedoras were particularly impressed with my progress through their country so far. In fact they couldn't believe it and waved me on with almost uncontrolled laughter of disbelief. The route was through several miles of thick fir forests to start with and I was beginning to wonder when and where the geographical spectacle of Yosemite would appear. I wasn't disappointed and once established on the valley floor, it was nothing more than awe-inspiring. There are probably not enough superlatives in the English language to describe this quite amazing place. I was provided with uninterrupted views of the granite domes of Sentinel Rock and Half Dome, towering majestically from the valley floor. Then the waterfalls and the thick forest. I got in close dialogue with a geographer from Pennsylvania who was still impressed with this place after a lifetime of visits over his 70 years. Apparently it's the walks and climbs away from the tourist viewing points that put you in a different world. He admitted only to have scratched the surface of this wonderful national park. A little commercialism was evident in Yosemite Village, a supermarket and a few gift shops and the like. I let these commercial trappings escape my eye in exchange for the mellowing couple of hours I spent down on the valley floor.

Leaving the park, my desired route east on the Tioga Pass road was still closed. That route would have put me in a great position to pick up 395 south for the Sierras. Instead, I had to exit south on 41, through a further curving coniferous-bordered route which put me in the bubbly little town of Oakhurst. It was 6 pm and I had had enough for the day. Having encountered high snow passes, undulating agricultural land and the delights of Yosemite, it was time to call a halt. My body was tired, but glowing all over after an incredible ride.

I had intended to stay one night in Oakhurst and press on to the Sierras first thing in the morning. It turned out to be three nights and I didn't get out of town until Monday morning. The weather was superb where I was; a weekend of beautiful warm spring sunshine and not a hint of wind. Not so at my destination. I desperately wanted to see the Sierras and Death Valley on my way to Vegas and beyond into Utah. It would require patience. It was the wind that was the problem over there all weekend. The breeze was blowing at a constant 40 mph with frequent gusts of 60 mph and the Weather Channel were getting excited about an isolated gust recorded of 88 mph in Lone Pine. That was my destination. I would have to sit this one out.

Oakhurst did provide a good weekend base. Set just to the south of Yosemite, the town is very much the gateway to one of USA's most impressive National Parks. The place was full of motels, bed and breakfasts, art galleries, boutiques, real estate offices and of course plenty of gift shops. Having digested the bad news of my destination weather forecast, I dug in for the weekend and relaxed with the locals. Set on quite a hill, tramping around the place from breakfast to lunch to browsing the odd shop turned out to be quite a workout. It was the many estate agents or rather real estate shops that attracted my attention. Property of all types for sale in the environs of Yosemite. Houses, cabins, condos, you name it. Made of brick, stone or wood, there was a type of place for all tastes. Prices appeared incredibly cheap considering the location.

I also had the opportunity to catch up on some current affairs with my downtime in Oakhurst and amused myself surfing the multitude of TV channels. It was quite a normal evening pastime in the motel life that

I was living on this journey. It was election year of course and whilst John McCain was out there selling his worth to the nation as Republican nominee, the complete opposite was happening with the Democrats. Hillary Clinton and Barack Obama were challenging each other on a daily basis, competing for the coveted prize of Democratic nominee to take to the November elections. If CNN weren't reporting on the election, they would have nothing to transmit! The National Geographic and History channels were far more interesting, but repetition of programmes was commonplace. What I saw in one state was shown again in another state and the next and the next. I had already cherry-picked a couple of semi-interesting shows and if you could bear seeing his trademark loud coloured braces-sorry suspenders, the *Larry King Show* was worth a few moments. Oh and thankfully CNN have a decent reporter in Anderson Cooper who puts together an interesting programme in his AC360 magazine broadcast.

Chapter 31

In the High Sierras

It is always nice to get back on the road and after exhausting the facilities of Oakhurst, joining the Interstate at Fresno for Bakersfield, for a short time actually seemed enjoyable. That euphoria didn't last long as I was passing through probably the least most interesting part of California. Bakersfield couldn't come quick enough, where I found route 178 heading north east towards Lake Isabella and onwards to route 395. 395 would then take me north past China Lake and into Lone Pine. The twisting road to Lake Isabella turned out to be fun. It was set almost on the floor of a canyon, with many areas having vertical walls. It was a fine balance between carefully navigating the curving road and simultaneously admiring the sheer cliffs and circling birds above. Traffic on this route was non-existent and in no time I was in Lake Isabella. The town of Lake Isabella, on the shores of its deep blue lake, is a mecca for fishing, hiking, camping, windsurfing and skiing. Only a day trip away from the urban monster of LA which lies 150 miles or so to the south. My fuel was low and I stopped at quite a rustic fuel station in town which doubled as a busy grocery store. Very soon I had quite a gaggle of locals, including a couple of Police Officers, surrounding my bike. It was interrogation time again and I had to field the usual what, where, why, when and how long type questions from the motley bunch. The conversation got quite political for a few moments as even residents in this small town were concerned who would be in the White House next year. They wanted my view. They wanted a Brit's view and in detail. They were a demanding bunch and one of them got quite animated about the weak US dollar versus the strong GB pound. That fuel stop certainly woke me up. Lake Isabella was the sort of town you could hang around for a few days and dig out the local bars and speak to some real characters. Leaving Lake Isabella, a quick climb and descent of Walker Pass led to route 395. I had got there and this was the road I could have picked up just to the east of Yosemite if the park exit on Tioga Pass had been clear of snow. This was the area that had suffered from high winds the other day, and looking around, there was absolutely no shelter. To my right, that's to the east, it was just completely flat, the completely featureless terrain of China Lake. It could be a view from a distant planet. Desert scenes, flecks of white from salt deposits and pale yellows dominated the landscape. Continuing north through the Owens Valley, very slowly I was beginning to see the rising terrain of the Sierras.

Arriving in Lone Pine, the high snow-capped Sierra Nevada mountain range simply dominates the area. Set in the middle of the tooth-jagged peaks is Mount Whitney and at 14,497 feet high, it's the highest mountain in the lower 48. The mountains seem in touching distance from the town centre. The normal gathering of motels, restaurants and gift shops, were centred on the board-walked main street giving almost a cowboy feel. I wanted a room with a view and the Trails Motel provided just that. I had the Sierras sitting there, almost at arm's length. Mr Patel the manager was very enthusiastic to tell me all the facilities of his motel. Free continental breakfast, free wireless internet, pool, refrigerator, microwave, coffee, king and queen beds and fax and all AAA approved. He mentioned nothing about the smell in my room. Apparently it was the chemical from the carpet cleaning. All the amenities were advertised on one of those lovely retro signs outside, the multi-coloured ones with big flashing arrows. It was very American and could easily have been the same scene in the 1960s. Mr Patel wanted to talk and talk and I had to make excuses to unload the bike, plug into the world and find the tourist office. So close to such a huge mountain range where some roads may be still closed and where the local area had recently received a bashing from very high winds, I needed some local knowledge.

I found the tourist centre quite close to the single-strip airport, a short ride down the high street. It was a new construction with high ceilings and walls covered with maps of the local area. Few folk were around and the girls behind the desk gave me their full attention. 'I should go here, try there, eat here and careful that road is not open yet, but Onion Pass is. You access it from Independence, the town up the valley road a bit.' The road that was still closed was Horseshoe Meadows Road that climbed up to 10,000 feet and gave great views of the Sierras and China Lake far below. That was a shame, but I was assured that the top of Onion Pass was equally as impressive, peaking at over 9,000 feet. The rest of the day I just rode the local roads and acclimatised myself to the local area whilst soaking in the unique environment. The forecast for the next couple of days was set fair and I would leave the climbing until the next day. At a 24-hour diner on the high street, I sat outside and took in the vista of the Sierra's over apple pie and a mug of tea. A refreshment with a view. Splendid. The visit to the tourist office was well worth it. It gave a real feel for the history of the place, which had a mining and railroad heritage and as the industry diminished, abandoned towns became ghost towns. This area of California has several well-preserved ghost towns including Cerro Gordo, Keeler, Swansea, Darwin and Tramway. These settlements, some perched high in the mountains, blossomed at the height of silver mining in the mid-nineteenth century. Today, some are well preserved, some have but skeletons of buildings remaining after decades of decay and wind blast.

After a leisurely dinner that evening, I found a saloon complete with swing doors and Stetson wearing locals at the bar. After the 320 miles from Oakhurst that day, a quick familiarisation of the local area and simply taking in the contrast of China Lake and the high Sierras made me feel somewhat overcome with the enormity of this country, never mind the state. Apart from a quick overnight in Nevada, I had been in California over two weeks now. One guy caught my attention at the bar and seemed to focus in on me when I spoke to the bar tender. He was in his mid-60s, well dressed and insisted he was a climber. He had a couple of cell phones attached to his belt and a bulging wallet. I got the impression he had been expecting me. Almost as if he was checking up on me. This surveillance thing had raised its head again. This area is surrounded by military bases and the occasional sound of jets could be heard echoing through the night sky high above China Lake. If I was being trailed, they would be sensitive about this area. The guy insisted on buying all my beer, so he was a friendly spook after all. We arranged to meet the next day for a late breakfast before he went climbing and I took off on the bike. However, he just didn't turn up. Locals I had met the night before denied all knowledge of his presence.

The next morning I took off on Whitney Portal Road out of Lone Pine and rode until the road stopped. This was a good warmer for the day and provided spectacular views of the Sierras and Mount Whitney standing proud in the middle. The snow-capped sharp mountains, dramatically contrasted against the foreground of scrub, dashed with huge boulders and the occasional red and yellow spring flowers. I was warned that this area was prime rattler country, although at this time of the year they would still be sleeping thankfully. I didn't see any signs of snakes and felt confident to tramp around off the road. Next, I just had to find Onion Pass and rode the short distance up to the town of Independence as advised by the tourist office. The road up to Onion Pass started as a gentle climb for five miles or so and then matured into a snaking steep ascent with many hairpins. The road was challenging enough without the debris and rocks to avoid from recent landslides. The road had not been swept since it opened for the season last weekend. It became so steep that it was just impossible to stop and photograph the views down to Owens Valley and beyond to China Lake. It was well worth the effort and the climb abruptly came to an end at 9,200 feet in a small loop, with adjoining parking area. A couple of vehicles were parked up, their occupants no doubt on a day's climbing. Maybe my friend from last night was out there? Close to the parking area, there were several large wooden padlocked crates full of rescue equipment. Other than that, there was no sign of any human influence. It was high and very still. All that I could hear was the trickle of melt water and the gurgle of a distant stream. The peaks of the range extended another 5,000 feet above me into almost a lost and forbidden world. It was an eerie place, where I couldn't even hear a bird song. My rumbling stomach forced me to break the tranquillity and I began the eye-watering descent back down to Independence. It had been such a mesmerising experience that I did not want it to end.

It was mid-afternoon when I returned to Lone Pine. The sky had filled with the most incredible high altitude lenticular clouds. The type of clouds you may have seen in a 50s or 60s sci-fi movie. Blue sky, strange clouds and suddenly a flying saucer lands, that sort of scene. Ghost towns, aliens and the wind whistling through the long high street!

Chapter 32

Descending into Death Valley

It was forecast to be 95F on the floor of Death Valley by 10 am. That was bearable, but I wanted to be through the valley and into Nevada by noon to avoid the frying time of mid-afternoon. So it was an early departure from Lone Pine and Mr Patel's continental breakfast of lukewarm coffee and stale cake didn't really delay my departure. The motel car park was busy with other early risers. A team of geologists were packing their equipment in preparation for their work in the desert, also before the heat of the day. In Lone Pine it would be another nice late April day, blue sky, a bit of cloud later and nearly tanning weather. Quite remarkable that less than a hundred miles away the climatic barometer would be reading something completely different. It was quite fitting that as I departed east for Death Valley, the snow-capped Sierras would stay in my mirrors for several miles. It was only when I started the snaking descent into the guts of the cauldron that I lost sight of them. Very soon I was in it. The hottest, driest and lowest. A desert of streaming sand dunes, snow-capped mountains around the rim, multi-coloured rock layers, water-fluted canyons and acres of stone wilderness. I had no cell phone coverage, which wasn't surprising and happened regularly, but with little traffic around so early in the season, this was not the place to breakdown. When I stopped to take photographs, I left the bikes engine running. Paranoia, but a personal thing. At the lowest point, I was 282 feet below sea level, an amazing contrast to the 9,200 feet elevation in the Sierras at Onion Pass only the day before. The temperature at night here has fallen to 10F and a record high, which is also a record high for the western hemisphere, peaked at an amazing 144F. Thankfully I avoided any extremes of temperatures like this and once through Beatty Junction and Indian Village, I was clear of the valley and crossing the state line into Nevada.

So that was it. Two weeks in California and with just a brief visit planned for Las Vegas, I would soon be taking on Utah and making ready to cross east through the middle of the country from Salt Lake City. Apart from the few days of high wind, I have been spoilt with settled weather since I entered New Mexico a month ago. It would be a different story crossing the middle of the country where phrases such as 'tornado alley' were sitting in my mind. There was no point in getting excited about that sort of thing at the moment. My weather briefing and checking regime seemed to be working. Forecasts on the Weather Channel, which I mainly accessed via the internet, were consistently accurate. Sometimes I felt I was being too careful adhering to weather warnings. However, having avoided that wind in Owens Valley and Lone Pine a couple of days ago and then to be told by the locals up there it was wild with no visibility because of blowing sand, I think I was treating Mother Nature with the required respect so far. I was still ahead of schedule and would continue with this planning system that seemed to be working.

I felt quite relaxed having just seen the magnificent Sierra Nevada range followed by an uneventful ride through Death Valley. It was still only mid-morning and I was content to just sit back and let the GPS take me on through Pahrump and down into Vegas. My mind was crystal clear and any mental demons that were percolating around early in my journey a month or so back seemed to have vanished. I would be in Vegas in time for a late lunch. The bike dealers had recommended a hotel to stay just south of the strip. So I was looking forward to getting parked up, checked in and changed to have a look at the scenery in the multi-casino South Point Hotel. Passing through Pahrump gave me great amusement. What a name for a town – Pahrump! It sounds like words to the *Pink Panther* theme, Pahrump-Pahrump-Pahrump-etc. Before I get into hot water, I must add that the town of Pahrump was first settled by the Shoshone Indians and slowly inhabited by Americans late in the nineteenth century. The name chosen comes from a local valley – 'Pah-Rimpi' – and means water rock. So named because of the abundant artesian wells in that valley. As Vegas grew, real estate speculation in the area also grew and facilities just had to be improved. They were and today Pahrump boasts a vibrant population of over 25,000. Arrival in Vegas was on my mind and once descending on route 160 through the Mountain Springs range, Las Vegas was laid out in front of me like a child's building brick toy. Visibility was unlimited and the characteristic shapes of all the glitzy hotels on the strip were easily identifiable from over 20 miles away. An adventure motorcyclist arriving at the entrance to a major casino hotel in Las Vegas was quite a spectacle and turned many heads. Other guests checking in, forming quite a long line, immediately gave way for me and I had no waiting. I even negotiated a great rate for a couple of nights with the duty manager. It was a cheaper rate than I was paying in an average motel around the country! That's Las Vegas for you and there was no mistake, this was a grand hotel. One of the bell boys wanted to park the bike for me. Not a chance, although he got my tip for taking my panniers to my room whilst I found the bike park on whatever level it was in the monster multi-storey car park.

Hotel activity was 24 hours. Casinos, restaurants, bars, shops, pool, sauna, massage and even a few shows. Hotels may come and go in this town, but the activities remain the same. It was a great people-watching arena and not a gambling person, after a good dinner a bar stool perch was my preferred lookout. I spoke to Jim from Colorado. Jim was in his second year at the South Point and remarked quite clearly that once you have a bartending job, you keep it. A good one is hard to come by and once in, you make the most of the tips that come your way. After all, it's a casino and guests here are reasonably relaxed and ready to enjoy themselves and tips just flow. Then there's the waitresses that serve the gambling tables. Michelle, an attractive blonde in her mid-twenties from California, commented we work long shifts, are always on our feet, however, our salaries are quite low and we work on being polite and getting those tips.

The following morning, the bike dealers were ready and wheeled the beast in for the treatment. I had an hour or so to kill and the tyre fitter, with a glint in his eye, strongly recommended a grill bar across the plaza. I didn't really question why he recommended it, but simply strolled across in that direction for my mid-morning coffee. It was a plush place with a comprehensive menu, obviously sparsely populated at such an early hour. I felt quite underdressed in jeans and biking jacket, but nonetheless was made more than welcome by the posse of waitresses who even twisted my arm to taking a cooked breakfast as well as a coffee. But even at such an early hour and some distance from the strip, the girls were dressed in Vegas style and ready for their Vegas day. A biker's recommendation indeed!

Part Four – Utah Red Rock

Las Vegas – Nevada to Salt Lake City – Utah

945 miles

Utah Red Rock - Las Vegas NV to Salt Lake City UT

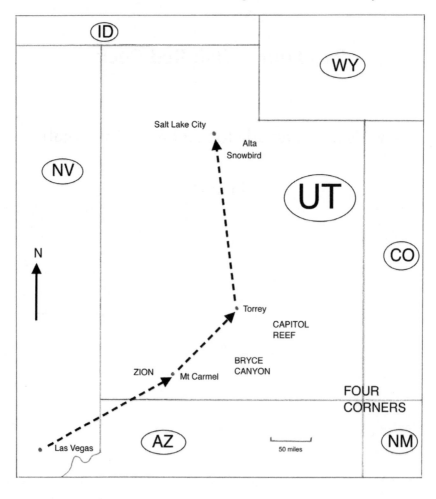

DATE	START	FINISH	MILEAGE	CUMULATIVE	COMMENTS
25 April	Las Vegas NV	Mt Carmel UT	200	9932	I-15/ US9 & 89
27 April	Mt Carmel UT	Mt Carmel UT	127	10059	Zion NP & local canyons
28 April	Mt Carmel UT	Torrey UT	250	10309	Via Bryce & Capitol Reef NPs. Scenic route 12
29 April	Torrey UT	Torrey UT	98	10407	Capitol Reef NP & local area.
30 April	Torrey UT	**Salt Lake City UT (16)**	243	10650	US24/72/10/31/89 & I-15
April Total				3690	
2 May	Salt Lake City UT	Salt Lake City UT	60	10710	Alta & Snowbird Ski Resorts.

Chapter 33

Art at Mount Carmel

With enough of Vegas in my veins and new tyres on the bike it was
onwards and upwards. Upwards through the country and into Utah.
Departure from the hotel was a similarly amusing scene as my arrival.
Whilst the bell boy, one of hundreds, carefully transported my panniers
down to the lobby, I collected the bike and made ready for departure
at the busy entrance to the hotel. There were about six lanes for traffic
to accumulate at the hotel entrance and the novelty of my hook up and
departure slowed the flow. Stretch limos to sedans to tour buses, it was
a congested scene and the morning was still new. Although it had been
a novelty, I was rather glad to get the hell out of there and back on my
route. I was heading for Mount Carmel in Southern Utah and it wasn't
a big stretch that morning, only a couple of hundred miles. Enough
distance to scrub the new tyres in and look forward to a lunch time beer.
Beer? I must remember I would shortly be arriving in Utah. Quickly
navigating through the busy Las Vegas Saturday morning traffic I was
soon established on Interstate 15 heading North East. The 'strip' was
close to the urban freeway and seemed to just flash by. It still looked
like a big toy or model from close up. It had been a brief, but amusing
48 hours in the desert gambling mecca. The Interstate took me through
desert and more desert. North East of Mesquite, my route even clipped
30 miles of the top left hand corner of Arizona, as if a reminder of an
interesting visit to that state.

Dan Shea, who I met for lunch back in California on that hot early April day, had put me in touch with art dealers Paul and Susan Bingham. Clearing the Interstate and passing St George and Hurricane, in no time I was in Mount Carmel and introducing myself to Paul and Susan over a late lunch at their Bingham Gallery. Not only do they own and run the gallery, but their estate includes the former home buildings of American artist Maynard Dixon. For over 50 years Maynard Dixon painted the life and landscape of the American West. In paintings, drawings and illustrations, he epitomised the beauty of the great scenery in this unique part of the country. Dixon recorded the ways of the west's settlers and the traditional life of the native Indians. His completely preserved home buildings in log cabin style, include a house, separate studio and bunkhouse. In the heat of the day, I was given an extensive tour and overview of the property set in multi-level grounds and gardens close to the new gallery. Dixon passed away in 1946, but his legacy lives on. Paul and Susan have retained the original exterior and interior of these fine buildings. Soon after the purchase of Dixon's Mount Carmel home and the completion of their new and stylish gallery, Paul and Susan started a non-profit organisation. The Thunderbird Foundation, as it is known, seeks to preserve the Dixon legacy and to encourage Western American art. Surrounded by the splendour and beauty of deserts, mountains, canyons and valleys, the facilities are frequently used by artists from all over the USA. The home and grounds are open to visitors for self-guided tours between May and November. It was still just April and Paul and Susan had kindly opened the bunkhouse early especially for my arrival. It wasn't the Hilton, but it was certainly better than the average motel I had been staying in so far! Introductions over, I insisted in popping down to the local village of Orderville to get some wine to go with dinner. I would get some fuel for the bike at the same time. I got a titter of laughter when I mentioned wine purchase. I must remember I was in Utah and alcohol availability is extremely limited. I found Orderville a couple of miles down the road and reduced my exuberant speed as I saw a patrol car sitting on watch opposite the two fuel stations and large grocery store. As I passed, the officer appeared to be in a trance and just staring straight ahead. Strange. Fuel for the bike first and what an experience. It was one of those places where the owner does everything. He's the mechanic, runs the cash register and sweeps the forecourt. His rustic establishment accepted my debit card and we exchanged pleasantries as the machine chirped and authorisation took place to complete my purchase for 5.366 gallons of his finest. Our accents just made us stare at each other with amazement. What a clash of cultures, but communication took place effectively. Next was the large grocery store, or rather small supermarket. It sold everything apart from booze and I would have to rely on Paul and Susan's generosity for a glass of wine with dinner. The guy from the garage followed me to the store and was taking every opportunity to listen to me talk again as I made a couple of purchases. Maybe he thought I was an alien from a Lone Pine movie scene? Passing the patrol car, the officer still had not moved. I was going to stop and try and have a chat, but thought better of it and sped back to the Bingham Gallery. Later that evening, it was a refreshing change not to talk about politics over dinner. The accelerating election campaign seemed to dominate talk everywhere I went, from diner to motel to gas station. Thankfully, Paul and Susan talked about art and the contents of their marvellous gallery over dinner. To complete the evening, a local artist of national repute joined us for a nightcap. It was a cultural evening and a contrast from the night before in a Las Vegas casino. The high moon in the clear sky cast long shadows on my short walk back to the bunkhouse. I could see the moon as I lay in bed and there was not a sound. It was so eerily quiet that it was noisy. Maybe I had become accustomed to the noise of my journey. Road, bars, restaurants, motel guests arriving and departing, all forming the cacophony of a journeyman. Tonight was so different. The fresh air acted as an anaesthetic and in no time I was in a deep Utah slumber.

The next morning I arose at 8 am only to find I had not advanced my timepiece and in fact it was 9 am. Passing through time zones was becoming quite a regular occurrence on this journey. An artist's open day was taking place at the estate and guests would be arriving shortly. They congregate to view the Maynard Dixon establishment and hopefully buy some art from the gallery. The gallery does attract passers-by on the highway, but organised groups can entice visitors to get their dollars out. Today's guests were all local and their day included a buffet and wine. Whilst the hosts played at being hosts, I assisted with the refreshments and my British commentary I am sure added to the day's entertainment for the guests who all left in good form and reasonably lubricated. It was the geography of the local area I wanted to explore the next day and close to Mount Carmel is probably the most visited National Park in Utah. Zion, an ancient Hebrew word meaning a place of sanctuary or refuge, is a prominent geological area consisting of canyons, escarpments, gorges and deep rivers. The park offers outstanding scenery and was a mere ten minutes ride from my lodgings. The clear blue sky was contrasting dramatically against the red and tan coloured Navajo sandstone. By riding down to Springdale for breakfast and then back to Mount Carmel, I got a double shot at the quite unique massive rock formations, which was my introduction to Utah red rock. It did occur to me that unless you are a geological fanatic or happen to be visiting Southern Utah, you may miss out on this national park and maybe miss out on this state. Most holiday-makers who want to point their camera at rocks invariably head for the Grand Canyon. Zion is an amazing destination and equally as impressive. A must-see in what is probably the USA's best kept secret state of Utah. There were few folks around so early on a Sunday morning. I was able to stop at my leisure and crane my neck skywards at the incredible sheer vertical sandstone walls. After absorbing the geological splendour of Zion, a ride down to the fun town of Kanab was enough rock and asphalt for one day. It was in Kanab that I met an Australian biker who was doing the American biker thing. A real Australian. He had flown in to the east coast and bought a second-hand Harley. In a couple of weeks he had ridden from New York to Utah and was finishing in the next couple of days in LA. We exchanged notes over a coffee and he expressed great amusement that I had been tagged as an Aussie in every state so far.

Chapter 34

Hoodoo Red Rock

It turned out to be quite a cultural break with the Binghams and I left Mount Carmel loaded with advice of what else to see in southern Utah on the way to Salt Lake City. Passing through Orderville northbound on 89, that police officer had not moved, he was still there. He had had a long shift. In the next town, I think it was Glendale, I passed another patrol car with another guy sitting there. It was very early and he couldn't be on a house call. I slowed right down and there he was. It was a mannequin! It must be the county police deterrent to show off to passing motorists, on what is a busy highway, that the police are out there!

Bryce Canyon National Park was first which was just off 89 and down 12 and 63 a little. This is where I had found the USA roads numbering confusing. One road can be given two numerical designations. Why? Even if they pass through different counties and maybe cross state lines, one identity would be enough. Thankfully GPS alleviated any confusion. But some roads entering and leaving large cities have a multitude of designated numbers and the sign can be huge and sometimes extremely confusing. 63 and 12, the same road, took me to Bryce Canyon. Bryce is just one of the many canyons which form a series of horseshoe-shaped amphitheatres on the edge of the Paunsaugunt Plateau in Southern Utah. Erosion has carved the colourful claron limestone into thousands of spires, fins, arches and mazes. Collectively they are called 'hoodoos' and these rather amusingly shaped formations are tinted with colours too numerous and subtle to name. All these structures are significantly smaller than any formations in Zion and hence make for a great contrast. What was particularly impressive on this late spring morning, was the dramatic contrast of the multi-coloured rock formations and the deep green coniferous forests against a lovely morning's blue sky and remnants of snow in creases and crevices. It was a dazzling vista, creating a rich photographic cocktail. It was route 63 that took me on a 20-mile scenic loop of the park through the Dixie National Forest. Next on my list for the day was Capitol Reef National Park. Not far to go and just follow route 12 was the advice. That was the advice from a non-biker, with no description of the road to expect. What a treat I was in for. 12 took me past the Grand Staircase at Escalante and onwards or rather upwards through Boulder followed by a gentle forest descent into Torrey. I peaked at 9,600 feet altitude, simultaneous to notching up 10,000 miles completed on the journey. 10,000 feet and 10,000 miles I suppose would have been too much to ask for! The views from the top made up for the lack of numerical co-ordination, which were just quite stunning across many miles of Utah red rock. The visibility was unlimited. This was heaven.

It was only lunchtime when I arrived in Torrey after a brisk 250 miles from Mount Carmel. An early start is so vital when covering a lot of geography. An arrival at the day's destination around 2 pm allows time to explore and chill out before planning the next day and all that goes with it. In Torrey I was ideally placed to have a couple of hours in Capitol Reef National Park, which would make two parks in one day and then I would press on to Salt Lake City the next day. The town had a lovely feel; one long street with a few restaurants and lodgings and one chain motel at one end. I hadn't done any research on this place and didn't know what else was available. Whilst riding down the one street and completely by luck, I found a delightful-looking motel tucked away from the side of the road. A quick snapshot of the surroundings, revealed two restaurants and a laundry within walking distance. I would stay here, decision made. The Boulder Edge Motel turned out to be a private motel. Earlier experiences had revealed private motels are either very good or not very good. This place was very good and I was greeted by a friendly lady and was the first to check in for the day. She was a Mormon and was only too happy to field my many questions about her family following. These private motels are certainly worth sniffing out and like the Boulder Edge, can be better and cheaper than their chain big brothers. My room was absolutely cavernous and I could have easily held a party for the rest of the motel guests. My challenge would have been seeing enough people to invite. It turned out I was the only guest that night. Torrey is on the doorstep of Capitol Reef and I could see impressive rock formations from my window. The park is another superlative tongue twisting spectacle, characterised by more deep canyons and gorges. The most dramatic feature is the 100-mile long Waterpocket Fold which extends like a rugged spine. At the west end of the fold close to Torrey, the rock is deep red and brown. Progressing east, the dark colours dilute to yellows and whites, before flattening out to the desert floor. I took a couple of hours to ride past the many colourful canyons, ridges, buttes and monoliths. I am glad we are in the age of digital photography where compression, edit and download is just a whizz of the fingers allowing mega image capture. The old days of using conventional film would have been a logistical nightmare on this trip, especially in photogenic Utah. I had shot in the region of 500 images on the National Parks of Southern Utah so far. Another exhausting but exhilarating day. Luckily the lady at the Boulder Edge recommended a fine restaurant within spitting distance. I could see the Café Diablo sign from my room and a menu of local rattlesnake, Utah Lamb and fruit pie, hit the spot. Gary, the owner of the restaurant, passed on advice for a great biker's route north into Salt Lake City.

I was awoken the next day by the wind. It could be deceiving, hopefully whistling through a gap in the doorframe making it worse than it was. My weather checking last night had not revealed anything to get stressed about, but alas, this time the forecast was wrong. It was very windy in Torrey and blowing a gale in Salt Lake City. My advised route from Gary climbed high through a mountain pass that I really wanted to experience. I could make it above 10,000 feet on this route which was a personal aim. So after a check on the next day's en-route weather, which looked good, Torrey it would be for an extra night. I just hoped tomorrow's forecast would be accurate this time. There wouldn't be a problem getting the room again that's for sure. I had the place to myself. It was safe to ride here, but along with the bright and blue sky, it was very breezy with frequent gusts stirring a lot of sand. On a local trip, eastbound through Caineville and as far as Hanksville, the wind became so uncomfortable that I was cranked over to compensate. It was okay for a short trip, but could have been dangerous at higher altitude. Returning through the Capitol Canyon back towards Torrey, viewing of the Petroglyphs carved into the rock face provided a brief shelter from the sand-stirring wind. Later, whilst refuelling back in Torrey, I met another BMW rider on a trip out of Washington State. He was heading east and was understandably concerned about the wind that had sprung up. I quickly added that my 100-mile local trip that afternoon had been challenging but not dangerous. Before pressing on to Moab, he extended an offer of lunch with his family when I made it to the north west. Another appointment in my mental diary. The surprising aggressive weather system that had hit central Utah today was charging east and should leave settled conditions in its wake tomorrow.

Chapter 35

Sara and Alana's Capitol

The weather people got it right. The next morning was set fair with a mixture of ragged cloud and blue sky and thankfully not an ounce of wind. But the morning had an angry feel to it after quite a bashing from the wind yesterday. An aggressive cold front had charged through the mid-part of the state yesterday and continued dragging its heels through the night. It was the calm after the storm so to speak. After chatting to the motel owner over coffee and pastry, and quickly loading the bike, I was off on Gary's route up to Salt Lake City. My GPS was coming out with 250 miles today leading me to the motel car park of my 16th state capital. I was taking a very scenic route and the mileage may be more. Route 24 took me north west from Torrey to Loa where I branched off north on 72. This was the beginning of quite a special bit that Gary had mentioned. Quite quickly I was climbing and at a convenient layover near the top of this pass at 8,500 feet elevation, I was treated with quite a spectacular view back to the east and looking down over Capitol Reef National Park. A bird's eye view of where I had been an ant down there for a couple of days. At this point to the north, the terrain turned lush and green and a complete contrast to the typical Utah rocky terrain. 72 descended and wriggled past a lake with no name and soon hit Interstate 70 at Fremont Junction. From here it was a quick couple of miles on the Interstate before exiting north on route 10.

The Google Maps facility was a fantastic planning tool and I remember scrolling through this part of the route and magnifying the Interstate area, whilst going through my planning routine the night before. At Ferron I pulled over for coffee and was joined by a posse of school kids on rollerblades. They were showing off a bit and doing circuits around my bike. Quickly their teacher turned up and continued to give them a look-and-learn geography lesson of the USA using the maps on my bike panniers. They didn't attend a school, but instead had lessons at home and hence were able to zoom outside on their blades for fresh air between lounge room lessons. They all accumulated in their garden and waved as I pulled away and continued north. Before I went, I mentioned I was taking the scenic route across the mountains. The teacher in the group was not sure if it would be open today after overnight snow. I did have a contingency route if required, but I decided to try the high route anyway. At Huntington, I branched off on 31 and entered the Manti la Sal National Forest. The locals called this road the Huntingdon Canyon and it climbed very quickly into another snowy and icy wilderness. The road was okay, but at elevation, snow banks were piled high on the road side up to at least 10 feet. I wanted to stop and take a photo of the bike against the towering snow banks, but I was quite concerned about the surface condition on the roadside which may have been icy. I pressed on using the centre of the road which was shiny and wet. It was the coldest I had experienced so far on the trip and the bike ice warning was flashing. I was freezing! This ice world continued for 30 miles or so, peaking at 9,800 feet elevation! I was urging the GPS to turn over to 10,000 feet elevation, but it just didn't happen! Maybe somewhere later. I was so cold that I had to stop and thaw out in the small town of Fairview. I was a shivering wreck and coffee just had to come first in the warmth of a fuel station diner. The waitresses were all having a good laugh at me as I clumsily struggled to find some money with my numb fingers. I mentioned I was looking forward to a few days in SLC and much to my amusement, they warned me it would be a good half-day's ride up to town from Fairview. Rather an exaggeration at just over a hundred miles to go. After my body had returned to what felt like a body, I quickly refuelled the bike and continued north. Snow-capped mountains from the Uinta National Forest flanked my right side all the way to the city. Reaching Provo, the traffic suddenly got completely crazy and continued that way for the rest of the ride into town. I had gone from a red rock rugged country into a snowy wilderness, to an urban monster, in just over half a day. Maybe with a population of 180,000, an urban monster is an unfair description for Salt Lake City, whose first impressions gave a fresh, clean and organised metropolitan feel.

I had made it into Salt Lake City one day ahead of my loose schedule. It was the last day of April and I was now on schedule to start east on time. My comfortable motel was snug in the downtown, allowing exploration of the city on foot. During the evening another rush of cold air passed through the state eastbound and my bike and the city had quite a covering of snow the next morning. My next states, Wyoming and Colorado, were getting a good thrashing with this wintry theme. I had heard rumours from travellers in the motel that Interstate 80 east was closed in several places and all motorists were advised to check routes and avoid travel. 'May was in like a lion', I think is an apt phrase here. Salt Lake City may have my presence for an extra day or so.

I could see the State Capitol perched upon a hill, from the motel. The organised, grid-planned streets made for easy navigation and in no time, I was climbing that hill. Unbeknown to me, I was about to have my first unsavoury moment in the USA. There were groups of people casing the city. They appeared to be part of a demonstration and, accompanied by fast cars with young men hanging out of open windows, were creating a lot of noise with air horns. I encountered such a group heading my way as I walked to the Capitol. They weren't Americans. As I passed them, one character on the edge of the group intentionally pushed into me. He nearly knocked me over and there was plenty of room to pass. I am normally calm unless provoked and I had just been provoked. I voiced my dissatisfaction to this guy's action and the whole group stopped and stared. I think my accent may have put them off their stride and when I asked where were they from, they shouted California, to which I replied, where are you really from. Going over the scene later, I think that was a brave statement, as who knows what they had hidden under their thick sheepskin and denim jackets. The ringleader gathered his group together and they continued down the hill, flashing their big white teeth in open grins as they left. I wonder what would have developed if a patrol car had been passing during this minor fracas? Shaken but not stirred, I continued my trek up the hill and had an enjoyable tour of the State Capitol. It had seemed ages since I was in a Capitol Building. It was only two weeks previous in Carson City Nevada. On my route east and onwards to the north east, the state capitals would come thick and fast. Utah's Capitol is a large and impressive example of an Italian Renaissance revival design. Many steps guide you to the multi-columned entrance, with 'State of Utah' engraved into the rock above the columns. Above, a huge dome is supported by a drum tower. Attractive gardens and fountains are hidden at the rear of this impressive building. In the main auditorium, a Jewish formal presentation of some sort was taking place. TV cameras and the media were hovering as I skirted past the group in search of a building plan. A rabbi in all his regalia was on the dais delivering a speech to an engaged audience. What a cultural cocktail in the colourful tapestry of life we live in.

Sara and Alana in the nearby visitor centre provided enthusiastic commentary on the many highlights of SLC. They included the Capitol I had just seen, the Cathedral of Madeleine, the historic Temple Square and Library Square, to mention but a few. They were also enthusiastic to apologise for the uncharacteristic demonstrations that were occurring today. It was May 1st and immigrant workers, were appealing for longer working permits in the USA in support of their eventual citizenship applications. Much to their surprise and slight embarrassment, I related my incident earlier that morning. Intrigued by my journey and photographic journal, Sara and Alana insisted in being part of my photographic record of SLC. They kindly posed in front of the Capitol Building, clear of demonstrations thankfully and we called the shot, 'Sara and Alana's Capitol'.

Back at the motel, I started planning my departure east for the next day. So far I had done the route as planned. However, a traveller I had met back in Torrey had mentioned Steamboat Springs in Colorado was a scenic delight and worth a diversion. Instead of hitting the interstate direct to Cheyenne, a little tinker with my route could get me east into

Steamboat, followed by Denver and then up to Cheyenne to rejoin my planned route. Some internet work revealed there was a lot of snow about and I-80 was still closed in several places. It would appear that the weather would continue to thwart my progress. If the Interstate was closed here and there, what would the roads be like leading to Steamboat and onwards to the Rockies and Denver? East of Steamboat there was a pass called 'Rabbits Ears Pass' to contend with as well. Hmm. Decisions. A quick call to a motel in Steamboat, coincidently called the 'Rabbits Ears Motel' gave further bad news. Snow was everywhere, the pass was blocked for four-wheel drive big boys, for a motorcycle forget it! I leaned back towards my original plan of east on I-80 and the forecast leaned towards an improvement by May 3rd. Hopefully I-80 would be open all the way by then. I found an Interstate 80 website and would use that as a go – no go decision tool. That meant another day in SLC, which was turning out not a bad place to be delayed.

Dropping into the visitor centre the next day, I was given a day's itinerary to fill which revealed why SLC and the local area is so unique. As we know, SLC is the headquarters of The Church of Jesus Christ of Latter-day Saints or the Mormons. That's how a lot of folk may know the place. However, mining and the first transcontinental railroad initially brought prosperity to the area that was titled the 'Crossroads of the West'. Today, much confident and overrated spiel from locals suggests that SLC and Utah are recession-proof. Very brave statements indeed, albeit a robust economy is evident by the established industrial banking that takes place in the central business district of downtown. SLC hosted the 2002 Winter Olympics as we remember and has since developed a very strong outdoor recreation industry primarily based on skiing. The local resorts of Alta, Brighton, Snowbird and Solitude are the most impressive attributes to the city. All are within 30 minutes' drive or ride for me from the downtown. I rode up to the 8,500 feet resort of Alta. From busy Friday lunchtime downtown traffic, I was high in the mountains within 20 minutes and into another snowy and very alpine scene. All the pistes were just full of snow and full of skiers. It is perfectly feasible for locals to take the afternoon off from the office and have a few hours on the piste before returning to their office or the shopping mall. Quite a quality of life here if you have the dollar. In the very cool air, looking around at scenes that a European winter sports person would die for, Utah was quickly becoming a very very attractive place to live.

Part Five – The Big East

Salt Lake City – Utah to Richmond – Virginia

3,598 miles

The Big East

Salt Lake City UT to Richmond VA

DATE	START	FINISH	MILEAGE	CUMULATIVE	COMMENTS
3 May	Salt Lake City UT	**Cheyenne WY (17)**	442	11152	I-80
4 May	Cheyenne WY	Cheyenne WY	20	11172	Local area
5 May	Cheyenne WY	Cheyenne WY	20	11192	Local area
6 May	Cheyenne WY	Estes Park CO	93	11285	I-25 & US34
6 May	Estes Park CO	Estes Park CO	46	11331	Rocky Mountain Park
7 May	Estes park CO	**Denver CO (18)**	61	11392	US36/92
7 May	Denver CO	Denver CO	30	11422	City & local
9 May	Denver CO	**Lincoln NE (19)**	501	11923	I-70/I-76/I-80
11 May	Lincoln NE	Lincoln NE	76	11999	SAC aerospace museum/ Lincoln & local area
13 May	Lincoln NE	Omaha NE	45	12044	12K service-BMW Omaha NE
13 May	Omaha NE	Lincoln NE	45	12089	Rtn to Linc only
14 May	Lincoln NE	**Topeka KS (20)**	167	12256	US75
14 May	Topeka KS	Topeka KS	21	12277	Topeka local
15 May	Topeka KS	**Des Moines IA (21)**	271	12548	Kansas & Interstates
15 May	Des Moines IA	Des Moines IA	27	12575	City & local
16 May	Des Moines IA	**Jefferson City MO (22)**	283	12858	Scenic route 63
17 May	Jefferson City MO	Jefferson City MO	5	12863	City & Capitol
17 May	Jefferson City MO	St Charles MO	117	12980	Lewis & Clark trail route US94
17 May	St Charles MO	St Charles MO	12	12992	Historic town area
18 May	St Charles MO	St Charles MO	53	13045	St Louis-Gateway Arch & St Charles
19 May	St Charles MO	**Springfield IL (23)**	111	13156	I-55
19 May	Springfield IL	Springfield IL	13	13169	Local & City
20 May	Springfield IL	Springfield IL	23	13192	Local & City
21 May	Springfield IL	**Indianapolis IN (24)**	200	13392	Route 36
21 May	Indianapolis IN	Indianapolis IN	13	13405	Local & City
22 May	Indianapolis IN	Indianapolis IN	20	13425	Local & City
23 May	Indianapolis IN	**Frankfort KY (25)**	163	13588	US31/7/214
23 May	Frankfort KY	Frankfort KY	15	13603	Local & City
24 May	Frankfort KY	Aberdeen OH	108	13711	US460/68
25 May	Aberdeen OH	**Columbus OH (26)**	112	13823	US62
25 May	Columbus OH	Columbus OH	9	13832	Local & City
28 May	Columbus OH	**Charleston WV (27)**	165	13997	US23/35
29 May	Charleston WV	**Richmond VA (28)**	311	14308	I-64
30 May	Richmond VA	Richmond VA	7	14315	Local & City

Chapter 36

Cool Runnings

I awoke from a deep sleep at dawn. Checking the weather revealed that Steamboat was still snowed in, but thankfully Interstate 80 was open all the way east. That was great news and the expectation of starting east across the country generated both excitement and slight nerves. The sky was clear over SLC and the early morning sun was glinting off the wet surfaces. Steam from central heating systems was rising vertically and creating white stripes against the morning blue sky. I had met quite a few travellers in my time at the motel and they were all intrigued as to my route decision. Quite a few of them were gathered around as I made the bike ready. There was the lady from Montana who was tracing her family tree in a local library, then the couple from Wyoming visiting elderly relatives and the Mormon couple from out in the Utah boondocks on a little spiritual weekend here in the capital. Quite a motley bunch and we chatted for a while over coffee. I had developed a new strategy when I fancied some local information about a particular state. It was quite a simple ploy and I would just target a car with a state licence plate of interest and pin down the occupants at a convenient time. Not literally of course, normally in a car park or fuel station. 'Excuse me, you have a Montana plate and I want some information about Missoula,' for example, was a great ice breaker and folks are only too pleased to tell you how good their town is and try that restaurant etc. That's how

I had met the lady from Wyoming here in SLC. She had given me some local information about Cheyenne that I would hopefully try out today. I like the idea of the state being identified on a vehicle licence plate. It makes for a great collection, which I must start. My Florida bike plate was already generating amusing comments about my geographical displacement in this part of the country. I wonder what the locals would say when I got to Alaska?

By the time I had checked out of the motel, steam was rising from the wet surfaces as the warm morning sun got to work. In short time I was on the Interstate and weaving through the city limits. Then very quickly I was clear of SLC and out in the countryside. Gently climbing to the east, it got a bit cooler and I had an uncontrollable shiver that made the bike wobble a touch. Someone had just walked over my grave. Glancing down at my GPS, it said 'next turn in 430 miles'. Hmm, quite some distance although I mustn't forget I was riding practically right across the state of Wyoming. This could turn out to be a really boring ride. However, being on a dry surface was far more appealing than taking on the snow of Colorado down towards Steamboat. I think it would be mind games time today. On such a long run on one road, I had to keep an active and alert frame of mind. Most folk I had spoken to said that I-80 east will bore you to tears. But what a pleasant surprise I was in for. Maybe boring in the metal cocoon of a car, not so on a motorcycle. The route consistently curved, snaked, climbed and descended, following the contours inch by inch. How could an Interstate be interesting? It was this morning and the bike was in its element. When you see a line on a road map, at first glance, it can be difficult to ascertain what elevation you may be at. I had studied the terrain this route followed and it appeared to be undulating, but not dramatically high. I forgot that I started at 4,226 feet in SLC and after a short climb east of town, I levelled off a touch, but it remained undulating, like a giant rollercoaster all the way to dinner. I felt high all the way east and it wasn't until checking finer details later that day that I surprisingly found that the en-route town of Rock Springs sits at 6,388 feet, Wamsutter at 6,772 feet and Laramie at 7,165. That's why it felt like riding on the roof of the world. I was elevated between 4,000 and 7,000 feet for 442 miles, with the high plains to the north and as

I progressed east, the increasingly large shoulder of the Rockies rising to the south. This was far from boring and crossing the Continental Divide on a clear and chilled early May Saturday lunchtime, on board a mechanical Teutonic marathon athlete, was invigorating. At certain parts of the route, I had the opportunity to race with some trains. Their length seemed to go on forever and ever, as the track twisted in and out of valleys and hugged the changing relief. I mustn't forget that this route was only fit for snowmobiles the last couple of days. It was a bonus to be making such progress east with no closures. Big metal gates with warning lights were at frequent intervals. 'If lights are flashing, turn around and return to last town.' Thankfully they were all open today and the route was clear of snow. The terrain was not and the white-covered mountains and rocks certainly transmitted a cool and isolated feel at these considerable elevations. Being a main arterial route east and west, there was plenty of life in the many vehicles on I-80. The same could not be said about anywhere else. Although I passed small settlements and many farms, I never saw a soul outside, until stopping for fuel around the halfway point at Wamsutter.

The bike would have easily had the legs for another hundred miles or so, but it was coffee and leg stretch time and the truck stop at Wamsutter looked the ideal place. It would be fuel followed by boy's room and then coffee and then off, in that order. Just a quick pit stop, as I was not anxious, but enthusiastic to get to Cheyenne by mid-afternoon. That was the plan on my first footfall in Wyoming. The site had two fuel stations, one of which was closed. Maybe this was a sign of the times, as I had already seen a lot of abandoned fuel pumps and boarded up buildings earlier that morning. The boy's room turned out to be cholera waiting to happen, as was the flu-ridden guy behind the cashier's desk, who proceeded to eject phlegm with alacrity and regularity into a bin beneath his counter. Welcome to Wyoming! Escaping also with alacrity from his virus-ridden capsule, I returned to the chilled outdoors, only to find a guy giving my bike very close attention. I was suspicious at first, however Rick Menolascina turned out to be a perfectly harmless creature. Quite a gentle giant, Rick was rather underdressed for the Wyoming chill in shorts and T-shirt. As a long distance truck driver, it was the map of my route on the bike that attracted his attention. He was intrigued or rather astonished at the miles I would be covering and we instantly hit it off sharing road tales. It was my first chat with an en-route truck driver and after all, it is these guys that pound the Interstate with freight of all kinds that simply makes the USA work. They make the country function. Rick was out of Baker City, Oregon and today was eastbound to Lincoln Nebraska and then further east. He would spend maybe a couple of weeks away from home and in that time tick off many states across the country. He showed me inside the cabin of his Kenworth truck. It was a challenge enough for me to climb up there. Inside, as I expected, all the mod-cons that make life bearable for these road kings. Upfront was satnav, radio, CD player and CB radio naturally. In the rear, a comfortable bed, fridge, TV, storage etc., everything but a 'john' I guess. Rick's 'rig' was a medium-size affair which seemed big enough to me. But some have more salubrious living quarters, almost like a small apartment behind the cab. Rick pulled away first and by the time I had finished my coffee and hit the road, he was a couple of miles further east. I caught up with him in quick time and formatted alongside the cab. I stayed on station just enough time for Rick to take a photo and then accelerated off. He was sitting at the optimum speed for best fuel consumption. Whilst talking he had emphasised that the increase in fuel prices was forcing drivers and hauliers out of business. 'You have to fine-tune everything these days and if it means sitting at 55 mph, so be it.' Not all truck drivers had that discipline. Thankfully it wasn't a consideration for me.

The rest of I-80 to Cheyenne flashed by and very soon I was passing Laramie and arriving in the Cowboy State Capital city by 3 pm. It had been a cool, but exhilarating ride. The biggest distance I had covered in one day so far, with stimulating en-route scenery thrown in. My first choice motel was just a little out of town. A quick recce of the small downtown revealed a place I would have loved to have hung up my boots for a couple of days. It was the Plains Hotel, steeped with cowboy history and elegant accommodations. I recall, it was the hotel that my Wyoming lady contact in SLC had mentioned. Alas, although their price was good, there was absolutely nowhere to park the bike. I instead went for a place with an equally appealing western name and checked into the Hitching Post. From the outside, it looked bland and boring, but this was thankfully not the case inside. I was welcomed into a huge lobby adorned with cowboy memorabilia and fantastic old black and white photographs. The motel-style accommodation was accessed at the rear, where I even had both a front and rear door to my quite huge room.

After completing my normal post-ride rituals, which included a very hot shower to melt the cool of the Wyoming day, it was straight to the dining room. I had put in a good shift today and propelled myself a good distance into The Big East sector. I treated myself to a huge steak, which was almost as thick as a door mat. A thick and pleasant deep purple Shiraz adequately washed down the meat and then it was a nightcap in the bar. It was quiet for a Saturday night, but just the right atmosphere to reflect on the day. I had a warm glow and a feeling of euphoria that was always there after a good day's ride. I also had the thought of a relaxing couple of days ahead in Cheyenne, with no big decisions to ponder. The lady bartender got talking eventually and when I remarked upon the lobby photographs, she went into verbal overdrive. 'Follow me and come and see the VIP dining room.' Now there was an offer I couldn't refuse and with beer mug in hand, I followed her. The walls were adorned with black and white photographs of former Presidents and guests who had visited the establishment. I lost count how far they went back, however, I recognised the Presidents from the last 20 years or so. A fitting end to another one of those exhilarating days in the saddle.

Chapter 37

Cowboy Capital

The blast from yesterday's journey and the evening's refreshments produced a sound sleep for my first night in the Hitching Post. Although I was just aware of a slight background noise which turned out to be next doors TV on low, but it was the sound of the railway locos that really got my attention and brought consciousness shortly after 7 am. It's that uncanny wailing sound of a loco's sirens that is so characteristic of the North American railway, or railroad rather. The woow wooow of the horn accompanied by the ding ding ding of a bell. A huge freight terminal was very adjacent to the motel and the clatter and rumble of freight trains was as common here as black cabs are in London. No need for a wake-up call in this city, which I found difficult to pronounce correctly, much to the amusement of the locals. I had to change the spelling to remember. Cheyenne became Shy Ann. It worked. The Sioux Indians who roamed the plains named the place, which in their tongue means 'aliens' or 'people of foreign language'. Fierce fighters, the native Indians were not pleased with the changes that started to take place. The first real settlers were men working on the great Union Pacific Railroad. Surveyors and construction crews ran the gauntlet with the Indians. Eventually the iron horse won and Cheyenne became a thriving western town. Initially it was very much a tented town and was dubbed as 'hell on wheels', but was quickly developing into a frontier settlement. Eventually, masonry structures replaced wooden buildings and the tents were no longer seen. Completion of the railway brought the entertainment industry as troupes frequently stopped over for shows en route to San Francisco from the east coast. It has retained its cowboy image right up to today and hosts the famous 'Frontier Days' rodeo event which of course the locals insist is the best cowboy event in the USA.

Exiting the rear door of my spacious room, I took several lungfuls of fresh air to get the circulation going, simultaneously giving the bike the once-over. To my surprise or maybe alarm, the car park was absolutely full of police patrol cars, trucks and pick-ups. White with big yellow writing. 'Wyoming State Trooper'. There must have been 30 or so police vehicles out there each with dogs, handlers and other officers. The sound of electronic voices emanated from many radios. They were all out of their vehicles as if about to assault a building or take on something. Short haircuts, streamlined sunglasses and baseball caps aplenty, they looked a professional bunch. But not in uniform – bulletproof jackets and jeans seemed to be dress of the day. What the hell was happening out there? It was Sunday. For one moment, I didn't think they were there on my behalf, even though I had frequently conjured this security thing in a few states. It could be the Wyoming Police force versus Gilroy. When they saw me, several looked away and began small talk. Some started to use their radios. I continued with my morning routines and even shouted the odd 'Good Morning' across their way. Some nodded, some waved.

I got the usual thing over first and rode through the quiet Sunday traffic to the State Capitol Building. It was only five minutes from the motel, although nothing is far away in this compact town. It was a smallish building with the usual drum tower and gold-gilded dome and cupola. What was really impressive and reminded me what part of the USA I was in, was the life-size bronze statue in the Capitol gardens. 'The Spirit of Wyoming' depicts a bucking horse in almost vertical stance. Loosely on board is a cowboy complete with dangling reins, furling chaps, hat and lasso at the ready. Whilst examining this hugely impressive work of art, all sorts of images and noises were provoked within. Alas, I was too early in the year to live that cowboy experience at the August Frontier

Days rodeo. However, a visit to the city's impressive museum housing more cowboyalia was sufficient to satisfy my appetite. Whilst riding back to the motel, signs for Warren Air Force base caught my eye. It turned out to be very close to the downtown area. But my logistical naivety of the US military inventory did not reveal the function of this base until chatting with some locals later that day. You could walk down Pershing Boulevard from the base into town. Missile Drive, Peacekeeper Road and Atlas Loop all offered bigger clues. In the late 50s, Warren became one of the first operational Intercontinental Ballistic Missile Bases. That must explain the white rockets standing guard at the entrance to the base. Today, missiles are siloed in several locations. The safe, secure and ready key commands are apparently all co-ordinated from Warren. Quite a chilling thought in such a small town with much frontier and cowboy feel. How the modern world has changed things. I wonder what the ghosts of the roaming Indians on the nearby high plains would think of Warren's function today.

Before I dropped into the motel bar later that evening, I could still hear the TV next door and a 'do not disturb sign' hung on the door handle. I wonder what they were up to in there? I had seen no sign of life from my neighbours since I arrived. This time the bar was boisterous and a few characters were draped around here and there. One guy clung on to my every word and was very impressed about meeting an Australian. Unprompted he continued to lambast Brits and British food for some reason. The lady bartender knew my true identity and grimaced in the shadows beneath the liquor. When I revealed my nationality to the garrulous American, he withdrew into an embarrassed shambles and wanted to be my best friend. It was so amusing and he left like a scolded dog after I threw some hearty banter his way. He added, 'I am going home to my wife and take-out food and God bless the Queen.' One nil England I think. The next group to take me on had heard all that. They had also been drinking since lunchtime and mixing a deep south accent with several bottles of Jack Daniels, reveals a drawl that the native Indians of yesteryear would have trouble deciphering. The three of them, one women and two men, were completely drunk as skunks. They were trying to eat, drink and stagger around the pool table and gained high scores for artistic impression in the process. I did get out of them that they were newspaper machinery installation technicians. They state-hop chasing contracts and today was their last day in town. The younger guy became so paralytic in my time at the bar that he turned quite insulting, but sort of amusing for a drunk. However, his bone of contention was against UK immigration on a past trip, who denied him access to Blighty because of drunken behaviour on arrival. I didn't disbelieve him. He was apparently returned to sender and had to re-board the same aircraft he had just arrived on. Now what really capped this series of exchanges was a local sitting alone at the bar. He had also heard all this verbal commotion and laid into the Louisiana drunk. A big guy with a face attached to a moustache, he was dressed in red checked shirt and wore a weather-beaten Stetson. His fingers were stained yellow with years from the weed and he grasped a large glass of whisky. It was as if he was defending me, much to my amusement. The Louisiana drunks withdrew from the bar, probably before their livers got out and walked. I never saw them again. I only went to the bar for a quiet meal and a beer and ended up in quite a charged atmosphere. The poor bartender lady was so apologetic, but I was quick to dismiss her concern. I was more interested in my cold beer and meatloaf and remembering a night in a real cowboy bar. She quickly added that if I wanted more of the same, she knew several places downtown that could compete. She was off shift imminently and offered escort. It sounded like more action, however, it was late. I had thoughts of saloons, glasses rolling down long bars and skirmishes from more uncontrollable drunks. Maybe another time. Some geographical advice came out of the bar talk. I mentioned I had been unable to get into Steamboat Springs and would have to make do with viewing the Rockies from Denver. Not so, a local added. 'Drop into Estes Park before Denver, you will not be disappointed.' I made a note of that advice and just maybe I could get above 10,000 feet on the bike!

I decided to stay one more day in Cheyenne. The permanent clatter from the railway sidings drove me to despair, which provoked some quick research on the history of Union Pacific. So close to the heavy metalwork, I couldn't really leave town without an insight. The small downtown railway museum set in the old train depot dating back to

1886 provided an ideal snapshot, including a vast collection of old photographs. Cheyenne certainly must have been some place in its rail heyday. One of the largest locomotives built, 'Big Boy' 4004, is on display in a city park. At 132 feet long, weighing 600 tons and capable of pulling a train five and a half miles long, there were 25 'Big Boys' built. This freight-pulling behemoth was finally retired from service in 1962. There is no longer a passenger service through Cheyenne. The USA is not known for an extensive rail passenger service and perhaps the comprehensive Interstate networks and plethora of cheap airlines have taken over as people carriers. But the freight trains still ply the east-west and north-south routes with regularity. My final ride around Cheyenne included a quick visit to the regional airport, which doubles as an Air National Guard C130 Hercules base. The terminal was tiny and served only Great Lakes Airlines, with flights to Denver and connections onwards. I had mentioned to the Wyoming lady I met back in Salt Lake City that I had some aviation in my veins and enjoyed old photographs. She quickly mentioned that I should go to the upstairs café bar at Cheyenne's airport and see shots of Amelia Earhart posing alongside her aircraft with Miss Frontier Days, then there's the Spirit of St Louis as well. 'Now don't expect much,' she said, 'the airport bar is not a glitzy joint like at JFK or similar. It's Cheyenne.' It's nice to follow up recommendations. The small bar was populated by a few locals. They were neither passengers nor workers. Just locals chatting over beer and sandwiches with the bartender, who was obviously part of their social set. I interrupted their flow and ordered a coffee and pastry. In the empty dining room next door were the pictures just as described.

I was awoken in the middle of the night. I could hear the TV next door. It was on low again and this time accompanied by the occasional loud cackle of a lady laughing. It didn't sound like a young lady. I thought maybe I was dreaming at first and then the loud reality of nearby railroad noise, including the wailing loco sirens, confirmed I was perfectly awake. I eventually drifted back into sleep, but remembered everything the next morning. When checking out, I recalled my experience to the reception clerk. I got a strange look at first and shuffling through hotel records, the clerk revealed no reservation of any guest in that room over the period of my stay. She showed me the blank screen and uncompleted booking docket. I left it there, but quickly mentally rewound to the stories I was told in the bar. I am not sure if the tales are true. The former long-term owners of the Hitching Post had passed away a few years ago. They had been at the place a long time and through many good years. It had been a sad affair when they died and some staff had allegedly reported eerie experiences and reports of ghostly apparitions in certain rooms! Maybe I was under surveillance from a variety of sources?! I was out of here and south to Colorado! This had turned out to be a little city with a big kick.

Chapter 38

Rubbing Shoulders with the Rockies

It had turned out to be an eventful stay in Cheyenne. I would re-enter Wyoming later on in my journey when going west across the top of the country. My three days had been a good appetiser for what I am sure is an interesting state overall. Close to the Hitching Post, Interstate 25 took me south and very quickly I was crossing the state boundary into Colorado. I very nearly left Cheyenne direct for Denver without even a look at the Rockies. Ria and Laurie in the Hitching Post Inn bar had persuaded me otherwise. I came off 25 at Loveland and followed 34 all the way to Estes Park to complete a quick 100 miles. Estes Park is a small town nestled in a high mountain valley sitting at 7,500 feet elevation. Undoubtedly a gateway to the Rockies National Park, the place was awash with hotels, motels and log cabins on the hill into town. A compact town centre had all the shops with the trappings for the outdoor person. This place would be mayhem in a couple of months but right now, in early May, it was almost a ghost town. The gargantuan visitor centre advised me that some of the accommodations would still be closed. They were right, however I found a basic-looking motel that was open and I was the only guest that night. The mountains were very adjacent, snow-capped and rugged, peaking at 13,000 feet. Entering the park on Trail Ridge Road, I was able to do a 50-mile circuit of the roads that were open. I got very close to the impressive geography, but again, alas, 10,000 feet eluded me and I only managed 9,800 feet elevation. The road ahead was gated with no further access to the highest public road in North America which tops out at 12,813 feet. I was about 100 miles east of Steamboat Springs and after that recent early May snowfall, a lot of the elevated portions of the road ahead were closed. One of the Park Rangers I bumped into mentioned the road closures up here can last all through the summer months. I was lucky to get up to where I was. So after an abortive attempt to get into Colorado via Steamboat Springs last week, I got into the Rockies after all. Not from the west, but from the east and nicely positioned for Denver. The full extent of the range is approximately 2,700 miles stretching from almost Mexico to Alaska. The Rockies of course are known as the backbone of the continent or the Great Continental Divide. I first saw them back in March when in northern New Mexico around Charma. That was the day a wolf ran across the road in front of me. I clearly recall that the lady in the visitor centre urgently advised me not to progress north because of snow-blocked roads. I didn't appreciate that nearly six weeks later, snow would still be causing travel problems. More recently, I crossed the divide a couple of days ago when eastbound on I-80 heading for Cheyenne. As I continue on my trail, I would be crossing the Rockies a couple more times, which really emphasises how they dominate the geography of North America.

Back in Estes, fatigue attacked me after the afternoon in the quite rarefied air. I again felt as if I was walking in glue. I now could identify this altitude sickness straight away. In some respects I was looking forward to getting down to lower levels as I progressed east through the plains. However, that change would bring flat and featureless landscape for a couple of thousand miles.

That was a very welcome and enjoyable close quarters Rockies experience, leaving only a short hop down to the Mile High City. It would be a visit to the State Capitol only, a quick walk around and then off east. Early in my trip a Denver biker had been in touch several times and was keen to meet for a ride out for a few hours and even lunch. That could be a possibility, but he had not answered any emails or phone calls as I approached. After passing Boulder, I dropped into Golden to the west of the city to find a motel for a couple of nights. Locals had recommended Golden. I had been warned that Denver was a city of distinct neighbourhoods and I had to be sure I stayed in the right one. Golden was okay apparently. Denver is an attractive place overall and has a pleasing blend of outdoor adventure and urban sophistication. With snow-capped peaks providing a spectacular backdrop, the city is as refined as laidback. After checking into a regular chain motel and unloading, I was off to familiarise myself with the Colorado capital city. This was the bit I was growing to like when I stayed slightly out of town. Bike clear of luggage and feeling light and frisky, GPS programmed for downtown, jeans and jacket only and off into the traffic! You never see these chunks of a city closely as a tourist that arrives at the airport and takes transportation direct to hotel. Urban Interstates, freeways, link roads, regional airports, parks and the grid of central streets and then quickly the high rise of the central business district growing on the horizon. After morning showers, the many glass-sided skyscrapers sat pretty against a blue sky backdrop with the Rockies within spitting distance. A pretty city. I recognised the central bits and easily found the State Capitol Building. The Capitol was full of school kids, however I managed to tag onto a noisy group heading for the climb into the dome. So I instantly added 276 feet on to the 5,280 feet elevation of the city. The Capitol's state flag was roaring in the keen breeze. It was a blue and blustery elevated view of the busy lunchtime criss-cross of roads, with the southern Rocky Mountains only 15 miles away. Just where I had been yesterday up at Estes Park and beyond. The 105th meridian west of Greenwich passes through Denver Union Rail Station, which marks the reference point for the Mountain Time Zone.

The spring sun was now extremely warm and a sandwich in the Capitol Gardens had to be the lunch venue. I just had to find a sandwich. I did within a short walk from the Capitol and ordered a sandwich and coffee to take out from a nice little grill bar. I heard a slight disturbance at the bar and saw a guy sitting there who was just staring at me with his mouth open. Eventually, nervously, he spoke. 'It's you, the Brit, doing all the states on a bike.' Would you believe, it was the Denver biker who had previously been in touch earlier in my journey and suggested he showed me Colorado. My accent, followed by recognition of my jacket badges, confirmed to him my identity. I think he wanted to dissolve into the shadows and he was embarrassment personified. A few excuses came my way. A quick email or call would have sufficed. He was a character who suggested and promised a lot and came up with nothing. Thankfully I had encountered very few like him. He left before I got my order and probably wished he had chosen a different lunch venue. I am glad this stranger would remain a stranger. The sandwich was enjoyable.

Chapter 39

Into the Plains

It was now becoming a very common theme of my journey. The weather. I had been told frequently that spring can be unsettled everywhere in the USA. Ground temperatures rise creating heat radiation, which conflicts with the ever-active weather systems charging about. This cocktail produces thunderstorms from hell, some with hail the size of baseballs and the dreaded tornado. I was forever looking out for the distinctive vertical snake that could spoil the day of the most resilient traveller. I had seen drooping and straggling clouds that looked like a tornado to the unfamiliar. But the distinctive cone which connects cloud and ground had so far escaped me, or rather I had escaped them. On a daily basis there are reports of tornados on the TV at this time of the year. Some days humans and buildings evade all damage as the hoodlum will rush through open ground. Other days they cause death and collateral damage. It's as simple as that. The tornado is almost considered a fact of life in the meteorological conundrum in this huge country. The next part of my journey, a little over 500 miles, was my first real encounter of tornado alley. It stretches from the Dakotas all the way south to the gulf coast, although a definitive geographical boundary varies from who you speak to. Leaving Colorado, I was planning to hop across the guts of tornado alley, through most of Nebraska and into the capital, Lincoln. Again a common theme, I had another down day. The next day's forecast all across southern Nebraska, was for one of thunderstorms with hail expected, wind in excess of 40 mph and rotation anticipated in the active weather cells. Rotation was a word that would ring alarm bells. Rotation meant the strong likelihood of tornado activity and the Weather Channel would get quite excited about delivering this part of their forecast. Quite rightly so. Their weather radar could pinpoint exactly where the action was taking place, not just in a state, but in a county and which towns were in the path of these demons. I was now a Weather Channel aficionado. I was almost becoming a storm searcher, but to search, locate and avoid! It was the weather or the election campaign that was flicking my TV switches on an hourly basis when I was not on the road. An extra day in Denver or rather Golden was on the cards, even though it was bright and blue here. I decided to give the bike a rest and stay local. A quintessential American breakfast followed my decision to hold the mobile action for 24 hours. As a great people-watcher, it's quite amusing watching American motel users come and go. Not all motels have an adjoining restaurant, but this one did. Breakfast diners varied from young kids to single mums, to sedate elderly couples unsure of their day's destination. Then there's the contract worker who shoves a huge plateful away prior to embarking on a day's work. I sat at the bar and whilst consuming a perfect omelette with toast, tea and OJ, observed with amusement as the meal orders came thick and fast. They were fielded by a gent who had a deep resonating voice that would be great on the radio. I told him he was in the wrong job, much to his guttural laughter. It was the no-nonsense dispatch of the orders that seemed an efficient process. The order on a ticket would propel itself above a single cook, who over a hot grill, was a blur of eggs, bacon, pancakes and the like. Replete from sustenance and the contents of *USA Today*, which didn't take long, I was nearly halfway through the morning. A stroll around the gargantuan nearby shopping mall, with the odd coffee here and there, got me through the rest of the day. It was weather check time.

With a lost day, it wasn't such a big decision to take the Interstate east. That's I-80 again. I had considered an assortment of smaller roads to the south, but I was conscious of another lost day and lost days could mount up. Progress expeditiously when possible was my mantra at the moment. After all, the scenery on this trail across Nebraska, whatever route I took, would be a mixture of flat and very flat. The forecast read brilliantly for the next day, with all meteorological dilemmas for the moment, clearing well to the east and away from where I would be. 500 miles, well about an hour in a plane, but around a full day for me and I divided the route up a bit for fuel stops and looked in detail at en-route weather for the towns of Sterling, North Platte and Kearney, just in case. With weather set fair, Interstate 76 took me out of Denver and the north east corner of Colorado, after which Interstate 80 looked after my navigation for the rest of the day. Leaving Denver and the Rockies in my mirror, I did have a gentle feeling of descent as the road ahead curved and meandered to lower levels. I had mentally programmed myself for another boring 'on the road' day. There turned out to be quite a few distractions. Unlike the elevated I-80 the other day in blue but chilled air, this was a contrasting portion of the transcontinental monster through much lower and rich agricultural areas. The Weather Channel got it right and it turned out to be a superb spring day. No wind at all and lines and lines of fair weather cumulus cloud ranked up with parade-ground precision as far as the eye could see. The type of cloud that is very white and very fluffy, with flat bottoms. Nothing looked threatening, but standing water in the fields was evidence of yesterday's tumult. To pace the leg, I divided the 500 miles into a stop at 200, a stop at 400, leaving a leisurely 100 into Lincoln. Being a first-class all-rounder, the bike was equally happy to sit at speed on long stretches like this, as it was roaring around the Rockies of Colorado or the desert roads of Arizona or Utah. At any speed in any gear, the mighty boxer twin power plant is happy to sit at any rpm, with any load, with no complaints. This engine is literally bullet, grenade and bomb proof. The only thing that suffered was the progressively stiffening muscles of the rider. Much to the amusement of passing road users, I had developed a few stretching exercises to combat such physical challenges. My concern was that when I thrust a leg forward at full stretch, it would stay there and I would be unable to retract it back onto the foot rests! Thankfully, I had avoided that dilemma so far. As the first 200 miles clicked over, I took my first stop and after refuelling, looked for some fellow travellers to chat with. My first contact was not human, but a lively young dog that was also intent on leg stretching and was running rings around me and the bike. He or she was also jumping up and required attention. I was slightly concerned he would jump up and place paws on hot exhaust which would make for an instant yelping canine barbeque. Thankfully, Piper was quickly rounded up by his young owners. Out of Oregon, both were medical students heading to Pennsylvania for further studies. They had a carload of life including a newborn baby. It turned out these young Americans led busy lives. Not only raising a family, studying medicine, but also learning to fly. Piper got his name after their training aircraft. But was he a Cherokee or a Warrior?! My meeting with the Oregon posse passed an interesting 20 minutes or so before starting the next 200 miles. The scenery was not as boring as I had anticipated. The Americans call the plains the 'Flyover States'. If you don't need to be on the ground, you fly over them! A little harsh I think. I had been quite surprised so far. It wasn't completely flat, but a bit undulating, lots of trees and copses, interspersed with huge farms with outbuildings the size of aircraft hangars. Cattle, well all types of cattle, long horn, short horn, black, brown, white face, you name it. I would like a dollar for every head of cattle I saw between Denver and Lincoln.

At the 400-mile stop, I didn't have to look for conversation. I was cornered by an old travelling couple. I had seen them taking coffee in the diner and they followed me out. They were in their late 60s or early 70s and, even the way they were dressed, you could instantly put them both in a 50s or 60s movie. Their mode of transport, an old square-shaped camper van, was from that era as well. Certainly not a modern machine. It had probably seen all of the USA several times over and I wouldn't like to guess the mileage it, or even they, had covered. The lady made for her seat in the cab and the gent followed me to the bike and started the talk. He was dressed in denim jeans, checked shirt and light blue denim jacket, complete with baseball cap on top of a craggy face. He had a tooth pick between his lips which he continued to propel from left to right with great skill and with no danger of losing it. Kneeling down at my pannier maps he commented, 'We are on a five-week trip, heading east to New York to see her sister, then up to Wisconsin to see my brothers and then a slow hike back home to Oregon.' That is quite a road trip and the second family I had met that morning who resided in Oregon. When I asked why didn't they sit back and let a plane take the strain over these vast distances and leave the long trips to young whippersnappers like me, he added, 'Hell no, flying and airports are stressful and boring. You see the real America on road trips. Anyway, I was a crew chief on C54 transports in the Korean War and saw a lifeful of aircraft then. We are getting a bit old these days and have to stop more than we used to for the bathroom and coffee. But it all makes for interesting experiences and our old camper van is one of the family.' We exchanged further travellers' tales, before he joined his patient wife and made off east. He was a sharp and polite old guy. These people were a real part of America and it had been learning experience to meet them. I wish I had recorded our conversation. Next time.

The final 100 miles passed very quickly and soon the State Capitol Building of Nebraska was visible like a Saturn V rocket on its launchpad in the middle of downtown Lincoln. What an unbelievable landmark on the low plains; tall and statue-like, reaching high up to the big sky. It was a clear day and I reckon I saw this leggy behemoth from at least 10 miles west. Arriving in the motel car park, the bike computer read 501 miles completed since leaving Denver. Walking around the air felt and smelt different. Even after sitting facing the front for several hours, I felt considerably energetic and was gulping lungfuls of thick, fresh oxygen. I wasn't struggling and walking around sluggishly like I had been at higher elevations back west. The lower altitudes of eastern Nebraska, not much above 1,000 feet, offered a revitalising feeling to my body, which was nice after 12,000 miles on the road. I was almost in the middle of the country, the guts of the great agricultural plains of the USA. Arrival in Lincoln, state capital 19 on my trek, had put me in an excellent position to start the state 'pinball' run further east into Virginia by the end of the month.

Chapter 40

Marooned in Lincoln

The capital of Nebraska territory had originally been Omaha. However most of the population lived south of the Platte River and it was decided to also move the capital further south towards Lancaster. Lincoln started life as the small town of Lancaster. It was renamed after the recently assassinated President Abraham Lincoln and became the capital of Nebraska with the admission to the Union in 1867. The great man himself would not have been happy with my first visions of his city. The next day the low cloud was zooming along at a great pace aided by a strong wind. Enough water to refloat several sunken battleships was hammering down to complete an awful day on the northern plains. The bike was getting a good wash. I managed a bus trip around the city and got drenched in my attempt to be the tourist. It wasn't worth it and after lunch in a quiet downtown grill, everywhere was quiet. I retreated like a drowned rat to my motel. At least I had a couple restaurants I could float to later in the day for dinner. The motel was a hive of activity and full for the weekend. The incumbents were a mixture of party-goers and families attending a college graduation

The weather thankfully graduated to a better grade the next day and greeted me with a crystal clear blue sky, not a sliver of cloud and a keen breeze. I don't think the wind had stopped for 24 hours now. At least the deluge from yesterday was nowhere to be seen and the land was dry.

After mopping excess water from the bike, I wanted to cram in as much as possible on this bright day. My first excursion was to the Strategic Air and Space Museum just up the road a bit at Omaha. I believe Nebraska's Offutt Air Force Base has been a bastion of air power for decades and the museum at Ashfield is within the same area. It was rather like a Duxford in England. A big, glass-fronted building, with a couple of rockets on guard outside and cavernous halls housing the usual suspects of air power over the years. It was nice to stroke the nose of an SR71 Blackbird, kick the tyres of the amazing B58 Hustler and reminisce at quite a sorry-looking Vulcan bomber which was in much need of tender loving care. Amongst the collection was a pristine example of a Voodoo, the type that my friend in Arizona so loved to fly in England. He could have flown this machine.

Leaving the museum and heading back to Lincoln, I very soon got sight of the amazing State Capitol building and headed straight for there. Lincoln's crown and jewels, in my opinion, really puts Huey Long's Baton Rouge vertical monster in the shadows. I can only describe Nebraska's State Capitol as an art deco skyscraper. This rare design for a Capitol Building is in complete contrast to the standard dome and cupola designs that I have seen around the country. Entering the place was like stepping into a Batman movie. Was I lost somewhere in Gotham City? Long, dark, marbled corridors, some studded with colourful mosaics, huge wall art and the usual collection of statues and inscriptions, all gave a menacing feel. A perfectly serviceable, but ancient-looking lift propelled me nearly 400 feet into the Nebraska sky and the viewing balcony. The day before, I would have been in cloud up here and needless to say, on such a clear day the visibility in all directions was unlimited. No mountains to see, but the criss-cross of streets and the many huge white crop stores were set out like pieces on a monopoly board. Looking out into Nebraska, it was difficult to get a perception of how far I could see. There was nothing to make a reference with. Looking skyward at an airliner's contrail, I have often wondered whereabouts a vertical line from the glinting metal aircraft would strike the earth. I was trying to put this exercise into practice right now as I gazed at a couple of distant participants in the experiment. I am glad that I am not a vertigo sufferer; straining straight down to the street, my bike looked like a metal ant at rest way below. Descending back into the bowels of Gotham City, the high ceilings continued to mesmerise. It would be quite easy to step in the shadows and remain unnoticed at locking up time in a building like this. This place left an impression. I like different things. Returning to the daylight from the cool interior, a walk around the sky rocket of a building concluded an impressive visit. Gazing up at the summit on the tower, a striking statue of 'the Sower' looked proud against the blue sky. He was casting his seeds into the surrounding plains of the Cornhusker State. An appropriate apex. The statue of the man himself, Lincoln, was a fitting closure. I passed my compliments to the man as he gazed down with a typical Lincoln stare from his elevated plinth in the Capitol Gardens.

In contrast the downtown of Lincoln did nothing else really to inspire. It contained the usual collection of high-rise buildings and businesses. Other than the Capitol Building, there was really nothing else to contain a tourist's interest. Although before leaving the urban area, I had been told to have a look at the Haymarket historic district. It is refreshing to see throughout the USA, that a lot of cities have made the effort to restore former industrial areas. Brick Town in Oklahoma City comes immediately to mind. Here in Lincoln, the Haymarket area is very similar, where many bars and restaurants have been added to the restored warehouse area. Antique shops and art galleries complement the district, not forgetting the once a week farmers' market selling local produce. Shutting out the noise of today, it is possible to walk around and try and imagine how it would have been centuries ago. Probably the clanking from the adjoining Lincoln railroad station, the clatter of horses' hooves over the cobbled streets and the chatter of shoppers as they went from the Milady Coffee Store, to the Apothecary, to Veith's Store and maybe calling into Jack's Bar for refreshment. Today, although authenticity is maintained, it's new chain joints like Lazlo's and Old Chicago that dominate. We should not live in the past, but not forget the past. The Haymarket was probably once the hub of Lincoln.

The next capital on my route was Topeka in Kansas, at just 170 miles south east. I had been cogitating a few new tactics with the map. I had contemplated using Lincoln as a base and heading down to Topeka for the day. That would be possible, putting Des Moines next from Lincoln. Alas another gale bashed Nebraska the following day. It was dangerous to walk outside, never mind ride a heavy bike. An expedition to the restaurant in the evening was hazardous on foot and I vividly recall having to hang on to road signs to keep upright! I was slightly concerned that the bike would get blown over and moved it to the lee side of a building. One good day, one bad day seemed to be a theme on the plains. I didn't even look at the forecast and tested my theory. It worked this time and the next day allowed the short journey to the bike dealership at Omaha for the 12,000 mile service. It was now mid-May and after a longer stay than expected in Nebraska, tomorrow it was into Kansas. So far on The Big East, I had only passed through four states, with nine to go.

Chapter 41

Kansas-Iowa Pinball Run

Although this big section across the country is generally east all the way, these states in the middle required a little deviation to route via their capitals. I had thought about refining my route a little to optimise my time. The outcome was to stick to my original plan, which from Lincoln meant going south to Topeka, north to Des Moines and then south again to Jefferson City. Progress required a bit of zig-zagging here like a hurtling pin ball through these states, but it was unavoidable. But progress was a nice word to introduce into the next day on the road. After being trapped in Nebraska by never-ending lashing rain and gales across the plains, progress was a beautiful word! The forecast for the week ahead looked settled and there was a realistic chance of getting through a lot of country in quick time. My memories of Lincoln would be of gigantic grain stores and that amazing Capitol Building. I saw both leaving the city, standing proud against the skyline. Heading east on highway 2 as far as Nebraska City and then branching off south on highway 75 took me through rolling green countryside. It was quite an enjoyable biker's route with an abundance of sweeping curves and delicious crescents, carving through the quiet Nebraska and Kansas geography. With only a short distance to do for a change, I would be in Topeka in time for a late lunch and stroll around the Capitol area. Consequently, with a no-rush feeling, it was a delight to have time to take in the small agricultural towns of Dawson, Sabetha, Fairview, Holton and Mayetta. They all had the same theme of serving the local agricultural counties. One busy main street with the usual shops and a smattering of eateries and hinged at either end with a couple of fuel stations and not forgetting the ubiquitous American motel. I had grown accustomed to the rural route and as Topeka approached, it was quite a culture shock to join a busy urban Interstate and navigate around another brick and asphalt colossus to my motel. A little unkind on Topeka, but compact as the downtown looked, Interstates 70 and 470 looping the city still had the look of a race track. Cars and trucks were everywhere and quite a contrast from the rural tranquillity I had just ridden through. Again the quiet countryside and then suddenly extremely busy urban areas was forming a nationwide common theme.

In complete contrast to the leggy State Capitol Building in Lincoln, Topeka is a city with another dome and cupola State Capitol Building. This dome and cupola Capitol was completed in 1903 and considered to be the most architecturally handsome around in the Union. There was an awful lot of copper on this large dome and climbing the steep staircase to the viewing platform at just under 304 feet up may have been too much for some. The climb was certainly not for the faint hearted and I overtook several potential balcony viewers who had vertigo on their mind. What was astonishing on the climb were the very low hand rails on the steep staircases that even a mountain goat would have found challenging. States have different rules for this and rules for that I am sure, however, I did consider this climb was verging on a health and safety issue, especially for kids. Reaching the top and emerging onto a narrow ledge like viewing area, Ara, the Capitol guide on her elevated early afternoon shift, instantly gave me a historical commentary of the state. She dismissed all my concern about the route to the top and made sure I enjoyed the view from the top! I couldn't argue with that and cautiously leant on the wall and listened with interest to her words. Kansas is named after the Kansa tribe and means people of the wind. Now that I could equate to after some of the wind I had experienced recently. A Kansa tribesman, complete with bow and arrow drawn, sits atop the dome. Kansas joined the Union in 1861 as the 34th State, which included a constitution prohibiting slavery. Settlers became known as Homesteaders and could claim 160 acres of land by living on it for five years. I had probably ridden through prime homesteader's country that morning. Today, Kansas is famous for farming, the aircraft industry and modern cities. Ara concluded by stating that Kansas is a proud and forward-looking state. I was looking forward to lunch, but enjoyed my brief and informative overview of the Sunflower State from an enthusiastic State Capitol guide. This confident, friendly and informative approach is common with Americans in general. They certainly are very proud of their country and what they do, whether it be a waitress or a manager. Everything is important and in America 'you aren't just a waitress, you aren't just a store clerk'. Mundane as they might be, these roles are important roles and everyone has an important function. Can we say that everywhere in Europe and England? As much as Topeka offers impressive tourist attractions, including 12 art galleries, delectable dining, unique shopping and not forgetting 3,000 hotel rooms, alas my attention was not contained for more than one night. It was all Lincoln, Nebraska's fault. If I hadn't been swimming up there for those days, I may have given Topeka and Kansas closer scrutiny. Instead, it was progress into Iowa.

I was on the road early the next morning. It was a beautiful spring day, lots of blue sky and I think I nearly got the smell of the odd flower between blasts of vehicle exhaust on Interstate 70. Interstate 70!! It was my first experience of paying to use a road in the country! I should have realised, I-70 is called the 'Kansas Turnpike' for a stretch. The title 'Turnpike' does have historical significance which I will come onto later in the north east, where there are lots of turnpikes. But for the moment I quickly learnt, turnpike means get your dollars out. It had better be worth it and fancy charging a motorcycle a toll. This financial intrusion was early in my day whilst still in Kansas heading east. The road surface was excellent. It didn't look far on the map on this bit up into Des Moines and Iowa, although it was nearly 300 miles. Therefore I didn't have the time to have a look at the 'city of fountains'. That's Kansas City or KC for short. Straddling the state lines of Kansas and Missouri and sitting between the rivers with the same names, KC today has a metropolitan population of around two million. From my seat it looked a monster, with quite an impressive skyline towering above. I followed instructions from Mr Garmin to the foot, and as if on rails, was soon hurtling through the bowels of the city on Interstates 70 and 635, before picking up 35 north. If you look at a map of KC, there appears to be more Interstates than urban areas. There's 70 from the east, 35 from the southwest, 29 to the north and 35 to the north, not forgetting city loops of 435, 470 and 670. Just as well I didn't plan a stop there on hindsight. Undoubtedly without the mapping magic of my GPS I may have still been on a KC circuit. I have recollections of multi-lane freeways, overhead signs the size of barns and wall-to-wall traffic. In very quick time I was in rural countryside, clipping the north west corner of Missouri heading for Iowa. Missouri would get better attention in the next few days. Established on 35 north and in the green rolling hills, it was another one of those Interstates that passed through quite beautiful countryside. The land was a lot softer and gentler than further west. It was prime agricultural land with huge dairy herds all out grazing in the warm spring sunshine. This was very European and if I wasn't on the right side of the road, I so easily could have been in an English county such as Surrey or Kent. The bike was just growling through the miles and passing Decatur City put me into the state of Iowa, leaving a simple straight run into Des Moines. The Iowan capital is somewhat smaller than KC I had passed through and around earlier that morning. Nonetheless, the urban high rise dominated the skyline as I approached the city renowned for politics, finance and insurance. What a bundle of fun could be in store here. It was another one of those places where all the accommodation was on Interstate spurs out of the downtown. I think I selected a decent area and my motel had rather a glitzy-looking bar and grill very close, which could be useful later. Whilst checking in and asking for a drive-up room, or in my case a ride-up room, my accent created quite a few raised eyebrows at reception. The receptionist was an Asian-Indian and wanted to practice her English skills, whilst a couple of cleaners were leaning on their brooms with a surprised look on their faces. Remarkably, or rather disappointingly, both the cleaners did not recognise the Union Flags on my shoulders and hence had no idea of my nationality. They both guessed I was from Canada. I had to pinch myself and not overreact to their international ignorance and remember I was in Middle America. Oops, is that a little rude? For the record, it turns out the traditional drive-up rooms in original motels are becoming less popular. They can encourage all sorts of crime including the world's oldest industry of course and families moving into a room, when young Jimmy has checked in as staying alone. So today, new builds are more like hotels with one main entrance and maybe a side door. At least my new Indian friend gave me a room with an access door quite close to unload my panniers with ease.

Des Moines was founded in May 1843 when a fort was built close to the Des Moines and Raccoon Rivers. Fort Raccoon nearly came into existence, but the American War Department suggested politely that Fort Des Moines would be more appropriate. The name was shortened to Des Moines when the capital was moved from Iowa City in 1857. As far as the name goes, Iowa City has a more fitting name to fly the capital flag, but history changed all that. To get into the Capitol area of Des Moines, or Desmond as I had nicknamed the city for ease of pronunciation, I had to take on the Interstate again. It was only mid-afternoon and the traffic was flowing very well in Desmond and I soon found Grand Avenue leading to the State Capitol. What a sight for sore eyes. Even though it had the normal or 'regular' main dome, it has four smaller domes. The sky was deep blue and sun was showing the five gold domes in the best illumination possible. The whole place stood out like an ornate Russian palace. All that was missing were the onion domes. The Iowan State Capitol building had accelerated into my top five seen so far and I was contemplating giving it the number one tag. When I got through the airport-style security, the interior was equally as impressive with highlights of marble columns, fine art and a gleaming bell from the famous 'Big Stick' battleship USS Iowa, dated 1943. Even an inscription from William Pitt – 'where law ends tyranny begins' – was deep in the marble close to faded battle flags. The security guard recognised my accent, which was nice for a change and bent my ear for ever about a trip to England he and his wife did over 30 years ago. London, the Lake District, the Cotswolds, Bath, you name it they had been there. Even

Edinburgh was thrown in complete with the incorrect pronunciation of the Scottish city that always trips Americans up. The Capitol is surrounded by delightful gardens and very poignant memorials. Whilst sauntering around the many stones and paths, I by chance and slight embarrassment came upon a couple at the Vietnam memorial. They looked the age to have maybe served there and most certainly to have lived through that era of American military campaign. They were standing at a particular part of the monument which had the names of victims inscribed into the marble. The lady had her hand on a name and the gent was head-bowed. The deceased, or maybe even missing in action, was obviously close to them. It was a heart-rending moment and I dissolved quickly into the shadows of flowering magnolias before they could see me.

For any serious petrol heads, whilst returning through Des Moines and back to motel, I notched up 300 miles done that day, accompanied by low fuel warnings. I wasn't quite on fumes, but uplifted seven gallons, with one gallon still sloshing around down there. This proved to be a great barometer for the fuel consumption of the bike now that it was more than properly run in. A quick guestimate and a bit of number crunching produced a range of about 350 miles, give or take, depending on my mood and the traffic's mood. That statistic gives a long distance biker an extremely warm feeling. On some isolated and long sectors of the journey, I had thought about carrying external fuel in cans. These figures suggested it just wasn't necessary. By the time I got back to the motel, the grill bar, which I could now see was called the 'Daytona' was heavily populated by the HD crowd. Quite impressive for mid-week and with nothing else seen in walking distance, the Daytona would get my vote for dinner. The menu turned out to be an everything-with-fries type menu. I dug out some spicy chicken which put my taste buds into a frenzied orbit, sank a cold beer and took in the surrounding action. It was a bikers' bar and had all the accessories for just that, wall art, old bikes suspended at impressive angles here and there and scantily clad waitresses skilfully manoeuvring between kitchen, bar and tables. I thought that type of waitress only came from Las Vegas? Obviously not so, they were here in Des Moines and a young guy at the bar reliably informed me this place was tame. 'You should try here, here and here and the girls are much better.' I believed him and we continued to talk about biking. With a spotted handkerchief tightly fastened around his head, this young man of 22 declared that not only was he a biker, but also a serving soldier in the US Army. He had already done two tours of duty in Iraq and if he kept his nose clean, he had been given the nod of early promotion to Sergeant. He was full of it and drank like a fish simultaneous to smoking like an industrial chimney. He was getting drunk and I started to show a little concern about him riding back to his garrison at Camp Dodge. It was close apparently, but that was not the point and I suggested he took a cab in the near future. 'Cab, hell no, I will be riding back to base okay, this is bikers' night and we all do it.' Eager to show me his HD and leading me outside, the busy parking area was now dominated by vibrating and clattering HDs of varying shape and size, with owners in attendance. They all looked to be in a similar state of inebriated brash contentment. To extend his bragging rights, my new friend fired up his bike to add to the roar of voice and machine.

Chapter 42

Show Me Some Celebs

Leaving Des Moines, I certainly felt that I had not really given both Topeka and 'Desmond' the attention they deserved. It's like a lot of places; I am sure there would be locals around that would show me the nooks and crannies and delve into secrets of history that would elevate these rather ordinary cities into memorable places in the USA. Alas, time and motion was on my mind. I climbed back onto the journey and rejoined the snakes and ladder-style route again that I seemed to following here in the mid west. This south easterly zig or zag was taking me out of Iowa and back into Missouri and heading for the capital, Jefferson City. It's another one of these state capitals that was declared the capital at the time of the coming together of the Union and after the civil war. In the meantime, JC's neighbour of St Louis has developed into a giant of an urban sprawl and some may think the city with the grand arch, standing on a couple of major rivers, is the state capital. Not so.

East out of Des Moines got me to Prairie City. What a delightful little name for a town. The name evokes all sorts of thoughts of farmers, homesteaders and settlers over a hundred years ago. Not forgetting that it sits in prime agricultural territory and this theme continued all the way down the 283 miles into JC. Oskaloosa was next and then Ottumwa, more absolutely tongue-manoeuvring names for more quaint little places. 'Where are you going, oh I am just going to the store in Oskaloosa.' It probably sounds very normal to the locals, but rather amusing to a roaming Brit. I was having a morning of picking out strange and amusing town names. It made for a good game as roaring south on scenic route 63. It's called scenic 63 and scenic it was. I was seeing it on a warm and then hot, mid-May morning. Bloomfield and Kirksville didn't score high in my game, but Queen City and La Plata regained an advantage. It was on this route that I had my first experience on this trip of the Amish community. I hadn't realised that they lived this far west, however, characteristic buggy tracks on the side of the road gave their existence away. Typically, Amish communities are concentrated in Pennsylvania. More very green agricultural land and small market towns were making for an enjoyable mini rollercoaster ride. There were enough curves and hills on the road to make it interesting but not challenging. Crossing Interstate 70 was a trigger for my imminent arrival in JC. Only 20 miles or so to go. I picked up the urban area intermittently as I followed the road contours and through the gaps in the trees. I was getting closer and closer, with no sign of the typical dome of the Capitol seen yet. Where was it? At the last moment and when I was almost in the city, there was the bronze statue of Ceres appearing through the trees, a last-minute shot so to speak. You can normally see the State Capitol from miles away. Today's approach to JC had been from the countryside and it was unique seeing the Beaux Arts style Capitol Building with central dome and cupola with a zenith of 262 feet, at the last minute. Ceres the goddess of vegetation sits atop the dome and looks over the fast-flowing Missouri River. That was three state capitals in three days. Reasonable progress and kept my list ticking over nicely. There are a lot of them about in this part of the country and my capital frequency was certainly a contrast to the days and weeks between capitals I had experienced on previous sectors.

Finding a motel room in the Missouri capital was challenging to say the least. Okay, it was Friday, but that had never been a problem and somewhere normally had a room for a lone traveller. The city was hosting a couple of conventions, a hockey match and a military event of some sorts. These affairs were dragging Missourians out of their normal weekend routines and into the accommodation in their capital city. I eventually found a room in a chain brand place which made do.

The waitress in the restaurant over dinner remarked that there is not much to do for kids in town. Most are either at school or college and pass evenings by getting a part-time job. I must admit that even on a Saturday morning the place looked very quiet with not a lot about. The city is dominated by the domed Capitol which rises from a bluff overlooking the Missouri River. Early adventurers Lewis and Clark passed through this area on their historic journey west, well before any settlers. I was finding that the displays in a State Capitol were sometimes more appealing than the history of the building. A dome and cupola from state to state, of various size and elevation, some with columns, some without, they were all melting into a State Capitol Building blur. JC was my 22nd and coincidently 22 is my lucky number, so I wonder if I would get any surprises inside. In defence of my rather disparaging description of American State Capitol Buildings, JC's was magnificent and a fine example. Maybe six years rather than six months would be a better timescale to get under the historical skin of the United Capitols of America. Informative guides pointed me in the direction of the crown jewels and that they were. Not only USS Missouri's giant bell, dated 1944, but some fantastic mural art by Thomas Hart Benton and a collection of superb bronze busts of Missourian celebrities. Benton was at the forefront of the Regionalist art movement. His huge paintings showed everyday scenes of life in the USA. The house lounge in the Capitol is a Benton gallery and displays many a scene in bold colours including home life, working life and even a gent in a bar being shot in the rump by an excited waitress. I am rather glad I haven't met any of her type around the bazaars so far. The chatty guide in the lobby mentioned that Betty Grable was in the Capitol last month. I gave her a strange look and continued on my tour and when I found the 'hall of fame', the penny dropped and I knew what she meant. It was still quite early in the morning. I think she must have meant that Betty Grable's bust was new and just arrived in the collection last month. There she was, with typical BG look over her shoulder. Born in St Louis in 1916, actress, singer and dancer, Betty Grable passed away in 1973. It was the second time I had met Betty on this journey. The first time was back in Chandler, Arizona, as a pin-up in blue swimming costume on the side of B17 bomber Sentimental Journey. Today, she had the same stare with those eyes and that tantalising pose. Close to Betty was another famous Missourian born in Independence in Jackson County. Academy award-winning actress and dancer Ginger Rogers was best known for her dance partnership with Fred Astaire which continued for 10 years. Complimenting the Capitol guides on an interesting visit, I was given an account of an unusual but slightly amusing event that took place in 2006. The chandelier that hangs in the dome was being lowered for cleaning and routine maintenance. Apparently it fell to the ground for the final few feet of its journey, making a hell of a clatter from the glass elements and ornamental chains. Restoration took place in St Louis and today, without this little tale, you wouldn't know any different. This story did tickle my Brit humour. It reminded me of a very famous scene from a TV comedy show when there was also a famous chandelier incident. But on that occasion, the descent was higher and more rapid! I shall let any inquisitive readers do their own research and view the scene themselves to enjoy the event. The only clue I shall give is that an actor in this Brit comedy has a nickname pronounced very similar to a US state capital city. So on a quiet Saturday morning, in a very quiet State Capitol, I had met some American celebrities, viewed some unique art and even had an amusing Capitol tale thrown in.

Chapter 43

Into Lewis and Clark Country

Checking out of the basic motel in JC, I recalled the comments from the waitress the night before. 'Don't stay in St Louis, it's an urban monster and some of the neighbourhoods are less than desirable.' She was participating in a dual conversation. Issuing me a tourist brief while simultaneously explaining to her partner that she had been put on the twilight shift in the morning to cover for a sick colleague. It was already 10 pm and she was back in at 5 am. Not an ideal way to start a weekend, but I guess she would welcome the extra money. By the time I left JC, she would have been back at work some four hours. I didn't have to stay in St Louis at all as it happened. My next capital was Springfield, Illinois, and I could exit Missouri and enter Illinois directly if I wanted. However, the urge to look into a bit of history and view the huge arch in St Louis were a couple of reasons to create the diversion. It wasn't that much of a diversion, but locations in my general direction of travel. St Charles, just west of the Missouri River, was my destination, putting St Louis only a very short ride away. Quickly clearing a sleepy Saturday morning JC, I found myself in prime mid-west countryside. It was route 94 eastbound, following the Lewis and Clark trail. Late spring had really got hold here and I was graced with deep green fields and very deep green thick deciduous forests. Every now and then, the fast-flowing Missouri River came into view on my right hand side. Meriwether Lewis and William Clark were great American explorers. President Thomas Jefferson had heard rumours of possible European exploration of the American North West. Jefferson selected Captain Meriwether Lewis to lead an exploratory expedition. Lewis selected Clark as his partner. The objectives of the three-year trek were to explore the Missouri River and study Indian tribes, botany, geology, terrain and wildlife. However, as military men, they were also carefully briefed to assess any interference from British and French Canadian hunters and trappers who were already established in the area. From 1804 to 1806, The Corps of Discovery, as the expedition was later named, provided important information on Native Americans and natural resources. But one of the significant findings was a clearer understanding of the vast geography, which in turn helped produce the first accurate maps of the area. The line across the USA the expedition followed is big history today and you know it when you are in Lewis and Clark country. Road signs, statues, gift shops, annual celebrations, you name it. I was on route 94 – the Lewis and Clark trail. It lasted a snaking 100 miles, which was abruptly spoilt first by crossing a busy Interstate and then arriving in buzzing St Charles.

St Charles' claim to fame is that it beat off competitors to be a temporary state capital, whilst Jefferson City was being built to fulfil that role. Not a just a Capitol Building being built, but the city to go with it. With quite a reputation for festivals, including a Riverfest, Festival of the Little Hills, Oktoberfest, Tartan Days, Irish Heritage Days and Bluegrass Festival, I was statistically well placed to arrive amidst such an event. That I did, but none of the aforementioned. I arrived in St Charles on a hot afternoon in the middle of a Lewis and Clark celebration. Lewis and Clark arrived here in 1804 with 40 men and three boats. They danced, dined, prayed and then continued west on their journey. The riverside celebrations laid on for me had enthusiastic locals dressed in costumes of the era and replaying scenes from the early nineteenth century. Tents lined the banks of the river, some selling local wares, some selling foods. There was even a drill squad of brightly uniformed soldiers complete with muskets under the command of an extremely vocal sergeant. Without these colourful celebrations, St Charles boasts a quaint main street with wooden-fronted buildings, containing a mixture of shops, restaurants, real estate offices and the odd bar. It was a lively little place and a good recommendation not to stay in downtown St Louis.

After immersion into a bit of serious American history and absorbing some play-acting thrown in, I felt historically satisfied and could move on into St Louis with no guilt. The next day was blue blue, making ideal photographic conditions. The ride into downtown was Interstate all the way. Even on a Sunday, traffic was agonisingly busy and I wonder if Missourian law makers have ever thought of a vehicle congestion charge. Thankfully, when passing the airport, vehicular volumes decreased a touch and I just put my feet up and followed directions all the way to the grand arch on the riverside. Before the arch stole the city's visual highlights, it was the bronze statue of Saint Louis on board his charger that was widely used as the city symbol. Today, St Louis is named the 'Gateway to the West' in honour of the many people who migrated west through the area on the Missouri River. Ironically, I got to the Gateway to the West from the west. I made it into St Louis on my 'Big East' sector from California, Nevada, Utah, Wyoming, Colorado, Nebraska, Kansas, Iowa and finally into Missouri. Completed in 1965, the Gateway Arch Monument is a component part of the Jefferson National Expansion Memorial, and is a modern contribution, honouring western pioneers. It was eerily quiet down by the riverside on a beautiful Sunday morning. A coffee seller informed me that the city was on flood watch. I had seen on the early news that poor old Iowa was floating. I had only been in that state a few days earlier. Roads were closed, rivers had burst their banks and one news item showed a young couple watching their new build home simply float away downstream a flooded river. The mighty Mississippi in downtown St Louis was flowing well above normal levels and was lapping or rather gushing extremely adjacent to the roadside. It added to the spectacle. Swollen river versus space-age arch versus brilliant blue sky. Quite a concoction. It wasn't quiet in the waiting area to take a ride to the top of the arch. A two-hour wait deterred my ambitions of an elevated view of Missouri. I made do with another chat with the coffee seller, whilst straining my neck skywards at the small space craft like windows, in the apex of the arch that certainly do not require curtains. No neighbours overlooking that lounge. Leaving the riverfront and navigating through the city centre, I didn't know what to prioritise, avoiding the traffic or the potholed side roads. Before a congestion charge, road repairs should come first. It was baseball match day, St Louis Cardinals against Tampa Bay. I also had to avoid programme sellers and young kids providing 'safe parking' for spectators, as they meandered across the roads plying their business. I could so easily have been back in an English city on match day, with similar shouts of 'park over here mate, I'll watch your car', 'hotdogs, hamburgers', 'programmes, match day programmes', but this time in mid-west accents and not Cockney, Geordie or Brummy tones.

Escaping the St Louis hubbub, I returned to the relative calm of St Charles. Historic events were still in progress and the town was bursting at the seams with weekenders taking in the atmosphere. I found refuge in a main street pub called the 'Lewis and Clark'. It had to be done! I learnt that my bar-side dining company were brothers and HD corporate men from the head office. We talked USA and biking for an hour or so. They agreed I was riding the right bike and should not contemplate my journey on an HD. This chance meeting got me a free lunch and a bigger insight into the HD world.

USA most Southern Point – Key West FL

Pelican Sunset – Key Largo FL

Tallahassee FL – Journey 1ˢᵗ State Capital City-Old Glory frames old and new Capitol Buildings

Baton Rouge LA – My first view of the mighty Mississippi-a river that would just keep on appearing throughout my journey

Baton Rouge LA – Huey Long views his unique Capitol Building

Don't mess with Texas! Austin TX

Jackson MS – Maritime history

50 State Crescent – Montgomery AL

Atlanta GA on a very cool and clear day

Grey and moody museum carrier flight deck USS Yorktown – Charleston SC-The impressive Ravenel bridge in the background

Weekend retreat! – Charleston SC

Columbia SC – Capitol Building

Raleigh NC – Capitol Building

'Life is like a box of chocolates' – Forrest Gump's park bench –
Chippewa Square – Savannah GA

*First sighting of mountains on my trail! Misty and moody Great Smoky
Mountains. Tennessee and North Carolina State boundary line*

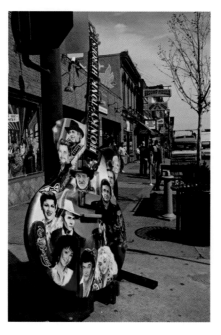

Nashville TN – The City of Music!

The Flying Fish – Little Rock AR – a great lunch venue

Oklahoma City OK – State Capitol Building

Amarillo TX – no takers for the Big Texan prize

Canyon country close to Amarillo TX

Route 66 Amarillo TX-was an important pit-stop on the historic route in years gone by

Santa Fe NM – unique Capitol Building

Spanish style in Santa Fe NM

Phoenix AZ

Sentimental Journey at Chandler AZ

After a week's break in AZ my thoughts pointed west to the CA coast and the Pacific Ocean

The Californian Pacific

The Big Sur – a curvaceous beauty of a coastal road following the Pacific – a bikers dream!

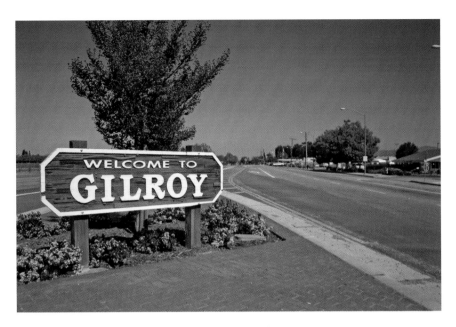

Gilroy was here! Gilroy CA

That bridge! Golden Gate with San Francisco backdrop

San Francisco CA – a city of challenging hills for the biker

Pony Express at full gallop-Sacramento CA

Lake Tahoe CA-Do the depths hold ghoulish secrets as folklore suggests?

Kit Carson in Carson City NV

Stunning Yosemite CA

Sierra Nevada range CA – pristine jagged peaks

*Rugged relief and enduro motorcycle-harmony achieved –
Sierra Nevadas CA*

Spring blooms with the high Sierras – close to Lone Pine CA

Mr Patel's Trails Motel-Lone Pine CA – what beautiful retro signs and sci-fi clouds!

Descending into Death Valley with the Sierras mirrored behind

Descending into Death Valley CA

In the guts of Death Valley CA

Maynard Dixon Cowboy lodgings – Mount Carmel UT

Towering escarpments – Zion UT

Red road and red rock – Zion UT

Reds, blues, greens and whites in the Bryce Canyon Park UT

Hoodoo red rock – Bryce Canyon Park UT

Capitol Reef Park UT

Sara and Alana's Capitol! Salt Lake City UT

Alta ski resort – close to downtown Salt Lake City UT

Cowboy Capital – Cheyenne WY

High in the Rockies-Estes Park CO – a road so close to 10 000 feet above sea level!

Looking towards the Rockies from Denver CO

Capitol Building of rocket ship proportions – Lincoln NE

Not for the faint hearted was the climb to the summit of my 20th Capitol Building-Topeka KS

Stunning and almost palace like Capitol – Des Moines IA

Vibrant art in Jefferson City MO

Unique city attraction – St Louis MO

Lincoln's final resting place – Springfield IL

Gasoline Alley revs up for the Indy 500 – Indianapolis IN

Frankfort KY – nearly a one horse town!

Columbus in Columbus OH

Beautiful dome-Charleston – WV

Washington in elevated pose overlooks my 28th – Richmond VA

Chapter 44

Hands Down to Illinois

It was an overcast, wet and warm Monday morning as I navigated through the usual high volume of traffic on American urban Interstates. I had given the map a quick once-over the night before, but the route was a 'no-brainer'. Interstate 55 was really the only way to get to Springfield, the capital city of Illinois, from St Louis. It was an extremely leisurely 111 miles to my 23rd capital. I didn't even put any route into my GPS, but followed the breeze north. Crossing the Mississippi for the fourth time on the trip, whilst still in the St Louis metropolitan area, immediately put me into Illinois. Thereafter it was quite a flat and unexciting ride through more agricultural land of the American mid-west and the internal plains. As much as the state appears to be all the same, there are three distinct areas. Chicago dominates the north and has an ever-expanding metropolis. If asked to rattle off as many Illinois cities as possible, I may struggle after Chicago. Who has heard of Aurora, Rockford, Joliet, Naperville, Peoria, Elgin and of course not forgetting the capital, Springfield? Moving on geographically, there is Central Illinois. It's an area of flat prairie and known as the heartland of the state, where agriculture is dominated by corn and soy bean growth. That leaves the southern part near the junction of the Mississippi and Ohio Rivers. This area is known for a slightly warmer climate and a more varied mix of crops. Quite a contrast of geographical zones, in what is not a particularly big state in comparison with the big boys in the west.

Springfield is in central state. The state capital carries a name which is so common throughout the USA that there is probably a Springfield of some size or other in all the 50. The British Times Comprehensive Atlas of the World lists 22 Springfields in the USA. These are Springfields of a decent size and then I am sure there will be a lot of smaller Springfields not listed. It's quite a nice refreshing name and I when I buy my ranch in a state yet to be decided, I shall call it 'Springfield Glacier View', or 'Springfield Valley', or simply 'Springfield'! I arrived in Springfield, Illinois around lunchtime and the morning rain had created a slippery sheen on the city roads. I was greeted by a friendly lady at the front desk in one of my normal motel choices. I had the pick of about 150 rooms and took my lucky number 22, which I am sure would be the same as the remaining 149 rooms. Whilst munching on a crisp green apple courtesy of the management, the lady expeditiously checked me in, simultaneous to giving a thorough tourist brief. I had intended only one night here and then off further east. I was persuaded that two nights would be better to take in the city's offerings. Maybe they were short of tourists here? Room 22 was fine and whilst unloading my world and plugging into the world, I noticed there were more motel workers around than guests. Also I had noticed from my personal demographic observations in the last couple of states that the African-American population was increasing somewhat the further east I was getting on this sector. There is some history of note in the city. In 1908, a large race riot erupted, known as the Springfield Race Riot. The disturbances were law and order events. The Governor had to use militiamen to end the disturbances. The riots held quite a symbolic and political importance occurring in Lincoln's home town. All the motel workers were African-Americans and I shared some banter with them as they went through their morning rituals of room service and the like. They all looked quite young and I am sure their historical knowledge of the riots exactly 100 years ago was probably quite slim. Maybe when the exact 100-year anniversary arrives on 14-15 August they may be more alert to this piece of Springfield history. By then, my journey should be mature and maybe even complete.

Springfield became the state capital in 1839 with the help of a young lawyer and politician named Abraham Lincoln. He lived in the city until he left to become the 16th President in 1861. From that moment on, the city's history and future have been inexorably linked to this famous, respected and well-loved American citizen. A visitor could spend a couple of weeks taking in Lincoln memorabilia. Varying from his preserved home to the impressive new visitor centre to his moving burial tomb area, you are frequently reminded that you are in the Land of Lincoln state. I started in the visitor's centre or rather Presidential Library and immersed myself into a morning of history. Arriving in the lobby area, a life-size mannequin group of Lincoln and his family set the scene and put you in the required mood. Thereafter, an extremely well choreographed history of the man Lincoln himself, starting from early political days and culminating in his abrupt assassination, are portrayed in pictures, maps, drawings, scenes, recordings and anything else that you can imagine. It was a fantastic collection and understandably the Americans are proud of how one of their famous Americans is remembered. What I found slightly confusing, was at the time of my visit, a local Amish group, complete in their typical clothes, were also on a tour. At first, I thought they were all part of the display and setting the scene. A very amused guide informed me they were not and simply on a tour as well! Lincoln is laid to rest at Oak Ridge Cemetery and after a walk through his unfinished life, it was fitting to visit his impressive and moving final resting place. Understandably, this historic site attracts visitors from around the globe as well as many Americans. My quick visit coincided with the ubiquitous American school kids' coach trip. They were released from their coach and grouped close up to the tomb, after which one of the guides got hold of a microphone and gave the historical sermon. It was well done and my ears to his speech filled in a few gaps following my morning's history lesson. I had been chatting with the guide before the kids arrived and he suggested he mentioned my journey to them. I nodded in sort of agreement, but left the gaggle whilst he was still around 1860 and hence avoided any potential questions from the semi-boisterous gaggle of teenagers.

My attention to Lincoln had diverted me from my usual priority of an inspection of the State Capitol Building. That came next and I learnt that Illinois has always been quite a battleground for the Republican and Democrat political parties. That was an apt finding considering it was about midway through election year and media attention of the usual suspects was now red hot, verging on molten and flowing over. Barack Obama and Hillary Clinton were still at it hammer and tongs in their political joist to gain the Democratic leadership. Meanwhile, John McCain had already been declared as the Republican party nominee and was strutting his stuff around national and international forums selling his political wares. There was nothing else on TV these days and unless you were about to land on Mars, or perhaps about to marry a Martian, you didn't get a look-in. Today, the state is very much under Democratic rule and BO easily won the state by a margin of 22% I heard. That number 22 was showing its nose again! 22 Springfields, Room 22 and a 22% political victory margin, completed a trio of 22s in Springfield. Maybe a good omen. Anyway, to break the sequence, my 23rd state Capitol Building does have one statistic to boast. With a total height of 361 feet, it is the tallest non-skyscraper capitol building in the USA, which makes it taller than the Capitol in Washington DC. Only the high-rise brutes of Baton Rouge, Louisiana, and Lincoln, Nebraska, are closer to the clouds. It's another dome and cupola affair, this time from a French Renaissance architectural style. Inside, the building has a fine collection of plaster friezes, bronze statues and stained-glass windows. No politics were in progress during my brief Capitol tour and I had the whole place to myself. Whilst walking around the quiet interior, it was another one of those extremely peaceful and thought-provoking experiences. The internal lighting was low, creating a moody feeling against the many art backdrops. I had noticed that you get one of two ambiences in a State Capitol dependent upon the visiting population. They are either jam-packed with politicians, school kids or even demonstrations on the steps, or completely empty, offering instant tranquillity. In Springfield, I was encountering the latter, which was an apt theme after experiencing much Lincoln history over a couple of days.

I was told that Springfield has a long affiliation with food and in particular, is famous for a 'corn dog on a stick' which is locally known as a 'cozy dog'. I didn't find one of these tasty snacks, maybe I wasn't looking hard enough. However, we all know that America is a huge melting pot for many nationalities, a lot of which hold high their home nations' culinary habits. Italians are a race with a large population in the USA, especially in the north east. In search of dinner on my last night in Springfield, I stumbled across an ordinary-looking Italian restaurant, only identified from the outside as Italian by a faded national flag above the door. Entering the diner, canteen or restaurant, I couldn't make my mind up which, I noticed that half the city's police force were consuming pasta. That was a good sign and if the local constabulary were trusting the menu, it would do for me. The walls of the place were awash with photographs of Italian football teams and photographs of Italy and in particular the Island of Capri. I later found this was the home island of the friendly Italian-American owner. In the large open kitchen, I watched my pizza expertly constructed as I was given a history of the owner's family, including how long they had been in the USA and other sibling restaurant locations. New York City has a big Italian population and I recall my new friend had a brother who served good fayre on checked tablecloths right there. I took the address, but was unsure if my journey would venture into the guts of Manhattan. My crunchy and exquisitely flavoured pizza was perfection. It just goes to show that the drab and ordinary-looking places don't always serve drab and ordinary-tasting food.

Whilst preparing to leave the city and watching the TV, I noticed the rather attractive blonde charismatic lady Weather Channel presenter was making strange hand movements. Further investigations and increased volume revealed that whilst talking about Illinois state weather, she was describing Illinois as the 'hands down'-shaped state. When checking her description with the shape of the state, I would agree, the outline of Illinois does in fact look like a hand pointing downwards. Wrist in the north and fingers in the south. Not that I had encountered the motion, she continued that some Illinoisans accompany their chat, with a hand pointing down movement. If I had been staying around a little longer, I maybe would have looked out for that trend, or even tried it myself. I think maybe an exaggeration could be occurring here that may accompany happy hour and alcohol. 'Yes, look at those guys over there, they are all from Illinois.' The presenter went on to describe and mimic the 'hands up state', which turned out to be Michigan, not a million miles from here. But at the moment, it was 'hands down' to Illinois!

Chapter 45

Indiana Gilroy and the Kasablanka Café

Setting course east the following day, as normal I programmed my GPS for the journey. As a bit of a laugh and to try and break the monotony from the generally mid-west flat geography, I decided to try and get lost. Simple, I just left the route and headed off to the south east for an hour or so to see if there was anything different out there. More of the same. Flat and very green agricultural land, interspersed with neat farms and small towns. It was worth a try and after I had finished my little game, I followed the GPS arrows back to my original route, which picked up highway 36. My deviation may have thrown off any parties in pursuit. However, I had not seen anything that looked like a tail for several states now. I think it was back in Wyoming when I had my last suspicions of being followed. I was successfully moving my 'box' along the route as if being sucked towards the east coast. Good signs and progress was excellent at the moment. This route was nearly straight as a die running east through more lush green land all the way to my destination of the day. At Montezuma, I crossed the state line into Indiana or the Hoosier State. Hoosier, what a strange nickname for a state and I never got an answer from any residents how that name came about. Apparently there are several suggestions to the origin, varying from folklore and banterous greetings to a boating term, to a name taken from a canal contractor way back. Whatever the origin, at Montezuma, I was in Indiana and the urge for caffeine around 11 am persuaded a brief stop, although Indianapolis was only another hour or so further on. I didn't need fuel, but the fuel station store provided the hot black stuff. Whilst inhaling that arousing steaming stimuli that can only be coffee, I was suddenly conscious of a hell of a racket close by. Montezuma was a quaint little place, consisting of a single main street with all the usual amenities. A couple of stores, grocery and hardware, diners, fuel stations and even a hotel. The noise was coming from a school. It was lunchtime and the normal clamour of kids playing was drifting across the high street. I got talking to one of the teachers from the school, as she marshalled her kids across the road to an ice cream parlour. It was the last day of term and the kids were all getting an ice cream treat prior to the summer break. Melissa McMullen and I talked for a while. She told me about her teacher training college days and we mused over the election campaign and who might be the President in 2009. Politics normally cropped up in my conversation with strangers. It was the buzz subject at the moment which wasn't surprising. Remarkably, and rather politely, most Americans wanted a Brit's view, which was quite nice. I always remained impartial to avoid potential conversational conflict. Sometimes I got that in a bar here and there and if I stepped over the mark, I would retract and declare international political immunity. It worked. There was no threat of animosity from Melissa, we could have talked all afternoon, but she had her kids to escort back for their last lesson of the term. I remarked I had enjoyed the morning's ride through prime Indiana agricultural land. Quite surprisingly, she mentioned that there is quite a bit of poverty in the local counties and not all kids come from big farming families. The type of places I had seen lots of that morning, big farm units with handfuls of expensive vehicles parked up in each yard, were not the places her kids came from. No, she confirmed that most of her kids come from poorer families and good jobs are hard to come by here. Some folks make the daily commute of 60 miles into Indianapolis for work. As a teacher, Melissa mentioned she was extremely fortunate to have a good job. Her husband worked for the Sheriff's office in Rockville, the next town east. Not everyone was as fortunate as the McMullen family and her comments were certainly thought-provoking as I continued east, through Rockville and onwards into Indianapolis.

Even though I had crossed back into Eastern Time and lost an hour, it was still only early afternoon as I sniffed out a motel on the western side of a compact looking city. I had arrived via the rural route and ridden through delightful green countryside all morning. Looking at the map later that day, it suddenly occurred to me why Indianapolis is known as the 'Crossroads to America'. The city is surrounded with an octopus of Interstates, highways and trunklines. Not to mention airports, mass transit railways and even a couple of ports on Lake Michigan in the north. I had been lucky to stay completely in the country and sneak in with no traffic problems. I nearly had problems getting a room for a couple of days. It was Wednesday and would you believe it, the annual Indy 500 race was at the weekend! My thoughts immediately went back to early April and that conversation in San Diego with that couple from Indiana. 'Indiana is the best state you have remaining on your trip and avoid the Indy 500 weekend.' I remember her words very well now. In a couple of days, I could pass judgement on the potential delights of Indiana. But in the meantime, I was grateful of a room at this inn for a couple of nights. Friday onwards and no chance as the city would be bursting at the seams with up to 500 000 race goers. Some stay in caravans and trailers and the like, most take up the city's beds – period. My arrival turned out to be excellent timing and I would make a quick exit before the coming of weekend metal and human mega congestion.

It was only a short ride into the downtown and the Italian Renaissance revival Capitol Building did not occupy much of my time. I did notice that the glass roof and marble columns on the upper floor would make an excellent location for large potted plants. Mature palms with draping foliage would look most desirable up there. I passed on my horticultural comments to the ladies at the visitors' desk, much to their amusement. Whilst chatting, and I cannot recall how aviation cropped up, one of the ladies proceeded to give me a full brief on her husband's pilot resume. I recall now, I had a newspaper under my arm with a Chapter 11-type headline showing, which normally meant an American airline was on the brink of financial catastrophe. She mentioned that her husband's airline was safe for the moment. He flew for a local regional airline and before that had been an Air Force jet pilot in many home and international locations, including a tour of duty in England. That could also have been the connection. Later, I did find some interesting words from George W in the State Capitol gardens. On a simple block of wood, the words, 'Terrorist attacks can shake the foundations of our biggest buildings, but they cannot touch the foundation of America – President George W. Bush September 11, 2001'. Nice words from George and the first words I had seen from him around the country since I saw him in his own State Capitol back in February.

Let's face it, there is only one thing to see in this city and it's the Indianapolis Motor Speedway. It's located in Speedway, Indiana, which is still in the city limits of Indianapolis and only a stone's throw from the motel I was staying at. It's the venue for the famous Indianapolis 500 mile race, or simply the Indy 500. The race is held annually over the Memorial Day weekend and is reputed to be the largest single day sporting event in the world with 260,000 seats and then lots of standing space for petrol heads. I took a look on the Thursday before race day and the place was beginning to rev up in preparation. A friendly guy on the gate greeted me and pointed in the direction of bike parking. There were one or two HDs at ease, but plenty of space available which would not be the case in 24 hours or so. Walking back into the arena, I spent a bit of time chatting to the same guy on the gate. His excitement for this year's approaching event was palpable. I got his history and the circuit's history before heading for the museum and weaving through more visitors with similar ideas. Close to the museum, a sign with a few words said it all. 'Constructed in 1909, the Speedway has contributed significantly to the advancement of automotive technology and the development of safety devices. It is unchallenged as the world's oldest continuously operated race course and the site of the largest one day sports event anywhere.' But where does The Brickyard come in? I had heard that phrase mentioned frequently about the place. Close to statues and plaques of Henry Ford, Caston and Louis Chevrolet and Tommy Milton, another historical marker revealed my automotive racing inadequacies. It was a sign next to some bricks looking rather like house bricks, which read, 'The Indianapolis Motor Speedway has been referred to by many over the years as 'The Brickyard'. The name is derived from the fact that the track was resurfaced with approximately 3,200,000 paving bricks after a series of initial races on the original surface of crushed stone in 1909. The race track remained completely brick for the annual 500 mile races beginning in 1911. Portions of the track were then paved with asphalt beginning in 1937 and the main straight on the west side of the course remained brick until resurfacing after the 1961 race when all but a 36-inch strip of the original brick was left at the start-finish line. This yard of brick is present on the race track today and will be kept there for traditional purposes'. That's The Brickyard explained. The museum is compact and a sight for sore eyes for motorsport lovers. Inside is a fine collection of cars of varying contours depicting many decades of technological and aerodynamical advancement. Chevrolet, Ferrari, Corvette, to mention but a few. Then lines and lines of 1960s, 1970s and 1980s race cars. There was even a motorcycle collection including some fine-looking Indians. I am sure they were superb machines in their time and immediately generated images of leather protective clothing, goggles and the smell of oil. Outside, the roar and screech of modern engines around Gasoline Alley signalled practice laps approaching. It was possible to get reasonably adjacent to the pit area as teams fine-tuned their machines in readiness for the weekend race. After close inspection of the race machines and the gorgeous contours of the new Corvette at the Chevy stand, my Indy experience was over.

I had just realised that another triple coincidence had occurred. I was in Indiana, it was the Indy 500 race at the weekend and Harrison Ford was strutting his stuff and airing his fedora in the latest Indiana action movie in the series. So, I make no excuse for the title of this chapter – but what about the café? Well, back at the motel and owned by the same gang, was a fantastic grill bar called the Kasablanka. It wasn't that common to have a decent eating and drinking establishment so close to my bed. The Kasablanka was an exception and served excellent food and an assortment of cold beer. A bikers' hangout with live music thrown in, what more could a journeyman biker ask for? A ticket to the Indy 500 would be nice. Quite astonishingly, several guys at the bar I had met over the two nights of my stay offered me a standing ticket at the event. Free! Should I? Shall I? When would I next be in these parts on race day? Hmm? No, sense and sensibility and progress was the only sensible option. The thought of 500,000 people and associated vehicles and trailers and similar descending on the place was not that appealing. As it turned out, my escape from Indianapolis was timely as race-goers were arriving in the city and checking into the motel before I had finished breakfast. For me, it was south into the rolling green hills of Kentucky.

Chapter 46

Into the Bluegrass State

In my attempt to find the most rural route south out of Indianapolis, I got lost in industrial and residential areas in the southern part of the city that would not have been on my visit list. I eventually picked up highway 31 which was particularly quiet and led through Franklin, past Edinburgh and onwards to the border town of Madison. Like a lot of other boundaries around the country, a river marks the state line. In this case at Madison, crossing the wide and extremely fast-flowing Ohio River and I was in Kentucky. The huge metal bridge crossing the river seemed to go on forever. Below, the mighty Ohio River was surging onwards, heavily swollen after a lot of recent spring rain. These rivers are so long in this country, that if it rains heavily in a couple of states upstream, a couple of states down will carry the excess water onwards and may also cause flooding on the way. The Ohio looked brown and menacing and it was a safe feeling to be across the bridge and into Kentucky. Just into my 25th state, I stopped for fuel and a leg stretch at Milton prior to taking route 421 down to Frankfort. The fuel station and diner were full of construction workers. It was lunchtime and the majority were eating either in the diner, or outside on picnic-style wooden tables. I got talking to a trio and between mouthfuls of sandwich and pies, they told me they were from Indiana and were involved in a school building project here in Milton. There was a lot of building going on in the area apparently.

After refreshment and confirmation from the workers where to find the junction for route 421, I continued south. Close inspection of the map the night before had revealed that 421 followed a twisting and snaking course. The map wasn't wrong and the twisting and snaking was around the undulating and hilly countryside of very rural northern Kentucky. I so easily could have been in gentle fell country of North Yorkshire or Cumbria back in England. All that was missing was the purple flowering heather plant on the roadside. I think these were the first hills I had seen for many states. The first since the mighty Rockies way back in Colorado. Although nothing like the Rockies, these Kentucky rounded hills I had found nonetheless did provide a welcome change from the flat terrain of the prairies and the mid-west that I had ridden through for the last few thousand miles. It was a beautiful, rolling and undulating landscape and very green. The recent heavy rain gave a lush feel, with fields of rich green vegetation. Taking the description of Kentucky grass as bluegrass literally, I would have been disappointed so far, as everything looked green. The experts tell me that bluegrass looks like normal grass and has green leaves and stems, but the name is derived from the seed heads which are slightly blue when the plant is allowed to grow to its natural length. So it's not exactly an agricultural phenomena that all the grass in Kentucky is bright blue as the term suggests. But when you see a field of mature grass in the late spring or early summer that is swaying and rippling in the breeze, you really do get a blue image. I was getting that vision from time to time heading south for the capital. Passing through New Castle route 421 became the Castle Highway. Further south the Castle Highway became Bald Knob Road. I was really out in the sticks, however, my GPS was getting excited and counting down the mileage quickly to Frankfort. All I could see ahead was a very rural scene, with absolutely no sign of anything looking like a city. Getting very close, I became slightly bemused and was wondering when I would see something which looked like a state capital city. I had heard that Frankfort was small and it was certainly hiding from me at the moment. Suddenly, between a gap in the trees, I saw the Capitol Building dome and there it was. I had actually descended into the place quite quickly from the north and was on and in town at rather short notice.

I had every intention of only one night in Frankfort before continuing east. I had a social appointment in Maryland at the end of this sector and time was marching on. Also, folks I had met were quite puzzled that I was actually staying in a place which wasn't red hot for the tourist. Everywhere seemed deathly quiet. It was Friday and I had expected a bit more action, however, even the motel was like a morgue. It had a small entrance lobby area and then three huge accommodation blocks at the rear. I had one of these blocks that must have had enough rooms to house an army battalion, all to myself. Only a short ride from the motel, I found the State Capitol with lantern style cupola, sitting on a hillside. It had quite an elevated perch and that's why I got the feeling of being so close to it when arriving in the city. Inside the State Capitol was also a dead hush where even Old Glory was flying at half mast. It was in respect for a local soldier that had recently perished in one of the global conflicts. I only saw one person in the building and she was getting ready to leave. A coach party of young school kids had just left and the place was eerily quiet. It was so quiet that I could have had a chat with Lincoln who was standing in the hallway. Kentucky was his birth state, however, I was now becoming quite accustomed to seeing his statues everywhere around the country. It was a grey afternoon and thankfully a colourful flower bed in bloom with spring flowers brought some colour contrast to the dismal sky. As I left, the visitors' desk closed and the lady kindly recommended I visit the Vietnam War Memorial. It was a short ride out of town and thankfully I overtook the coach carrying the school kids that had just left the Capitol. I guessed they were heading the same way. I got there first and had the place to myself before the hubbub arrived. It was fitting that it worked that way and this memorial had to be seen in tranquillity. Based on a giant sundial, the sun's shadow would cast a line on the exact time that a Kentucky soldier was lost. The soldiers' names were inscribed in time order on a huge marbled surface of the monument. It was a well-constructed and tasteful shrine. Unfortunately the afternoon gloom did not provide a hint of sunlight to show the process in operation. What a surprise downtown was. Frankfort is so small. The centre is literally one street with what looked like a disused railway line in the middle. I found one or two places open, including a pizza restaurant, a couple of shops and a combined bookshop café. This was a real backwater and I am sure the residents must heavily rely upon the out-of-town malls. It was 4 pm and I did the English thing and had a cup of tea and healthy slice of chocolate cake and watched the quiet Kentucky life go by for a short while. Around the corner, I did stumble across some interesting history that linked to earlier places. The Frankfort newspapers, *The Palladium* and *The Western World*, were the first to print news of explorers Lewis and Clark's safe return from their great expedition. The journey's details were then circulated nationally and hence Frankfort gained some editorial notoriety in very early media days. Other than the old State Capitol Building and the Frankfort School of Ballet, I couldn't really get excited about anything else to see in such a very quiet place. Maybe it was a public holiday or something, although I don't think so. The afternoon was nearly over and I retreated back to the motel. The same receptionist that checked me in earlier in the day could not recommend anything close by for dinner. She suggested I head out to a mall and rattled off several fast food places. Surprisingly, a vibrant Chinese buffet-style restaurant was next door. The receptionist obviously assumed I didn't like Chinese food. The place was full of travellers all tucking in to enormous amounts of the usual stuff. 'One price, as much as you want mister, please go around again and again,' the pretty oriental waitress with bright red lipstick uttered as I took a seat. It was all freshly cooked and very good. Maybe the motel receptionist didn't like Chinese food either? It was dark when I left the restaurant and not far away I could hear the sound of country and western music banging away. I found an ordinary-looking door in an ordinary-looking building and parting with a $5 door charge, entered into an amazing place. It was like entering a Tardis. Small on the outside and huge on the inside. It's what I would call a typical American bar, the population drinking bottled beer, some playing pool and draped over the bar, others sitting at tables scattered around and cosy couples getting close. In the corner was the source of the music, a five or six-piece band in full swing, or rather full country and western. This place had some real atmosphere and real attitude and certainly represented quite a chunk of Americana. It was Friday night and apparently a hot spot for locals far and wide. A cheap restaurant with good food and a music bar with gig in full session. I wonder why the motel lady didn't mention either of these places to me?

Amongst other things, Kentucky is well known for bourbon distilleries and thoroughbred horses and horse racing. I gave the liquor a miss, but a ride through horse country was on my agenda. Most race-goers in England would have heard of the Kentucky Derby, pronounced as *derby* and not *darby* as in my tongue. Heading north out of Frankfort gave the opportunity to ride through prime horse-breeding country. It was a very warm Saturday morning and following the Maysville Road north in the middle of the month of May was quite apt. It was beautiful rolling green countryside, studded with neat farms and paddocks full of expensive-looking equine stock. This industry is big in this part of the USA, as it is huge in Great Britain. The heat of the day was obviously generating the flies and bugs around the horses and they were wafting their tails in attack. It was quite a scene from the roadside looking through the white fences at the multi-coloured horses and onwards to the expensive farms. This scene continued for much of the way between the small towns of Clintonville, Fairview and May's Lick. I didn't choose to take on the large Kentucky cities of Louisville and Lexington, however; I had been recommended a stop in Maysville. Sitting just south of the Ohio River, Maysville holds historic significance and has celebrity notoriety. The colourful buildings contrasted quite dramatically against the spring blue sky. Some buildings were white with typical columns and verandas. Others were red brick high rises complete with original faded business titles on the elevated walls. The small town, with such a pleasing collection of buildings, created quite a special atmosphere. Walking around the neat streets, I found the famous Russell Theatre which holds the annual Rosemary Clooney Music Festival. Actress and singer Rosemary Clooney was born, married and laid to rest in Maysville. Strolling around a corner, I came across elderly couple May and Charles Jackson. May is a fitting name for this place. Both in their 80s, they were relaxing in the sun on the veranda of a fine home. Beneath their opulent home was once a historical secret of the town. An underground railway network passed through Maysville connecting safe houses. Operating between 1810 and 1850, the railway was used by black slaves escaping north. Thousands fled to safety on the underground rail network. My experience of Kentucky was completely over ground. I arrived into Kentucky heading south and crossing the Ohio River. Leaving the state, I was heading north crossing the same river and into the state of Ohio.

Chapter 47

In Search of the Great Explorer

Almost before my wheels had turned one revolution, I had left Kentucky and was over the state line into Ohio on a beautiful late spring morning. Ohio is another one of the states that joins on to the Great Lakes area in the north. My rural route on highway 62 was north through the agricultural lands of the Central Lowlands part of the state. The en-route towns of Russellville, Macon and Hillsboro all had a sleepy Sunday morning feel. Activity pepped up a bit after just over a hundred miles and arrival in a bright and breezy Columbus. I had chosen a motel right in the downtown of the city, adjoining the attractive German Village neighbourhood. The lobby of the motel had a curry smell, signalling that this was a place run by an Asian-Indian family. It was; there were about three generations of them from grandfather to grandchild frolicking around in the morning sun. I was given the choice of a room and the attentive duty manager of the family ensured all was in order including the internet. I felt I had a bit to explore in this city and decided to get my ritual out of the way first. The State Capitol! I could have walked there, it was only 10 blocks or so up the street, but if the bike could talk, I knew it would be telling me to ride there and do some posing on the way. The bike enjoyed these short frisky rides without the heavy luggage. The ride got the vote. Arriving at the Capitol, I had to take a second take. It didn't look finished, it wasn't the full picture. Apart from a couple of lanky Capitol Buildings I had come across, the rest were the standard cupola with dome on top. They vary in size and if they have steps and columns etc, but to the non-architectural eye, they do really look quite similar. I could be getting into hot water here. Quickly moving on, the Ohio State Capitol doesn't have a dome. It's Greek Revival of course and features a large flat-topped drum tower covering an interior domed ceiling. No dome on top of the drum tower. There were plans for one, but they were abandoned. I declare I am not becoming an aficionado on the architectural design of USA State Capitol buildings, although as my journey was maturing, I was becoming quite familiar. Inside was the usual and impressive collection of art, statues and marbles. I again found Lincoln, but this time a bronze plaque marking the spot where he addressed the locals in 1859. It was his first Ohio speech defining that a house divided cannot stand. I had arrived at a moving time. Under the central ceiling, a large art collection depicting Ohio soldiers lost in the Iraqi conflict was on display. Serving soldiers and several families were paying their respects and understandably, there were a lot of very wet eyes. Although my priority on this journey was my safety and route completion, I was only too aware that whilst splicing this huge country with my navigation, I was experiencing not only the geography, but an awful lot of American life. It was right in my face every day. Real people and children, news, media, the election, war, conflict, life and death. It paid on occasions like this just to slow down my sprint and share what the nation is enduring. Some of the families I met here were only too keen to chat, especially when I related my journey and the American veteran charity I was supporting. But sadly, when you examine things closely, although the military are volunteers, the victims are normally young men and women. They leave life only a fraction complete and leave mourning families in the process. In complete contrast to the families inside the Capitol Building, a carefree bunch of high-dollar bikers on custom-built machines, including a tricycle, were viewing the military memorial in the gardens. They were calling the information number on their cell phones to get a run down on history and events. Idle chat revealed that none of them had done military service and didn't want to.

The city of Columbus does have a number of very distinctive neighbourhoods and the rather quaint German village area was next door to my motel. Back at the motel and with the bike refuelled and checked over for the next excursion, I could walk and explore this unique cobbled street area. It is very much a historical area and was settled by a large number of German immigrants a couple of hundred years ago. During the Prohibition era, the community went into decline, but with almost local village governing, the community was resurrected as a vibrant place to live. Today, it is considered one of the most desirable places to live in town and the neat red brick dwellings with expensive cars outside certainly give that image. Amongst the grid of cobbled streets are restaurants, bars, cafes and some shops. I dined in Schmidt's Sausage Shop and was maybe treated to the best sausage in the country. I so easily could have been in a high-class restaurant in Munich or Frankfurt. The full dining room was a barometer of just how good the food was and it was excellent. My portion of whatever sausage and all the trimmings I chose was too much. I think it was the first time I had asked to take the leftovers away with me. 'I'll have a box with the cheque please,' is quite a common heard thing in the USA and not typical in Europe. It always amuses me why Americans insist on taking their meal leftovers away in a box. Is it because they have paid for it, they may have it for tomorrow's lunch, give it to the dog, or just throw it away? Probably a combination of all. On this occasion and against my normal conventions, I took some sausage home along with a slice of apple strudel to munch on through the late news. At the southern end of the village, Schiller Park provides a nice green contrast against the dark red brick buildings. Joggers, dog walkers and kids feeding the ducks are a plenty in a well-used park. But the main attraction was the open air theatre, which hosts regular plays, especially Shakespearean summer performances. Rehearsals were in progress as I strolled around the couple of days I was there. Another quite tasteful attraction on the edge of the village and opposite my motel, was the collection of large Victorian-style houses set on the side of Thurman Avenue. Several are converted into high-class bars and restaurants and offered alternative hang-outs to the choices in the village. What a gem of an area I had chosen to stay in, at a reasonable rate and with not a fast food joint in sight – so far!

On a couple of occasions whilst in the German village, a police helo complete with search light, camera and other dangling apparatus, was circling quite low in my vicinity. This first happened on a quiet Sunday afternoon and again the next day. I had become quite blasé if I had been attracting surveillance, but unless I had missed other low-level flights, this was the first time I could be under the spotlight from the air. On one pass the helo was quite low and slow and almost in a hover. I pointed my camera his way and offered a big wave. No wave was returned. This helo just seemed to pop up when I was out walking. Maybe I should have called this book *Under Surveillance*! It was certainly a theme that had conjured up itself with no personal anticipation of anything like this.

The following day was Memorial Day and an American public holiday. The city was deserted. The sky was deep blue, with not a trace of cloud or helos, but a strong wind was developing as the day progressed. The wind was heralding the onset of storms rushing east. That would be worth checking on later; tomorrow was east into West Virginia. I always find cloudless, very windy days quite special. The wind seems so out of place with no cloud and rain as company. Columbus would have met the title of 'windy city' certainly. The almost-gusts were surging around the high buildings creating eerie whistling and occasional thuds as windows slammed shut under protest. Plastic bags and other litter were airborne and being hurtled around. The few pedestrians were walking at angles to combat the wind. The wind was rushing through the large metal sign of the Ohio Dispatch, creating tones rather like a harmonica being played. I did ask the security guy in one tall building if I could take the elevator to the top to take in a few panoramic images of the city. He declined my request and returned to his newspaper. I made do with a walk down by the river and found the huge statue of Christopher Columbus. The city was named in honour of the great navigator and explorer and the immense figurine was a gift from the citizens of Genoa, Italy. I wonder what Columbus would make of the high-tech navigational equipment that the modern world uses. From a simple GPS I was using, to marine and aviation navigational aids, to space craft computers, I am sure Columbus would be astonished at the technological contrast to the sextant and stars in use in his day.

Returning to motel, I caught quite a bit of the Indy 500. I must admit, the arena did look ridiculously congested and aerial shots of the city showed gridlock. I think it was a good decision to escape Indianapolis and view proceedings from the comfort of my own space. The winner was Scott Dixon from New Zealand and afterwards he gave several TV interviews. His accent was unmistakably from Australasia, with not a hint of anything British. It made me smirk a touch and I hope the Americans who aren't good at accents were watching and listening carefully. I did feel sorry for an American lady driver in the race who got obstructed whilst manoeuvring in the pit area. After a collision with the offending car, she had to withdraw from her strong position in the race. After the race ended, she was pictured marching towards the offending driver's pit area, obviously with the intention of throwing some carefully chosen words his way. At the last moment an official intercepted her to prevent conflict. This incident hit the media all over the country and replaced election headlines! How refreshing!

Politics did come my way the next day. It was my birthday and I decided another day in Columbus would be a relaxing alternative to the road. Anyway, wind and thunderstorms were forecast en-route, a good excuse to put my feet up for another day. The Indian manager got a bit stressed when I declared usage of the room for a further night. He got quite hot under the collar and I don't think it was his last curry. 'We have Government guests arriving and you are in one of the regularly requested rooms. I will move you to another room, we have plenty.' I objected to the move. 'Move them, it's my birthday and I am staying put.' He agreed after a few head wobbles and we both got on with the day. Later the car park was a bit busier and I saw a few cars with 'Senator' on the licence plate. One car was parked next to my bike and the lady occupant was unloading into a room next door and casting glances of derision my way. I introduced myself to Senator Teresa Fedor and we talked for a while. The Indian manager was right after all; his motel was a gathering place for senators on business. Good rates, the German village around the corner and the State House a few blocks away were the attractions. Teresa did mention she normally stayed in my room and I of course offered her the spare bed for the night if she had become so attached to that particular set of walls. She declined and went on to tell of her life and that she classed herself as a Vietnam veteran. At first glance, she didn't look old enough. She then elaborated that it was military service straight from high school and her duties remained stateside, however, support involvement in the campaign enabled veteran status. Thinking about Teresa's possible age and the fact that it was my birthday, I suddenly realised I was carrying some interesting personal milestones along my journey. I started the lower 48, whilst 48. I would be getting to the 49th state whilst 49, and finally, in my 50th year, I would be visiting the 50th state. Still a long way to go to achieve this little conundrum, but interesting numbers nonetheless.

Chapter 48

Fried Green Tomatoes at the Bluegrass Kitchen

After a suitable rest on my birthday it was up and off. I was finding the distances between the capitals over here in the mid-west were only short half-day hops. I was fast approaching the end of this sector as I neared the mid-Atlantic area of the USA. The mid-Atlantic sounded nice and it wasn't that long ago that I was charging around the Rockies and forging across the Great Plains way, way back in the west. It was warm and clear with a sizzling 75F forecast by lunchtime at my destination. My route was just a 160-mile south east diagonal jaunt through some more pretty and green land on highways 23 and 35. I left Ohio at Henderson and then simply followed the Kanawha River all the way down into Charleston. It was quite nice for a change just to have a simple route to follow without a plethora of road changes and towns to look out for. If I smoked, it would be feet up with a cigar and follow the arrows all the way to my bed. Talking of which, I had decided to have a slightly belated birthday treat and sample a slightly more expensive pillow for the evening. Up until now, the motel had more than adequately provided all my needs. The country is awash with motels and inns to suit all pockets and has a superb infrastructure for the traveller. As a slight diversion from my norm, but at double the normal price, tonight was a bed and breakfast. 20 or 30 years ago, B&Bs over here would be quite average accommodation and probably quite rare. Now, they command a unique nationwide brand. They are normally elegant houses full of traditional furnishings, with extremely comfortable rooms completed to a very high standard. I had chosen to stay in the Brass Pineapple in downtown Charleston's historic district and arrived at lunchtime after a gentle ride through the countryside. West Virginia is entirely within the Appalachian Mountain range and nicknamed the Mountain State. I hadn't seen any mountains on the way into town and would encounter them further east towards Virginia. Lisa greeted me at the Brass Pineapple and was probably rather surprised to have a biker dropping by instead of her normal business professional clientele dressed in city suit, shirt and tie. We exchanged the normal pleasantries as she was checking me in. I noticed she had the cutest American accent that I had ever heard and I assumed that she was from the deep south somewhere. No, she was born and bred in West Virginia and that's how she spoke. She told me so quite directly. So, that was me told. Who am I to talk about accents? My room, complete with internet, was on the ground floor and sumptuously appointed with furnishings and drapes fit for royalty. The room was overdressed for a biker. My private bathroom was a short hike down the corridor and had an amazingly deep bath tub that almost needed a ladder to descend into the depths. It would have been home to a submariner. It was quite rare for the bike to be resting in a private car park and not lined up with other cars outside a motel. My first B&B experience was superb. The price was the only restricting factor that would preclude the whole trip themed on this level of comfort.

After the civil war, pioneers migrated west into what was then the western part of Virginia. It became a contested territory and with authority granted from President Lincoln, was eventually admitted to the Union as West Virginia 1863. West Virginia is a small state and looking closely at the map, it must have had some connection to Virginia way back. With important natural resources close by and after a bit of toing and froing with Wheeling, Charleston became the preferred state capital. Like a few Capitol Buildings around the country, fire destroyed the original building and the present Capitol Building was completed quite recently in historical timescales. I could see the gold dome from Lisa's place and the Capitol gardens were literally five minutes' walk away. After the unusual style of the Capitol Building in Columbus, in Charleston, I had returned to a central circular drum tower, capped with golden dome and cupola. I must add, the dome is particularly attractive with ornate gold accompanied with black gild design. It just seemed quite strange seeing the Capitol Building at the end of the street, with telegraph poles and overhead domestic electric cables criss-crossing the vista. A statue of Abraham Lincoln greeted me in the grounds. His figure depicts the President who was in office at the time of the state's incorporation. He is dressed in robes over his suit, and with head bowed, portrays a typical Lincoln pose. Security was non-existent in the Capitol and I accessed it with ease for a quick visit. Lisa had mentioned I should try the new Capitol Building basement café for a late lunch. In an attempt to find some human activity, I did and was most surprised. Finding a large cafeteria-style diner in the basement of a historical building was unique. I am not sure if the facility was meant for staff only, but no one was about apart from the chef and I had to stalk someone down to pay my bill. Normally you find a vending machine hidden away somewhere, but rarely a comfortable eating place. It was a good recommendation. Following a few hours in the saddle, a healthy lunch and a quick historical injection, a walk was in order to circulate the oxygen. I think the forecast was quite accurate, as the temperature had risen to the mid 70s. After a stroll down the banks of the Kanawha River and into downtown, I was sweating. The route down the river turned out to be another short history lesson boasting further Charleston chronological bookmarks. Passing the Governor's executive Georgian-style mansion brought me by the grave of industrial pioneer Joseph Ruffner. Thereafter the route passed the statue of Charles Glendenin after whom Charleston was named. Further on, there was a sign for the original site of Fort Lee, before passing the site of the first gas well where Mr Ruffner was undoubtedly involved. Quite a trail in a mile or so, before arriving in the downtown area dominated by a mixture of modern high rise and old tall brick blocks dating back a century or so. The historical signs from the riverside were replaced with modern trappings such as Happy Shores Insurance, Legends Bar, Julie Js Boulevard Lounge and Sam's Uptown Café and Bar. It wasn't a busy place with only the usual activity of folks going about normal afternoon business. One sign that did catch my eye with much amusement was 'Long Term Wife Insurance'. It was above a jewellery shop, which also boldly displayed 'we buy gold'. So over one roof, you can go and insure your wife and buy her gold!

I later learnt that Lisa also ran an outside catering business and hence was well qualified to offer local culinary advice. Her dinner recommendation was first rate. It was the Bluegrass Kitchen just around the corner. It's the sort of place I always enjoy. Quite a posh dining room, but as is typical in America, complete with a big wide bar area where folk can perch and enjoy good fayre and a gargle, whilst watching the diners in action with small talk and clattering irons. I quickly engaged in some great repartee with the owners Keeley and Jon. They made my decisions from the menu and after fried green tomatoes on toast, it was a slab of a chicken sandwich 'loaded' with all the bits. Jon and I chatted about his recent visit to Belize in Central America. Ah, we instantly had some global geography in common and I reminisced about my six-month spell in that tropical paradise some 20 years back. Jon gave me some route advice for my trip into Virginia and onwards to Richmond. Looking at the map earlier, the area was just riddled with highways and byways and I must admit, I was quite confused about which option to take. If in doubt, just take the Interstate, you will not be disappointed, was what a couple of guys said. I was also given en-route contacts to look up in Hartford, Connecticut if I could later co-ordinate. Much to my embarrassment, Keeley insisted that I drop by the next morning to pick up a packed lunch for my onward journey. She left a note for the morning staff to prepare something special.

Next morning in the elegant dining room, I joined a couple of other guests that the Brass Pineapple had gathered whilst I was out the night before. The younger of the two guys was a recently qualified cardiologist and was travelling to his first job further east. The other guy was also a doctor of some sort and was giving a presentation at a local medical institute on the role of doctor and patient communication. We didn't dwell on his day ahead. Fresh fruit followed by piping hot quiche went down a treat and I still had my free lunch to look forward to. Returning to the Bluegrass Kitchen, it was all there waiting for me. Meatloaf, cheese sandwiches, soup and biscuits. What a treat. I didn't risk transportation of the soup into Virginia, but the rest got the treatment later that day.

Chapter 49

Big East Complete

I had allocated all of May to get across the country and it was the 29th. Things looked good to do that, leaving June for the north east and then all of July for the final bit across the top. I was still a month ahead of my original planning calendar. Following chat the night before, I decided to take the Interstate the full 300 miles east into Richmond, Virginia. I had pored over the map again and again and picking a route out of the spaghetti-like clutter of secondary roads could have been challenging. With a tent and no deadlines to meet, I could have spent two weeks on this run drifting from scenic area to scenic area. Although as it turned out, I was not disappointed in seeing the area in one journey. It was another one of those quite epic biker's routes, even though it was all on Interstate. The route was through parts of the Blue Ridge Mountains and the Shenandoah National Park and was flanked by thick deciduous forests throughout. The first hundred miles seemed quite lofty and was a continuous blend of curves, climbs and descents. It was rather like an inland version of the elevated ocean highway route down to Key West. The bike was in its element and it was so tempting just to open her up and ride at excessive speed. The curves were delicious and not dangerous, traffic was light and I could see for miles ahead. The occasional hidden patrol car tamed my exuberance and I kept at just 10 mph over the legal speed limit which I had found didn't give the police high blood pressure. What I had noticed in a lot of states was that the police, or state troopers, hide behind their cars with a speed gun concealed. I had seen a few of these at the last minute and my cheek of throwing a friendly wave their way, so far had deterred pursuit. I had not had a brush with the law since February back in Louisiana. The second hundred miles when across the state line and into Virginia was pretty much more of the same, but flatter and not as undulating. The final 100 miles into Richmond was straight and again flanked by thick wooded areas on the roadside. It was like riding through an arboretum for mile after mile. With a population of over one million, Richmond was the largest city I had encountered for several states on this sector. Passing into Virginia I would complete this haul across the middle of the country and into a state with a coastline. The last time I saw the ocean I recall was back in California. That seemed a long time ago.

I think my excitement of completing the Big East could have taken a bit of shine off getting under the skin of Richmond, my 28th state capital. I just wanted to get in and get out and get into New England. It was quite hard to remove this mindset; however, I was also guarding against diluting any part of the trip which would not be ideal in order to complete the full trail with all objectives met. I would give the place a couple of nights and then move on at the weekend. That was a simple decision made and I checked into a motel on Dickens Road in the North West part of the city. This place was not a normal motel, but more like a huge hotel with many floors. The elevated car park was ramp-accessed and had a swimming pool in the middle. It had peaked at 80F with high humidity all the way across the state and the pool looked inviting. Alas, maintenance was in progress and the talkative guy who was filling the pool, painting and mopping up, all at once, told me it wouldn't be ready for a few days. 'Next weekend this will be the most used pool in town sir, do come back and look at the scenery.' He had a sense of humour which I liked and he added that my bike would be perfectly safe on his high car park. It was high and along with the big swimming pool, it gave me the impression of being on an aircraft carrier's flight deck. When I found my room, which was even more elevated, I had views from the clouds looking down on the pool and the car park. It wasn't my ideal choice of place to stay, but would do for a couple of nights. What a contrast to the Brass Pineapple of 300 miles west! It was a bus ride into the downtown, but a local Greek restaurant and sports bar provided a suitable evening's entertainment for my first night in Virginia.

This motel or hotel was one of those places that throw in a free breakfast. The standard and content vary from place to place, but I was told that the breakfast provided here, was enough to keep you going for a week. Some places you got the basics of a pastry and coffee, some throw in fruit and yogurts and the more expensive places also gave a cooked option. Approaching the dining room, I could smell cooking, but it wasn't the bacon and sausage. Jammed bread in the toaster was burning, sending thick black smoke up to the ceiling. It was inevitable that a smoke alarm was imminent and before I had dashed across and unplugged the toaster, the alarm sure enough yelped out with a high frequency resonance. I hadn't started eating, so made my way out to the lobby area. The rest of the diners were reluctant to move and it took the cacophony from three huge fire engines screaming up to the premises with claxons blaring to eventually persuade them to evacuate. It was quite an exciting scene with masked firemen rushing around, hoses being unfurled and the loud chatter on radios. All because of burnt toast! The fireman soon declared the dining room fit for rehabitation and the offending toaster and incinerated bread were removed. I desperately wanted to talk with some of the fireman, however, they were in such a rush to make up kit and return to their HQ that they declined. They undoubtedly had better things to do on a Friday morning, but before they roared off, the crew-chief did mention that this happened frequently.

The state of Virginia has much colonial and revolutionary war history. Catching the bus downtown, I would make do with a look around the historical part of the city and had no intentions of examining the many neighbourhoods of the burgeoning metropolitan area. Richmond is very much a business city with many industrial companies providing high commercial index ranking. After the excitement of the motel toast fire, action in the State Capitol just didn't compete. Although the State House is another diversion from the domed norm, its low-gabled, roofed Neoclassical design, with several low boxy appendages, just did not seem right. It went through major restoration between 2003 and 2007 which focused on retaining the Capitol's 1906 appearance. A new edition to the building was a public entrance built in the hill beneath the portico on the south side. Inside is a new reception area, exhibition area and offices. Everything was bright white on the outside and bright yellow on the inside and looked so, so new. It was more like looking around a brand new museum than the State Capitol. The historic art just didn't look right against the pale yellow walls. I am sure it was expertly designed by Thomas Jefferson and painstakingly restored very recently, however in comparison with my previous 27, this one lacked character. Sorry Richmond and Virginia. Your Capitol did not score highly on my survey. One consolation I did find was the magnificent statue of George Washington inside and, a similarly magnificent life size bronze of GW on horseback in the Capitol Gardens. Whilst photographing the garden area, I was slightly amused by an elderly group of Americans who were trying to master the controls of Segways. The Segway is the two-wheeled, self-balancing electric vehicle that you see around the streets in many roles these days. City police, parking officials, sports officials and in this case, a tourist party. The group leader was demonstrating how to use them to this loud and motley bunch, as they jerked around in circles without making much progress. They were not 'simply moving', as the machine's motto suggests, and GW's downward stare today, I am sure may have been one of disgust. Leaving the Capitol area, with a few smirks after my free entertainment, I very nearly got into some hot water myself. A police car was outside a large city building and without a map and needing directions, I thought the officer would be a good source to ask for some quick advice. When he finished on the radio, he did speak, but seemed distracted. No one else was on the pavement near where I was, although it had not been cordoned off. In a flash, two other patrol cars arrived with lights and sirens. Quickly a lot of police with hands on guns were rushing around. I don't think this was a Friday morning drill. This was similar to something from a cop programme on the TV and at the moment I appeared to be in the middle of it. Very quickly, I extracted myself from that part of the street and made off to the solace of a café for an injection of reinvigorating caffeine. I had got so far on this journey and did not want to be in the wrong place at the wrong time! The city evening news did not reveal anything exciting from that morning, so who knows what the action was about. I am sure it was a commonplace occurrence for any American city.

That was enough excitement for one day and for one sector and over dinner I reflected on the last 3,500 miles. I had passed through 13 states and their capitals. Starting in Utah, it followed Wyoming, Colorado, Nebraska, Kansas, Iowa, Missouri, Illinois, Indiana, Kentucky, Ohio, West Virginia and finally Virginia. It had been quite a ride through the month of May. I had encountered one or two weather delays here and there, caused by strong winds and thunderstorms, but generally it was a good run east. I was lucky and seemed to get to places just before or just after a meteorological dilemma. It was the flooding in Iowa that I was so fortunate to miss by a mere couple of days. The swollen Mississippi in St Louis was evidence of the drenched mid-west, where homes, businesses and lives had been washed away. As well as meeting capital city objectives, it was the changing geography that was the highlight. The map of the continent dramatically changed. From the elevated Salt Lake City with surrounding winter sports resorts, it moved to the high plains of Wyoming on the north side of my route and the Rockies emerging to the south, as I approached and crossed the Continental Divide. The highlands gave way to the low plains and the real flatlands in the middle of the country. I enjoyed the patchwork quilt agricultural lands of Nebraska, Kansas and Iowa. One outstanding memory of the terrain was the gentle rolling hills of Northern Kentucky. The first contours of any significance for over 2,000 miles. Quite remarkable. Continuing east, the impressive rolling and much wooded states of West Virginia and Virginia concluded my months ride. New England is next for June. Here the states are much smaller and I shall have fewer capitals to pass through.

Part Six – North East Gridlock

Richmond – Virginia to Augusta – Maine

2,177 miles

North East Gridlock - Richmond VA to Augusta ME

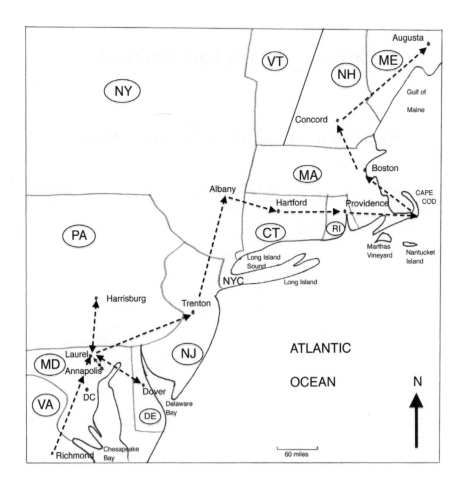

DATE	START	FINISH	MILEAGE	CUMULATIVE	COMMENTS
31 May	Richmond VA	Laurel MD	138	14453	I-95
May Total				**3803**	
2 June	Laurel MD	**Annapolis MD (29)**	28	14481	32/I-97
2 June	Annapolis MD	Laurel MD	27	14508	I-97/32
3 June	Laurel MD	**Harrisburg PA (30)**	102	14610	I-95/695/I-83
3 June	Harrisburg PA	Leola PA	43	14653	30
3 June	Leola PA	Laurel PA	118	14771	30/I95/695
5 June	Laurel MD	**Dover DE (31)**	94	14865	301/302
5 June	Dover DE	Laurel MD	94	14959	302/301
6 June	Laurel MD	Chantilly VA (Washington Dulles)	50	15009	
6 June	Chantilly VA	Laurel MD	50	15059	Washington Beltway
8 June	Laurel MD	Hightstown NJ	164	15223	NJTP
8 June	Hightstown NJ	Belmar NJ	37	15260	33/ocean front drive
8 June	Belmar NJ	Hightstown NJ	37	15297	33
9 June	Hightstown NJ	**Trenton NJ (32)**	21	15318	33
9 June	Trenton NJ	Hightstown NJ	21	15339	33
9 June	Hightstown NJ	Phoenicia NY	174	15513	206/I-287 & I-87
10 June	Phoenicia NY	**Albany NY (33)**	88	15601	28/42/23/I-87 Catskill drive
10 June	Albany NY	Albany NY	10	15611	Local & City
11 June	Albany NY	**Hartford CT (34)**	141	15752	I-90 & I-91
11 June	Hartford CT	Hartford CT	20	15772	Local & City
12 June	Hartford CT	Newport RI	91	15863	134 rural route. Newport for **Providence (35)**
12 June	Newport RI	Newport RI	30	15893	Ocean drive, city & local
14 June	Newport RI	Provincetown MA	139	16032	Day on Cape Cod
14 June	Provincetown MA	Marlborough MA	139	16171	I-495
15 June	Marlborough MA	**Boston MA (36)**	43	16214	I-495 & MTP
15 June	Boston MA	Marlborough MA	42	16256	MTP & I-495
16 June	Marlborough MA	**Concord NH (37)**	79	16335	I-495/3
16 June	Concord NH	Concord NH	8	16343	Local & City
17 June	Concord NH	**Augusta ME (38)**	142	16485	202 rural route
17 June	Augusta ME	Augusta ME	11	16496	Local & City

NJTP   New Jersey Turnpike
MTP   Massachusetts Turnpike

Chapter 50

Hubbing Maryland

At this stage of the journey, it is a good idea to introduce Bruce and Diana. Way back in February when I was passing through Stone Mountain, Georgia, I met furniture business man, Jim Trovato. I subsequently stayed with Jim and Pam in their delightful North Carolina rural home. In conversation, they mentioned family in Maryland which would be a convenient route stop when I got up there. I completely forgot about their offer until heading east across the country from Salt Lake City. Through the electronic ether, Bruce tracked me down and we subsequently exchanged emails for a few states. An invitation was on the table for me to use Laurel, Maryland as a base for a week or so and I was heading there after Richmond.

Over the last couple of weeks, the weather had become extremely hot and settled. A huge area of high pressure was sitting over the north east of the USA. This early summer weather feature was absolutely static and not budging an inch. It was covering about eight states. The normal rush of other systems east from the plains and south from Canada had remarkably dried up. There was nothing to move this brute out of the way. As the days progressed, it became hotter and hotter, with humidity building to uncomfortable levels. All this humidity was the mechanism for localised afternoon thunderstorms that banged and flashed, drenched the place for an hour or so, after which it was safe to return to the veranda. They were isolated to start with, so it was hit and miss if you got clouted. But as this period of hot weather continued, there was so much humidity around that the storms started to develop sometimes before lunchtime. On the morning of my departure from Richmond, violent thunderstorms were forecast all along the east coast by 9 am. Three weather channels had all sorts of warnings out and the day looked doomed for the traveller. I didn't want to waste a day in a motel watching TV and decided to make an early start to get ahead of the weather. It was only 130 miles to Bruce's place, so I could crack that in a couple of hours and get ahead of any potential deluge. When I went down to the car park to load the bike at 6.30 am, it was already uncomfortably humid and the sky was full of tall storm clouds tinged pink against the dawn sun. To my amusement, my bike was surrounded by police patrol cars, although I had other things on my mind to start thinking about any security issue. The lady at reception had mentioned that the local police use the car park and don't be alarmed if it resembles a precinct parking lot out there. Fair enough. I was on the road before 7 am. My destination of Laurel sits between Washington DC and Baltimore. To get there, I had two options: either around DC, or straight through the middle. Bruce had mentioned that so early on a Saturday morning, the central option would be okay and I would see all the sights. I elected to do that and headed north on Interstate 95, looking for 395 to pass just to the west of National Airport, across the Potomac and then 295, followed by 95 leading me to breakfast. It sounded easy. Approaching DC I was confronted with road works, lane closures and some confusing signage about bridge closures. The traffic had built up considerably heading towards DC and I quickly decided to take my secondary route all the way around. I looped off on to the Capital Beltway, Interstate 495, passing east of the metropolitan area, passed Andrews Air Force Base and soon linked to 95 for Laurel. It wasn't a bad run at all really and it was one of those trips where a route contingency plan is always worth having up your sleeve. Laurel is not a continuation of the DC metropolitan sprawl, but is almost in the countryside and seemed to be very much in a natural green belt.

It was just after 9 am when Bruce and Diana welcomed me into their spacious condominium. I later found out that B&D's place was two condos knocked into one, giving the opportunity to find your own space and get lost in quick time. It was huge. Retired engineering manager and business manager, B&D spent the day asking questions about my life, including past travels and the reasons for the trip. We talked and talked. The storms arrived at lunchtime, a little later than forecast, but in quick time the network of roads in the neat green neighbourhood resembled a paddy field. All that was missing were rice pickers in conical hats and roaming water buffalo. From the lounge balcony, I was frequently treated to views of white-tailed deer, varied bird activity, confident feeding squirrels and croaking frogs the size of dinner plates. With the hot and humid weather accompanied by daily thunderstorms, I could easily have been somewhere in Asia. It was hard to believe I was a mere 50 miles from Washington DC. Also big international travellers, B&D had amassed 135 countries in their passports at the time of my visit. But what is particularly impressive about Bruce's wanderlust are his frequent solo expeditions into North America. He heads off to visit friends and relatives across the lower 48, simultaneously searching out varied cultures, rare agricultural methods and other points of interest one normally associates with National Geographic. In a compact study, all their travels from the last 35 years are documented in incredible detail with notes, photographs and brochures. It was both impressive and embarrassing when I mentioned a small place I had passed through. Bruce would be up in a flash and straight to the file for this remote town. 'Ah yes, I was last there in 2003, they were doing this, I stayed there and here you are, see for yourself.' Not many Americans have the enthusiasm and attention to detail for travel, especially in their home country than Bruce. At the time of my visit Bruce was preparing another road trip across several states around the Great Lakes area.

My first weekend coincided with a social extravaganza. Part of a large social set, B&D and other group members take it turns to host events from supper parties to BBQs. The next day we hit the road by 10 am heading for Frank's place deep in rural southern Maryland. After leaving the southern remnants of the DC metropolitan sprawl, it was at least another hour south way down into the part of the state that looks like an old man's nose. Just to the west of the nose is the mature Potomac

River as it snakes off towards Chesapeake Bay and the ocean. We found Frank's place eventually, although B&D's familiarity with this part of the state was surprisingly slim. It was a delightful, but a rather isolated house set in its own grounds and surrounded by thick, broad-leaved forest. Frank had already gathered a few other members of the group by the time we had arrived. An afternoon of idle gossip, beer, food and geography followed and the group insisted that I pin my map to the wall and go over territory covered so far. I felt a bit like a military man giving a mission briefing: 'I have been here, here and here, I am now here and going there next.' We did have some opportunity to view the spacious grounds as Frank was hard at work over the BBQ, however dark clouds and the onset of a lengthy downpour cooled down food and outdoor activities considerably. It was the afternoon and monsoon season after all.

Chapter 51

Capital Returns from Laurel

Annapolis-Maryland

It wasn't until looking at the map that I realised what a fantastic base this would be for my state hopping in the north east. We put a plan together which would encompass the capitals of Maryland, Delaware and Pennsylvania. All were easy as day trips from my new home. I chose my new home state first and at the start of the week made off for Annapolis, the capital of Maryland. I was now firmly established in the Mid-Atlantic region of the USA. This motel and road trip existence was almost becoming a way of life, interspersed with the kind hospitality I was receiving from time to time. With an informal nickname of 'America in Miniature', Maryland is small but diverse and boasts a varied geography. You can find sand dunes and sea grass in the east, marshlands around Chesapeake Bay and rolling hills covered with oaks and pine groves in the Piedmont region of the west. A local motto of 'smart, green and growing' is quite apt. It was only 28 miles into Annapolis and I was there in a flash. The place just gave off that lovely cosy historical ambience straight away. An avenue of fine tall red brick, rather official-looking buildings led me to the historic district and the Georgian-style State House. The attractive octagonal wooden drum tower, capped with dome and cupola, framed by tall trees, all contrasted quite splendidly against the brilliant blue June sky. I learnt that the Maryland State

House is the oldest in the nation still in legislative use and is the only State House to have served as the nation's Capitol. From this spot, the peace treaty ending the Revolutionary War was signed and, later on, the Annapolis Convention issued communications to other states that led to the constitutional convention. It was pleasant to take in the morning sun over a coffee and gaze around the many cobbled streets that spoked out from the Capitol. Several had small shops, delicatessens and cafes and a rather chic-looking hotel complete with concierge on parade, overlooked the circle. I noticed one shop sold naval officer attire and I remembered that Annapolis is the location of the famous United States Naval Academy.

To further my maritime knowledge, a short ride to the city centre and the harbour area, revealed more pretty scenes. With the water full of expensive-looking yachts and a harbour area full of tasteful restaurants, it was soothing to the eye. It was so neat and tidy that it resembled a life-size model of a future show town or show harbour area. I even found a parking area that was exclusively reserved for motorcycles. Annapolis boasts a maritime heritage and today is one of America's premier sailing capitals. A sea food lunch overlooking the harbour was an apt venue. It was an amazingly beautiful location, with an almost movie set feeling. Frequently in the scene were officers from the Naval Academy dressed in brilliant white dress uniforms attired with a variety of gold bars and numerous lines of medal ribbons. They were out and about in the compact town doing lunch time chores no doubt. The early June sun was hot. The ubiquitous American baseball cap would be useful now. I found the entrance to the Naval Academy in the centre. I was able to roam freely throughout the most impressive grounds, which is almost like a small town within the city of Annapolis. I was encouraged to walk around the full site. Access to a lot of buildings is even allowed, which I found surprising but particularly interesting. Groups of cadets were moving around in rigs varying from starched whites to pressed sports kit. What a different and quite refreshing culture here, where cadets were only too enthusiastic to speak to the public. One young man threw a salute my way as I was strolling towards a huge hall. 'Yes sir, go straight ahead and have a look, it is a fine building and worthy of a few photographs for you.' I very nearly returned his salute, which would have looked a bit strange coming from a biker in jeans and T-shirt. Flanked by large cannons, I was entering the impressive Memorial Hall. I came face to face with former graduates, who became political figures. Each had a 'then' and 'now' photograph, which proved to be a good identity quiz back at my hosts. Much in the news in election year was the youthful and unmistakable face of John McCain, an extremely boyish portrait of Jimmy Carter and a smiling Ross Perot. They were all graduates from the academy. The four-year course that cadets follow is a gruelling cocktail of all naval matters and academia. Graduating as officers, they also graduate with an academic degree and probably a life-long career.

Harrisburg-Pennsylvania

I was back in the groove immediately the next morning, this time a slightly longer trip of 100 miles north to Harrisburg, the capital of Pennsylvania. After a good ride up the Interstate on another warm, sticky and humid morning, I got my first glimpse of the Capitol whilst crossing the fast flowing Susquehanna River. The skyline is a mixture of high-rise buildings, with the Italian and French renaissance style State Capitol Building sitting in the middle. It's another dome and cupola Capitol, complete with a golden statue, named 'Miss Penn' or sometimes 'Leticia', sitting proud on the top of the dome. The Capitol does hold some international notoriety and it is said to be a half scale replica of St Peter's in Rome. My arrival in the Capitol area was at the same time as a local TV crew. They were covering some veterans' event and all and sundry in jacket, ties, medals and forage caps were waiting for their turn to be interviewed. Inside the Capitol was no different from outside, people everywhere, with at least three events in progress. I had picked the wrong day to visit and movement inside was like picking your way through the crowds at a ball game to get to the refreshments bar. I met a suited gent loaded with files and associated paperwork under his arms. He agreed with my comments about the congestion and added that it was difficult to work in the place with so many people around and why don't they use the City Hall or the library? Anthony Frank Barbush was obviously a man on a mission, but he took the time to talk and invited me to view the inside of the House which was just about to restart a session. It was a huge room, decked out with the usual collection of ornate art and furnishings. Raised voices and the bang of a gavel were my signals to leave. My impromptu guide returned to his microphoned desk. That's another reason why the Capitol was so busy; the place was full of politicians. It was certainly a contrast to a lot of the Capitols I had seen, where sometimes there wasn't enough visitors to make a football team and even in certain cases where I had been the only visitor.

Leaving the Capitol after a brief visit, I still had the afternoon to fill and it would be a shame to return directly to Maryland when so deep in a quite special part of the USA, which is farmed and inhabited by a unique group of people. I had already encountered the Amish in small groups in a couple of states back. Their concentration is much more evident in Pennsylvania and after advice from my hosts, I headed for Lancaster County. The Amish are an Anabaptist Christian denomination, formed in 1693 by Swiss Mennonites led by Jacob Amman. They live in the United States and Canada and are divided into several major groups. The Amish use horses and mules for farming and transportation, dress in traditional manner and forbid electricity and telephone in the home. Most Amish speak a dialect called Pennsylvanian Dutch, although English is widely spoken. Arriving deep in Amish territory just after lunchtime, I found Diane's Deli and country store in the small village of Monterey. The store was staffed by some young Amish girls dressed in traditional long gowns and head scarves. It could almost be a film set. They prepared a perfect sandwich and over coffee, I watched more Amish folk at work in the gardens of local homes. Although non-Amish Americans in normal cars, vans and trucks were using the store and driving here and there, I noticed immediately that nothing mechanised was in the hands of the Amish. The creaking of the shop sign in the now keen breeze, whilst an Amish Lady in traditional dress, pushed an old grass cutter over her lawn, provided quite a spooky feeling of yesteryear. I chose to visit a nearby farm in Leola which was close. It was a beautiful-looking farmhouse with tidy outbuildings and finely manicured grounds and gardens. Everything about the premises appeared to be immaculate, which typifies their organised lifestyle. The approach road to the farmhouse was through a white-railed paddock where several large mules were grazing in the hot early afternoon sun. The head of the family was more than content to speak to me, as long as I de-personalised his people in any writings and avoided close up photography. We stood in his barn and talked. Inside were his animals including a herd of milking cows, several ponies, a few newborn calves and a German Shepherd with a huge litter of new pups. The farmer was an extremely young-looking 50. With glasses and typical long beard in the shadow of a straw hat, he was dressed in normal working clothes of homemade trousers complete with braces, over a baggy white shirt. One of six children, his young son looked on and listened with interest. Born, raised and married into the Amish world, the farmer has a total of six children and six grandchildren. In Amish terms, his farm of 36 acres is considered quite small. To supplement income, his family sell quilts and crafts from a shop on the farm site. Surprisingly, the shop had an electrical supply including credit card facilities. Was this a one-off example to enable better commercial facilities, or are the Amish becoming modernised? I chose not to ask the farmer, but I was confidently told that the Amish are well known for producing and selling crafts and fine furniture. The furniture has a market throughout the USA and is available for export. More locally to this farmer, his herd of 35 cows produce milk and his acres produce maize and alfalfa. The mules I saw when approaching the farm, tall and muscular in appearance, were his work animals. The ponies in the barn were used to pull the characteristic black buggies along the tracks that run down the side of the public highways here in Amish country. When asked if adolescents from the community are permitted to diverge into modern society, his reply was quite open. Although not encouraged, they can. Most return. I listened with interest, but it was quite hard to imagine a life away from the global technologies of today, where modern transportation and of course the faster and faster internet dominate our lives. It was a fascinating interview which was abruptly ended when a tourist coach pulled into the yard and the tranquillity of Leola Farm in Lancaster County suddenly vanished. A loud gaggle of Texan school kids emerged and made for the craft store and the barn where I was standing with the farmer. A couple of young girls saw the dog and pups and immediately entered her pen and tried to pick up some of youngsters. They got a shock. The protective mother turned from content canine to an aggressive protective animal, snarling and baring teeth. Quick as a flash, the farmer slammed the pen door shut and rather politely told the kids that their intentions were not a good idea. I do hope these quite brash visitors spent a lot of money in the shop, but it was time to leave. The farmer shook my hand as I made off. He was about to start milking the cows. His wife, daughters and young son watched with curiosity as I left the farm. In a nearby field, a young Amish boy was in control of six mules pulling a manure spreader. This was quite a photographic opportunity and possibly my last experience of this distinctive lifestyle before returning south. Stopping at the side of the road, the boy drew his mule team to a halt and prepared to turn them and the equipment around, before starting the next run. Approaching, he threw a wave my way and we talked for a while. He could only have been fourteen, but was quite bright and alert and showed an independent and mature personality. He insisted I didn't photograph him, but mentioned his mules wouldn't mind attention. Our chat drew the attention of the boy's father, who joined us in the field. We talked for 10 minutes about Amish life, the world and the universe and then I left. Within 10 minutes, I was on a busy highway and the exclusive Amish world seemed a million miles away.

The next day was a day off the road. As if with pent up vengeance for not raining for twenty four hours, violent thunderstorms and flash flooding engulfed the Delaware and DC areas all day. The day was not lost and there was much to talk about. Election fever was building dramatically in the country. Barack Obama was all but the elected Democratic Party leader as he sustained his nationwide party popularity over rival Hillary Clinton. It had to be Obama now and I am sure his slick speeches, intelligence, conviviality and popularity would get him through to the election. That gave the prospect of an interesting contest to observe between McCain and Obama on the run up to the November election. Bruce was very much a current affairs and political aficionado and whilst strutting and marching around the condo glaring at the monsoon outside, he frequently erupted into a tirade of what he would do if he was President. 'Just give me the opportunity for a couple of months, that's all, I would do this this and this and get the country out of the mire we are in.' Diana remained quiet and floated around providing us refreshments as the day matured. After catching up with my photos and writing, Bruce pinned me down in front of the TV. I was required to watch recent recordings of several current affairs and chat shows. We watched the Glenn Beck show on CNN headline news, the Bill O'Reilly show on Fox News and Fareed Zakaria's GPS programme where he interviewed former British Prime Minister Tony Blair. These shows were entertaining and varied in professional performance. Concluding our viewing, we watched with interest an interview with Sarah Palin, the Governor of Alaska. Interesting. It sparked my thoughts of getting up to Alaska on my journey that would only be in a couple of months. Bruce was commenting that she was an astute political figure and may contribute to the Republican campaign trail in the near future. She actually refused to comment on this subject when asked by the bold interviewer and I must admit at the time, I was more concerned about getting to the 49th state than assessing Sarah Palin's political credentials.

Dover-Delaware

The rain had stopped and the floods were gone the next day. There was no blue sky, but the sound of the forecast was good. It was to be 100 miles east into the Atlantic Coastal state of Delaware and the capital, Dover. It was extremely overcast and very humid after the deluge the day before. There was no wind to push away the grey and gloom that was still hanging around. I am sure the Delaware weather is much influenced by the Atlantic Ocean and maybe it was grey and gloomy all the time here? Heading east through Maryland, I had my first taste of the very long and impressive Chesapeake Bay Bridge, that as the name suggests, gets you across Chesapeake Bay. It was two or three miles of riding on a big metal grid, until landing back onto asphalt around Stevensville and Chester. Highway 301 led to 302 and through the western part of this quite small state and into the very small city of Dover. Although not raining, there was so much moisture in the air that I was convinced that I would be leaving vapour trails from my shoulders in my wake. Several glances in the mirrors did not confirm my theory, however it made for a reasonable mental thesis as I rode through the flat agricultural land of what is the second smallest state in the Union.

Delaware is known as the First State and for such a small area, is steeped in Native American, colonial, American Revolution and slavery history. Today, banking, chemical companies and agriculture contribute significantly to the state's economy. Also a main player in the economy is the Dover Air Force Base, located adjacent to the city. The base is one of the largest in the country and is the home of USAF Air Mobility Command.

I found the Georgian Revival Capitol Building nestled in the historical part of the city. Garden workers were out in masses tending to the many acres of lawns bordering the collection of neat buildings around the green. The air was filled with the sweet smell of freshly cut grass. I was the only visitor in the Capitol Building. It was another one of those experiences when the Government workers in their small offices were quite intrigued to see who was browsing the galleried walls this time. The colonial interior had the feel of an old family home with a wooden staircase and some wood-panelled walls. Prior to leaving, the security guys suggested I walk across the green to the Golden Fleece Tavern, have a look at the old Capitol Building, prior to a ride out to the aviation museum at the base, followed by a late lunch downtown. That would do for your Dover day. Why not an early lunch in the Golden Fleece? Alas, it is no longer a functioning tavern. The Tavern did however have significant history and no doubt holds many a secret. A visit to the original State House across the green concluded my historical morning. A couple of enthusiastic uniformed guides gave me another potted history and personal guided tour of the immaculately restored building, before I escaped back into the twenty-first century. The humidity was becoming unbearable as the heat of the day began to add to the already sweaty temperatures. With the smell of the shrubs and grass, the city had a feel of being cocooned in a giant greenhouse. A ride out of the city centre on highway 1 to the coast did provide some cooling, influenced by a keen breeze from Delaware Bay. My journey back to Laurel was a reverse of the morning – a gentle ride through the Delaware countryside, back into Maryland, across the metal bridge and home. On a state and state capital note, mission accomplished in this area – three planned and three done.

DC

All that remained from my most convenient base for the last week was to give the nation's capital a visit and then it would be north bound. My research did reveal yet another aviation museum, a Smithsonian overflow is now at Dulles and very adjacent to the international airport. Many folk had intimated that it is the best in the country and unmissable. I decided to ride out to Dulles and have a leisurely stroll around DC on my last day. The route out to Dulles just had to be on 495 the Capital Beltway. There was no other option really. After skirting around the north west of the city on 495, 267 would take me directly to destination. It was a mere 50 miles and I left mid-morning on a Friday and expected to get to the museum by coffee time. I had nonetheless underestimated the traffic congestion and even on a bike, it was stop-start, stop-start. To get off the beltway onto 267 couldn't come quick enough. It came eventually and thereafter it was a very quick run to the museum car park which was already filling up quickly. Looking rather like a huge spaceship, complete with high stainless steel conning tower, the museum or rather the Steven F Udvar-Hazy Center, met all expectations.

On the way home, traffic was moving very well until I hit 495 and then became a standstill. Gridlock. My bike computer indicated the air temperature was 92F and with the jungle-like humidity which I had forgotten about in the super air conditioned museum halls, very soon I was overheating. I was picking my way slowly and skilfully through the mainly stationary multi-lane traffic, when suddenly another biker pulled up alongside and indicated I should follow. He pulled off on to the shoulder of the carriageway and I followed hot, very hot, in pursuit. My escort knew what he was doing and frequently he pulled back into the crawling traffic. Patrol cars were everywhere and they seemed to be operating in teams pulling motorists over for apparently doing the same as we were doing. We continued to run the gauntlet for the majority of 495 and didn't attract the attention of any patrol car. My escort peeled off into the north of DC, leaving me a couple of miles to solo on the beltway before turning off on 95 and dropping back into Maryland and Laurel. That friendly biker turned 50 miles of hell into quite an exciting zig-zag ride through steaming heat and the metal gridlock of Friday commuters. I had decided the name for this sector of my journey in the north east of the USA, will definitely be 'North East Gridlock'; that's far more accurate and certainly after my experiences on the capital beltway, was very appropriate.

On my last day I had every intention of riding right up to the steps of the nation's Capitol. Diana had been doing some local research on my behalf and had other ideas for me. Not only were the local temperatures expected to peak at over 100F, but the city centre was going to be closed down for a ladies' charity early morning running event. I left the bike in the garage and took the sensible option which was a ride on the metro into downtown DC. The heat and humidity were ridiculously oppressive again. I think the order of the day would be to do a walking loop of the Mall, ending at a grill bar for a late lunch that Diana had recommended. Her words had been, 'You will not be disappointed with the location and menu.' I started in the Smithsonian. I had an appointment with an old acquaintance. I made for the Apollo 15 crew displays and photographs. I met astronaut Jim Irwin at a military presentation in England back in 1982. He talked to us at length about his test pilot days and lately his training and experiences as a lunar astronaut. I recall Jim was a gentle man, short in stature and slight in build, yet still carried a formidable persona. I was the first to shake his hand after an enjoyable talk that evening and he gave me a signed print of him standing on the moon next to his spacecraft on the Hadley Apennine landing site.

'What shall I write for you Nick?' he asked me.

I shrugged my shoulders and said, 'Your name will be fine thanks.' He signed the photo 'to Nick with love from the moon, Jim Irwin'. It remains with me today.

Later I found the Old Ebbitt Grill. A fine establishment and an excellent recommendation from Diana. Over lunch, I got talking to the couple next to me, who turned out to be on a political mission or conference from Austin, Texas. Austin, Texas... that seemed such a long time back on my trail and Keats Norfleet was rather disappointed to hear his home city did not really score high on my list. As I thought, quite a few White House employees and Presidential representatives frequent the Old Ebbitt. One of them had just sat next to me and was advertising his connection to the President himself. He was sitting at his normal place and had his normal plate of rich food and large glass of red wine. I was told he was as regular as clockwork in the Ebbitt. He cut a large figure to be polite and was wearing expensive clothes including pinstripe trousers held up by colourful braces, a striped shirt and paisley tie and of course cufflinks and all the other associated metalwork a city gent could add to his attire. But around his neck was a tape measure! Yes, a tape measure. It seemed a bit odd, however the attentive bar staff discreetly pointed out to me that this gent was the President's personal tailor. Over dinner back at Laurel, the blue sky turned to grey and then black and the most violent thunderstorm erupted for the next two to three hours. When was this weather pattern going to change and what of tomorrow?

Chapter 52

Atlantic Shore Breeze

Steam was rising from the ground the next morning. The place looked a mess after the violent storms of the night before. Branches from trees and shrubs that had been ripped off their stems were scattered around. Even healthy green leaves had been strimmed from their stalks and lay on the ground. Remarkably, the ground was only damp and all standing water had dispersed. I was still unsure how far to progress north today. My next state capital was Trenton, New Jersey. My master plan was to go directly to the state capital of Trenton, spend a short time there and then continue to Albany, New York State. That was 370 miles and with a healthy pit stop in the middle in Trenton, was easily achievable on a Sunday, whilst brushing past several urban monsters on the way. I did however have a contingency plan to break this up just a bit and would check things out once mobile. I was loading and preparing the bike dressed in shorts and T-shirt in an attempt to stay dry from perspiration before donning my riding kit and departing Diana's place. Bruce had already left a day or so back on one of his mammoth USA rural trips and hence I was leaving Diana on her own with the Sunday newspapers to digest. When I was fully dressed and ready to go, it was already 85F, with 100F forecast with the humidity of a sauna. I recall I had almost decided on plan two whilst bidding farewell to Diana. It had been a great stay in Laurel where I was able to charge around the geography of several states whilst being treated like family in a lovely home by hosts who were complete strangers a week ago. Departure from Laurel was quite simple. I passed to the east of Baltimore and took the JFK memorial highway or I-95 heading north east, with the north part of Chesapeake Bay on my right. Crossing the Delaware River and picking up the New Jersey Turnpike, I had already made my mind up it would be plan two and I glanced down at a couple of small towns I had written down on the lower windscreen that were quite close to Trenton. I had already programmed them into my GPS. It was hot and extremely uncomfortable riding. Bikers might find this hard to comprehend. In some parts of the world, especially in the cool months of the year back home, many pray for hot weather. It is hard to explain, but all this heat bouncing off the asphalt and buildings and the excessive humidity made for an unpleasant cocktail and was quite tiring in all the kit on a loaded bike. It's the humidity that's the killer and the dry heat I had experienced back in Arizona is a completely different and more manageable animal.

The 'turnpike'! I recall I briefly mentioned this type of road earlier on in my journey. In the north east of the country they are quite common. The Pennsylvania and New Jersey Turnpikes are examples and also major routes in the area. A turnpike is a toll road and you get your money out to make progress. That may be at the start or end point where you join the route, depending on the position of the toll collection booths. Historically the 'turnpike' is the gate or barrier preventing access on the road until the toll has been paid. This term was particularly common from the 16th to 19th centuries around the world and is still used here in the north east USA. Toll roads are of course common around the world, however most other places have dropped the name 'turnpike' and simply use 'toll road'. When paying to use a road, you expect a good surface. I was not disappointed so far and the surface was as smooth as a baby's bottom. I was on the New Jersey Turnpike on the east side of the Delaware River, with the sprawling urban monster of Philadelphia on the west side. Visibility was good and the extent of Philadelphia filled much of the picture to the west. Sunday morning aviation was lined up on approach to the international airport, which is extremely close to the river. The urban sprawl of Phili continues north east and almost joins on to Trenton. I saw Trenton on the skyline to my left and after only 170 miles I had had enough for one day. Plan two it was and the thought of progressing into New York State was just too ambitious. Hightstown got my vote and I exited the turnpike and found myself in quite a pretty little town. Hanging baskets on red brick homes, a neat town centre splashed with an assortment of small shops and restaurants, all gave a rather warm feeling. After 10 days with my hosts in Laurel, it was a slight shock to have to find and pay for a motel. However, as normal, I found a place quickly and checked in nice and early. The check-in lady mentioned I ought to ride out to the coast and rattled off a few beach towns that may be worth a visit. I took her advice. The thought of an ocean breeze was very attractive after the hot run up from Maryland. Without checking the map, I simply headed due east with the objective of hitting the coast at some point and taking it from there. I made for an area where a couple of light aircraft were pulling advertising banners. They must be flying up and down the beach. It worked and a most body-quenching Atlantic breeze told me I had made the right decision to break the journey after all. It was quite hard to compare the mile after mile of asphalt, concrete and brick I had seen in the morning and now I was staring at the deep blue ocean on a gorgeous coastal ride. I went as far north as Belmar which seemed to be quite an upmarket seaside town. It was 100F and the huge beach was crammed full of residents dressed in not a lot, frolicking and bathing in the early June heat. Even the police were in the spirit of things, rollerblading and cycling around on duty in the most discrete uniforms. Belmar got my attention for a coffee and a sandwich and then it was back inland, where the temperatures quickly increased without the cooling coastal breeze.

Hightstown made for an interesting but quiet evening, leaving the next morning only to have a quick look at Trenton. My intention, regardless of the temperatures, was to continue north at lunchtime. Not exactly the right time of day to be embarking on the day's journey, but some research the night before had revealed a couple of options. I was so close to New York City and would die for a biker's escort through Manhattan and over the Hudson a few times. Alas, the promise of an escort had not materialised. It would be me and the GPS if I wanted to do it. Shall I or shan't I? Or shall I stay boring and stay to the west of NYC and remain rural? A decision I would make before embarking north at lunchtime. In the meantime, it was a quick 20 miles into Trenton. The 145-foot high golden dome of the state Capitol stood out proudly against the surrounding buildings and I was very quickly turning into a security car park in the Capitol grounds. The Capitol had airport-style security at the entrance, but with it being so early in the day I had the place to myself. One of the secretaries was quite impressed with my capital city itinerary and that Trenton was 32 on my journey list. 'Gee, we are number 32 for this crazy Brit guy folks.' Leaving she piled me high with information leaflets and a rather smart lapel badge. After a walk around the Old Barracks dating from 1758 and a glance at the war memorial with impressive floral metalwork, it was time to go. My next big decision had to be imminent; was it to be Manhattan or not? The journey back to Hightstown may have contributed to my decision. Traffic was stationary on 195 and the Turnpike was not much better. I ended up deviating into the countryside around Robbinsville and Windsor, passing through fine agricultural land, in order to beat the traffic and get back to my motel. It was noon and 110F. Some truck drivers I spoke to in the car park said that traffic on the Turnpike was not moving. There was stationary traffic north towards NYC. Maybe my decision had just been made.

Chapter 53

Al's Seafood Bar and Walter G Crump

The lady at check-in said to me, 'Well are you gonna ride through Manhattan today on the way north?' I laughed and reminded her of the temperature outside and then pointed towards the turnpike. We could both just about see it and the traffic was stationary with none of the normal noise of passing traffic heard. Traffic was stationary. Returning to my bike after checking out and bidding farewell to the chatty clerk, the metal surfaces, especially the panniers, were now too hot to touch. Decision made, it was a no-brainer; NYC could wait for me. It was still a touch disappointing as riding around Manhattan crossing the Hudson and playing with traffic around Central Park along to big Frank's 'New York New York' or even Don Henley's 'New York Minute', did hold some appeal. Next time. The prospect of mixing it with wall-to-wall traffic in one of the world's largest cities and in sweltering temperatures was just not appealing. I had a rural route planned through Princetown and Somerville, which would get me onto I-287 and I-87, passing to the west of the metropolis. I-287 heads north east and acts as a boundary to the conurbations of New York and Newark, which were a mere 10 miles over my right shoulder. It was a shame I wasn't able to have a ride in downtown NYC, however I was more than content to be experiencing free movement with no traffic congestion. It was still disgustingly hot. I could feel my head boiling and sizzling rivers of sweat were pouring south. Rather than risk overheating, I pulled off the Interstate into a service area, which even had a shaded car park to escape into. I was a hot and very sweaty biker again and quickly drank a couple of litres of warm water. So warm had the water got I was carrying, that it so easily could have been used to brew coffee or tea with no anticipated complaint from any drinker. However, it hit the spot and provided instant hydration which made me feel much better and almost energetic all of a sudden. The bike was again proving to be an all-weather athlete and was thriving in these conditions. Temperatures again peaked over 100F, with no complaint or murmur from my steed. I had every intention of pressing on to Albany. However, I vaguely recall some comments about a national park close by that was worth a visit. I had forgotten the name of the place, but I didn't want to miss it and was mentally straining to remember what the place was called. Then I saw a sign – Catskill State Park – that was it, the Catskills. It is sometimes a strange name that is difficult to recall. I eased off the Interstate at Kingston and was very quickly in a hilly and forested park – The Catskills. I was feeling a little adventurous at making such a short notice decision and diversion, but a night stop here would not delay any progress north. I would continue to Albany the next day.

I went from busy Interstate into beautiful countryside very quickly. Ahhhh tranquillity and the anxieties of heat of the day and all that traffic were evaporating quickly. I had no idea where I was aiming for and decided to stay in the boundary of the park and drop into the first town or village that looked like supporting my evening needs. After 174 miles from leaving Hightstown at lunchtime, I rode into the small town, or village really, of Phoenicia around about 4 pm. With one high street dotted with the usual stores, restaurants and a couple of motels, this would do. The town, as everywhere else close by, was surrounded by hilly forestation and had quite an enclosed and isolated feeling. I was the only guest in the Cobblestone Motel and arrived just before they were about to call it a day. What of the Catskills? The area is rather like a huge raised plateau, dissected frequently by valleys and rounded mountains. They are sometimes called an extension to the Appalachians reaching out into upstate New York. They attract lovers of the great outdoors for activities such as fishing and hiking in the warm months and skiing in the cold months. In very early days, the Catskills had a reputation as a destination for the wealthy urbanites from NYC. Many country homes and fine hotels were built to cater for these trends. Alas most of them have been lost to fire and redevelopment and a lot of the history has vanished. Today, the local economy, including that of Phoenicia, survives on the through tourist traffic using some resorts, inns, lodges and camps. Although it was early June, it was Monday and the place was very, very quiet with only the locals going about their business in the one-street town. I found a lot of locals in Al's Seafood Bar, where I was welcomed by a no-nonsense waitress who pointed to the seafood buffet then the dining area then the bar. 'Eat as much as you like, sit where you want, what are you drinking?' I was quite surprised to stumble across a seafood place stuck here in the middle of a country park. I had images of venison steaks, pheasant and other game meats aplenty on the local menus. However, I was not disappointed and the seafood was abundant and delicious. The dining area was mainly populated by local couples and foursomes enjoying Monday evening. There was one old boy dining alone and his familiarity with the menu and wine list obviously placed him as a regular. After enough fish and shrimp to last me a week, I retreated to the bar and glass of wine in hand, the old boy followed me. He introduced himself as Walter G Crump, a boatyard owner from California with a country place right here in the Catskills. We got talking about this and that over a couple of drinks, after which he withdraw to his truck and two pug dogs waiting outside. He gave directions to his place not far away and suggested I drop by for coffee the next morning.

I found Walter's place with no dramas, although it was tucked away amidst undulating hills and was certainly not covered by my GPS. The gravel approach road to his multi-building estate was challenging to say the least and I very nearly came to grief. Whilst parking up on his driveway and taking my attention to greet him and his two dogs, I so nearly miscalculated the adverse-gravelled camber. Was I to have my first spill due to my carelessness and not the actions of an errant motorist?! When the side stand eventually made contact with the ground, I was over at such an obtuse angle that Walter had to push me back up to the vertical. That was quite some feat considering the combined weight of me and the fully laden bike. Embarrassing to say the least. Walter then rushed off into one of his sheds and brought back a chunk of wood to put under the stand. It was still a bit dodgy and very wobbly, so I retreated to some flatter terrain down the track a bit. After my embarrassing arrival, Walter proceeded to show me around his place. It was huge and consisted of one small cottage that was his main dwelling, a turreted multi-floored castle with embattlements, a swimming pool and several outbuildings. Alas, other than his cottage everything required extensive renovation. Walter was taking the whole task on himself with limited local help. He looked tired and worn and this was not the ideal lifestyle for someone of his years. He should be on the deck on one of his boats back in California enjoying life at a gentler pace. He asked my opinion on the whole matter and I suggested he should sell the entire estate and enjoy the rest of his days back west. He didn't agree or disagree, but wanted to keep the place in the family and selling was not an option at the moment. It had been in the family for over a hundred years. Walter took pride in showing me the poetry inscribed on all the walls throughout the cottage. The writings were over a hundred years old and maintaining this history was very important to Walter. In the hot mid-morning sunshine on his multi-levelled lawns, we viewed the quite spectacular panoramic contours of the wooded Catskills. It was this setting that gave Walter the energy to continue with his arduous renovation task in the summer months, retreating to mild California in the winter. But the work required to return the whole place to its former glory would require gargantuan application.

I extricated myself from Walter's place with a little more dignity than my arrival. As I was manoeuvring down the gravel roads back to the highway, I couldn't help but feel a little sorry for Walter. A widower of 75, he was such a quiet gent and cut quite a sad image through his tanned and creased face. He was exceedingly glad to welcome me to his estate and after an hour or so with him, dispatched me on a scenic ride through the northern edge of the park and onwards to Albany. As well as invaluable local information on further geographical gems in upstate New York, he also gave me contact details of a boat owner friend in

Washington State to look up later on when I get out there. He actually tried to call him whilst I was there. He didn't answer. He was probably cruising somewhere and out of network coverage. Anyway, that would be a useful contact and I looked forward to the prospect of getting out west, which wasn't that long ahead. In short time I had arrived in the capital of New York State. The busy crossroads city of Albany was somewhat a contrast to the rural Catskills. Roughly equidistant between NYC, Montreal, Buffalo and Boston, Albany is a popular stop-over for the journeyman. The city offers an active artist, festival and entertainment community and proffers exactly that image if you take time to look through a normal city skin. The ride downtown from one of my usual-suspect motel selections passed through an attractive residential area, with shops, bars and restaurants scattered around here and there. The place had quite an English feel although the history of Albany has very much Dutch roots. The New York State Capitol Building is extremely unique and unlike any other in the country. It was nice not to see the usual domed Capitol and while parking the bike I confirmed with a local that this actually was the Capitol I had located. I got an affirmative reply and entered something that I can only describe as a huge palace. It is said that the Capitol was originally modelled on a hotel, but actually finding fact to back up that statement is quite muddled. However, what's for sure is that the architectural design is a mixture of French Chateauesque, Italian Renaissance and Romanesque styles on the exterior and Moorish Gothic styles on the interior. I was given a colourful map for a self-guided tour of the high ceiling and multi-columned dark and cool corridors. After my circuit of the impressive rooms, galleries and ornate art, I reported back to the guide at his desk and asked for further city advice. He quickly suggested I should walk down the internal plaza to the Erastus Corning Tower and access the observation deck for a bird's eye view of the city and surroundings. I took his advice and was amused to find that the plaza, or rather a huge walkway, was accessed from the basement of the Capitol Building. The walk was almost underground. My Capitol guide had called ahead to the Corning Tower reception crew and I was expected. 'The English guy has arrived.' After a quick photo and instant production of a company

ID, I was pointed in the direction of the elevators and told to hit the 42 button. The observation deck on the 42nd floor of the tallest building in Albany provided stunning views of the city and the Hudson River snaking below. Storm clouds were gathering on the horizon and forks of lightning were dancing towards the state many miles away. It was an eerie scene. Bright blue above and in close proximity of the city limits and then a grey and moody periphery. I was in an elevated goldfish bowl. I chatted briefly to the security lady before I descended. She candidly stated she was scared of the forecast bad weather that afternoon and couldn't wait until closing time when she could descend to the relative safety of street level and home. She didn't have long to wait, it was already 4 pm as I dropped the 42 floors towards Mother Earth. I stayed over ground for my return back towards the Capitol and walked down the Empire State Plaza and past the amusingly egg-shaped performing arts centre. It is simply called The Egg because it is shaped like an egg! Returning to my bike parked on Washington Avenue, I spotted a lady traffic warden about to pounce. I was sure I had fed enough quarters in the machine to last my excursion and on inspection, I had over an hour left. But would you believe it, the lady was ready to give me a ticket and her excuse was she wouldn't be around this area of the city again today and wanted to make sure. Thank you very much for your over-efficiency! I had to have a little laugh as I eased through the late afternoon traffic which was building up to commuter hour. I just wanted to make sure indeed! Ah well, if I got a ticket they would have to pursue me for the fine across a few states that's for sure. I had no intention of hanging around.

Later that evening I found a nice sports bar close to the motel. It was the sort of place that had a TV in every available space on the wall, showing every possible American sport. If you didn't like football, then try basketball, if you didn't like basketball then try baseball. I sat at the bar and took in the busy scene. It was obviously a popular meeting place and watering hole for folks on the way home from the office. The menu was a bit limited, but after an ostentatious selection of seafood the night before, burger and chips and a couple of cold beers did the trick. In short time, the guy sitting on my right told his life story in detail and in colour. He was recently separated and juggled time and money between his former wife, his children and his new partner. Wow, he went into detail and to me, a perfect stranger. He was en route to a girly bar a couple of blocks away and urgently requested my attendance. My sobriety declined the offer and I bade farewell to this very open stranger. But quite honestly, that is a huge observation of Americans in general and everywhere I have been. They are very open about themselves, their families and their lives. Discretion and privacy is uncommon. Is this a good thing or a bad thing? A balance between being open and private is my answer. The afternoon upstate storm eventually got to the city. Thankfully I was close to motel and after a mad dash through the quickly forming floods, I observed the tempest, which was literally overhead, from the relative safety of my room.

Chapter 54

Constitution State

It was whilst munching over my free motel breakfast and shuffling through my mental filing system that I suddenly remembered I had a local business card from that senior couple I met way back in Key West, Florida. It was in that chic sea food restaurant when I had been eating at the bar and watching the growing line of diners awaiting a table. Dick and Maureen had joined me at the bar for a short time and passed on the card of their son Richard, the General Manager of the Embassy Suites Hotel in Marlborough, Massachusetts. 'Give him a call, he will give you a good rate on a room'. I took the card, but at the time, I couldn't really think and plan that far ahead. It was Connecticut today, followed by Rhode Island and then Massachusetts. I would be there in a few days and Marlborough would be an ideal place to stay to access Boston. I would call him, why not, nothing to lose. He could have course have moved on or deny all knowledge of the connection, so the situation may not click – but it did. He answered the phone immediately; 'Hello Nick, my parents did mention they met you in Florida. I have had the odd look at your website, when are you arriving?' Game on, communication had taken place!

'At the weekend by the looks of it Richard,' I said, and briefly went through my itinerary in the meantime.

'Good, make sure you have a look at Cape Cod before you come here, you will enjoy the unique location'.

'Thanks for that and what deal can you do for me in your hotel' Lets get the important question in!

'Well, how about this, what rate are you paying for motels as you move around the country?' There was no room for manoeuvre here, he would know the price of motels being the GM of a global chain-I couldn't waffle.

'Anything from $50 to $80 dollars a night depending where I end up Richard'.

'Okay, I will give you a suite for $50 a night here and you can stay as long as you want, I shall let the reception team know.' Excellent, I am sure two days would be enough, but two days in relative luxury would be a nice change.

'Many thanks Richard and see you at the weekend.'

Well done Dick and Maureen!

For some reason I already had a mindset that Hartford and Connecticut wouldn't be a stellar visit. I shouldn't really pre judge a place, but I think it would be a quick visit. I had already decided to stay in a small town called Wethersfield just to the south of the city. For some unknown reason, I got lost getting out of Albany and went around in a couple of circles on the city's looping Interstates. I hadn't done that before, but I was relying on nose and dead reckoning navigation rather than Mr Garmin. I think the couple of stationary patrol cars and toll attendants thought it was quite entertaining, when they saw me again and then again. I eventually found Interstate 90 and when it changed from the New York State Throughway to the Massachusetts Turnpike, I knew I had jumped states. Turning south at Springfield and picking up 91, I quickly jumped states again and had arrived in Connecticut. Very quickly and at the confluence of several interstates, the downtown high rise of Hartford stood out against the blue sky. The mercury had dropped a bit today and it was a cool 85F with a keen breeze. A cool 85F! – but riding conditions were heavenly in comparison with the recent weeks. I was through the city centre in quick time and continuing the short distance south to Wethersfield.

My motel routine was well established now. On arrival, I would quickly plug into the world by means of internet and TV. The Weather

Channel was always worth a watch, albeit their forecast could be quite general and not localised. Their website was much better for my planning purposes. However, when I turned on the Weather Channel, the attractive blonde presenter was getting very excited about regional variations. She was reporting flooding in Iowa after more torrential rain – *passed through there with no problems*, continuing to be very hot and humid in the north east – *yes thank you, I have had that in my face for what seemed weeks*, and snowing in the high ground in Montana. *Snowing in Montana? It was mid-June for heaven's sake and I would be there next month.* The fickle weather patterns of the USA, or rather, the enormity of this country and the dynamic nature of the weather systems had again been illustrated to me. I didn't fancy snow in Montana in July.

It was bright and breezy when I returned to Hartford, this time getting off the downtown Interstate and heading for Bushnell Park. About 400 years old, it's one of the oldest cities in the USA and after the Civil War, had the reputation of being one of the wealthiest alongside New Orleans. Mark Twain commented, 'Of all the beautiful towns it has been my fortune to see, Hartford is the chief.' Continuing on a historical note, Hartford claims to have the oldest public art museum and the oldest continuously running published newspaper, *The Hartford Courant*. So there are a few historical gems out there after all. Today, there is a mix of old and new in the centre, with the Old State House at State House Square rubbing shoulders with many high-rise neighbours. A lot of these high rises house the several insurance companies that have given the city the nickname 'the Insurance Capital of the World'. Not the most exciting nickname to have, but that's what makes the place breathe. With the corporate and insurance image, Hartford did have a reputation of being a rather stagnant place. However recent redevelopments alongside the river front have injected a new life and today, it is not an unattractive area to live and work.

Fair weather cumulus cloud was being pushed along quite quickly past the gold-leafed dome of the Gothic and French Renaissance Revival State House. Sited in the elevated Bushnell Park, the 257-foot tall building added to a rather imposing position. It overlooks the city and many new builds below. The interior has the usual art and accessories decorated on high walls and around marble columns. The politicians were in session and the place was buzzing on several floors. Bushnell Park offered a suitable retreat away from the crowds and the breeze was a most welcome refreshment. Today walking around had suddenly become comfortably normal with less humidity. I did a circuit of the park and ogled at the nooks and crannies of the tall Capitol before heading down the hill to retrieve my bike. I was just thinking that I hadn't had a brush with the law for many months and many thousands of miles when a patrol car went past me. It hit the brakes and came to a screeching stop opposite my bike and momentarily put the blue lights on. Blast, that was tempting fate a bit just thinking about the law, but I was still on foot and not yet astride my bike. I wonder what he or she wants? It was a he and police officer P Lewis from the Hartford Police greeted me on the roadside in a friendly manner. He was a slightly built guy dressed in uniform shorts and T-shirt with his unit badge emblazoned on the front. He looked quite strange in shorts with a sidearm on his hip. Not exactly Clint Eastwood. I was not being apprehended and I was not a felon after all. My new friend had heard somewhere about my trip and simply wanted to chat for a while. He quickly added that he was also a biker and completely unannounced, swung a leg over my bike and tried it for size. His actions took me completely by surprise and I tried to remain cool but cautious at the same time. The bike was too tall for him and I was relieved when he dismounted and the bike became supported by its stand and not his tip-toes. He turned out to be quite an interesting guy, but like a lot of Americans, he couldn't comprehend the enormity of my trip. He mentioned he and his family had never even been to Niagara Falls, which wasn't a million miles away from where we standing. Niagara was his immediate travel ambitions and the thought of doing the 50 states were simply out of space and out of reach. A former military man, he described to me in detail his first parachute jump from a sky crane helo basket when serving in the US Army. Not for me anymore; I once had the ambition to jump from a serviceable aircraft and float to earth. That was in my enthusiastic youth and today I prefer permanent contact with terra firma. He laughed at my comments and added he now had similar feelings. We got talking about the city and I mentioned it looked attractive and peaceful at the moment. That's the deceiving part of this place, he added. You picked a good place to stay, I mean out of the downtown. Even some of the good hotels are used by people working drugs and prostitution from their rooms. Shootings are also a problem in town; we have had several this year already, but not all are fatal. I wonder if that has anything to do with the Colt Firearms factory being in Hartford? He wasn't really amused by that comment and tersely added, it's the same all over the country. I couldn't comment on that, but maybe as I had been passing through the USA, I have been completely unaware what crime was really happening all around me and probably sometimes quite close by. Maybe I had been lucky so far.

At least I had confirmation from the city police that I had chosen a good place to stay, even though it was only for one night. Since my illuminating experiences in Jackson, Mississippi, I had initially been cautious of where to stay in places. I think I had come to terms with the country quite nicely and was almost operating with the confidence of a local.

Chapter 55

Maritime Arrival into Number 35

Back in Maryland, Bruce and Diana had bombarded me with geographical highlights to visit and additionally had set me up with people to stay with further out to the west. One of their must-see areas was the coastline around the ocean state of Rhode Island. Newport was the place to go for a couple of days apparently. That's exactly where I was heading when east bound out of Hartford. I was in one of those moods to get lost and not even dream about taking the most direct route or the Interstate. It was only 100 miles to Newport and I picked my way east through the pretty countryside. I was deep in the countryside not far east of Hartford, passing Hebron, Lebanon, Versailles and at Voluntown, crossed the state line into America's smallest. Despite being called Rhode Island, the majority of the state is on the continental mainland. The name Rhode Island originates from colonial times and is the name for what is now called Aquidneck Island. Along with Middletown and Portsmouth, Newport is located on Aquidneck Island, which is the largest of several islands in Narragansett Bay. After Voluntown, it was Centreville, then the small town of Wyoming, West Kingston, Bridgetown and the strong smell of the sea indicated I was getting close. All that remained was to get across the bay and I would be in the resort town of Newport. The long and high-arched Jamestown and Newport Bridges took care of that, whilst providing spectacular views of yachts carving white furrows in the cobalt Rhode Island Sound well below. Between the bridges is Conanicut Island, lying quite isolated in the bay, with big brother Aquidneck at the end of the second bridge.

I was greeted by the English manager of the Sea View Motel, which was reasonably close to the centre, but still had a secluded feeling. The ocean was just visible from the car park and the strong breeze was filling the high-flying Stars and Stripes. It was intriguing to meet someone from England that was actually working over here. I am sure there are thousands, but this was the first I had met. Originally from the county of Norfolk in England, she had been in the USA for over 20 years and had started her travels and work here in Rhode Island. After that, she spent a long time in Colorado before re-locating back to Rhode Island. It was the yachting world that captured her interests and lust for the oceans. She enjoyed several jobs on yachts and boating delivery jobs, frequently crossing the Pacific and in and out of Fiji. Quite an adventurer herself, she actually admitted that she was unsure of a return to the UK and was quite content to stay in the land of opportunity. 'It's a country that suits any personality over here, easy to fit in and quite a melting pot of personalities and nationalities.' Her final comments as I was unloading the bike were amusingly refreshing: 'Its almost been like a long vacation for me!' Good if you can get it and fit into that lifestyle I reckon. I guessed that her age was mid-30s, she was mid-40s, so the Rhode Island air had done her good over the last two decades. I think two nights were in order in this rather attractive little place and remarkably, I almost felt as if I was on holiday as well. A ride around the island followed by a late lunch seemed like a good plan. I heard that parts of the town were quite famous for a boulevard of mansions and fine estates overlooking the ocean. Newport has the highest concentration of colonial houses in the nation and as well as being scattered around the coastline they are located in the historic district downtown. Riding down Bellvue Avenue was an eye opener, where many mansions are located. Most of them are gated properties and set back from the road in their own grounds. Newport was known as the city of some of the 'Summer White Houses'. Presidents Dwight D Eisenhower and John F Kennedy both had homes in the area. JFK actually got married in St Mary's church in

Newport. Lucrative living continued all the way around the southern tip of the island. Following Ocean Avenue, several properties of varying architectural shape and design are positioned around the bluffs and coves overlooking the ocean. The nearest connection I could make to these places was to toss a stone into the water and watch it skip across the surface until eventually sinking well before my target. The question is, if I had the available greenback to purchase such a property, would it be Charleston South Carolina, or here? I think I would prefer Rhode Island at the moment. Continuing my clockwise loop, Ocean Drive continued past Brenton Park, Newport Country Club, Fort Adams and then back into the compact and colourful Newport town centre. A combination of the historic colonial buildings, the mosaic of colours from the waterside hang-outs and not forgetting the hundreds of yachts on the deep blue water, gave this place quite a special feeling. It was a unique ambience and probably did get my vote over Charleston. Bar 22, that number again, provided a first-class lobster sandwich, washed down with cool aqua. The waitress started some geographical verbal sparring and quickly thrust into the conversation that she was a '46-stater'. That was a good score for someone that looked 24. She turned out to be 34. She tried to guess my age and I flippantly replied I was somewhere between 21 and death. That brought a laugh from her and a couple of giggles from another table. Thinking on the spot and hoping my tan would get me through, I said I was 35. I was in my 35th state and should use this system for the remainder of the route if questions are asked. It worked here, or was she being polite? When I get to Alaska and if asked the same question, I will not be lying. It must be the sea air that keeps the complexion of these gals looking fresh. She was brought up by one of those families that were forever on the road with the kids. School holidays, half terms, long weekends, you name it, she recalls they were always state hopping. Her comprehensive coverage of the USA for someone so young was probably quite unusual. Walking off lunch on the waterfront boardwalk, I came across Bill sitting under a parasol overlooking the bobbing yachts. Wearing a floppy sun hat to protect his tanned face, he was well into retirement and passed his day as a local guide and ferryboat information man. His office was inside, but he had a small table outside which he moved around depending on sun direction and temperature. Today the temperature was a most comfortable 80F and I was not sweating like a racehorse that has just completed the Grand National. It was heaven. We chatted for a while and I mentioned I was heading for the capital tomorrow and guessed it was about 30 miles on the bike. Bill immediately suggested I leave the bike at home and get the ferry into Providence. That was great advice direct from Newport Rhode Island staff. A maritime arrival it would be. Before retreating back to the Sea View, I took a little ride over Memorial Boulevard and out east to Sachuest Point. It's the most south east corner of Aquidneck Island, with Massachusetts not that far to the east. It was a hot and clear afternoon and families were out walking and playing in the surf. I even sampled a Dels soft frozen ice cream lemonade – *'refreshingly different from Aquidneck Island'*. It quenched my dry throat from the hot day as I took in the beach scenes. It was all quite different here. I was getting to grips with the reasons why maybe some Americans are not that well internationally travelled. They live in such a geographically diverse country. Here I was on the beach next to a pretty little town. Not far away are several large metropolitan areas and from the many airports, the desert, the mountains, the plains or even a bit of gambling are all but a few hours away. There is even snow in Montana again today and skiers and snowboarders would be getting late season exercise on the piste. For today, I was happy with the blue sky, the ocean breeze and tolerable temperatures as I rode down Purgatory Road back to the motel. Purgatory. Hmm – maybe that would be an apt title for the weather patterns I had been enduring.

It was an hour's ferry trip mainly through the wide Narragansett Bay the next morning. We passed a few small islands, avoiding many yachts enjoying the perfect sailing conditions, before the channel narrowed into Providence River at the head of the bay as we approached the city. A trolley bus met the disembarking passengers and whisked us all off from the port area to the main bus station downtown. It wasn't a bus station from hell as I have discovered in other cities, but merely bus lanes positioned around a pretty green square, flanked by the high-rise buildings of what is a very compact city centre. I think everyone else had the same idea as me; it was to be a daytrip to Providence. It's quite a unique name for a city and my research revealed that it was named by Roger Williams in 1636. He was a religious exile from nearby Massachusetts and named the city and county in honour of 'God's merciful Providence' and broadcast that it would be an ideal place for his people and followers to settle. My ritual of finding the State Capitol was first. It was located on a hill on the north side of the river and quite close to the Amtrak station. Arriving in the state gardens, I reflected that it was one of those special beautiful blue summer days, with flowers in bloom and the buzz of bees as they moved gathering nectar. It may have been a different vista with a grey sky, but the stunning State House with tall central dome dominating, certainly completed the picture. It would have been a great setting for a film shoot or even a wedding this morning. I captured a special shot of the blooming roses against the white-marbled 225-foot dome. It was a quiet and serene setting. The cool interior of the Capitol boasted several historical displays including many a battle flag, a Gettysburg Gun and stunning art all over the high walls. I thought that after 35 so far, my enthusiasm for visiting the State Capitols may be waning. This morning I had some increased enthusiasm and vigour. Maybe it was the sea air or maybe I was mentally preparing for completing this section of the journey in the north east and could actually say 'I will be in Maine in... five days'.

Lunch al fresco on the patio of Joe's Bar and Grill completed a full morning. I chose meatloaf and trimmings and watched the Providence downtown tick over on a busy lunch hour. There were a lot of very young and exuberant office workers about. I wonder how many of these young Americans had been to Europe and even how many had been out west, or even out of New England? I was people watching and casting a critical eye again on this nation. Before I knew it, the afternoon had drifted towards bus time and I made my way through the busy streets back to the pick-up point. I arrived a little early and the square was busier than it had been in the morning. Busy enough for a mounted policewoman to be on duty. Was that just routine or for visitors like me to photograph? I got talking to the lady on board. 'England, do you still have food rationing over there?' She wasn't joking.

The breeze had picked up considerably in the late afternoon and the trip back to Newport, an exact reverse of the morning, was exhilarating. Brave passengers took in the marine views from the upper deck. The upper-deckers were a real mixed bunch; I think the majority of them were relaxing after a day in Providence and the enjoyable prospect of returning home or to hotel at the end of the day. I was sitting amongst a few folks who were in fine form and enjoying a wedding weekend stay in Newport and exploring the smallest state in the Union at the same time. I hadn't been called Australian for a while, until I met Joe Kaminsky, a real estate consultant from Scottsdale, Arizona. He was part of the wedding group and we chatted for the whole trip. It was politics mainly and we both agreed it would be a Democrat Government at the helm next year. But before we decided who the next President would be, we were passing under the Newport Bridge and berthing at the quayside close to Bill's table. We said our farewells and made off in different directions. That's the way things have been on this journey so far. Talking with strangers, few become friends and then goodbye to strangers.

Chapter 56

The Cape

It was a Saturday morning and the weather was set fair by the looks of it. The sun was already penetrating low stratus that was fudging over the deep blue water of Buzzards Bay. Interstate 195 took me to highway 6, that is the main arterial route inbound to the unique geographical feature of Cape Cod, or simply the Cape, in Massachusetts. If viewed from above the Cape looks like a crooked index finger. Is it a peninsula, a promontory or an isthmus? There are some interesting satellite photos around of this interesting chunk of the Bay state and it should make for an interesting day trip whilst being so close. The Cape is completely separated from the mainland by the Cape Cod Canal and you cross over on the Bourne or Sagamore Bridges, depending if you arrive from the mainland from the north or the south. I crossed from the south and joined the Mid Cape Highway east bound along the crooked finger. The Cape is divided into four areas: the Upper Cape which is nearest the mainland, Mid-Cape, Lower Cape and finally the Outer Cape. I was heading for the end of the finger, or the fingernail really, to Provincetown on the outer cape. Once past Barnstable Town, I cut off to the north and ended up on very narrow roads, passing through Yarmouth Port, Dennis and Brewster, before rejoining the main highway all the way to the end. It was 140 miles from Newport, Rhode Island to Provincetown, Massachusetts. On the Cape, there is certainly a diverse assortment of communities and properties. In some of the isolated villages on the north shore, fine colonial homes are set back from the road in neatly manicured gardens. Then there are a mixture of small towns, lots of tacky fast food roadside diners and as expected a plethora of motels and wooden cabin-style accommodation nearing Provincetown. With its unusual geography and ocean proximity, the Cape area is a certainly a tourist attraction and is a summer haven for hoards of Bostonians – 'Come to Cape Cod and feel inspired'. The usual outdoor activities attract visitors, but with 560 miles of pristine coastline, the Cape has become a favourite retreat for the beachcomber. 'Come to Cape Cod and let yourself go and let it capture your heart!' Interesting national statistics boast that Cape Cod is named in the top 25 most-visited sites in the USA. As the crow flies, Boston is a touch over 50 sea miles or so from the rather touristy Provincetown.

I arrived in Provincetown around lunchtime and it seeped with characteristics of a tourist town, with a bit of history thrown in and a smattering of top quality hotels as the cream. It was a cocktail of quayside fast food outlets, red brick historical homes and a few expensive-looking lodgings. It was obviously catering for all types and only 90 minutes across the ocean from Boston, probably gets all types. The quaint harbour area was full of expensive looking yachts, mixed with scruffy-looking fishing smacks unloading their morning catch. I parked up near the shore and was immediately joined by a group of other bikers that had been following me down the finger. We all parked up in a neat line rather like an advertising shot. They were all residents on this special geographic part of the state, including a couple from Martha's Vineyard and Nantucket, which are a couple of other islands that lie to the south of the Cape. The guy from Nantucket Island was riding a day-old HD and I was intrigued what happened on his small island. He was a builder and commented that there was enough work for him on the island alone. He also rode a five-year-old BMW GS, but with such gutsy machines, it must be so frustrating having minimal roads to exercise them. Both Martha's and Nantucket have ferry services and small airports, so maybe they are remote, but remain connected. Regarding properties, this motley bunch of ebullient bikers, euphoric after a good ride in good weather, confirmed that the Cape area and local islands are for the wealthy. You need a lot of cash to get a place here. Maybe that's who kept the builder in a job? The bikers made off to a bar and I tracked down a small diner and took in some local fish whilst sitting watching Saturday lunchtime Cape life go by. It was still early in the season and the crowds hadn't properly gathered yet. Provincetown is only small, so the place must throb when they do gather. After lunch I rode as far as I could before getting my feet wet. The Province Lands Road, almost single track, meanders through tall grass and marshland to the small municipal airport. It became cool and breezy all of a sudden. Across the ocean to the North West would be Boston.

I had one other thing to do before leaving the Cape. The Kennedy family, so prominent in American politics and life, have had family homes at Hyannis on the southern shore for decades. With a long-standing dedication to public service, the Kennedy family have been described by some commentators as the American royal family. The family has had many triumphs and deeply personal and public tragedies. Loses through assassination, aircraft crashes and illnesses, have placed their dynasty as a very sad historical segment of the USA. I wanted to have a quick look at the family property before rejoining the mainland. Just to see it, not touch it or go in the grounds. Hyannis lies just to the east of Barnstable Town and very close to the small airport. Saturday afternoon traffic was now heavy, but I was able to slide through the main street with ease and reach the quayside. It was enough for me just to observe the Kennedy compound in the Hyannis Port historic district. The area contained the homes of Joseph and sons Robert and John. It was used as a base for the presidential campaign and almost as a summer White House and retreat. That ended my day on the Cape and, crossing the Sagamore Bridge this time, I followed the coast north towards Boston and beyond into Marlborough. Over my right shoulder I got the occasional glimpse of the mighty Cape through the haze of the late afternoon.

Chapter 57

A Grey Tea Party

I could see the attraction of life on the Cape. The ocean, many secluded beaches, small communities and then extremely isolated communities. I had enjoyed a full day on the Cape. I must remember to start tracking towards Marlborough and not end up in the sprawl of Boston. I started to veer off to the north west and picked up signs for Marlborough. That's something special, unique or just strange up here, the Boston accent. For example the locals pronounce Marlborough as MALL-bro, sometimes MAH-bro, or even Marl-burrow! Marlborough is steeped in colonial and civil war history. From a village to a staging post. As trade in the area grew, it became a favourite traveller's stop thanks to many inns and taverns. George Washington himself is said to have frequented a particular tavern when passing through the area. I found my hotel with ease and drew up outside the opulent-looking place. It was somewhat different from my usual choice of motel. Instead of sharing the car park with jeeps, trucks, trailers and other charrabangs associated with the traveller, for this weekend I was rubbing shoulders with limos and expensive-looking German cars. Richard was true to his word and I was expected and checked into my suite with alacrity by an efficient team. It was like my Vegas arrival. The bell boy here was keen to assist, however I preferred management of the panniers myself and he was certainly not parking my bike. The room, or rooms, were quite ostentatious to say the least. I had a lounge and a bedroom and then of course a large bathroom. All very nice. It was one of those places that even put chocolates on your pillow. I must pass that on to the motel chain people. After a day of sea air, I would leave exploration of Mah-bro and Boston for the next day. I found a steak house in the mall just around the corner. A vacant stool at the bar invited my attendance and in short time I became established on my perch browsing a typical steak house menu. First, a cool Sam Adams very local ale direct from Boston was the priority. Thereafter it was a chunk of meat which wasn't a culinary delight, but did the job. It was a regular steak. During my meal my attention was drawn to the guy on my right. He was drinking like a fish and admitted to be driving home at the end of the evening. He was brave taking on the busy network of Interstates after a bucketful of Sam Adams. We got talking about biking and he added he was a biker. He had a new HD Fatboy. Hopefully he wasn't on two wheels tonight. A common theme over here I have identified is that a lot of folks are bikers. Everyone is a biker! An awful lot of guys and gals have a bike as a secondary mode of transport. Some are serious users and real bikers, some are extremely occasional users and light the fires only a couple of times a year when it's dry and hot. The rest of the year they caress the battery and shine the chrome. This guy I interpreted was one of the latter. His Fatboy wasn't getting much exercise at all. He admitted to be a casual bike user and blamed the distraction of wife and young family. He was dreaming of a long road trip after the kids had left the nest. Everyone dreams for this marathon road trip in the USA. Even the locals.

Whilst retrieving my bike from the car park the next morning, it suddenly occurred to me that something was very strange and out of place. Something I had not experienced for well over a month or even six weeks. It was grey, completely overcast, cool and with a hint of drizzle in the air. The area of high pressure so static over the north-eastern USA for the last few weeks was breaking up and petering out over the Atlantic. The formerly impenetrable barriers of the high were being broken down by a real shambles and mess of little weather systems heading east from the plains. We were now in a very unsettled weather regime, albeit still typical June temperatures, but no sizzling heat and muddy humidity. Consequently it was quite a cool 50-mile ride into Boston and it felt quite delicious after so many weeks feeling like a spaceman overheating on Mars. The bike was snarling in appreciation. Some say the city should be the capital of New England. It's the largest and has a reputation of a vibrant social scene, a thriving economy, cultural excellence and not forgetting was at the forefront of a lot of serious American history. Everyone should have heard of The Boston Massacre, the Boston Tea Party, the Battle of Bunker Hill and the Siege of Boston, which were all notable historical events that took place during the American Revolution. The Boston Tea Party, still has an iconic and slightly amusing place in American history. It is also rather ironic that even after all that tea was discharged into Boston harbour all those years ago, it's still challenging to get a decent cup of tea in the USA!

The cool day was not ideal for any tea party in the park on this gloomy Sunday. There were some bright bits however. The city is mad on sport and colours of the famous Red Sox base ball team and Boston Celtics basketball team, were all over the city as I carved through the many freeways, underpasses, overpasses and dark suburban tunnels. Traffic was light, giving freedom of movement rather like on an urban F1 circuit. The cooler weather was certainly a contribution to the enjoyment I was having zooming around the turnpikes, tunnels and expressways, down by the harbour, past the common and close to the districts of Chelsea, Cambridge and Charleston. I even got a glimpse of Harvard University. I hadn't had this boy-with-a-toy urban feeling since I did a similar circuit in San Francisco back in April. Only the hills and the blue sky were missing today. When I found the Massachusetts State House, I think the sports advert thing had gone too far. A huge Celtics Basketball banner was draped over the front of the federal-style Capitol Building. The fine architecture and gilded dome was reduced to a sorry-looking backseat. A sports banner on the State Capitol Building in the city of Boston! Around the corner, I got talking to a buildings manager who was leaning on a stone balcony reading the local rag and chain smoking by the looks of it. He turned out to a bit of a traveller and photographer himself. Mike Bowman's first comments to me were one of an apology for that banner hanging on the State House: 'It's not an ideal thing for a visitor to see on that building and we get a lot of visitors in Boston.' Mike had just returned from a tour of the southern states and we exchanged notes, comments and camera chat for a while. He went through several more cigarettes in short time. The afternoon had whizzed by, literally, and it was time to find the Massachusetts Turnpike and MALL-bro. The traffic was still very light and the journey west was swift. I would not like to be this piece of asphalt in a few hours at the peak of a Monday morning rush hour.

My final night in the relative opulence of Richards Hotel. As a treat I thought I would dine in the lobby or rather atrium restaurant in the evening. It was buzzing with fashion-conscious diners and the odd solo business person caressing QWERTY on their Apple Macs. I made for the bar and sat next to a blonde lady. She had a laptop and a large glass of red on the go. By the looks of her stained lips, she had been on the grape for a while. An attractive lady dressed in a smart business suit she proceeded to talk, drink and do laptop simultaneously. She was on a business trip from Iowa and luckily her community had escaped the incredible floods that had washed through there a few weeks back. I admired her multi-tasking as I ate dinner and tried to catch her up on the wine stakes. She became hooked into my conversation and attracted to my accent, however, I think the wine got the better of her. With a clatter of her purse, laptop and other accessories, she made off and retreated to the elevations of her suite. Before I called it a day, the barman and I shared a couple of night caps and had a chuckle over the Iowan. He was a law student from Harvard and earning a few bucks for his social life, school fees and also, as a biker, maybe one day that dream road trip.

Chapter 58

Supersonic New Hampshire

The next morning came around far too quickly, even though I had eight hours' slumber. Progressing through my morning rituals, it suddenly occurred to me that I was experiencing the first hangover of my journey. What was worse, it was a red wine hangover. They are the worst and my maroon tongue was the evidence of the fine Chilean Shiraz that had done the damage. I didn't consider it a fine wine at the moment and in an attempt to shrug it off, I think I tried to rush my departure. I should have ejected myself from the social scene the night before at the same time as the blonde lady from Idaho. I wonder how her head was this morning, considering she consumed a few basketfuls of grapes? Instead I had continued to talk with the Harvard student and between us discuss the whys and wherefores of the American legal system. The American legal system! My normal bar talk consists of motorcycles and travel. Apparently my Harvard student barman friend had considered my views worthwhile and had suggested I visit his class to give a talk. What a compliment, he had obviously been drinking as well. Thanks, but no thanks. Maybe I should drink more red wine and become a professor. My hangover was confirmed when I uncharacteristically consumed a huge cooked breakfast from the buffet selection. So early in the morning was not my normal habit for gargantuan portions of calories. In quick time I was packed and propelling one of those trolleys with my panniers on board through the atrium and out to my bike. I was always so careful when preparing the bike to leave in the morning. Oil, tyres and fuel of course were checked the night before as normal, but morning checks included engine start to get the bike breathing. Then I would check my primary and secondary routes were in the GPS and cycling okay. I would also check that all route roads and town names were written on the lower screen, in an order I could read if the GPS failed as I had experienced way back. I always had a contingency and a contingency. Then it would be the panniers. The bike would be on the side stand for this and loading would take place in a strict sequence. I was particularly careful about checking pannier security and would double and treble check that they were attached and locked before moving off. My nightmare would be a heavy metal pannier detaching and saying hello with alacrity to the windscreen of a vehicle behind me. The ensuing circumstances would be unimaginable and litigation would undoubtedly follow me to my grave. My departure checks were extremely limited this morning, I banged the panniers on, started the bike and off, GPS warming up as I entered the highway. Yikes! This was so unlike me. Very quickly I was in extremely heavy traffic and became stationary as I mixed it with the Monday morning commuters. My only view of Massachusetts in the first few miles were the wheels of giant trucks either side of the rather vulnerable piece of space I was occupying on Interstate 495. Why had I rushed off? I didn't even get the opportunity to meet Richard, who had very kindly given me the cheap suite. My guilt had quickly subsided on that matter as the pretty check out girl had informed me he always had meetings on Monday mornings and would not be around. Thankfully by the time I crossed into New Hampshire, got off 495 and joined highway 3, the traffic had thinned out considerably and was moving freely. Whew, I felt much better now and albeit perfectly in control of my faculties with complete spatial awareness, I did not want to breathe on anyone for the next few hours. Especially a police officer. No, I think the bouquet of a Maipo Shiraz would not be appreciated so early in the morning and any recipient would not require a wine tasting before noon. Passing through Nashua and Manchester, it suddenly occurred to me this short 79-mile ride north to the New Hampshire capital also had other challenges. Not only was it overcast and cool, but raining very heavily. Spray from the traffic was building, but nowhere near as I had experienced in North Carolina back in February when the road was nearly diluted into liquid asphalt. No, today was manageable and quite enjoyable. The bike was again demonstrating its appetite for absolutely anything and the *sssssssss* and swish from the surface water admirably complemented the snarled note of the mighty boxer twin. Quite remarkably I had arrived in central Concord, checked into a motel and was cornering locals with Brit chat by 10.30 am. Almost a supersonic arrival into Concord. Tremendous!

The motel staff looked Chinese, which was a first. Through their glinting teeth and oriental smiles, the couple were only too happy to check me in so early and made rushed walkie-talkie transmissions to the housekeeping staff to ensure my room was ready. It was. We continued some chatter for a couple of minutes as I lounged over the reception desk and wiped the rain from my forehead. My conviviality and exuberance was not shared by the gaggle of bikers that were moping around the lobby. Their bikes were under the protection of the motel awning and they were obviously so concerned about rain versus chrome. Chrome, that's the giveaway: they were all HD riders in the area for a bikers' meet which had the potential of simply being washed out. This was the opportunity for some healthy banter and I went on the offensive immediately. I bellowed a mighty 'morning' their way which didn't get any response. Following that verbal volley, I added, 'Not good weather for you Harley guys, eh?' I was pointing to several of them outside who were polishing their chrome as the rain lashed down. This time I did get a response. 'Not good weather for any biker, how many miles have you done?' As quick as a flash I replied, '16,343.' I had noted my journey total as dismounting earlier. That was a little cocky, but it would test their sense of humour. As it happened, they didn't appear to have a sense of humour and they didn't respond. I left it there. I'd had some fun with some HD chapters here and there and did not want to tempt fate. Some of these guys had a lot of tattoos and ear rings and I didn't want to provoke them too much – but afraid of the rain, for heaven's sake you guys, get real or go and live in Arizona. In comparison to their relatively gleaming machines, my bike looked good with mud and dirt flecked around here and there. There may even be a Florida bug down there somewhere.

After my less than diplomatic exchange with the New Hampshire HD chapter who was obviously aquaphobic, the small and compact city centre of Concord beckoned. By the time I found the federal-style Capitol Building just off North Main Street, it had just about stopped raining. The interior of the Capitol was quiet with few folk around. Chatting to the gift shop attendant, I quickly learnt that city became state capital because of its central state location and efficient river transport provided by the wide, deep and navigable Merrimack River and canal systems, allowing connection as far away as Boston. Other than that, Concord became famous for furniture and granite mining. The latter industry providing the 'Granite State' nickname and the State Capitol is constructed from New Hampshire granite quarried in Concord. You cannot get any more local than that I guess. Two oil paintings caught my eye. One was of General John Adams Dix, where the inscription below says, '*If anyone attempts to haul down the American flag, shoot him on the spot.*' Now that's a decisive order and I am sure had much historical and colonial connection. Which gives me the opportunity to comment on the American and their flag today. Everywhere I have been and New Hampshire is state 37, I have seen national flags flying from home to restaurant to shopping mall to trailing behind a Harley Davidson. Everyone flies the Stars and Stripes. The flags vary in size from handkerchief size to tablecloth size to gargantuan affairs that you can wrap a battleship in. In the USA it appears the exception rather than the rule not to have a flag flying. The other painting of note brought my historical infusion a little more up to date. Standing proud in rather a Flash Gordon-looking space suit of the 1950s is astronaut Alan B Shepard of the United States Navy, who was born in East Derry, New Hampshire. Shepard became the first American in space in 1961, piloting the Freedom 7 spacecraft to an altitude of 116 miles. Before launch, it is reported that Shepard said to himself, 'Don't fuck up Shepard', which he later said was a misquote. This phrase later became known as the 'Shepard's Prayer'. I have used the 'Shepard's Prayer', or rather the 'Gilroy Prayer', frequently throughout my life and this journey and I had absolutely no idea it was shared by an astronaut when I was two. Before leaving the building, I pinned down Walter Sword, the combined security and information guy at the main door. I asked him his opinion on the American and the flag issue. General Dix's quote had got me going. Walter couldn't really give any comment other than saying 'it's just the way we are'. Walter turned out to be an interesting type and claimed to have Scottish heritage. Walter has produced nine children, which in turn have produced 26 grand children and two great-grandchildren. My word, I am not surprised he escapes to the relative sanctuary of the State Capitol on weekdays. A former US Marine, boat builder and truck driver, Walter had been around the block a bit and was trying to reckon up if he had been to all the states in his working and travelling life. I left him undecided.

Before searching out lunch, I descended below street level into a brightly lit barbershop. It was time for a trim and barbers tend to be fair game for a bit of chat. What else have they got to do? It was one of those places I would call a typical gents' barbershop. Black and white tiled floor, rigid chairs that could pass for a dentist's or God forbid an executioner's electric chair and lines of glinting razors. I was greeted by the young owner, who thankfully had less hair than me. My usual trim only took a few minutes after which we talked about the New England Patriots football team. It was quite difficult to compare European football with American football. Of course, football as we know it in Europe is called soccer in the USA. That wasn't controversial, but when I broached the subject of all that padding and protection American footballers wear, the conversation did heat up a bit, including a few barbed comments from the guy in the next chair. I am glad my hair job was done by then and I humorously suggested they ought to research the game of rugby before my next visit, after which we could continue our debate. It turned out to be a fun and maybe getting slightly past fun. Over lunch I became the centre of attraction for a couple of kids belonging to a friendly mum. The boy was called Liam and his younger sibling was securely harnessed into his or her stroller prior to leaving the restaurant. I recall that Liam had bright red or ginger hair and without prompting, his Mum firmly added that they were all from Irish heritage. These New Hampshire folk certainly liked broadcasting their roots to any available European. Talking of the heritage thing, the town or city did have quite a European feel. The main street could just about pass for an English market town like Marlborough or Hungerford with a bit of Devizes thrown in – maybe – so we had some connection. A ride around the now dry streets of the compact New Hampshire capital, concluded my relatively brief but enjoyable afternoon. I took the backstreets back towards the motel, as was always a habit of mine in new towns during daylight. It was always good to try and get just a little deeper under the skin of a place, rather than remaining along the main drag and associated historical areas. Concord was no different to anywhere else. A lot of houses in the neighbourhoods around Clinton, Downing, Monroe and Fayette Streets were flying the Stars and Stripes. Arriving back at the motel, the HD crowd from the morning was still on site. They were still swaggering around their bikes, polishing chrome and making sure their flag was flying!

Chapter 59

Made it into Maine!

It was another cool and overcast day as I left New Hampshire northbound on rural route 202. Very quickly I was clear of Concord and into very green and forested countryside and crossing the state line into Maine. I had made it into Maine! The top right hand corner of the USA and the end of this particular sector. North East gridlock was coming to an end. As if made to order, once in Maine, which is aptly called the Pine Tree State, it was mile after mile of forests, lakes, float planes bobbing on choppy waters and neat restaurants. I could almost smell the lobster and seafood. My incursion into Maine was a mere thrust into the capital of Augusta. I wouldn't have the time or opportunity to explore the majestic extent of the jagged and rocky Atlantic coastline and mountain ranges in the north towards the border with New Brunswick. The scenery that was thrust upon me was certainly transmitting a feeling of isolation, and one of maritime isolation. I have had similar feelings elsewhere around the globe and occasionally I got just the hint of the Falkland Islands when seeing the deep inlets and rocky landscapes. 202 took me through many small towns including Sanford, Gorham, Gray and Auburn. Occasionally the rural and isolated feel was lost, as the busy Interstate 95 snaked by in close proximity and reminded me of the modern day and masses of traffic. All this traffic was coming in and out of this quite beautiful state as well. The forests and lakes were appearing so pristine and virgin-looking it was almost a disgusting introduction to include the traffic.

My rural treat was spoilt and came to end rather quickly around lunchtime as I completed the 140 miles from Concord and rolled into Augusta. Excellent, sector complete and quite a milestone. All that remained was the ride across the top of the country to complete the lower 48. Then of course there was Alaska to reach. I think my euphoria of completing this sector probably made up for the quite ordinary state capital city of Augusta. There is not an awful lot to get excited about, other than it is the most eastern state capital in the USA. After the usual history of colonial disputes and after Maine joined the Union in 1820, Augusta developed into a mill and lumber town. Today, as with a lot of State Capital cities, it's the government that generates a lot of business. The imposing Greek Revival State House with tall tower and dome, houses all the government types. It's another domed Capitol Building, which I have to admit looks extremely impressive on the outside. Alas, it has a rather sterile feeling on the inside, probably caused by extensive refurbishment and redecoration. It didn't seem to have a State Capitol feel at all and lacked the colour and depth of history I had experienced in several of the previous 37. The museum across the street stole the show with its fine collection of Maine historical and modern day exhibits. Before leaving the Capitol area, a stroll around the park close by was in order. The best views of the State House were seen from the park, with an avenue of deciduous trees forming a natural access to the pillared eastern aspect of the building. Through the trees, a path to the steps and main door was flanked by many national flags. I counted 15 Stars and Stripes flying. It gave an almost summer fete feeling. Why not just one national flag alongside the state flag?

After a riverside ride south to Hallowell, I had exhausted the delights of Augusta and its environs. Like many state capitals, not a lot really happens about town other than politics. I must remember that Maine is undoubtedly a state to spend several weeks in and explore the delights of the great outdoors. On the way back to the motel, I was deciding what to do with the rest of the afternoon and in an attempt to fill half an hour or so, I pulled off Western Avenue and took Airport Road up the hill to Augusta State Airport. It was out of curiosity really; everywhere seems to have an airport in the USA and sometimes I question if there are enough customers to make them viable, especially a small place like Augusta. A quick look in the very small terminal building revealed that the airport is served by mainly one national carrier flying twin prop Beech commuter aircraft. I had arrived between flights and a couple of the local pilots looked to be helping out with check in and other terminal duties. They were wearing gold bars on their shoulders, so I guessed they were pilots. My assumption proved to be correct after engaging in conversation with a very young pilot who eagerly told me he was a captain at the age of 23. That is some achievement. He was originally from England, but had lived in the USA for most of his life. Our conversation got on to the national economy rather than politics for a change and it was probably my first realisation that the USA was experiencing extreme fiscal difficulties. This was having a domino effect around many global markets. The world was a struggling economy and it was something I had never really given any thought as I progressed on my journey. I had other priorities. Undoubtedly I would be returning to an economically depressed UK. That made for something to look forward to! The depressed economy here in the USA was having a huge dampening effect on the airline business. Aviation normally suffers first in such climates and the young pilot reflected that things were certainly not rosy at the moment. Several companies had instigated massive staff lay-offs or enforced furloughs I think they are called. Unpaid leave of absence basically. Some of the established low-cost, no-frills airlines with a robust business model were still buoyant, but several major airlines with hundreds of airliners and thousands of staff were teetering on the brink of bankruptcy and applying for chapter 11 protection. He mentioned he would like to pursue his career onto larger aircraft, but the big boys were just not recruiting and for the moment his aspirations were on hold. An articulate and concise appraisal from a well-informed young man. It all made for depressing times and being such a grey and dismal day, it would be so easy to go back to my motel room and lock the door and sit in front of the TV for the rest of the day. But no, I had completed 16,500 miles on this ride, just finished another journey sector and a celebration was in order. Maine lobster was in order.

As anticipated, I had traversed the 10 states in the north east quite quickly. The states are quite small and journeys short. I had been arriving at my destination by lunchtime most days which was allowing a lot of exploration and down time. Without knowing it I was re-energising my body in readiness for the vast distances across the top of the country and into Canada and then Alaska. On reflection, I think the name of this sector, 'North East Gridlock', has been justified. The map of the north east is dominated by the sprawling and sometimes overlapping metropolitan areas of Washington DC, Baltimore, Newark, Philadelphia, New York and finally Boston. There is indeed a lot of asphalt, brick, concrete and metal down there. Over the last few weeks, I have been in it, on it and over it, so to speak. You have to pick your time to travel and even then you cannot be guaranteed movement. My experiences on the Washington DC beltway immediately come to mind. I agree that my title for this sector may be unfair to the wide open areas, like upstate New York and Maine where I am at the moment. However, on reflection, I think a fair title. The whole area has a huge population density in comparison to other parts of the country. I even got caught up in extremely heavy traffic moving through Cape Cod, Massachusetts on a Saturday morning. It was a hot weekend and one and all were off to the beach at the same time. I was nevertheless surprised with the traffic mass in what is a relatively isolated part of that state. I have now gone firm of my objective to do the lower 48 whilst remaining in the lower 48. Having studied the map carefully and as a bit of a shortcut, I do have the option to dive into Ontario and go north of Lakes Ontario and Lake Erie and then back into the USA around Michigan. However, I am going to stay south of these lakes and remain stateside, which I think is an appropriate objective for the ride. I will see enough of Canada riding through British Columbia for Juneau-Alaska later.

From Maine, 'Across the Top' starts in Montpelier-Vermont. Moving west I shall take the ferry across Lake Champlain and enter the Adirondack Park in the Lake Placid area. Thereafter, my route will track the southern shores of Lakes Ontario and Erie, before turning north into Michigan for Lansing. Grand Rapids will lead me to Muskegon for the Lake Michigan ferry crossing to Milwaukee and onwards to Madison.

Then it's a straight line to the metro monster of Minneapolis-St Paul. This is quite an important geographical point, as west of the twin cities the states start to get damn big again. The Dakotas are next and then Montana, where I will make a direct track for Glacier National Park in the North West part of the state. Leaving Glacier heading south east, my route will pass through Missoula for Helena and then further south east to enter the north west corner of Wyoming for Yellowstone and Teton National Parks. This puts me in a great position for Boise-Idaho and then further west into Oregon, before turning north into Washington State to complete the lower 48. There are fewer state capitals to pass through on this sector, but greater distances.

Part Seven – Across the Top

Augusta-Maine to Olympia-Washington State

5,279 miles

Across the Top - Augusta ME to Olympia WA

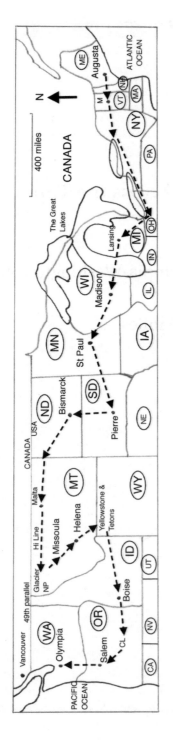

Key:

M-Montpelier
CL-Crater Lake

DATE	START	FINISH	MILEAGE	CUMULATIVE	COMMENTS
18 June	Augusta ME	**Montpelier VT (39)**	202	16698	Scenic route 27 & 2
19 June	Montpelier VT	Sackets Harbor NY	219	16917	Lake Champlain Ferry/route 3 west
20 June	Sackets Harbour NY	Erie PA	315	17232	Lake Ontario & Erie- Shore Scenic Highway
21 Jun	Erie PA	**Lansing MI (40)**	330	17562	Multi Interstate
22 Jun	Lansing MI	Lansing MI	45	17607	Local & city & Potterville
23 Jun	Lansing MI	Muskegon MI	100	17707	To Ferry Port for Lake Michigan crossing.
23 Jun	Milwaukee WI	Huntley IL	100	17807	Various highways
24 Jun	Huntley WI	**Madison WI (41)**	105	17912	County roads & Interstate
25 Jun	Madison WI	Appleton WI	105	18017	151
26 Jun	Appleton WI	De Pere WI	25	18042	**18K service & new tyres @ NICK's BMW De Pere WI**
26 Jun	De Pere WI	Appleton WI	25	18067	
27 Jun	Appleton WI	**St Paul MN (42)**	288	18355	Route 10
27 Jun	St Paul MN	Minneapolis MN	7	18362	University Blvd
28 Jun	Minneapolis MN	Minneapolis MN	1	18363	Fuel & Beer run-city
29 Jun	Minneapolis MN	**Pierre SD (43)**	402	18765	169/99/14
June Total				**4312**	
1 Jul	Pierre SD	**Bismarck ND (44)**	207	18972	83
2 Jul	Bismarck ND	Malta MT	419	19391	I-94/200S/200/ 24/2
3 Jul	Malta MT	St Mary MT	282	19676	2/89
4 Jul	St Mary MT	Missoula MT	210	19886	2/93 VIA Glacier National Park
5 Jul	Missoula MT	**Helena MT (45)**	114	20000	I-90 & 12
5 Jul	Helena MT	Helena MT	20	20020	City & Local
6 Jul	Helena MT	Gardiner MT	180	20200	12/89
6 Jul	Gardiner MT	Mammoth Hot Springs WY	7	20207	Yellowstone Visitors Centre & local area recce
6 Jul	Mammoth Hot Springs WY	Gardiner MT	7	20214	
7 Jul	Gardiner MT	Jackson Hole WY	165	20379	237/191/22 via Yellowstone & Teton Parks

DATE	START	FINISH	MILEAGE	CUMULATIVE	COMMENTS
8 Jul	Jackson Hole WY	**Boise ID (46)**	348	20727	22/33/31/26/20/ I-84 Via Craters of the Moon NP
11 Jul	Boise ID	Chemult OR	374	21101	20
12 Jul	Chemult OR	Yachats OR	335	21436	Via Crater Lake NP &101 Oregon Pacific Highway
13 Jul	Yachats OR	**Salem OR (47)**	106	21542	101/22
13 Jul	Salem OR	McMinnville OR	27	21569	County roads
13 Jul	McMinnville OR	Salem OR	27	21596	County roads
15 Jul	Salem OR	**Olympia WA (48)**	168	21764	I-5
16 Jul	Olympia WA	Fife WA	33	21797	**Oil & Filter change & safety check @**
16 Jul	Fife WA	Olympia WA	33	21830	**South Side BMW Fife WA**
18 Jul	Olympia WA	Mt Rainier WA	71	21901	County Roads to
18 Jul	Mt Rainier WA	Olympia WA	71	21972	View Mt Rainier
19 Jul	Olympia WA	Lynden WA	203	22175	Scenic coastal ride

Chapter 60

Verdant Vermont

I felt a little guilty leaving Maine after only one day. Everyone talks about Maine when you get talking about the USA, especially Europeans. Have you been to Maine? Did you see much of the coastline? Did you go hiking and fishing? Did you take a float plane ride and of course did you sample Maine clams and lobsters? It has quite a reputation and certainly stands out from the states further to the south in the north east of the country that are overrun with urban monsters. I think my satisfaction of starting the final sector of my journey in the lower 48 made up for any geographical anxieties. It was pouring with rain as I manoeuvred through the morning traffic and picked out route 27 northbound. The temperature was only forecast to peak at 65F which was mild to say the least. 65F! What a contrast to the sizzling and ridiculously humid 90s and 100s I had experienced for most of the month. That all seemed a long time ago now and today I could smell real Maine weather. By the time I passed Long Pond on my left and Great Pond on my right, the rain had nearly stopped and the heat from the morning sun was piercing and breaking up the stratus revealing lots of blue bits. It was going to a nice day I think, although heavy showers were forecast all long my route west into Vermont. The next couple of days I would be doing a bit of state-hopping as I progressed west. After Maine, it would be New Hampshire – *been there already* – then Vermont – *new state*, then New York State

– seen some of that – then very briefly into Pennsylvania again – *damn big state–* then across the top of Ohio, before going around the corner into the 'hands-up' state of Michigan. Very soon I would be able to look over my left shoulder and imagine my easterly trail across the middle of the country back in May. It was now mid-June and I had six weeks to get across to Washington State and exit the USA into British Columbia. I should be okay. What is for sure in the next couple of weeks is the variation of the country I will be encountering. I will be leaving New England and getting back into the mid-west around the Great Lakes where the burgeoning cities of Detroit and Chicago account for much economic contribution to this mammoth nation.

Joining route 27, I was now making mainly a westerly course and this road would lead all the way into Montpelier. It would be a nice gentle ride through the countryside, with views of Mount Washington to the south if the low cloud permitted. I was passing through some fantastic-looking little towns on the route. Livermore Falls, Canton, Dixfield and Rumford in Maine. Wooden-slatted homes and shops lined the main streets, stores piled high with provisions and accessories on racks outside and all busy with cars and locals going about their morning routines. Then into that northern sliver of New Hampshire, Shelburne, Gorham and Lancaster, before crossing the border into Vermont. These little places seemed to have a lot of character and couldn't really be anywhere else in the USA other than the extreme north, within just an hour or so of Canadian territory. Some of the larger towns looked to have a bit of industry as well, evidenced by tall smoking chimneys next to a fast-flowing river. However, not all the towns portrayed a postcard image. I can't recall the name of the place, but the highway snaked through one town and passed through a small neighbourhood that I can only describe as poverty stricken. Broken windows, litter strewn around and wrecked cars. These images were always a great leveller and reminded me not everyone has an opulent life in this country. I cannot remember which state – it was on route 27, as I passed through the northern bits of three – but I encountered a mammoth chunk of road construction where the asphalt had been removed for what seemed about 10 miles. The surface was simply rubble and mud, awaiting a new hardtop I hope.

The bike was in its element, but cars and trucks were struggling on the wet and slippery surface caused by the morning's heavy showers. I was first in the line at one set of traffic lights through this road construction and got chatting to the 'stop-go' sign man. He was dressed for the rain in a long yellow coat that would also be useful on a fishing trawler. He carried a radio which crackled into undecipherable tones from time to time. I was listening carefully for the 'go' word which didn't appear to be imminent looking at the opposing traffic. The sign man told me he did this for a nine-hour shift for $9 an hour. That was his working day, with very few breaks and he certainly relied upon idle chatter with passing motorists to alleviate the boredom. He was also a man with attitude and continued to tell me that he considered himself poor. *'Anyone earning under $30,000 a year in this country is poor and how will the old people get through the winter? It is very extreme in this part of the USA you know. We are very close to the Canadian border and winters are harsh. It's all George Bush's fault that the country is in this struggling position. Maybe you don't see it being on your great journey, but we are in a hell of a mess and looking forward to the next President.'* Good heavens, this guy let me have it with both barrels! Normally I get a bit of idle chatter from road teams but not an oration on the nation's economy. Good on him and he shook my gloved hand as I pulled away through the earth-moving trucks and scrapers.

I wish I had got that stop light guy's name, but I never thought of it at the time. Another great leveller this morning and it was good to see the roots of this country. I was getting the opportunity to see the real America with relative ease on such an expedition. It was approaching lunchtime and my priority was a roadside cafe in the near future. I had left Maine and I think I was still in New Hampshire and had not yet crossed into Vermont. It was a bit confusing as to where exactly the state boundaries were. I should look out for the big *'welcome to...'* signs. I was getting glimpses of the White Mountains to the south, however the showers and low cloud were still bubbling up and preventing unrestricted views. Alas, the highest mountain in the north east USA, Mount Washington, was totally obscured. The mountain peaks at 6,288 feet. I was still in New Hampshire and found lunch at Lowe's Store, quite close to where you would normally be able to see the White Mountains and maybe just Mount Washington. Doubling as a garage with fuel and light maintenance, Lowe's Store hadn't changed since the 1960s and still retains an abundance of character. The lady at the counter and her excited Labrador were only too enthusiastic to greet strangers. By the looks of the accumulated population, the store was also a meeting place. My coffee was dispensed from a relic of a machine which had large knobs and buttons and nothing electronic. It worked and the coffee was great! The boss appeared briefly from the adjoining workshop and added that the place was available for sale if I was interested. I shared a few words and laughs with them and then continued west on highway 2, through Lancaster, crossing into Vermont and onwards to the smallest state capital in the country.

Arriving at my first-choice motel, I was rather glad I always had a second and third choice up my sleeve. It looked a sad and tired place and when I eventually got the attention of someone, I immediately decided to move on. I felt sorry for the guy who emerged from somewhere in the accommodation area. Walking with extreme difficulty and looking if he was still recovering from a night on the town, I was greeted with, 'You just arrived in town?' Thank you for stating the obvious I thought. He then uttered, 'You new in town?' This was almost a mini interrogation and not the normal greeting at a place where I may part with money. Thankfully he added, 'Anyway, check in is at five.' Check in at five! It was already four; I wanted to unload, rest my bones and look for a decent steak. 'Thank you and good afternoon,' I added and rode off into the city centre to find a second choice. Crossing the small river on Main Street, I saw 'HOTEL' written on a bricked building, which was obviously the rear of the facility. Why not, it would be a change from a motel. I headed for there and turning into Theodore Roosevelt Street, found the front of the building which turned out to be the Capitol Plaza Hotel. A rather grand name and a rather grand-looking building. However, it was in the middle of the town, with the Capitol Building and a museum across the street. Shall I, shan't I? I did and with a few persuasive words negotiated a room with a view of my bike parking area, cheaper than that motel! The hotel was full of business and conference-type people. If they were all here, who was running the city and the state of Vermont this afternoon? It's not a big place. It won't surprise anyone to discover that Montpelier was named after the French city of Montpellier. That was received well as the French gave a helping hand in the local area during the American Revolution. The village grew as a trading and manufacturing centre. With the fast-flowing river and falls, industries developed and produced lumber, flour and furniture. Today, government and of course tourism in this very green state are the main businesses. With a population today of under 10,000, Montpelier is the smallest capital in the country. Nearby Burlington on Lake Champlain is a bigger urban brother. Close to Montpelier is the city, or in my definition another small town, called Barre. Montpelier and Barre form a local micropolitan area. Very micropolitan, which the locals refer to as the 'twin cities'! Now there are twin cities and twin cities in the USA!

It was extremely unique walking literally two minutes from my place of residence to the State Capitol. It was just across the road and behind the Capitol looked like wooded open countryside on the northern boundary of this petite city. It was Hubbard Park and yes, there is no city beyond that. What a remarkable place. With impressive summer flowers in bloom at the front and woods behind, a feeling of a garden city capital was broadcasting a most agreeable atmosphere. The Greek revival State House has a drum tower capped with a gold-leafed dome supporting a statue of Ceres, the mythological goddess of agriculture. She stands at 136 feet, commanding one of the few elevated views in the city. I was the only visitor in the small building and the guide mentioned he was closing up very soon. Could I make it a quick visit please? That was not a problem and I quickly navigated around the halls and corridors. Now this place was oozing history and State Capitol atmosphere that I didn't detect back in Augusta. Maybe it was the compact size, the fine art, wooden floors and creaky stairs that gave this historical feeling. It was after 5.30 pm when I emerged back into the June sunshine. The showers had gone east leaving a very warm end to the day. The Capitol gardens had attracted a few families and kids playing around here and there. A couple of young girls, probably only 10 or 11, were in front of the building doing handstands on the grass next to a couple of historical cannons. They confidently asked where I was from and what I was doing and would I take their photograph. They were on the first day of their summer school break and looking forward to the weeks ahead. I was always careful about taking photographs of people, especially kids and would always seek consent. These two were into posing for the camera by the looks of it and keen to tell their parents of a meeting with the English journeyman. An interesting meeting with some junior Americans. The tree-lined high street, also had a summer and fete-like feeling. Tall, square, red-bricked buildings occupied the compact town centre, with office buildings, shops and a smattering of restaurants plying their trades. But it was all so small and extremely compact and with the unique setting of the State Capitol, the city almost had a dolls' house feel. It took less than half an hour to walk around the town. This condensed feeling continued into the evening. I had dinner in the buzzing Plaza bar and, on an elevated track going around the bar, there was a model railway! A fitting end to my visit to the compact and attractive Vermont Capital city.

Chapter 61

Across the Adirondacks

I remember Walter Crump's geographical advice very clearly. We had been pouring over an old map of New York State. The map was spread out on the front of his truck in his gravelled driveway. I remember the scene as if it was yesterday; It was only 10 days ago. 'When you get to Montpelier in Vermont and that city won't delay you that much, head for Burlington and jump on the ferry across Lake Champlain. That will put you back in New York State and you can get across the Adirondack Park in a day easily, drop down into the finger lake area if you have time and then you will be in an excellent position for the Great Lakes. The small town of Sackets Harbor on Lake Ontario may interest you for a stopover.'

The next morning a gaggle of Canadian bikers were heading off just before me. We exchanged notes for a few moments and obviously they were full of Canadian geographical advice for a future trip. I kept forgetting how close I was to Canada, less than a hundred miles and across this sector I would see and meet more of the Canadian population. So, it was up and off on Walter's suggested route. The run down to the ferry terminal in Burlington was only 30 minutes. In short time, I had paid for my ticket, parked my bike and warming up over coffee. It was still quite early and the overcast and gloomy weather with moisture hanging in the air was making it feel quite cool. Lake Champlain looked grey, choppy and very cold. It was a pity it wasn't a blue morning. The ferry turned up on time. I was joined on board Adirondack-1913 by two cars and two other bikes. It wasn't anywhere near a full vehicle load and with only a few foot passengers we all had a lot of space. The bikers, a couple and a solo rider, were from Canada which didn't surprise me. They were heading west through the park and then north into Canada and back to work tomorrow. We decided to ride along together and break for lunch somewhere. In the middle of the lake, we crossed back into New York State. I felt I had seen quite a lot of this state when I considered I had already been through the Catskills and the capital Albany, before veering off east to take in the collection of states in the extreme top right of the country. I think I had optimised that part of my zig-zag quite well and passing through some states, especially big ones, a couple of times was inevitable. The rain had just about stopped when we all disembarked at Port Kent. We rode a westerly slice through towns of Lake Placid, Saranac Lake and Tupper Lake and a couple of other smaller places I had written down on my screen. It was highway 3 all the way. Progressing west, blue sky with quite bright sun was beating down and the whole complexion of the lakes and forests changed in a flash. The smell of summer rain, intermingled with a hint of pine, got into my helmet and filled my nostrils. 'The lands now or hereafter constituting the Forest Preserve shall be forever kept as wild forest lands,' is a tourist motto of the Adirondacks and with hundreds of lakes, thousands of miles of trails and majestic high mountains, it is a haven for the outdoor pursuit folks. It is the largest area in New York State that doesn't have a city. It is a stunning area and is the largest park in the contiguous United States. It's about the size of Vermont that I have just left, or greater in size than Yellowstone, the Everglades, Glacier and Grand Canyon National Parks all combined. That's quite some backyard and in the winter months, the greens and blue vistas of pine forests and deep lakes are replaced by a frosty landscape of snow and ice. That's when resorts like Lake Placid become extremely active and host the many alpine sports enthusiasts that congregate in the park. In contrast, in June it was relatively quiet and extremely tranquil. Riding conditions were superb. Lake Placid, well known for hosting the 1932 and 1980 Winter Olympics, seemed dead and at odds without snow and crowds of folk dressed in brightly coloured ski kit. The tall Olympic ski jumps looked completely out of place in the summer views and resembled abandoned rocket launching silos from a bygone era. We didn't stop in Lake Placid, or Saranac Lake, but pressed on to the small town on Tupper Lake. It was a good choice, however all the towns and villages seen so far looked as equally attractive. Most are on a lakeside with a smart collection of shops and restaurants in the centre. We chose a lakeside diner and my new Canadian biker friends bought me lunch. Although I had not yet done 200 miles since leaving Montpelier, I had the feeling of having made significant progress west and had covered a lot of ground. Maybe it was the contrast of scenery, from the quick run through green Vermont to Burlington, an hour on the ferry and now, well into this monster of an afforested park, studded with deep lakes. After lunch, the Canadian trio headed north on highway 56 towards the border and onwards to Montreal, or was it Toronto, I cannot remember. I continued west on 3, passing Cranberry Lake, Star Lake and exiting the park at East Pitcairn. The splendour of the Adirondacks abruptly came to an end. The scenery changed dramatically and roadside views were reduced to gorse bushes, scrubland and small copses. I had decided to miss the finger lakes area and press on to Sackets Harbor as Walter had suggested. After picking my way through the centre of Watertown I found the small village on the north east shores of Lake Ontario. My first encounter with the Great Lakes.

After riding through busy Watertown, my day was quickly returned to serenity by riding around this beautiful lakeside village. The heart of the village has a well-preserved collection of 19th century buildings. In the natural harbour, yachts and boatyards were aplenty. Traffic was non-existent and at first I felt guilty riding my noisy machine past lines of quiet and splendid-looking homes bordered by immaculate gardens. Further on, I passed the village green where a school sports event was in progress. It all seemed so peaceful and undoubtedly this would be the sort of place God would choose to live. I think God would also choose to live in one of those fine houses on the water front in Charleston, South Carolina! He could have a weekend home and a weekday home. Whatever, God had failed to provide me with a motel in Sackets Harbor and after covering the neat streets a couple of times, I saw plenty of places to eat and drink, lots of pretty gift and craft shops, but nowhere to rest my head. Not even any bed and breakfast signs anywhere. A last I spotted the Ontario Place Hotel. It was getting towards cocktail hour and I wonder if they had a spare cot for the evening? I was greeted by David Moxon the General Manager and was ushered into a roomy and comfortable lobby. A room was available and in short time I had parked up immediately outside the hotel in pole position and established myself in a comfortable room. David was full of conversation and questions about my journey and was extremely enthusiastic to provide a guided tour of the village. A tour of the village, what else is there to see? I would be surprised. 30 minutes later, David was waiting at the entrance to the hotel in one of those four-wheeled golf buggies primed and ready to go. Climbing aboard, I felt rather like a golfer at the Masters or a White House Presidential guest. This was VIP treatment. I was given a comprehensive overview of Sackets Harbor by an enthusiastic guide. 'This happened here, this happened here and then this. These are the original buildings and plans are to convert into a hotel if permissions and monies are available.' David continued, 'We want this place to be an exclusive resort for the sort of clientele who will appreciate such a beautiful place. It's an ideal weekend break location you know – fit for God.' He said it, not me – I wonder if David was also a Gemini and we had aligned thoughts? He wasn't wrong about Sackets Harbor; I was impressed and not only was given a snapshot of the future, but also the past. Further research revealed that Sackets Harbor holds a significant historical background. Quite surprising for such a small place. In 1812 and 1813, the harbour was the site of two battles where shore batteries repulsed marauding British Ships. The Americans convincingly were the victors during these heated conflicts. Walking around later, I viewed the battle areas and many historical information signs. I wonder what the many ghosts and spirits from past skirmishes would think of my Union Flags on the streets today? Original military buildings, including barracks at Navy Point, are still standing and it was these that David mentioned are under scrutiny for potential renovation and return to life. Well done Walter, good advice – New York State is a fine piece of the USA.

Chapter 62

Great Lakes Seaway Trail

A huge sign and map of the Great Lakes Seaway Trail caught my attention the next morning and helped plan my day. I would follow this route and skirt the southern shores of Lakes Ontario and Erie. My next capital city was Lansing-Michigan, some 650 miles west. That's quite a hike and I am not in New England now that's for sure. Michigan, that's the state that is in the middle of the Great Lakes. Huron to the east and Michigan to the west, with just a bit of Erie to the south west. I didn't fancy a 600-mile day and decided to break the journey to Lansing somewhere mid-point around the city of Erie. That should work and actually it didn't look far on the map. Avoiding the Niagara Falls and Buffalo area, I would try and follow the shore of the lakes as much as possible.

This Seaway Trail is a total of 518 miles long and designated a National Scenic Byway. The west end is on the Ohio/Pennsylvania border just to the west of the city of Erie. The east end is on the USA/Canadian border near Massena-New York State. Leaving Sackets Harbor, I was already established on the trail, being downstream or downlake to the south west of Massena. The route is mainly in New York State, which is a lot bigger than I thought and, then right at the end, is that little portion of Pennsylvania that abuts Lake Erie. It's like a small peninsula and not a panhandle! I am sure Texans and Oklahomans would have something to say if it was called a panhandle. Passing through Oswega and Sodus, I was able to keep Lake Ontario in sight. It was an overcast and windy start to the day and the Lake could really have been an ocean. Ontario is one of the smaller of the Great Lakes, but it was still impossible to see Canada across the 50 miles of lake. There is a lot of water out there. Continuing west, I skirted through the north of Rochester. If I had continued in this direction I would reach Niagara Falls in short time, and I had to decide when to cut off to the south for the Buffalo area. I stayed on Lake Road, as it is called on this bit, as far west as Wilson and then cut due south through South Wilson, North Ridge and then I had no option. It had to be around the Buffalo eastern Interstate to get further south. Rather like an orbital, Interstate 290 got me clockwise around to the south of the urban sprawl, after which it connected with Interstate 190. 190 led to Lackawanna and very soon I was back on the waterside, this time of Lake Erie and following highway 5 on the shore. By lunchtime, the grey sky had turned to blue, but accompanied by an extremely brisk wind. Waves were forming on the lake, which now unmistakably could be the ocean. Before Buffalo was completely out of sight, I pulled off the highway and rode down to a beach area. The car park was deserted and only a few folks were out and about walking dogs in the surf. I think it was around Pinehurst or Highland at the eastern and narrow end of the lake as I could easily see the Canadian shore to the north. Towering cumulus nimbus clouds were forming and dominated the skyline, along with the high rise of Buffalo and menacing-looking wind turbines. The turbines were hard at work and making full use of the strong wind. Looking west the weather continued to look clear and blue. Highway 5 took me the remainder of the way through New York State, passing Angola, Silver Creek and Dunkirk. All these places looked quite idyllic with yachts and fishing boats moored close to homes. The highway was mysteriously and quite eerily quiet. It was mid-week and maybe this shore route gets more use at weekends? Interstate 90 parallels the highway and the lake. I guess a lot of traffic was on that. At Freeport I crossed the state line and was in the top left stub of Pennsylvania. The Keystone State is large and has a lot to offer. My visits are limited to the Philadelphia environs and Harrisburg. The remaining countryside I am sure is worth exploring, not forgetting the industrial city of Pittsburgh which lies less than 200 miles south of Erie where I had just arrived. Erie was simply a pit stop and nothing else. Lansing was quickly coming into focus. I made do with a normal-choice traveller's motel slightly out of town. I think I had been spoilt the last couple of nights staying in nice establishments in Montpelier and Sackets Harbor. The motel I chose was perfectly okay, but functional, a traveller's stop. The noise of people and a band warming up intrigued me. Where was it coming from? It wasn't the TV in an adjoining room. I soon tracked it down and at the end of the car park found a fantastic bar grill. It was early on a Friday night and already the place was absolutely bouncing. When I prised myself into the busy bar, it was obvious the rowdy population were not travellers. They were locals and this was a Friday evening hang out bar without a doubt. The band quickly set up and played 1980s covers for a couple of sessions. It had turned out quite a long haul today and not a quick lakeside jaunt as the tourist sign had suggested back in Sackets Harbor. These are big lakes and getting down here by lunchtime was a complete oversight. It had taken most of the day to do the 320 miles from Sackets Harbor-New York State to Erie-Pennsylvania following the Seaway Trail.

Chapter 63

Gizzard City in the 'Hands-up' State!

The last serious thing I did in Pennsylvania was check the weather for the next day. My route would take me west along the shores of Lake Erie, almost immediately crossing into Ohio and then around the corner into Michigan. It was another one of those trips that didn't look far on the map, which was misleading bearing in mind the size of the Great Lakes. It was a good 300 miles and probably quite a bit more by the time I found Lansing. The forecast was for a hot and humid day, with aggressive thunderstorms developing all around the Great Lakes area. The cool relief of the last couple of days had gone. Tornado activity was even mentioned further west in the Dakotas. Thankfully that was out of my area, however thunderstorms and heavy rain were enough to contend with. Earlier on in the trip, this sort of weather would have kept me off the road for a day. However, the forecast was the same for several days and it was simply a case of going for it and if it gets dangerous, then pull over and sit out the squall and get drenched. Ever-conscious of the forecast, I left Erie very early in the morning and crossed into Ohio before 8 am. It was a humid and grey start to the day, with only hints of blue sky stained with storm clouds. It wasn't a day for en-route sightseeing, so I decided to take the Interstate all the way to Lansing. Hence navigation was extremely easy following I-90 west, through Cleveland and Toledo and picking up I-69 north bound into Michigan. It is still alarming, if not a little exciting to be making progress at Interstate speeds through a city centre with the high-rise buildings extremely close by. Cleveland was another perfect example of this unique feeling, where I could almost reach out and touch the downtown buildings. Saturday morning traffic was flowing rapidly and again, it's that sense of speed whilst passing through the high-rise that is extremely unique, especially on a bike. Advancement through Cleveland was a perfect example of an Interstate charging through the guts of the city. Passing through the downtown, the city airport and Cleveland Browns stadium almost appear to be sitting in Lake Erie. Looking north across the water, the Canadian shore is 50 miles away and Detroit 90 miles to the north west. Once west of Toledo, after having dominated my northerly views for a day or so, I left Lake Erie behind. From Buffalo back in New York State, I had been following the southern shore for over 250 miles. Before turning north into the 'hands-up' state, I just clipped the north east corner of Indiana which did surprise me, I hadn't expected to see Indiana again, even though it was for a mere five miles or so. The 'hands-up' state, it's another shape thing. If you look at the outline of Michigan, it does look like a gloved hand pointing north with the thumb on the right. It's almost a hand wearing a mitten. So it's 'hands up' to Michigan and as already experienced, 'hands down' to Illinois! When you consider how close Michigan is to the Great Lakes, it is not a surprise to hear that a state resident is never more than six miles from a natural water source, or more than 85 miles from a Great Lakes coastline. Additionally, the state has thousands of inland lakes and the boundary of the state extends north and west of the mitten. Needless to say, there are a lot of recreational boat owners around. Thankfully, the lakes didn't get a top up from the heavens on my day of arrival into the state. The thunderstorms had been lurking everywhere on the horizon and thumping around quite close to my route, but quite remarkably I had stayed dry. I was lucky and felt as if I had been in a protective cone from above that followed my 330 miles. I was being watched over. The day had gone bright and dark and bright, with lots of traffic with lights on and looking wet, but my timing must have been just right.

It was a Saturday night and the city of Lansing in mid-Michigan was filling up quite quickly with weekenders. A lot of people will wonder why

Lansing is the State Capital, with the much bigger brother of Detroit not far away. It all goes back to 1847 when the constitution decreed that the capital be moved from Detroit to a more central state location. Detroit was too close to British-controlled Canada and although originally formed from three villages, the mid-state location of what is today Lansing was considered a much better location for the capital. The city was still relatively unsettled at the time and citizens viewed the choice with scepticism, believing the decision was a huge joke that had backfired. At first, the place was called 'Town of Michigan' and not named Lansing until after the first political session. Today, Lansing is an educational and medical centre, as well as supporting governmental businesses as one would expect being the state capital. Of particular notoriety, the Olds Motor Vehicle Company developed in Lansing, which was one of the nation's first automobile companies. I recall as a child having an Oldsmobile Toronado toy car and I am sure the real thing originated from this very place. The university covers a huge area in the east of the city and I have seen many a T-shirt around the country bearing the title 'Michigan State University'. I think it was some sort of graduation weekend for the education side of the city, as a lot of students and families were in town. The motel I selected for a couple of nights was nicely placed for the downtown and had a huge shopping mall across the street with the usual amenities. The manager, an Asian gentleman, was commenting I had arrived at the right time; rooms were filling quickly with only a few left for hire. He could only offer me a deluxe room with Jacuzzi. However, he kindly sold me the room at the basic rate, with discount thrown in, as well as a couple of vouchers for cheap drinks at the bar and a parking spot for the bike in security camera cover. A bar, that was unique for a motel and so was the smart swimming pool I noticed on the way to my room. This was a motel with attitude! I later discovered a wedding party in full swing and guests were spilling out into the gardens at the front of the motel. Yes, this place had function rooms as well and was not my normal experience of a motel in USA. It was a multi-function place. I was a little concerned about some of the guests, complete with drinks and loud conversation, as they congregated around my bike. Thankfully they seemed to be quite safe and assured me they would look and not touch. They actually invited me to join the wedding party, which I did for a quick beer, before heading for a diner the motel manager had recommended. It was across the mall's car park and 'don't be deterred by the other function of the place', the manager guy had said. At first, I thought he had sent me to some seedy pole dancing girly bar, but that was not the case and I entered a huge gambling joint. Windowless and full of smoky rooms each with different games in progress, it was like a mini Vegas betting den. I cut through the smoke and active tables and made for the bar. The menu was basic but the beer was cold. My accent got a few interesting and amused looks from the other occupants scattered around. One guy in particular tuned in and immediately started conversation. He was an amusing-looking guy in his mid-thirties, with a baseball cap on back to front. He had a friendly moustached face and continued to smoke throughout our chat. But the most amusing thing was his cigarette never left his mouth. He had the most skilled technique of propelling the cig from one side of his mouth to the other, simultaneous to inhaling, exhaling and communication. It was a humorous, almost cartoon scene. My bar companion turned out to be a fireman and was enjoying one of his days off between shifts. What really surprised me about this guy was that he comprehensively and intelligently gave his opinion of the state of the nation and of Europe in the most eloquent and informed manner. He was undoubtedly in the wrong job and would certainly make a better TV political commentator than some of the less than professional types I had encountered over the last five months. He accepted my compliments, bought me a beer and continued with his cigarette trickery. We did actually touch on the finer points of the less-than-salubrious bars for men's entertainment in Lansing. He seemed quite an expert. When I asked why he wore his baseball cap on backwards, he quickly replied that there was no sun in the bar and it was a big American thing to wear these hats. I had to agree with him there, I have seen them globally, but in particular in the USA. Everyone wears a baseball cap and not just at games, but in restaurants, parties, on the beach and at airports. Kids, students, sportsmen, travellers and even businesspeople all wear baseball caps. I think I will be justified in saying that the baseball cap, although specifically associated with the game of baseball and originating as far back as 1860, today is certainly a piece of Americana. For many they are simply a fashion statement. Sometimes they are even used as sun protection. I didn't get down to the analysis of the American versus the baseball cap to my fireman companion, who proceeded to finish his beer and cigarette, turn his baseball cap around so the peak now faced forward and went on his way. He was maybe going to one of his bars? Whilst chatting to this guy, I had not noticed the small party of three ladies that had gathered next to me. They were undoubtedly sisters, which was confirmed after I got talking to one of them. Black American girls, at first glance it would be easy to confuse them for one of those trio singing groups of the 60s or 70s. The something sisters, let's call them. 'The Lansing Sisters'. The Lansing Sisters were immaculately appointed in fashionable styles, hairdos from the best salon, expertly painted fingernails as long as a ruler and make up ready for a film set. Maybe they were actresses? It turned out they were all completely normal and local and having a couple of pre-nightclub drinks. It was Saturday night after all. They were all quite astonished about how many miles I had done today and completely blown away with my big picture. All mothers, none of them had left the state of Michigan. I left the gambling grill feeling reasonably content after my chat with some locals. Heavy rain had eventually arrived and the walk back to the motel involved avoiding large puddles that had formed. The vibrant wedding party had subsided and the die-hards had retreated to the shelter of the poolside bar. Thinking about my conversation that evening with the girls who hadn't travelled and didn't see any urgency to travel, got me pondering again about the American and travel again. Maybe a lot of the population are put off by the size of the country and stay local to where they live. Many find enough to see in their diverse home nation. Some don't have jobs that require travel and some bring up families, which simply doesn't allow travel. Quite a lot of the population would ask me why why why? Why all this travelling and especially around the USA – are you crazy? Not easy and not difficult to answer. I think once a traveller, always a traveller. I would never criticise habits and interest of others – after all, we are all different. But yes, I was encountering a lot of national and international geographically deficient Americans in this vast country. The debate could continue.

Next morning, the downtown was deserted and walking between the State Capitol and the Supreme Court, which is quite a hike, I didn't see another soul. It was a bright, blue and a hot day and obviously other visitors were still in bed, or visiting places scoring higher on the interesting list. I soon discovered why. The Capitol Building was closed and I had to make do with a view of the spired domed building from Capitol Avenue and the pretty front park area. The streets resembled the aftermath of a population exodus and maybe there was something I didn't know about Lansing on Sundays. It was eerie, very eerie and almost movie-set eerie. Where were the wild dogs and mortified population? Were they all hiding and awaiting the shelter of darkness before prowling the streets? My imagination was running wild; this was not a movie set, it was downtown Lansing, Michigan, on a quiet Sunday morning. I was racking my brains what to do next when the words of Bruce back in Maryland came back. 'When you are in Lansing, drop into nearby Potterville and have a look at Joe's Gizzard City.' I was here and I would. Potterville was very close, but of Joe's Gizzard City, I had no idea what to expect. All I knew was that gizzards are secondary stomachs in birds, sometimes containing small stones that are used to grind food. I found Joe's Gizzard city in the small town of Potterville only about 10 miles south west of Lansing. It was a restaurant specialising in these little delicacies. The town was quiet. Almost dead, similar to what I had just experienced in the capital. Only a few diners were in Joe's and before I could have a look at the menu, the visitors' book was slid in front of me. I wasn't brave enough to go for the gizzard 'full monty' main meal and made do with a gizzard sampler, followed by a chicken sandwich. At least I followed the theme and stayed with chicken. Amber the pretty brunette waitress enthusiastically took my order, poured me a Coke and then made off to the kitchen. Locals boasted of a recent gizzard-eating festival that attracted crowds from far afield, filling the small restaurant and spilling out onto the streets. So what of these gizzards to the non-specialist? Well, deep fried in a little batter and with chilli sauce on hand, they didn't taste unpleasant let's put it that way and quite ideal as an appetiser. Like dark chicken meat with a stronger tang and slightly unusual texture. I have had worse. Intrigued, I was interested why Joe's place had become legendary. Legendary I guess for the type of traveller and diner that require distractions just off the beaten track a bit. Amber proudly passed me a booklet outlining the brief history. This place has been in the family since the 1960s and boasts the best chicken gizzards around, in fact the best in the world! We could have a World Series gizzard-eating competition right here in Potterville, Michigan. Preparation of the gizzards was once a closely kept secret. Not so now as I read on. Joe's place has been preparing deep-fried gizzards for over 40 years. Only a special species of chicken is used originating from South America. They are called 'Elle Pollo Bonita', the beautiful chicken. The chickens are processed in a timely manner and the gizzards are marinated in a delicious blend of herbs, seasoning and beer. When marinating is complete, tenderising takes place after which they are coated with a delicate batter and cooked until golden brown. Golden brown they certainly were. Served piping hot, gizzards are an ideal accompaniment to a cool lunchtime drink, as I was finding out admirably. Complete with a complimentary 'Joe's Gizzard City' T-shirt, I vacated the premises feeling suitably replete after a unique and rather unusual, if not chewy, Sunday lunch. Potterville was still extremely quiet, although I did find one other resident. It was Max Glum, a 'book pusher'. He was pushing his broom on the street outside his small book and gift shop. We chatted for a while before he showed me around his small store. A store with no customers. I asked Max how he would define a typical American. That was my question of the day. He gave one of those stares and then said he would have to work on that, before he gave me an answer. Come back tomorrow and I will have a response for you. A charming comment from a guy in his small shop, in a small American town, typifying the real America. Who needs to be in Detroit this afternoon when you can be in Potterville? On the way back into Lansing, and with a dip in the motel pool in mind, I got a drenching prior to arrival. An afternoon thunderstorm had developed and turned the sky black over the city. I was racing the storm that was moving in the same direction. The tumult from the first crack of thunder which was directly overhead, felt earth-shattering through my helmet. What a blast; this little meteorological beast was another thunderstorm from hell and not the type to encounter when miles out in the open. As quick as it arrived, it passed clear to the east and left steaming ground after the clatter of machine gun rain. I had an early maritime departure planned in the morning and hopefully would be well ahead of any further violent attacks from the elements.

Chapter 64

Across the Lake

I named this chapter 'Across the Lake', after a hero of mine. Donald Campbell from the famous Campbell racing family met his fate whilst record breaking in Bluebird on Coniston Water in the English Lake District back in the 1960s. It was a 100-mile dash from Lansing via Grand Rapids to the small port of Muskegon on the Michigan side of the lake. Lake Michigan was my water to cross this morning. Arrival into Muskegon was extremely timely, but to my astonishment, the programmed ferry port address in my GPS took me to a cemetery! Was fate trying to tell me something? Some local workers gave directions to the port which was a further three miles on. It was a tiny access road to the terminal where one security guy was on duty at the gate. A loaded HD was ahead that had Quebec plates. I guess the crew were French Canadians. They got told to dismount and had their luggage comprehensively searched. Was I going to get the same treatment? It was early in the morning and the only proof of booking I had was the reference number scrawled on my hand. When it was my turn to advance, I yelled a 'morning sir' to the security guy and he replied with the same and pointed to the terminal, 'Morning to you sir, ticket awaiting, enjoy the ride.' It worked, excellent. Needless to say, I got a couple of foul looks from the French Canadians, who refused to engage in any conversation when I parked up. Their conversational deficiencies were made up for by Dennis who pulled up on another HD. We hit it off immediately. The majority of passengers were waiting inside the terminal which was probably bigger than the vehicle parking area. After collecting my ticket, I studied a huge detailed map on the wall of Lake Michigan and the adjacent states. When the ferry arrived, it dwarfed the small quayside. It was a huge twin-hulled jet catamaran. The bikes were boarded first and in quick time we were manoeuvring out of Muskegon Lake and entering in comparison, the vast waters of Lake Michigan. It's 68.5 miles across to Milwaukee in Wisconsin and saves considerable time getting west of the Great Lakes. The alternative would have been to go south, around the corner of the lake, bypass Chicago and take it from there. I had no appointments in Chicago and the ferry it was. The cat was comfortable and spacious and with the bikes lashed down, it was chill-out time in the lounge and café area. I was pleased the bikes were lashed down; the first part of the crossing was quite choppy and as the cat built up speed, there was a distinctive thump thump as she cut through the waves. Lake Michigan was stirring. About mid-lake point and crossing into Wisconsin, it became as smooth as silk for the remainder of the journey into the former brewing capital of Milwaukee. I was sharing a table in the coffee lounge with a mixed bunch. Dennis turned out to be a marine veteran and was on a mammoth biking trip connecting with former Vietnam colleagues. He talked quite openly about his time in Vietnam and shared a couple of stories with us. In particular, he had us all listening intently as he related a helo arrival into enemy territory. Bullets were literally pinging around the cabin of the helo and the young marines were terrified, confused and unsure exactly what was happening. His stick of men had to jump from the helo whilst it was still at 10 feet in the hover, giving the helo every opportunity to get the hell out of there. They all got out. The tale ended there, what became of the patrol we didn't find out. He told the tale with a stern look, but with absolutely no emotion. Young men sent to war. That was a long time ago and now retired, Dennis spends time giving talks around the country to kids who are thinking of joining the military. On these visits he takes a fully laden pack and tells them, look, this is the weight of kit we had to take into combat in those days. Try it for size. Dennis added that back then, they quickly got used to the weight and they had many other priorities, like staying alive! In complete contrast and rather less exciting than Dennis' tales, the other guy sitting at the table was a road construction engineer. That was interesting and I related my tales of woe about my continued experiences of poor road conditions in many states. He absolutely agreed. However, in defence of the poor roads and trying to remain impartial, I did offer my points of sympathy, including that it's a big country to repair, traffic is heavy and severe winters break up the surfaces. Then the cost and how does the revenue get down from federal, to state to county level for distribution? He accepted these points, albeit whilst remaining firm in his views that the USA has poorly maintained roads. He became quite adamant about it and I hope he wasn't making a show for me the journeyman and visitor.

I had three contacts to stay with in the Wisconsin and Northern Illinois area. I was invited to drop by all if my itinerary allowed. I had been thinking which was the best geographical method of attack. Hence the reason for studying the huge map in the Muskegon ferry terminal. With some mental juggling on the ferry whilst gazing at the quickly enlarging Milwaukee skyline, I decided to drop in and see Caryl Fabian in Illinois first. It was about a hundred miles south and wasn't much out of the way. I had made no firm arrangements and once clear of the ferry and disembarking traffic, pulled over and got my notepad and cell phone out. I had noticed a black limo behind me, but mysteriously I had not seen the car leave the ferry and wondered where it came from. I had stopped safely but rather abruptly and 50 metres ahead, the limo also stopped abruptly and pulled in at 45 degrees to the curb. The smartly dressed gent driver didn't look my way and proceeded to use his cell phone. I hadn't experienced any tails for some time, but the behaviour of this guy refocused my earlier journey suspicions. Surely not after all this time? I was nearly 18,000 miles into this journey and I couldn't still be attracting attention – could I? Where did this car come from this morning? If I was being tailed on arrival into Wisconsin, this guy was not discrete to say the least. I got hold of Caryl and she was expecting me later that afternoon. I set off, checking to see if my black limo tail was in pursuit. After my chat with the road construction engineer on the ferry, coincidently I encountered lots of it on the way down to Huntley.

Typical. I pulled into the driveway of Caryl's large modern detached estate-style house a couple of hours after leaving Milwaukee. I didn't see my tail at all. He probably got lost in the road construction. I was surprised to meet this sprightly lady in her early 80s and was even more surprised that she was content to host a stranger for a night. After Caryl insisted I put the bike in the roomy garage, we chatted over a sandwich and exchanged life stories. Caryl had survived the loss of two husbands which was quite sad, however she was more than happy to talk about some memories. Whilst she prepared dinner, I acquainted myself with my quarters in the basement. It was like a self-contained apartment in essence and extremely comfortable. After dinner, we continued to share stories and this incredible lady drank tins of beer at my pace. She wanted to drink more when I decided it was time for the sack and descended to my bed. Caryl was up hours before me the next morning and had breakfast on the table before I knew it. It was a tour of her little community and exclusive sports centre that followed. Undoubtedly activity is so essential when you gain seniority in life and Caryl certainly subscribed to that. Her diary was busier than the average CEO of a large company, with activities such as bridge, sailing, tennis, golf, gym, swimming and skiing – yes skiing. She is an action gal to say the least and made my leisurely ride through the Union seem quite sedentary in comparison. Caryl desperately wanted to show me off to her social set over dinner in her club that evening, but with time and motion ever on my mind I bade farewell to this quite incredible lady. The Lady of Huntley, Illinois. Caryl Fabian.

It was north back into Wisconsin and the capital Madison next. Contact 2 in this area was an ideal mid-morning coffee stop. It was Zoe in Delavan just north of the Illinois state line. Zoe also turned out to be an interesting character, but extremely different to Caryl. In her 70s, Zoe was a lively, thoughtful and quite philosophical lady. She was also a no-nonsense, analytical and quite serious person. With much of her life spent as a nurse and peace worker, Zoe has a history of international assignments including West Africa and Central America. We chatted over coffee and doughnuts and she offered great encouragement for me to complete my journey.

I left Zoe and continued north through the Dairy Land state towards the capital of Madison. The run north was through prime agricultural land and producing more dairy products than any other state, Wisconsin appropriately gets one of its nicknames – 'The Dairy Land State'. Arrival into Madison maintained the lake feeling that is so prominent in this area. Sometimes referred to as the City of Lakes, the city has a unique location where the slim downtown is on an isthmus, flanked closely by Lake Mendota and Lake Monona. This finger of land was originally swamp and forest and reclaimed to provide an area to build a city. The territory of Wisconsin had just been created and the legislators were tasked to choose a capital. This location was chosen even though construction was not complete and the city was very much still on paper. Its central state location got the vote ahead of Milwaukee in the east, Prarie du Chien in the west and Green Bay in the north east. A college city, Madison today has a cosmopolitan feel. Micro brewery bars and many restaurants line the streets that all lead to the Capitol sitting atop the isthmus. As well as Nick's Restaurant, I found the Great Dane Pub and Brewing Company amongst many others. I was assured that all premises use locally grown staff as well as locally grown hops. Milwaukee was once the brewing city of the nation and it wasn't surprising to find good ale in the state capital, especially from the Capital Brewery – 'America's number 1 rated brewery!' The city also has an industrial heritage and I stayed in the Rubie Marie on Wilson Street, a converted Victorian-era railway building and now a tasteful downtown inn retaining many rich heritage features. The inn was a mere stone's throw to many places to eat and drink and by early evening the city was busy with diners. It was warm enough to dine outside and my choice of Italian restaurant on the hill gave excellent views of the Capitol dome brightly shining in evening floodlights. From a distance, it could have been the nation's Capitol Building.

I had already had many external views of the Beaux Arts-style State Capitol building with impressive dome and cupola standing at over 285 feet tall. Sitting on the hill it looked taller than other office buildings around Mifflin, Pinckney, Main and Carroll streets. A view from the Capitol balconies gave a good outline of the radiating streets below and the unique geographical isthmus location with Lakes Mendota and Menona beyond. It was whilst leaving the viewing area that I met Capitol guide CJ. He was in charge of a display up in the gods of the building and not in the lobby or downstairs as normal. Dressed in jeans, polo shirt and sneakers, CJ gave me a stare through squinted eyes that said he wanted to talk. I thought he was a hustler at first, but my views were diluted after we engaged in a short interesting chat. I had to see the Pneumatic master clock made by Hahl Automatic Clock Co. Chicago dated 1909, if it was the last thing I did in Wisconsin or even the USA. Why? CJ said so, that's why. A man of 79, CJ was enthusiastic to tell me about his hobby or passion, which was collecting memorabilia from old American gas stations. The old places well before the big chains took over as we know today. We exchanged a few notes and when I spoke about my journey, he whooped with excitement, stating you would have passed here, here and here, these places still have the original gas stations in use. He was multi-tasking and whilst talking to me and greeting other visitors, he was desperately trying to reach his buddy, the photographer for the local newspaper. 'We'll get him here and get you in the paper and I will be in the shot as well – okay?' I chuckled with his enthusiasm and I think he was happy. Leaving the Capitol for the Rubie Marie, I asked him to ring me if the photographer turned up. I didn't think any more of it, but CJ did ring. He couldn't find his buddy but instead requested I join him and the Capitol police for a couple of photographs before I left town. 'Just ignore the parking restrictions and drive right up to the steps, you won't get shot, you are expected'. I did just that and posed a couple of times for CJ as he scampered around with his camera to the amusement of passers-by. Who knows if that photo with L M Corcoran of the Madison Area Capitol Police Division ever made it into the press?

Leaving Madison, I was heading north for the small town of Appleton. In the Fox River Valley, Appleton may be unknown to many. More familiar to some is the busy airport of Oshkosh just down the road and home of the Experimental Aircraft Association. Oshkosh also hosts an incredibly busy annual general aviation meet which aviation buffs may have heard of. Tempted but not convinced, I had seen enough aviation for the moment and continued north to find my third contacts in this area west of the Great Lakes. I was hosted in Appleton by Tom and Sue Becker. They live with their daughter Ericka and lively Labrador, Cooper, in a single storey, three-bedroomed ranch-style house in a smart middle-class neighbourhood. Travis, their eldest son, has moved on and combines a college and working life. Tom is a machine operator in a local paper mill. The area was once awash with paper mills. Now there are few, the industrial complexion of the area has changed. Sue fills busy days as a plans and inspection coordinator for a fire protection systems company. They are a hard-working family unit that take nothing for granted. Perhaps they represent the real small town America. Appleton is removed from familiar tourist areas and bursting metropolitan cities. It's a normal working town. How fortunate it was to be experiencing more of real America. There was much evidence of outdoor pursuits in the Becker household. Boat, fishing rods and similar, neatly stored in the garage, provide the tools for Tom's passion in the great outdoors of the nearby attractive Wisconsin countryside. He enthusiastically commented over a beer in the backyard on a lovely sunny afternoon, 'Fishing, shooting and hunting are a big part of life here. It can be a great escape into the country after a work shift, even for an afternoon. Camping trips up state can account for longer trips, but further afield excursions are few. Maybe a family meet once a year or so down south a bit. Our interests and what Wisconsin holds keep us all content and close to home.'

We dined on venison and wild trout over my two-day stay and Tom insisted on my return we would go on a fishing trip. Tom and Sue gave me a short trip around the area including a few hours in Green Bay, which is the state's oldest city. The city of Green Bay is at the southern tip of a stretch of water called Green Bay, which juts off from the north west of Lake Michigan. We viewed Green Bay through the reeds from Nicolet Drive, looking north towards the Michigan border and beyond to Canada. It was a hot and sunny day and I my thoughts advanced to winter, where this part of the country has the reputation of being extremely cold to say the least. Water in the Bay freezes. As a casual NFL follower over the years, I had already heard of what else the city of

Green Bay is famous for. I had seen photographs of the team performing during those winter months covered in snow. Green Bay Packers was founded by Earl 'Curly' Lambeau and George Calhoun in 1919 and is one of the oldest clubs in the country. Lambeau successfully got funds from his employer, the Indian Packing Company, to buy players' kit and hence the title was borne, 'Green Bay Packers'. The Packers are part of the North Division of the National Football Conference in the National Football League. Followers will recognise the Packers in their distinctive dark green and gold uniforms. Concluding an interesting visit to the area, we paid a visit to the impressive Lambeau Field Stadium and Hall of Fame.

Chapter 65

Strawberry Fields in the Twin Cities

I was running out of map! Once west of the twin cities of Minneapolis and St Paul, I would be making serious progress towards the finishing line of the lower 48. I even had another contact up my sleeve to stay with in Minneapolis. Whilst putting my things together the night before my departure from Appleton for the 300 miles west across Wisconsin the following day, as normal the weather was on my mind. It had warmed up again and a cell of thunderstorms, including rotation and a positive threat of tornados, was moving south east through Minnesota and Wisconsin. I had been hoping throughout my trip that tornados would keep to tornado alley. Weather systems don't follow lines drawn on the map. This bundle of fun was well to the east of tornado alley and could spoil my day if I got mixed up in it. Undeterred I decided to head off anyway. It was always something I thought about. If I saw the distinctive snaking swirl of a tornado, which has to be in contact with cloud and the ground to be designated a tornado, what would I do? Whilst loading the bike the next morning and exchanging banter with Tom, I mentioned the tornado forecast for the day and I think he replied something along the lines of 'that should be fun for you'. Although best avoided, Americans tend to take tornados as a fact of life. They are not a freak weather event and are as seasonal as strawberries and cream. Non-bikers never consider the dangers for bikers I guess and Tom was merely remaining in the humorous theme of our early morning chat. My plan if I saw a tornado in my area would of course be to try and ascertain its direction of movement. If it was heading my way, get the hell out of its path and if possible look for solid shelter. That could be a lottery as can anything be called solid shelter when a tornado is around? My last chance saloon survival plan would be to lay the bike down and hide behind it and wait for the beast to pass. That should work. I had a plan and after bidding farewell to Tom, left Appleton in a reasonable frame of mind, but still dwelling on the thought of a positive warning of tornados on my route. Highway 10 was my route all the way west across Wisconsin and into Minnesota. Once clear of Appleton, the traffic thinned out considerably and passing Waupaca, I was really out into the countryside. Stevens Point and Marshfield were the last large towns on the route and afterwards, I only encountered quite small places like Neillsville, Fairchild, Osseo, Mondovi, Durand and Plum City. It was overcast and humid, with the odd spot of rain. No meteorological demons seen so far, but the cloud base was solid and low and it would be quite difficult to make out anything that would bite. Wisconsin is a big state out to the west of the Great Lakes and just mile after mile of agricultural land. It all looked extremely green and the patchwork quilt of farm boundaries and uniform fields and paddocks was easily defined. It was similar to riding through the great plains eastbound back in May. But up here, everything was a lot greener. It was beginning to get much brighter, the cloud base was lifting revealing a nice blue sky. The profile of thunderstorms and the like would easily be seen now if there were any out there. By the time I pulled into Plum City for fuel, it was a different day and I couldn't believe if there would be any weather warnings still out there. The friendly lady attendant in the fuel station had the weather radar on her TV and pointed out that the culprit had marched through very early and was now in the northern Iowa area. There maybe a few rogue cells hanging around over the twin cities, but nothing earth-shattering. Iowa was getting it again. The news was a little relief and my accumulated adrenaline diluted. I didn't really want to take a photograph of a tornado, although the opportunity may still present itself when I pass through the Dakotas. Lunch was in order and

I bought a sandwich from the spacious and gleaming supermarket at the fuel station. The lady attendant had that huge smile on her face that transmitted that she was proud of her position and of her well-stocked and modern store. What a contrast to Lowe's fuel station and store that I passed by back in New Hampshire close to Mount Washington. Everything has its own character I guess. I had gone much further than had anticipated without taking a stop. It's the long legs of this bike that just make you go on and on. St Paul was less than an hour to the west now. Nevertheless, taking a breather next to the large pond in the village of Plum City was a welcome break. It gave me the opportunity for some journey meditation and to try and focus my thoughts on the American people. My journey was maturing and I wanted to start to firm up my demographic views. What box can I put them in? Not one box, several boxes I think. It is difficult to paint them all with the same brush. They are different people to Brits and Europeans, but I think we have to make the distinction between Americans as a population and Americans as families and individuals. I could almost say that the USA is a country of immigrants. That's accurate isn't it? They all dwell on their connections to Europe and Africa, to mention but a couple of places. More to the point, it was early afternoon on a Friday and I had to plan my arrival into the urban monster ahead. I think the best approach would be to head to the State Capitol Building in St Paul now, do my normal rituals there and then sneak across to Minneapolis where I was expected for a couple of nights.

Highway 10 continued to propel me west and soon I was passing the mighty Mississippi again. I had lost count how many times I had passed the Mississippi and had forgotten it snaked through Minneapolis and St Paul. As I got closer to St Paul, which is the easterly of the twins, the traffic got busier and busier. My navigation to the Capitol deflected me onto an urban Interstate and very soon the striking Italian Renaissance Capitol was easily seen in quite an elevated position. But trying to get the correct link road off the horrendously busy Interstate was mayhem. I went past the correct exit at least twice and had to double back, before eventually getting it right. It was a relief to find Dr Martin Luther King Jr Boulevard that led me to Capitol Centre and far from the Friday congestion only a few moments before. Hot and sweaty after 300 miles through the rural Wisconsin, with a bit of urbananity at the end, after changing I joined the last organised tour of the Capitol of the day. I didn't fancy a self-guided stroll and tuned into the commentary from an expert. There was only a dozen of us, a couple of retirees, a young couple with some toddlers and one or two singletons. I have three distinctive memories of my visit to the St Paul Capitol Building. The first is the magnificent gold classical statues of four horses and figures on the balcony overlooking Constitution Avenue. The gold was a superb contrast against the brilliant blue sky and cityscape to the south. The second was the unique and unmistakable skyline of Minneapolis only a few miles to the west. It just seemed so strange to be viewing a city so close from a city. I chuckled when I recalled the reference about Montpelier and Barre in Vermont as being called the 'twin cities' by some locals. That was really put into perspective right now. My final memory was meeting a young Australian lady who had just qualified as a lawyer. In celebration of her recent graduation, she was on a global tour, but a global tour with a difference. Although she had an air ticket to whizz her home when she got fed up, she had nothing else planned and desperately little money. She was relying on accommodation by participating in a scheme called 'couch surfing'. It's a website-based facility where people offer a place to sleep for travellers, which normally turns out to be the couch. One of the criteria for participation is that the staying person must also make reciprocal services and become the receiving person if called upon. We chatted for 10 minutes about her adventures, after which she headed off to her couch for the night, wherever that was. Including her footwear, she was dressed for the beach, but had walked miles around the Twin Cities. They make them quite strong down under and this young lady was certainly no couch potato.

The Twin Cities are unique and one may ask why two huge cities so close together? Both grew up around Native American settlements as trading and transport areas. A significant asset to the area is the abundance of lakes and major rivers, which served as arterial transport links and aided industrial development. But why St Paul the state capital and not Minneapolis? It got ahead of its twin by becoming the capital of Minnesota Territory and was declared the state capital when Minnesota entered the Union. The twins tend to merge together today as business hubs, industrial outlets and cultural centres. With a combined population of over 3 million, I was certainly getting the feeling of being in one of the 'country's biggest'. After bidding farewell to the Aussie coucher, it was time for me to switch twins and find my couch. The Lady of Illinois, Caryl Fabian, had fixed it for me to stay with her daughter in Minneapolis. My network was extending. Would it go any further I wonder? The attendant back in the fuel station in Plum City was right. She commented there may be a rogue urban thunderstorm around 5 pm. She was spot on and the blue turned to black. The gold statues on the capitol balcony turned from majestic to menacing against the gathering gloom. Thunder was in the area, forks of lightning on the horizon and the rain was imminent. I clocked just seven miles from St Paul to Karen's 100-year-old town house in central Minneapolis. By the time I had garaged the bike, unloaded the essentials and drank a mug of tea, it was a deluge outside. I made it just in time – again! I chatted to Karen as she prepared dinner and welcomed me into her home. Having met her Mother only a couple of states back, I did feel more comfortable staying with another stranger. A family affair, a family connection. Karen talked about her life and family. She related to the challenges of bringing up a family. I had the choice of two places to rest my head for the weekend. A couch upstairs or a couch downstairs. I took the latter option and descended to the basement, the guts of this friendly home, complete with wooden veranda, front lawn and back yard. Was this the quintessential American urban residence? The sort of place you have a hammock swinging in the summer and catch the newspaper as the boy on his cycle throws it your way before speeding off? In the den of the basement, my sofa bed was surrounded by central heating pipes, boilers, piles of magazines and kids' toys from generations past. It was so cosy and a welcome contrast from the characterless motel rooms I had become so accustomed to. I had experienced an amazing selection of accommodation over the past few months. From basic motels, to smart motels, to city inns, exclusive hotels, to the comfort of private homes. I even had a strong wi-fi signal in Karen's basement. Whilst smelling and listening to the evening summer rain clatter down onto the gardens and paths above, I fell into a deep slumber for my first night in Minneapolis.

After breakfast the next day, I tagged along with Karen and her son Spencer out to the west of the city. We were almost on the city limits and spent a couple of hours picking strawberries at a local fruit farm. We arrived reasonably early, however, the crowds were gathering and pickers were closely marshalled into picking lanes by ebullient young kids with walkie-talkie radios. It seemed strange to be participating in such an activity. I was a biker charging around the country at a great rate of knots. If someone had suggested to me 18,000 miles ago that I would spend a Saturday morning picking strawberries in Minneapolis, I would have considered them crazy. It was however a therapeutic and relaxing way to while away a sunny morning. Any planning considerations for the next day were at the extreme rear of my mind and I just went with the flow and sampled the odd strawberry at the same time. We returned home laden with baskets of fruit and after a leisurely lunch, Karen fussed over the food preparations for the planned evening barbeque and Spencer cut the front lawn. Simple things by normal folk in their normal lives. It was good to see these activities just to take stock. It was approaching mid-afternoon and hard though I tried, I could not dismiss preparations for travel and had a sneak preview of the weather across Minnesota and into South Dakota for tomorrow. I recall way back in Fort Myers Florida, the owner of the bike shop clearly told me, be careful in the Dakotas, it is always windy and you will be riding cranked over at an angle whatever time of the year. My reply to him is extremely fuzzy after all these miles, however, his words were now loud and very clear. Today that region was experiencing winds of 50 mph, gusting 60 mph. That's just ridiculous; you cannot ride safely in such conditions. I only hope the abating forecast of 30 mph for tomorrow was accurate. I would plan to go anyway and as usual check the weather first thing in the morning. In preparation for the planned evening social, I made off to a local liquor store to buy some beers. It was just up the road and was one of those places piled high with bottles and cans to the ceiling. My selection was a pack of some local ale and returning to my bike, a crowd had gathered from the stores customers. Firstly they couldn't believe seeing a Florida plate up here and secondly, they thought the bike was a one off machine made for a movie or something. 'Was it out of a sci-fi movie, like an up-todate Blade Runner urban street bike?' Now that was some imagination. Even though there are dealers nationwide, a lot of folk either hadn't seen this model, or didn't realise BMW made bikes. After a walk down the steep banks to the Mississippi, it was food time. The evening was spent amongst good people and good food. As the daylight faded and the population drifted home into the Minneapolis dusk, in complete stillness with only the gentle rustle of leaves, I was alone on the balcony. What would tomorrow's weather bring on the northern plains?

Chapter 66

The Dakotas

Descending to my bed, I had wind on my mind. It was the winds on the Great Plains of the Mid West over the next 24 hours. I wanted to get to Pierre, the capital of South Dakota, the next day and that was 400 miles west. It was pointless looking at a general forecast for such a big distance. Again this was one of those days when I would have to break the leg down and check the weather at several places. Dividing the route up into quarters, I used the towns of Jordan and Sleepy Eye in Minnesota and Brookings and Iroquois in South Dakota as weather check points. The last thing I wanted was to be caught out there in winds of 50-60 mph with no shelter. Early the next morning the first thing I did was of course check those towns, which would give a reasonable reflection of what it was going to be like out there. All were giving morning winds of 30 mph, reducing throughout the day. A huge improvement from the 60 mph of yesterday. My decision was to go; the winds were from the west, which would be a headwind and considerably better than from the left or right which makes riding extremely uncomfortable, if not dangerous. I had packed and loaded the bike before anyone else stirred in the house. After a cup of tea in the garden and bidding farewell to a sleepy Karen, I was quickly departing a sleepier Minneapolis and heading south west. It always seems strange experiencing a big city and associated arterial roads absolutely dead and in complete contrast to the weekday congestion. The route was simple and extremely rural. After highway 169 for 50 miles to the south west of Minneapolis, it would be highway 14 all the way to Pierre. Once on 14, I was completely out in the sticks, in the wilderness, in the boondocks, of the very agricultural Great Plains. It was a bright and very breezy morning. However, as I progressed west, the wind just dropped off completely. By the time I crossed the state line into South Dakota and stopped for fuel at Brookings, the wind was but a warm zephyr gently stirring the green trees and summer blooms. It had turned into a lovely late June day. Whilst pulling out of Brookings, I noticed that I had my first bike failure of the trip. A headlight bulb had gone. Not bad considering it had been illuminated for 18,700 miles. Highway 14 was a single carriageway road all the way. Much of the time, the boundaries of the fields were very close to the roadside, with herds of grazing cattle almost in touching distance. For many sections, the road was completely straight and although it was possible to make excellent progress, there was no feeling of boredom like on some of the interstate routes I had taken. Small en-route towns broke up the journey considerably and offered interest and distraction, rather than just long distances of speed with tedium. At one point, the sky was full of lines of flat-bottomed fair weather cumulus cloud in every direction. This wide-angled vista completely wrapped around the road and appeared to show the curvature of the earth. It has to be seen and I certainly felt a miniscule part of this huge scene all around me. To an extent I now understand this 'big sky' term that is talked about; I was getting a feel of it even in South Dakota well before I had arrived in the 'Big Sky State' of Montana. After just one stop in Brookings and quite an exhilarating run through the plains, I rolled into Pierre, in the middle of a warm afternoon.

Historically dominated by agriculture and a settling place for the Native American Sioux, the arrival of Americans and Europeans gradually increased and the state of South Dakota was ceded to the Union in 1889. Perhaps the most significant and much talked about historical incident was the Wounded Knee Massacre on the Pine Ridge Indian Reservation. This was probably the last major conflict between the forming United States and the Sioux Nation. Today, the state is sparsely populated, dominated by an agricultural economy and very much a rural lifestyle. I had seen all of this on my run west. Contributing quite significantly to the economy of the state is the large Air Force Base at Ellsworth. It has continued to surprise me that big military establishments can not only contribute to a city's economy, but in this case the state's economy as well. That clearly illustrates that other than agriculture not a lot else happens out here. If young people are not involved with agriculture, what is there to keep them in the state? Pierre was another one of those state capitals that I couldn't get lost in. I reckoned it was only slightly larger than Montpelier in Vermont, which didn't exactly make it big. The city was selected as the state capital because of its central location and is much smaller than Sioux Falls, which is the state's largest city today. Pierre was originally set up as a fur trading post. Huron, Aberdeen, Mitchell, Sioux Falls, Redfield and Watertown were among six other contenders in the ring to be the state capital. This contest soon became between Pierre and Huron as the others fell away. Pierre had to fight off another attempt by Mitchell, but got the prize because of its geographical centre. Location, location, location proved to be the winning ingredient even back then. The domed Greek and Italian Renaissance Revival State House sitting on quite an elevated position overlooking the Missouri River is a real jewel. The building is constructed from granite, sandstone and limestone. The interior is complemented by large murals, mosaic floors, ornate plasterwork, carved marble and stained glass. It was another one of those occasions when I had the place to myself; I didn't even see anyone at work in any of the offices. Close to a small lake is an impressive war memorial covering several conflicts. Life-size statues of uniformed men and women are saluting, overlooking the Flaming Fountain marble wall with many inscriptions recording the details of local souls lost at war. It was very tasteful and nicely appointed with one national flag flying alongside the state flag. A centre piece to the memorial and with talons extended and wings spread, I was able to capture a perfect image of the sculpture of a landing eagle. Against the blue sky, with the dome of the Capitol in the background and the national flag flying, it couldn't have been choreographed any better.

A walk around the dusty streets gave quite a western and frontier town feeling. Looking at some of the old buildings down Pierre Street and Fort Street and with a bit of imagination, you could so easily turn back the clocks a hundred years. Today they are trading as Hardware Hanks store, small book and gift shops, utility stores, real estate offices and a few restaurants. Even on a weekday there were very few people around. Pierre, pronounced Pier by the locals, was not a ghost town but not the most vibrant place I have encountered. It made a refreshing change to some of the bustling urban centres. It was pleasurable to walk and ride around without having to negotiate crowds and cars. In keeping with the western image, I was attracted to Mad Mary's Steak House and Saloon for dinner on one of my two evenings in town. It was simply the name and humorous sign of Mad Mary dressed in cowgirl attire and holding a rifle on the relatively scruffy-looking building that attracted me. I wasn't disappointed. The smoke from the sizzling steaks drifted into the dining room and along with the thump of beer mugs on the solid wooden bar and the chit-chat from diners, all contributed to a fine cowboy atmosphere. On arrival into the relatively dark dining room and before I hit the bar, I noticed a table of four bikers. They were obviously the crowd from the two HDs at the front. When I entered, their table went quiet and conversation continued in near whispers. I had said nothing; maybe they knew a stranger was in town – a stranger not on a HD! They finished their meal and made off without chat. I did however meet a biker in town that was the complete opposite and wanted to talk on behalf of South Dakota. It was Ed in the city post office and I was buying stamps on his final day behind the counter. He was retiring and in celebration was joining a biker group on a ride up to Montana the very next day. I was invited to tag along and we exchanged cell numbers. However, I had a small geographical dilemma to overcome. Which way shall I go next? I knew that Bismarck was the next capital and that was due north, but how many national parks shall I try and squeeze in? With a little over four weeks left, my six-month clock was ticking down rapidly. I desperately wanted to see Glacier National Park in Montana and then drift down into Yellowstone and Tetons in Wyoming, before heading for the west coast and the chequered flag in the lower 48. So did

I have the time to see the Black Hills and the Badlands in the south west corner of South Dakota, not forgetting Mount Rushmore? If I tried to do it all, it could turn out a hell of a rush and take away the enjoyment. I think something had to give.

The decision came reasonably quickly. I would miss out the Black Mountains and the Badlands of South Dakota and put them top of my shopping list for a future visit. It would be north into the upper mid-west and the Great Plains of North Dakota next. I just had the urge to make positive progress and get into Montana as quick as possible. With this route preference made, I had plenty of time to complete the lower 48 on time and maybe have a few days to put my feet up in Olympia before heading north. Whilst checking out of the Governor's Inn in Pierre, I was telling the attractive blonde clerk my plans. She was a college student and earning a few dollars for spending money. Spending money to enable her to hire a small motorcycle for the remainder of the summer. She was full of questions about my strange-looking bike and miles covered. Strange looking bike eh? If it wasn't HD it was strange-looking. That's a common statement over here. Her father was a biker and she was looking forward to seeing some nooks and crannies of the Dakotas with him over the following weeks. I wonder if her father was in Mad Mary's last night?

North Dakota is sometimes referred to as the High Plains. Once across the border and in the Peace Garden State, I did have the feeling of climbing, although the majority of the route was flat with only occasional undulating sections. Maybe there was a bit of psychology coming in here. I was northbound in the north of the country, in the geographic centre of the American continent; I must be going up! It was a beautiful, warm, blue summer's day and the light breeze was creating swathing patterns in the fields of long grass. It was a re-run of my entry into South Dakota the other day. Miles and miles of fields, farms and nothing but agriculture, with the occasional view of the broad Missouri River on my left. Cattle and haymaking seemed to be the main themes up here. I suppose you could really be in any part of the agricultural states of the USA. I am sure the North Dakotans would disagree and stress North Dakota is unique to anywhere else. I would. Once through the small agricultural towns of Strasburg, Linton, Temvik, Hazelton, Moffit and Sterling, highway 10 paralleling Interstate 94 took me directly into Bismarck, the state capital.

For anyone with a German interest, after originally being named Edwinton, the city was renamed Bismarck after the German chancellor Otto von Bismarck. It was an early marketing ploy in an attempt to attract investment and possible German immigrants to settle in the city and bolster the state's sparse population. Ironically, most immigrants were instead attracted to the gold fields of the Black Hills in the south west corner of the state. The area I had chosen to miss out this time.

In accordance with some advice I received from a lady back in Raleigh, North Carolina, I never really did any research on the next state capital city and State House. National parks and similar yes, but the capitals I would normally take them as they came and hope for a surprise. Arriving into Bismarck, I headed for a motel which was close to a tall skyscraper building that I had seen for miles and there was probably a good bet it was close to the downtown area. I mentioned at check-in that I would like to see the State Capitol and she said, 'You're right there, follow your nose around the corner, you cannot miss it.' Around the corner was the flat-topped 20-storey tower that I had gravitated towards for my final navigation into the city. Walking over a stretch of grass and what looked like scrub area, I was confronted with this tower block which was the Capitol Building. On closer external inspection, there was a bit of art deco and international style thrown in, but a flat-topped high-rise it was. Towering over the city, it is the tallest building at nearly 250 feet high. So along with Baton Rouge and Lincoln, albeit with an adjoining legislative wing with curved frontage, Bismarck joins the short list of unconventional Capitol Buildings that have a high-rise structure. The building was not completed until the early 1930s and art deco architecture had by then become very popular. A breath of fresh air and a pleasing contrast to the domed Capitols. My surprises continued when entering the building. A suited gent with a bundle of files on his lap looked up and asked if I needed any help. It turned out to be Merle Boucher the Minority Leader. Merle proceeded to give me an impromptu tour of the Capitol, simultaneously greeting friends and colleagues and introducing me along the way. I am sure the majority of the 20 floors contain routine state and administrative offices and my brief tour with Merle only included the important bits down below, which are decorated with a blend of foreign and domestic materials. I left Merle as he greeted more friends in the lobby. Any thoughts he had about having a quiet read of his legal documents soon fell by the wayside! Before leaving the Capitol, I had a most interesting conversation with Gene who was running the information desk. He mentioned that the downtown was about a mile's walk and with only a shopping mall and a small historic area, it wasn't worth the sweat in the afternoon heat. He suggested a look at the adjoining museum and heritage centre would be far more interesting. He was right. Gene began to quiz my journey and objectives. I fielded his queries and decided to throw a few questions his way. When I asked him what Americans strive for and have in common, he smiled and quoted, 'We look for variety and new opportunities.' Interesting and this linked to my identification of the American endeavour for freedom and independence. Freedom and independence in the land of opportunity.

The grass and scrub I had walked over to get to the Capitol area I later learnt was quite a special piece of native prairie of North Dakota. Almost sacred ground. It is a one-acre remnant that has never been ploughed and over the years more than 50 plant species have been recorded growing there. Native prairies created North Dakota's fertile soils and once supported thousands and thousands of bison. I didn't walk over it on the return to the motel, but took the long way around. I hope I hadn't stirred any spirits from the past. So as a geographical recap, here in Bismarck, North Dakota, I was in the centre of the Great Plains, with the Rocky Mountains to the west and the Great Lakes to the east. Canada and the provinces of Saskatchewan and Manitoba lie to the north. Although only quite recently, I have left the Great Lakes far in my wake and will be very soon revisiting the Continental Divide, this time in the north west of 'The Big Sky' state of Montana.

Chapter 67

The Big Sky State

I stirred my bones quite early the next morning. Glacier National Park in Montana it would be. But at 700 miles from Bismarck to the eastern gate of the park in the top left hand corner of Montana, an overnight on the way would be sensible. I decided to leave North Dakota on the Interstate, crossing into Montana at a small town called Beach and then go completely rural at Glendive. My introduction to the Big Sky State was one of a grey sky and showers. After refuelling and slurping free coffee at Glendive, the whole scene looked rather depressing. It could only get better and it did quite quickly west of the small town of Circle. The low cloud and drizzle soon gave way to bright sunshine. Anywhere looks better with a bit of sun and Montana is no exception. But the roads were so quiet and lonely. On highway 24 for 60 or 70 miles or so, I didn't see one other vehicle. Not even anything agricultural. Just acre after acre of prairie, full of cattle and sheep. It looked a barren land and I am sure would be extremely cold and bleak in winter. It was a little relief to get Fort Peck Lake in sight, after which I joined highway 2 westbound. This route, known as the 'hi line', runs across the northern part of the state all the way to the Idaho border. Mainly flat prairie, it is an extremely unique part of the USA and several small towns are spread out along the route. The names of many of the towns are quite amusing. Glasgow, Harlem, Havre and Chester to name but a few. There may have been a method to this random naming madness. Running alongside the road is quite a busy freight rail route. A hundred years back, most of the towns grew up as rail service stops, supplying water and fuel for the locomotives. Originally the towns were small and carried a number as a designation. Refuelling stop 5, 6, 7 etc. Eventually as the towns got bigger and started to provide services to the local farms, it was decided to give them a name and it seems to me that they were christened at random from global selections, by almost spinning a globe! I may be wrong, but it seems a good theory! 400 miles after leaving Bismarck, North Dakota, I arrived in Malta, that's Malta, Montana. It was mid-afternoon and a short ride around the town proved to be a good idea. I saw quite a few motels on the approach to the town, on the main road and sitting right next to the railway. Tucked away a few streets back, I found the Maltana Motel and this was my selection for the night. I recall I was the only guest and when checking in, the lady owner remarked I had made a good decision. She would say that of course. She stressed that the noise from the freight trains in the other motels resembled an orchestra of clanking metal, bells and horns and I would get little sleep. I could even hear them from the Maltana. Later on whilst refuelling the bike, the whole town suffered a power cut which was quite unique and quickly reminded me how remote and at times how literally cut off this sort of place could be on the hi-line. It was like a play or a film set – 'We'll just take a pause and a little break there folks, talk amongst yourselves for a moment.' There were a couple of vehicles alongside also stranded mid-fuel flowing and I got talking to a young couple in the car next to me. They were originally locals from Hinsdale just down the road. I had passed through there earlier and it looked a lot smaller than Malta. This family had just driven 14 hours from their home in Fort Collins, Colorado, making an annual pilgrimage to family still living in Hinsdale. It was agricultural festival weekend coming up in Hinsdale and overnight, the population would increase from 300 to 1,000. Hinsdale would creak at the seams just for that weekend and then return to a lonely prairie town for another year. They seemed a nice family and by the time we had finished our chat, a buzz and clatter from the fuel pumps indicated the power had been restored. We finished our rituals and departed.

This small town of Malta looked an interesting little place and worthy of pedestrian exploration. The town is dominated by the highway and the railway. With wide streets, high grain stores, tired-looking shops, as well as a couple of hotels, bars, steak houses and even a casino, there was just a little cowboy town feel coming through. Just around the corner from the Maltana, I stumbled upon a Ford-Mercury car dealers from yesteryear. I am sure they hadn't been trading automobiles there for years. It is now almost a museum with a line of rusted 1940 and 1950s Chryslers, Dodges and Fords stranded from a bygone era. I could almost conjure a title to a photograph to accompany this line of auto relics, 'we don't have much trade here anymore', or 'we don't sell many cars now in Malta', or even, 'ring this number for the salesman and then check in to a motel and await his call'. It was the railway that attracted further investigation and during my short walk around the compact town centre, several freight trains had forged through east and west. All of them were hauling double-decker container cars, plying the regular route from Seattle to the urban centres around the Great Lakes and return. With 'Evergreen', 'Seaco', and 'Italia' and other usual suspect-named containers on the incredibly long trains, most of them are in excess of a mile long. It took an age for one train to clatter through town with the associated squeal of metal, clang of bells and screech of whistles. The rail route is also shared by an Amtrak passenger service and a small building directly on the rail lines is the passenger terminal and station. You could walk on the lines without knowing it and I guess the locals get used to the close proximity and the potential dangers from the huge metal monsters passing through. Whilst photographing the area, I was abruptly reminded of the frequency of these dangers. Loco 4060 hauling a container train westbound gave a long blast on his horn, instantly elevating my blood pressure and causing near apoplexy as it approached. I saw him and was clear of the tracks, but it was obviously on the driver's mind that I hadn't seen or heard him. He was shifting to say the least and created a lot of turbulence. The trees shook. An opposite direction train held off just outside the town until this brute was clear and then proceeded at a much gentler pace. By the time I got back to the Maltana, I realised I had made a good choice of motel, especially after my Cheyenne experiences. Anything closer to the railway line would have led to a sleepless night with the frequency and racket from these mechanical behemoths.

After dinner in the Great Northern Hotel steak house, the adjoining Stockman Bar attracted my attention. The entrance was via swing doors and with the wooden frontage and pillars, this looked a real cowboy bar. Alas, Chevrolet and Ford pick-ups at the front replaced horses and ponies that would have been tied up in years gone by. It was quite rowdy for a Monday night and the drinking population, dressed in checked shirts, jeans and leather boots, complete with stained Stetsons, were obviously all local farmers. I got chatting to Jon and Jeanette Carman, who were local goat ranchers. They mentioned that this is a growing trend, even in a cattle-dominated area. Their main market for the goat meat was in the ethnic centres of Billings right here in Montana and Chicago, Illinois. Their agricultural network is far and wide in the area. Everything is far and wide in this area. Our conversation diverted to cattle ranching and original cattle rearing methods. Here, annual branding days are a big event where typically a young bullock is pinned down by the 'wrestler' and given close attention by the 'brander', who may castrate and inoculate the beast as well as sizzling the farm identity into his rump, all at the same time. Then there is the rest of the herd. A 'supervisor' on horseback looks on and many other 'helpers' corral the cattle as the event unfolds from dawn to dusk. It's a physical day, managed by an organised and expert team from several ranches. It's a big team event and resources are shared. This was a priceless conversation and insight into Montana ranching methods, which are still practiced in adjoining western states. My stay in Malta was an eye-opener into the small town life on the hi-line. Some of the towns are smaller and some are much bigger. Agriculture is obviously the main theme up here and cattle and wheat farming are the two main commodities. Other light industries have developed, including small oil and gas plants around Shelby. But the question again I was conjuring whilst riding through these big open states was this: if children are not from an established agricultural family, what is there to keep them in the state? The Colorado family I met at the fuel station are a perfect example. They had shipped out of Montana for work and to bring up their kids elsewhere. In future generations, will these hi-line agricultural communities continue to exist?

The next day it was back on highway 2 of the hi-line again and westbound. More or less all similar, I passed though the towns of Dodson, Harlem, Chinook, Havre, Kremlin and Chester. All looked smaller or bigger versions of Malta. It was the railway again that dominated, running parallel to the road. I cannot remember seeing any trains westbound; my good progress probably prevented any catching up. It was refreshing and quite interesting to see that the speed limit up here was 70 mph. I don't think I had seen that anywhere else, even on an Interstate. Every 15 minutes or so, an eastbound freight train would pass and after throwing a friendly wave, most would give a long blast of their horn. It's that wailing 'woh-woooh' that I mentioned back in Wyoming that is synonymous and is a thought-provoking slice of Americana. It can give an eerie feel. What can the mind conjure when you hear the sound? It reminds me of the movies and a train passing through a city at night in torrential rain. When I see and hear these huge trains, I am now reminded of the states I have passed through and witnessed them at work. Passing quarry trains in northern Arizona, racing freight east out of Utah, awoken by the marshalling yard in Cheyenne-Wyoming and startled by fast-moving freight in Malta-Montana. A couple of occasions on the hi-line, I met a train as it snaked around the contours close to the road. A loco on the apex of the bend would for just a moment, just a smidgen of time, fill my vision, but not completely fill the big sky. They were big orange and yellow locos, dual locos normally, hauling a mile-long train of containers and tankers. Without knowing it, the American railroad was becoming a sub-theme to my journey. I left the hi-line in Browning. I had thought about staying there overnight, but was deterred by the extortionate cost of a very, very basic motel and less-than-friendly manager. He was more concerned about the raucous meeting or party he was having in the back room than tending to guests. I forgot I was approaching one of the country's most visited national parks and prices for everything would immediately increase. I continued the short distance to the small resort area of St Mary's. Someone had mentioned there are a couple of places to stay there and the entrance to Glacier National Park is extremely adjacent. It was dominated by a large resort-style hotel, with accommodation in the main premises and in adjoining cabins. It was obvious that the place used young and under-trained holiday staff. They appeared rude and not really bothered about anything that resembled customer service. Quite strange for the USA. 'Yer, we have loads of space for tonight. Discount, you will have to speak to the manager, he is on walk about.' The young guy behind the desk called the manager on a radio and he agreed to meet me outside. When I found him, he was leaning on my bike. I didn't like that one bit. Any biker will agree that it is just not form for a stranger to be touching your bike, especially a non-biker. Leaning on it is at the extreme end of tolerance. My bike was my office and my mobility and some arrogant stranger had no right to be resting his bulk on my best friend. He removed himself when I sent a few carefully selected words his way. He was a young man and certainly not a good advert for a manager and someone meeting and greeting the public. He uttered, 'I have had the call from the front desk, no discount tonight, cheapest room rate is $175'. He looked a mess, with a double chin resting on his shirt which was stained with the remnants of his last meal. With an enormous girth, which is a polite description, this guy obviously gave diet and exercise absolutely no priority. He was a disgrace and his audacity continued as he had the nerve to photograph my bike from several angles. I was very disappointed with this character and his general slovenly behaviour was not befitting his role as duty manager for this resort. Although I was slightly annoyed that he wouldn't negotiate any discount my way, my thoughts at the time were that he didn't deserve this job. I make no apologies for writing about some bad experiences. Not everything is good in this country. Needless to say I moved off quite quickly and still with no action plan of where to rest my head that night. I hope my unfriendly encounters with accommodation management in Browning and St Mary's, would not be a sign of things to come. Had I made the right decision to come all this way to the far reaches of Montana? Should I have indeed gone to the Black Hills and Badlands of South Dakota after all? It had been nearly 300 miles from Malta and at 2 pm, I didn't really want to ride through the park now.

That would give me more opportunity of places to stay further west. However, I wanted to enjoy the beauty of the park fresh and alert in the morning. Arriving in St Mary's, I had seen a large colourful sign for a motel with big arrows and writing pointing 'this way'. It could be an option and the sign took me up the hair-pinned Red Eagle Road where the motel was sitting next to a local restaurant. This would do. The motel turned out to be extremely basic. Wi-fi – forget it, TV signal – no chance. But with clean sheets and hot water and a damn good price, who cares. I recall my priorities after wi-fi were clean sheets and hot water. I didn't have the former, but after my less-than-friendly encounter with Mr Mess the manager from the resort down the hill, I cared not.

I think it was the morning chorus that had awoken me. It was Independence Day. It was clear and cool at 05.30 and the Lower St Mary Lake looked striking in the dawn light. There wasn't another sign of life and I was a little guilty that the sound of my bike starting up would disturb the local community. I left the gravel car park and eased carefully down Red Eagle Road and entered Glacier National Park at 06.30. The morning chill helped to blow my cobwebs away and I felt quite human in comparison to my fatigued body of yesterday. This state wasn't going to get the better of me. It's not the largest; it's the 4th largest behind Alaska, Texas and California. I hadn't got to Alaska yet, but I think the diverse geography, huge open spaces and sparse population certainly gave the Big Sky State the edge over the other two I had seen. I had already been Californicated, there are too many people there. As for Texas, well there's the USA and then Texas so they say, so I shall count that as a different country. Montana just could be the 'last best place'. I hadn't realised just how close I was to the Canadian border in St Mary's and the mountain ranges in the park are an extension to the Canadian Rockies. It was a surreal experience riding on the 'Going to the Sun Road' with mountain goats as the only traffic joining me. It was too early for the crowds and apart from the odd early morning Park Ranger patrol, I had the whole place to myself. I think it was worth the deviation all the way up here just to take in the spectacular scenes I had heard so much about. Many Americans had said if there is one park to get into, it's Glacier in North West Montana. So far, I was experiencing very much what is 'said on the tin'. A land of jagged peaks, rolling mountain ranges, deep blue lakes, thick forests and meadows full of summer flowers gently wafting in the early morning breeze. It was certainly a sight for sore eyes. What was so special about this experience was the total lack of people and vehicles. The early bird catches the worm indeed. This time of the day was certainly the best viewing time and I even had lots of time and opportunity to stop and breathe in the pristine air and photograph the breathtaking vistas. Whilst crossing the Continental Divide at Logan's Pass, I could almost touch the rugged mountains and surging waterfalls. This was GS bike territory without a doubt. As with all good things in life, it was all over rather quickly and passing down the side of Lake McDonald and through West Glacier, I was out of the park by 08.30. It had been a two-hour geographical extravaganza and not to be missed. The celebration day visitors were gathering and by the time Flathead Lake came into view, northbound traffic was building up to gridlock. Congestion and people would spoil that amazing experience I had just had. The park does not deserve vehicles and people and I hope the abundant wildlife, including many bears, would not be disturbed. I felt quite honoured to have been so intimately close to one of the most beautiful places on earth. I needed time to reflect and a first-class breakfast on the shores of the lake was the ideal refuge. In a busy diner, the tranquillity of the great outdoors quickly dissolved into banter and joviality with locals and travellers. Everyone was in party mood and had every intention of revelling as Independence Day matured towards midday.

Everything seemed boringly mundane after the morning exploits. What next in Montana? Well, I kept my spirits high with the expectations of a night stop in Missoula. Then it would be Helena and south into Yellowstone and the Tetons in Wyoming. This journey was really like a fine bottle of wine and I wasn't going to rush whatsoever. Especially as I was getting down to the last glass or so. Quite a few people had asked me if I had got any inspiration from anyone to do this journey. I did get some inspiration from two people. Two celebrities with huge slices of Americana in their blood. One was a writer and the other was a writer and broadcaster. Both regretfully are deceased now. Have you guessed yet? Well the first is the novelist Jack Kerouac who wrote the epic novel *On the Road*. Kerouac, of faded jeans, workman's shirt, boots and rucksack, conjured up a sort of modern-style hero in that book and most travellers and adventures, along with *Zen* and *The Art of Motorcycle Maintenance*, have a copy. I was carrying an edition with me and at low moments, a few Kerouac words would give a fillip of inspiration. The other person must be coming into focus now, of course. Alistair Cooke. The iconic Americanised Brit that delivered the unmissable *Letter from America* for decades. I used to hang on his every word and his Sunday radio delivery was a highlight of my week, any week. I feel I have the unconventional sides of Kerouac and the refined aspects of Cooke within me. Traveller certainly, writer I hope, broadcaster, who knows. In Cooke's *American Journey*, the lost manuscript that his secretary found after his death, he talks about Missoula. I had to go there. I think the name also persuaded my visit. Missoula-Montana – its got quite a ring to it, as has Anaconda-Montana. Behind Billings, the garden city of Missoula is the second largest city in the state and home to the University of Montana. It was very quiet on arrival and I had no trouble finding a motel in the middle of downtown. Walking around, I instantly got a nice feel to a compact city with wide streets lined with tall, red brick buildings, bars and restaurants and a busy railway station and freight depot. Parking on the streets was abundant. Maybe the public holiday had pushed everyone into the countryside and Glacier National Park. Whatever, I studied a parking meter to check if I was reading it correctly. One quarter for two and a half hours! That is incredible and not seen anywhere else. Another example of how things change in this melting pot of the USA. It further qualifies my views that the states could almost be independent countries. That would please Texas. A couple of things have come out of this state worth noting: the speed limit of 70 mph on the hi-line highway and very cheap parking in Missoula. Come and live in Montana folks. On a serious note, the first settlers were American Indians who didn't encounter any whites until the Lewis and Clark expedition passed through the valley. It became a trading post in early days and quite remarkably, the success of the city was helped considerably by the development of the university. It is quite unique for education to be at the roots of a city rather than the civil war and politics. Today much evidence of student life is in town. As one would expect, the majority of serving staff in the many bars and restaurants were motley-looking students dressed in varying apparel. I sampled a few hostelries in the evening. In one pub a group of locals introduced me to their chum. He was a giant of a bartender. It turned out that he played football for the college side and was a huge brute of a guy, as wide as he was tall. Standing next to him put my five foot ten inches in stocking feet into mediocrity. It posed a question, if all these football players are so big, bulky and muscular, oozing masculinity and machismo, why are they helmeted and have to wear all that padding? It didn't go down well and I didn't receive a free T-shirt this time. No, it was late, the bars were bursting and getting extremely rowdy with Independence Day party-goers. I retreated to my motel room balcony and viewed the celebratory fireworks over a glass of Shiraz.

In contrast, the highlight of the state capital day was the 100-mile journey to get there! It was east over an elevated pass on route 12, through Frontier Town, followed by a rapid descent into quite an ordinary-looking place. I think I would be ticking a box here and moving on. That would be a shame as the romantic name Helena in such an impressive state conjured up so many visions of an exciting cowboy town surrounded by mountains. I was a little disappointed with Helena, which had little to rival the vibrant atmosphere of Missoula, a city with attitude. The town was established following the discovery of gold along the Last Chance Creek and at one time had more millionaire residents than anywhere in the world. That's quite a statistic to boast. The precious metal transformed the city into Montana's golden capital. The considerable wealth did however account for significant culture, including varied and impressive architecture in some neighbourhoods. St Helena Cathedral and the Greek Renaissance Revival Capitol Building are fine examples. I think it is always the people and sunshine that make a place. It was a grey Saturday in Helena. However, I did meet a couple of interesting personalities, the first of which brought a firm religious theme to our lengthy conversation. It was the motel maintenance man who cornered me as I was unloading the bike. It was obvious he was extremely religious from the onset. His views were extremely strong on a couple of issues that were hitting the press at the time. He accounted for the wild fires in California as God getting annoyed with couples indulging in same-sex marriages. He said, 'God is not happy, it is an unnatural thing and in annoyance, he has created the fires on his sacred earth in that state.' We talked for 15 minutes and he brought religion into everything we were discussing. When I asked him if religion was the common theme in this country or Montana, or for him, he would not commit to an answer. I had heard that before. Some folk are full of opinions, but sometimes not backing them up with belief and commitment. He added that all states are different which also corresponds to my frequent thoughts. Different countries using the same currency is one way to look at it. It was whilst musing around the State Capitol, which incidentally had the flag flying at half-mast for another war fatality, that I met an interesting couple from Virginia. Touring Montana, they had met Barack Obama in Butte the day before. He was on the election trail and had been freely walking amongst the public and greeting perfect strangers. Now as the Democratic Presidential nominee, BO was certainly becoming the man of the moment in the accelerating political and election frenzy. The country was warming to the man who could be a breath of fresh air in Washington.

After Helena, it was off on the national park trail again. The next state capital on the route was Boise, Idaho, then Salem, Oregon, leaving Olympia Washington State to complete the lower 48. With about three weeks left to do that, it was looking good. First, I had an appointment with the North West corner of Wyoming to view Yellowstone and the Grand Teton Parks. They also hold much geographical spectacle and reputation. I had studied the area and my plan was to proceed to Gardiner, Montana at the northern entrance to Yellowstone. A day should get me through both parks before turning right for Idaho. From Helena, routes 12 and 89 took me through more diverse scenery of the Big Sky State. Prairie, forests and mountains, most of which again were under-populated with few settlements and little vehicles. It was big cattle country out here and undoubtedly a way of life to survive the harsh winters and hot summers. I had heard that Gardiner gets busy with travellers all with the same plan as me. It was one of the few times I rang ahead and booked a motel. After 180 miles, I arrived in the quaint but quite basic town of Gardiner. The motel was expecting me which was nice and I was greeted with coffee and nice smiles. What a contrast to St Mary's. Gardiner seemed a bit more gritty and down to earth in comparison to a tourist rip off I had seen in St Mary's. After a lunchtime stroll, my views were confirmed – gritty and down to earth it was. Over lunch, I met an interesting guy in a small bar who appeared to be having trouble with movement. He was the barman and on closer inspection, it was apparent that he had only one leg. He was hobbling around using many surfaces for support. He was doing rather well and produced a perfect sandwich and coffee in no time. As I ate and drank, he became quite open about his disability which was the result of a crab boat accident in the Bering Sea. He agreed that Missoula is a great little city and told me how he divides time between there and Gardiner. Montana is his favourite state and when I asked why, he said it's the geographical diversity and the open spaces. He added that these little towns next to the parks can get a bit pretentious and over-priced and to look out in St Mary's and Jackson Hole. I exchanged notes about my experiences in St Mary's and it didn't surprise him. As I was leaving the bar he shouted, 'Gardiner is different, you will enjoy your stay here.' I was still feeling a bit fatigued. I again put it down to the altitude. In Gardiner I was up at 6,000 feet and had been at elevation in Montana for over a week now. I was convinced it was the altitude in addition to my reasonably arduous schedule. I had done 1,200 miles in Montana alone which exemplifies how big this state is. How many Rhode Islands, Delawares and Vermonts would fit into this piece of country?! Anticipating an early departure the next morning, I bought my entry ticket in advance for Yellowstone and rode the short distance to Mammoth Springs and the visitor centre. After a succinct chat with the informative ranger, it was clear that I could pass though both Yellowstone and Teton Parks easily in one day and maybe stay in Jackson Hole at the other end. He added the earlier the better, keep west and watch out for the bugs, they get big at this time of the year. I don't think he was meaning the roaming bison. I experienced more of rustic Gardiner in the evening, including a first-class steak cooked right in front of my eyes on an open grill. The bars did seem quite rough, populated by guys in jeans with handkerchiefs on their heads, smoking cigarettes with that different smell shall we say. My appraisal of the place would not make glossy brochure headlines, but it made for an entertaining evening. Prior to turning in, I became a tourist guide when a loaded vehicle screeched to a halt next to me. In an accent that couldn't be from anywhere other than Mississippi, which was confirmed by the licence plate, the driver shouted across, 'Where is the welcome to Montana sign?'

I replied, 'There isn't one here, trust me, I have done a recce,' 'Thank you and it was nice to meet someone from Australia tonight.'

No comment. I did however have one more opportunity to exercise my Brit tones that day. An old industrial building caught my eye at the end of the village. Close by was a building that could only be an accommodation block; it just had that look. It was and a few folk were milling around outside in the evening sun, including a huge African-American guy and his most petite partner. They were from Texas and Oregon. What a couple. Things would be interesting in their lives. They confirmed the building was the bunkhouse for workers in the park and it was end of shift and relaxation time. The Texan was full of grins and giggles and to his credit he correctly identified my nationality. That was a refreshing change. Before we went our ways, he wanted me to say 'bloody hell' in that British way. He had heard it said in movies and clips from British TV. It was his interpretation of a typical Brit phrase. I of course obliged in enthusiastic style throwing a few examples his way, resulting in more Texan giggles and guffaws. Bloody hell it's bed time.

Chapter 68

Return to the Cowboy State

It was back in early May that I was last in Wyoming. That was on the Big East, 2 months and 10 000 miles ago. At that stage of my journey, I wasn't sure if I would be re-entering the state to see these 2 National Parks. But here I was in early July primed to run south through Yellowstone and Grand Teton. It was another dawn departure from the cosy little motel in Gardiner. Regretfully, the guests of the full motel got an early morning call courtesy of Mr BMW and the crunch crunch over the gravel parking area. So be it, progress had to be made. The park had just opened as I passed through the Roosevelt Arch, showed my ticket to the sleepy ranger and crossed the state line back into Wyoming. I had been as far as Mammoth Springs the day earlier and passing there again and joining the Grand Loop Road south bound, another geographical spectacle began to open up. I had read that the main Lewis and Clark Expedition had passed by the area and merely sent a small scouting party to explore the region. It was an area settled by Native American tribes and later, mountain men and fur trappers. Some early travellers nicknamed the area a place of 'fire and brimstone' and there were numerous reports of boiling mud, steaming water and petrified trees. Were they rural myths or accurate? Progressing south, the words of my reading came off the page and into reality. They were not myths and what I was observing on a quiet and still July morning just after dawn, could have been a couple of hundred years ago. Steam rising from soft undulating hills, the gurgle and glug from active volcanic pools and that pungent smell, were all so atmospheric. Maybe the asphalt road and modern park signage were the only bits of today's world in the picture. Yellowstone is centred on a 7500 feet high plateau, the caldera of a former volcano. It's probably the volcanic properties, particularly hydro thermal activity creating steaming pools and bubbling mud, that make the park that much different from others and so popular to visit. These impressive attributes are complimented by mountain ranges, gushing rivers, steep canyons and many deep blue lakes. Stopping the bike and turning off any connection to the modern day, it was so easy to drift back into another century. As my journey had progressed into the west, I had received many cautionary words about the wildlife and be careful out there, you are very vulnerable on a bike. Are you armed, are you carrying a hunters knife? Those chats were normally in a bar and the seriousness of the threat from the Grizzly and other big beasties was normally diluted by a couple of beers. Yer, thanks I'll look out and be ok. I thought I could leave the warnings about wildlife until getting into Northern Canada and Alaska. However, in Yellowstone a lot of those words of advice reappeared. I was seeing big groups of bison and huge herds of deer. They were all enjoying early morning grazing and thankfully well clear of the road at the moment. I had heard tales of tourist cars having altercations with bison and the car always coming off worse. Vulnerable and unarmed I was. I was particularly careful to make sure no wildlife was lurking close to where I pulled over for photographs, or so I thought. Whilst taking some shots of a thermal area, boiling water and unstable ground, I heard a noise that was animal and not mineral. Returning the short distance to where I had parked up, a Bison was having a good sniff and snort around my machine. He, yes it was a he, was particularly interested in the shark's mouth nose which up until now had only attracted miscellaneous swooping attacks from avian directions. I approached as close as I dare and Mr Bison looked my way through those brown eyes, almost studded onto his very thick set head. We exchanged glances for what seemed an age and he eventually returned from whence he came. Thankfully he didn't glance past my bike, from which his bulk may have caused upset and calamity. No, he trudged back into the fir trees in search of more nourishment and frolicking no doubt. He was the first close contact to anything living I had experienced so far that morning. A little close for comfort. However, crowds of humans were re-introduced into my day around Old Faithful, the famous geyser named way back in 1870. So famous has the geyser become over the years, that the area is designated a historic district and along with its impressive hydro thermal properties, the site is also a tourist magnet. It was before 9 am when I arrived and the place was already bustling with visitors. An eruption was imminent which I viewed far from the crowds and whilst sitting on the bike. It was still impressive and a predictable eruption interval of every 90 minutes or so, justifiably attracts the hoards. It is not however the tallest geyser in the park, that title belongs to the less expected spurts from Steamboat Geyser. Continuing south I had nearly run out of Yellowstone on the west side. The tranquillity of Lewis Lake attracted my attention for a leg stretch, a call of nature and few photographs. It was right here where I remembered the comments from the Park Ranger, the bugs were damn big and were becoming attracted to my smells. They were undoubtedly after my blood and the only relief was to replace my helmet and move on. They were hideous and creating a horror show type buzz as they homed in on my odours.

Approaching Jackson Lake I was clear of Yellowstone and into the next park. The Grand Teton National Park. Quite a contrast. Part 2. The blue summers day with a few flecks of cloud bouncing off the mountains, were ideal conditions to view the spectacular landscape of jagged peaks and pristine lakes. The mountains appear to abruptly rise, almost vertically from the valley floor. Beautiful yellow summer flowers flirting in a light breeze, provided a fitting foreground to the snow capped peaks and blue sky. Thankfully all the traffic was north bound, probably heading for Yellowstone. That left a free run south, stopping frequently to view Ranger Peak, Doane Peak, Mount Moran and Grand Teton, towering up to 7000 feet. The area is a haven for the outdoors type, with climbing and rambling routes to suit all standards. A log cabin with a view of the mountains, lakes and fir trees, I would almost place in the heaven box. Traffic was still heading north and purring along at a sedate pace, not in any rush, the John D Rockefeller Jr Parkway meandered down the east side of the mountains and dropped me off in Jackson Hole. It was only mid afternoon and I had ridden through one of the country's most impressive parks and down the side of a huge alpine like mountain range in but a few hours. The blue sky undoubtedly made the day. It may have been different in grey. Anyway, from the outside this little town looked neat, compact, full of amenities and hopefully good fun. However, it turned out to be both touristy and grossly expensive. What did I expect next to these 2 parks? However, it still irritated me to pay over the odds, way over the odds for a basic motel. Some of the locals appeared pretentious and unfriendly. 'Here's more visitors folks, lets fleece them for all the dollars they have'. Maybe I was being unfair, but was I seeing the Jackson of 20 or 30 years ago? I don't think so, winter sports, the beauty of the parks and the proliferation of the electronic world, has transformed Jackson's skin into a different colour. Give me Cheyenne any day. One thing about this journey, I was seeing a lot of places and justifiably able to compare and contrast. I would place Jackson in the Sedona-Arizona genre. A commercially orientated town in the middle of stunning geography. These sort of towns do not represent the real America, whereas the geography does. Thankfully I have experienced few similar places. Bikers Tony and Lill Pospisil I met in the motel, did not share my views. They loved Jackson and returned to the same motel when passing through north west Wyoming. With a Honda Goldwing towing a trailer, Tony and Lill represented a different style of biker. But cover the ground they do. Every year they embark on a 10-12 000 mile journey from their home in Massachusetts and connect the isolated regions in search of unique pieces of Americana. We chatted for ages and they were impressed with my trail through their country, albeit quickly reminded me they were both already '50 staters'. That didn't surprise me. I was a '45 stater' at the moment. Going over my route, I mentioned some places that I had passed by without closer examination. I recalled my dilemma about whether to stay in Tuba City way back in Arizona, or continue to Sedona. I continued to Sedona and was disappointed with the swamp of tourism as similar to right here in Jackson. Tony let out a long sigh, followed by a longer laugh. Apparently, Tuba City was a great stopover, steeped in Indian history and worthy of a travellers scrutiny. I had missed out on a gem that day, only to be drawn towards the commercial town of Sedona. We all shared something however, that was the washed out bodily feel that had been lurking. We agreed it was the local elevations and distances covered that were to blame. A second opinion is always worthwhile. Without prompting Tony mentioned that Americans especially long distance bikers seek to achieve freedom and independence. That was interesting and in line with other comments I had received in my urge to discover what Americans strive for. Tony's calming dialogue in Mid-Atlantic tones, soothed my perhaps unnecessary lambasting of little old Jackson. But they both agreed they had seen the changes over the years towards the commercial spot that it is today. Folks have to make a living I guess, however more smiles and conversation would be nice from the town that is keen to get your dollar. It dawned on me as turning in that night, that in the last couple of days I had perhaps over dosed on the great outdoors and stunning national parks. Maybe I was expecting too much. It made a change from 'od- ing' on the state capitals that's for sure. Talking of which it was west into number 46 the next day, Boise Idaho.

Chapter 69

What about Boise?

What lay before me was one of the most geographically diverse rides of the 20 000 miles covered so far in this country. There were a lot of surprises packed into the ride across the middle of the state of Idaho. Tony and Lill saw me off and very quickly I was clear of Jackson and in the countryside climbing up to 7500 feet across the southern tip of the Teton Range. The road was flanked by thick forests, extremely steep slopes and valleys. Over the top and leaving Wyoming and crossing into Idaho, it was a rapid descent into the Swan Valley where the terrain quickly changed to gentle rolling green hills and fast flowing rivers. By the looks of the many parked up RV's close to the river, I am sure this was big fishing country. Leaving the Tetons behind and progressing west, it was almost like another world, another country, certainly another state. Idaho Falls, a busy commercial and agricultural town was next. Then crossing the wide and fast flowing Snake River and continuing west, the geography changed again. It was a gentle climb out of Idaho Falls and at about 5000 feet, I was on the moon. Greens turned to yellows and browns of the scrub and sand of the high desert. I had never really associated Idaho with the desert, in this case the high desert, considering its location in the country. Rugged mountains, valleys, rivers and plains yes, but desert up in the North West? Highway 20 levelled off and with the increasing heat of the day and complete lack of traffic, it suddenly became a very very lonely ride. St Mary's Nipple,

East Butte and Middle Butte broke the flat and rather nebulous scenery up a little to the south of the route, but other than that there was nothing but scrub and sand. I am sure these huge lumps of rocks would have made excellent landmarks for the early pioneers. But arriving in this barren featureless land from green lower elevations and exploring this desolate landscape would have been a challenging experience to say the least. Atomic City was sign posted off to the south. Atomic City? What an apt name for a town up here. If I saw a strange building, craft or alien I wouldn't be surprised. The dramatic cloudscapes from Lone Pine would have completed the picture up here. Maybe the heat was getting to me? I was looking forward to reaching Butte City and Arco to reintroduce myself to some sort of civilization. That experience came earlier, when completely out of nowhere, I was brought to a halt at some road construction. The stop guy who was dressed in a lot of protective kit which astonished me in the heat, told me there would be quite a wait and I should switch off and stretch my legs. He was a young man from the town of Arco that I was approaching. My first question to him, was why on earth was the resurfacing in progress? The road looked fine to me and some of the best I had ridden. I related to him my general comments about roads in the USA. He assured me it was in bad condition after the winter and had to be done. It must be the end of the financial year for the local county and they have dollar to dispose of. From nowhere, we were shortly joined by a long stream of cars out of the heat shimmer from the east. I hadn't realized others were behind me. The lady driver of the first vehicle got out, slammed her door and approached the stop man with a look of disdain. I smelt conflict, but she thrust some snacks his way, added a few complimentary words and made off. That was nice, which the stop guy I think appreciated. We got talking about my trip and studying my route on the side of the bike, I mentioned I was getting towards the end of the lower 48 and would be heading towards Alaska soon. 'Alaska, how are you going to ride up to Alaska, are there roads up there?' I didn't quiz his geographical knowledge of this part of the world, but it was obvious this young man was not really sure if Alaska was connected to the American continent. Not to worry, he was young and lived on the moon. The 'follow me' truck arrived and motion was a relief to the increasing heat of the day. West of Arco, the occasional Butte I had seen earlier, gave way to the rugged Sawtooth Mountain range to the north. Yellows and browns and lacking any trees and vegetation, they were in complete contrast to the alpine like snowcapped relief of Glacier National Park and the Teton's. Suddenly the earth turned black and covered in the cinders of huge lava fields. I had arrived at Craters of the Moon National Park. At 6000 feet on the Snake River Plain, this collection of crunchy rock and cinder would be heaven for volcano specialists. I was surrounded by the finest examples of lava fields and basalt found in the Americas. A twisting small road prescribes a looping circuit of the rugged site, which has the remnants of several volcano cones reduced to rubble. Rainfall up here is extremely limited, however, I was surprised to see sagebrush and yellow flowering vegetation scattered around the rocks. From a distance, the vegetation is not seen and as I left the park and rejoined the highway, I got an impression of total black desolation. The site would be an ideal place to film a sci fi movie set on some distant planet. Although I am sure the geologists would object. The Sawtooth Mountains provided an impressive backdrop to the north, in contrast to flat and nothing more than desert to the south. The small town of Carey appeared out of the heat shimmer and I took shelter from the scorching day at a fuel station which had all the amenities. Fuel, food, coffee, sandwich bar, you name it. I was back amongst the services of the modern day. West of Carey, the desert became the high agricultural plains. The yellows and browns quickly turned to shades of green, giving the impression of a much more civilized and utilized world. I had left the moonscapes behind and was passing through an area rich in cattle, horses and hay making. The agricultural theme continued as I passed Picabo, Magic Reservoir, Fairfield and Hill City. Granite and Bennet Mountains were a final reminder of the magnificent contours in this area and descending down Tollgate Hill took me to Mountain Home for the final run into Boise. That had turned out to be quite some 350 miles. From the lofty Teton's, crossing west into the lowlands of Idaho, climbing into the high desert and passing towering buttes and lava fields, further west across rich agricultural plains and finally, a gentle descent into the state capital.

Well what about Boise? Pronounced Boy-zee, Boise is the capital of the geographical diverse Gem State. Gem State because it is one of 2 places in the world where star garnets can be found. Gem State not because of the geographical gems I had encountered on my way across from Wyoming. The city's origins go back to 1862 as a settlement used by pioneers passing on the Oregon Trail. The original site had a forest by a river which was a truly welcome sight in comparison with the surrounding arid desert areas. I concur. The name was originally given by French trappers – Les Bois – meaning 'the woods' and although there may be some doubt as the years unfolded, Les Bois may have been miss spelt or referred to as Boise. 'The City of Trees'. That's one explanation that would make a good question in a pub quiz. I am sure there are others. Boise won the capital rights from Lewiston in the north of the state and the sandstone State Capitol building was completed in 1920. It's another domed capitol, Italian Renaissance Revival, capped with a statue of an eagle. The Capitol is Idaho's most significant historic structure and a building that reflects the state's political, social and economic history. Due to extensive refurbishment, I was prevented access to view the interior. After a similar experience in Annapolis, Maryland, this was only the second time I had encountered a 'no entry'. That wasn't a bad statistic considering Boise was my 46th state capital. I was able to have a virtual tour on my lap top from the comfort of a poolside table at my motel. Incidentally, moon rocks from the 1969 Apollo XI lunar flight are on display in the Governor's Office. I found that an amusing coincidence after riding through a lunar landscape across the high desert the day before.

Sitting at just under 3000 feet, this mid size city similar in size to Des Moines and Providence, certainly has a buzz and an attitude. It's a clean and compact place. I noticed immediately that I was at lower altitudes after quite some time elevated in the mammoth Big Sky State. It was a pleasurable feeling to have my body back and not to be walking around as if suspended in glue in an exhausted doldrum. My theory of Montana altitude sickness may be correct. Trees and parks dominate Boise giving a refreshing feel. The abundant street side cafes and convivial locals express a cosmopolitan culture. Included in the multi-cultured capital is a large Basque community, whose vibrant festival, transforms the downtown Basque Block into a frenzy every 5 years. I missed out by 2 years, but could still anticipate the feel from the general atmosphere oozing from the plentiful eateries close to the Basque Market. Along with a jazz and theatre scene, Boise gets my vote and may just appear in my favourite top 5 state capitals so far. 4 still to go, final analysis to follow. The downtown is neatly divided into the Capitol District, a Cultural District with theatre and galleries and Old Boise's Historic District. The pedestrian friendly city centre is easily navigable on foot or even on an efficient public transport network. In every section, elegant brick faced restaurants and shops are plenty. I passed on the invitation to float down the swollen Boise River on a rubber tube. It looked fun and is apparently a local tradition, which I left to the locals. The attractions of an unpretentious and enjoyable city did however persuade an extras day stay. During mid-July scorching summer days, I attempted to chill out-literally-and enjoy a city with a unique combination of architecture and cultural districts, blended with a distinctive selection of specialty boutiques and restaurants.

Chapter 70

Return to the Pacific Coast

To avoid the forecast high temperatures of the day, I was up and on the road by 0630. The last few days had been hot and hotter, but thankfully with no humidity. It was dry heat and peaking around 100F. The weather was creeping in to my planning again. My objective from Boise was to take up a westerly track to the coast, which was still a good hike away and maybe stop en route and pick out any other nuggets hiding out there. I did have an invite to drop by and share a beer with Rick the truck driver I met on my first cut through Wyoming in early May. He was in Baker City, but busy with work and hence I had to skip that one. From a sleepy Boise, I headed north for a while and then turned left into Oregon on route 20, with the intentions of carving through the guts of the state as far west as my energy would allow. I had heard that Oregon has a diverse landscape, rather like Idaho, with a coastline thrown in. I wanted to see the coast and the Pacific before heading for the capital. Before the ocean I would see more high desert, the rugged and glaciated Cascade Mountains and maybe even dense evergreen forests. The Oregon Central Highway, route 20, took me west into more of high desert country. It was quite similar to Idaho the other day, but not as arid and harsh. West of Harper, the road climbed and snaked through a mountain pass and then levelled off onto quite a high plateau past Elephant Butte and King Mountain and onwards to the small town of Burns. This was my first stop at around mid morning and I took some fuel from the first station I found. It was a small place on a corner, where refuelling was supervised by an old boy dressed in blue overalls. He was in charge of operations on the forecourt and chatting to all, I am sure he knew all. When it was my turn, I think he was a little thrown and his chatting slowed down to 'morning' and 'come far' type comments and nothing more. That was enough fuel for the rest of the day and getting to minimums on this full tank would be a good barometer when to call a halt. West of Burns, a huge convoy of assorted military trucks was heading the opposite direction. There must have been over 50, lights on and tall aerials flexing in the slipstream, they were in an awful rush. Route 20 continued west, undulating through the high desert which was getting hotter as noon approached. I was desperately looking for a coffee and leg stretch stop and came across what looked like a single building with a few bits added on here and there. It turned out to be Brothers Stage Stop and US Post Office 97712. But it was everything, post office, café, store, restrooms, fuel, bar, vending area, you name it, it was there. Not modern and glitzy, but exterior paint peeling from the high desert sun, plastic tablecloths on simple tables, a wooden bar and ordering area, a variety of foods populating the cluttered shelves, another bar for evening use and even a piano thrown in as well. This was probably the only meeting, greeting and eating place for miles around. Baseball caps and branding irons were hanging from every available place on the ceiling. It just stunk of character and by the looks of the clientele, used by local characters. Mike Knuckles and his wife were out the front looking at their cruiser bike, in debate about something by the looks of it. It turned out they were desperately short of fuel and the pumps had run out. Delivery awaiting-or had they stopped supplying fuel, I cannot recall. They didn't have enough to get the short distance to Bend the next town west and had relied upon fuel here at Brothers. I offered some from my recently replenished tank, but a local farmer had beaten me to it. He returned from his ranch with a jerry can of fuel to save Mikes embarrassment. Conversation continued inside where 2 extremely hospitable ladies multi tasked post office duties, running the kitchen, looking after general sales, simultaneous to walking around with the coffee jug and talking for Oregon. Marvellous! They reliably informed me that the military convoy was heading for California to help fight the bush fires that had increased and put the state in an emergency situation in certain counties. I lost count how many refills of coffee I had, which may have just been instrumental in how far I progressed. The whole place was perfectly clean, but just with a fantastic rustic feel. It was like a big version of Lowe's store I had encountered way back east. Many locals were in and out and some were having lunch of the day which looked like giant pork chops. One guy came in and I swear he must have tied his horse up outside. He was dressed like a real cowboy. Jeans, leather chaps, boots with spurs-yes with spurs, checked shirt with leather waistcoat and of course impressive weather beaten Stetson perched upon a stubbly face. All that was missing was a sheriff's badge and a shooter on his hip. I was impressed by the authenticity of this guy and Mike reminded me that I was in the west and at Brothers Stage Post Stop, the Wild West! After all the coffee, a visit to the restrooms was a prerequisite before saddling up again. Even they had character, wooden slatted creaky doors and old porcelain. This was the sort of place I always looked out for rattlers and scorpions hiding before getting comfortable. Luckily nothing encountered. Departing Brothers Stage Stop, Mike Knuckles fired up first, obviously the fuel was good and we chatted more as his bike ticked over and his wife got comfortable. They were out of Eugene and heading home after a trip down to Yellowstone. Cigarette perched on his lower lip, he waved and shouted 'independence and freedom are my meaning to life my friend' and made off westbound with a small Stars and Stripes flapping in the wind. It had been a busy 30 minutes at Brothers.

How could I better that experience? Rick the truck driver had mentioned that Bend would be an interesting stopover with motel and restaurants a plenty. Did I want another place like that after having an enjoyable R&R in Boise? No, I needed somewhere non tourist and local for the night. The Crater Lake was on my agenda before the coast, but after 380 miles in the heat since leaving Idaho, it was time to find a bed for the night. Fuel was sloshing around on minimums below. With the snow capped Cascade Mountains in sight to the west, I decided to by pass Bend and keep south until I found a small town. I passed a couple of very small linear places south on route 97 and stopped in Chemult which looked to have fuel, food and bed. Gidget and Don welcomed me into the Featherbed Motel set in 6 acres just off the highway. I got the potted history of their business, including an introduction to a couple of horses in an enclosure, whilst an exuberant dog circled and barked. Gidgit and Don were a hardworking couple that got the Featherbed up and running after some inactivity. It's a frequent stop for truckers especially loggers. Chemult had origins as a logging town. They even gave me some contacts for Juneau Alaska, which may prove to be useful in a couple of weeks. I was beginning to look at the extreme north west of the map now. It looked to be an interesting community, on the busy highway and also an Amtrak railhead on the Seattle-Sacramento scenic route. After a walk around in the afternoon heat, it was obvious that I had chosen to stay at what is today simply a trucker's stop. Everything was hugging the highway, including several fuel stations, lodgings, stores and a few diners. Competition and the recession had forced some of the businesses to close, which was evidenced by some empty diners and the like. 'Drive up for ice and chilled beer', but alas some signs were still attached to the empty properties and no ice or chilled beer was available today. Some with broken and boarded up windows reflected Chemult was no longer booming. Locals told me later, that the opening of a modern travel centre including fuel, mini supermarket and restaurant, operating with highly competitive prices, had simply forced oxygen out of the smaller fry. A shame and harsh, but a sign of the times in today's modern business world. Logs for sale at most of the open stores, indicated that there are extremely cold winters in this part of the state. My hypothesis was proven when I discovered a collapsed roof on a fuel station was caused by heavy snows. It wasn't all doom and gloom in town and I found a good steak house for dinner. It was a diner and bar and the manager who was on patrol greeting eaters and drinkers, reliably informed me he gets the best steak in the country from an outlet up the road in Bend. He wasn't far from the mark and my hunk of rare flesh was juicy and tasty and could have been cut of the beast's rump and floated over the grill 5 minutes before. The karaoke had fired up next door, trucks and RV's had gathered outside and the local population were adding their names on the list to become a Friday night entertainer. One lady who was obviously a karaoke expert and regular, sang well. Others were awful. You need to be inebriated to participate and enjoy this pastime which I had no desire to do. Even in Chemult. Between the caterwauls from the increasingly intoxicated contestants, I did manage some conversation with truck driver Doug. He tended to agree with my sentiments of the evenings entertainment, but it was mildly amusing nonetheless. Chemult was a regular stop for Doug who hauls paint out of Reno Nevada and covers all the western states. With lots of time spent in the cab, he was a real current affairs aficionado, both national and international. What's more he tried to tune into the BBC World Service when he could. He mentioned a few of his favourite programmes, including 'From our own Correspondent', so I am sure he hadn't said all this simply to impress. I quickly went into interview mode and started with the questions. 'What's a typical American, what of the future, who will be the President next year?' Quaffing his beer and looking me straight in the eyes, he replied, 'Americans are greedy, Americans are arrogant, education is not a good standard and the country needs an injection of great innovators, or else we will go to the dogs'. I don't think I had hit a nerve, but I got the impression Doug wanted to get that off his chest to a non-American. After our mini debate, he made off to the comfort of his truck bunk-probably the size of my apartment and I headed off to my featherbed.

The next day dawned blue and very breezy. I had heard about the spectacle of Crater Lake and headed that way the short distance from Chemult. It was a Saturday morning and surprisingly the looping road around the lake was free from the tangle of any other trippers. It's the setting that is so eerie and thought provoking. At 7500 feet elevation, the lake is surrounded by tall vertical walls that cast shadows and reflections on the menacing looking surface. The lake was formed when a massive eruption of Mount Mazama 7700 years ago caused the mountain to collapse, leaving a steaming caldera. Centuries of rain and snow filled the huge void creating the lake. Deep blue and almost black at a second take, it is a little under 2000 feet deep and the deepest in the western hemisphere. Some years ago, a helicopter crashed in the lake and sits on the bottom with occupants on board 2000 feet down in the gloom. Their final resting place and tomb is in the icy depths of Crater Lake. I wonder if the lake holds any other secrets similar to those of Lake Tahoe in California? I spent a good hour at the lake prior to heading off further west in search of the Pacific. It was back in mid-April when I last saw the Pacific Ocean. It was when I was leaving San Francisco east bound for Santa Rosa and Sacramento. Since then I have done 13 055 miles across the middle of the country, traversed the smaller states of New England and most lately passed right across the top. An oceanic coincidence, it was on the 12th of June I was tossing stones into the Atlantic Ocean at Newport Rhode Island whilst gazing at expensive and exclusive looking properties. Exactly a month to the date later, the Oregon Pacific coast greeted me on a very breezy Saturday afternoon in the seaside town of Yachats. Pronounced Yah-hats. It was quite a dramatic and rather moody scene as the white surf from the deep blue ocean, was crashing onto the rocky shoreline, against the backdrop of a clear summer sky. The temperature on the way from Crater Lake to the coast had risen to 95F and cooled rapidly and dramatically to a meager 65F on the coast. Yachats was a pleasant little place and one of many attractive towns that dot the Oregon coastline. Like any other seaside town, people were out walking, beach combing with infants and throwing sticks for exuberant canines reluctant to get their feet wet. Whilst gazing out to the west across the miles and miles of water, my thoughts went to reaching my 50th state. Hawaii was out there somewhere, a mere 2 or 3000 miles or so, it would be a long swim. Walking further on, I returned to reality and nearly tripped over the easel and paints of an artist at work. He was a huge guy and seemed to be living and operating from a large camper type van. Hidden under the brim of a floppy hat, he didn't notice my near collision, but continued to concentrate applying thick lines of bright paint to his latest masterpiece. To compliment my maritime location, it had to be fish on the menu in the evening and there was plentiful choice. I chose quite an average looking establishment with a dining room overlooking the ocean. The fish was good and washed down with Oregon beer from the adjoining bar, completed a good day.

Coincidently, I later met the painter in the bar, he was perched on a stool dressed in tracksuit pants and Hawaii shirt, drinking gin and tonics out of a cocktail glass. I mentioned I had seen him that afternoon at work and he admitted not to have noticed. Obviously concentrating on his canvass and thinking of his first evening drink. He started to talk about his days in the military as a special forces Ranger and then quickly diverted back to today. It turned out that his home was in Washington State which wasn't a million miles away. He lives in the motor home in the summer, earning a living by painting coastal murals and restaurant signs. Work comes and goes he added and, most of the money he sends back to his wife to pay the bills. Apparently he was always running the gauntlet with local Sheriffs who would move him and his motor home on at an annoying regularity. An interesting coastal character. A coastal tramp. Later I mused over some local tourist maps of the coastline. It hadn't looked that far on the map, which was quite normal, but the trip from Chemult via Crater Lake, across Oregon forests and fields and finally joining the Pacific Highway, had accumulated to 360 miles. From Jackson Hole to the coast via Boise and Chemult had been over a thousand miles. I was looking forward to the short distance to Salem and Olympia, to recharge my batteries prior to taking on Canada.

It was a cool start the following day and low cloud and fog shrouded the ocean. Passing north through Newport, Depoe Bay and Lincoln City, the sun was beginning to burn off the offending blankets of grey, revealing glimpses of the Pacific. The ocean was still out there somewhere. Just north of Lincoln City, I left the ocean behind and headed inland to the state capital of Salem. Temperatures recovered very quickly and 20 miles inland, it was like riding into the hot air of a greenhouse. Salem became the capital after Oregon City and Corvallis and today is the states 3rd largest city behind Portland and Eugene. What happens in Salem? Well, some of the locals call their home 'Snailem' which may give an indication what they think of the place. Unsurprisingly, the state government is the largest employer, in addition to light industry. The downtown area is compact and on a grid pattern of streets, navigation on foot or wheels was surprisingly easy. The present Capitol Building was completed in the 1930s. Previous buildings have been lost to fire and columned segments from the first State Capitol are on display in the Capitol Gardens. These columns could have been from Rome. Pleasingly, the present Capitol Building does deviate from the norm by having an art deco design, with large flat drum tower-no dome. A distinctive gold statue of the Oregon Pioneer, sits atop the imposing building providing impressive reflections in the garden pool. One of the highlights of my journey through Oregon, was a ride through the vineyards to the north of Salem and on to the aviation museum at McMinnville. Maybe a last look at American aviation. It was one aircraft that attracted my attention and one only. Moved from its former home in California, Howard Hughes' 'Spruce Goose' is now fully preserved and a main exhibit at the museum. Other display aircraft looked like ants scattered around the hall in comparison to the bulk and sheer enormity of the Goose. I was allowed to go on board and sit in the Captains seat, in Howard's seat. Just for a moment, quite a special moment, I was able to reminisce about the wealthy American entrepreneur and the unsuccessful Goose that flew only once. I felt the spirit of Howard Hughes very close.

Chapter 71

Across the Top Complete and the Lower 48 in the bag!

I could have dawdled up the Pacific Coast into Washington State and the capital Olympia. It may have made for a scenic arrival into my 48th capital via the seaside towns of Rockaway Beach, Seaside and Astoria. No, I had that mindset of just getting there, crossing the finishing line and kicking my tyres after doing the big lump of the continental USA. I had seen enough scenery for the moment and Canada planning was very much on my mind. So, it was an unmemorable 170 miles north on the Interstate into number 48. Interstate 5 did carve through the guts of Portland, which made for some distraction. It was another 'slot car' feeling as passing by the urban high rise, before being spat out into Washington State when crossing the Columbia River. Folks in Salem had mentioned that Portland was very much the action city of Oregon and Salem the quiet neighbour. I could get that feeling even from the road. I hoped that Olympia would maybe offer a bit more than Salem. On arrival, it looked small but appealing and after a quick ride around the compact and neat centre, I selected a motel just on the edge of town. I would be there for a few days and wanted to get things just right with my planning before heading north. It was a regular chain motel with a pool and usual amenities thrown in. I got chatting to the friendly janitor, who gave me a few top tips. 'Go and have a sandwich and a beer in the Japanese Garden just around the corner. You will appreciate the tranquillity after your journey'. If only he knew the full extent of my journey! 21 764 miles. 'Oh and by the way, just walk a few blocks down from the garden and you will hit 4th Street where all the action is'. He wasn't wrong and 4th Street provided a mix of all styles of bars and restaurants which handled evening events very well during my stay. Live music was even thrown in. I later found the Japanese Garden. It was postage stamp size immediately off a busy city street. But it did provide tranquillity and an ideal place to reflect.

What can I say about my 48th State Capitol Building. Set in nice gardens? *Yes.* A big dome ? *Yes.* Adjoining official buildings? *Yes.* It gets a big tick in the 'very regular' box for State Capitols. However, they are all different and it would be completely unfair simply to give Olympia that tick in the box and then move on to the bar. For starters, the verbose guide left an impression with me. He passionately talked, gesticulated and even at times remonstrated about the state of the nation. His views were too extreme to convert into words, but it was all hard core politics and what ifs, what when's and with who. 'Roll on the election and please come back and discuss the new government with me'. It was hard to get away from him. However, slightly refreshing as quite a lot of the population are not as well informed as this guy. My walk around the Beaux Arts Style Capitol was brief, but entertainment continued in the administrative area where a posse of girls were attracted to my tones. We talked for a while and they pulled up my website. Doors opened and others joined the gathering that had suddenly erupted into slightly raucous tenors. I hope I hadn't disturbed any meetings or similar, but no, it was a Friday afternoon and I am sure one and all were looking for distraction, looking towards 5pm and looking forward to a cocktail in a 4th Street bar. Every Capitol is indeed unique and the girls enthusiastically informed me that this was the only Capitol that had suffered 3 earth quakes in its history. The first in 1949, the second in 1965 and most lately in 2001. All caused damage to the Capitol building that required improvements and renovations. The huge dome's position originally relied upon gravity. Along with supporting columns, during one of the quakes, it moved! The dome is now fixed to the building, but its security has yet to be tested by any subsequent seismic action. I rather hoped this would not be assessed until I was well north and across the 49th parallel.

Olympia proved to be an excellent base for a few days before continuing north. What with the vibrant 4th Street and lively lakeside eateries, an interesting downtown and a decent motel, I had all that I needed. I still had over 2000 miles to get to Juneau, Alaska, number 49. There were maritime alternatives rather than taking on the roads of British Columbia. I could watch the west coast go by on board a boat. But the thought of sitting on a large ferry full of loud tourists held no appeal. No, if I could ride there, there was no option. Then after Juneau, there was still over a thousand miles to Anchorage. It is big country up there and I was far from finished. I wouldn't see another bike dealers for 3000 miles and took the opportunity of getting a local dealer to give my machine a quick inspection. All was well and the beast was given a fit bill of health, which was quite a testament considering all that had failed so far had been a headlight bulb. A couple of long distance riders were hanging around the dealers and offered excellent advice for my Canadian and Alaskan ride. My bike would apparently gobble up the roads, any type of road and the only concern that was offered, was look out for bears. They may gobble me up! Whilst the bike was in dock, I was reacquainted with Keith Keller. I had met Keith in Torrey Utah, back in early May. A man of his word, he took a day off work and arranged and paid for a fine lunch in a Tacoma restaurant overlooking Commencement Bay. I thought it was the ocean but this area has quite a complicated geography of inlets, bays and mountains, before you hit the Pacific west of Olympic National Park. I talked with his family for ages in the hot July temperatures. This meeting was probably the highlight to my 4 days in the area. We talked about the diversity of the USA and what the country offers to the traveller, the professional and the entrepreneur. Economic recession in progress yes, but hidden potential for all was not far away if you took the initiative. Upbeat and confident, Keith's closing remarks to me were, 'if there is a problem, it can be fixed, that's us in America'. Before leaving Olympia, Mount Rainier, part of the Cascade Range got my attention for half a day. My first sighting of the Cascades was from the high deserts of Oregon a few days before. It was a unique sighting of the rugged saw toothed snow capped peaks whilst still in the scorched and bleak deserts of Central Oregon. Mount Rainier boasts several impressive statistics. An active volcano, it is the highest peak in the Cascade Range. A food delivery guy I met over coffee, recommended an ideal viewing point. 'If you just want to take photographs, don't pay to enter the park, ride around to this car park which will give you the best views of the peak in the area'. Mount Rainier was the last significant geography I saw in the lower 48.

I was still 200 miles from the Canadian border and my planning and advice from Keith had revealed the best border crossing was via Aldergove, east of Vancouver. It was said to be a quiet border post and free of trucks and heavy commercial vehicles. That sounded good advice and an early morning crossing, would undoubtedly be the best plan in order to progress well up into British Columbia on my first day in Canada. That gave a spare day and the opportunity to look up a contact that Walter Crump had given me. Dear old Walter Crump I had met in Phoenicia-New York State. I remember him well from my visit to his rambling rural estate. As we poured over a map, he said when I get to Washington State, 'drop by and say hello to Craig, he will probably entertain you on his boat, he is often in La Conner which is very nice'. That sounded a plan and Craig was ashore the day I had decided to drop by. But it was picking a route west of Puget Sound and finding a ferry to the chunk of the state where La Conner is located, that was the challenge. It was a Saturday morning and once clear to the west of the Seattle-Tacoma sprawl, traffic was mainly light, probably weekenders heading towards boats and waterside restaurants. Washington State Ferries from Port Townsend to Keystone, provided the island hopping required and a scenic ride followed down Whidbey Island towards La Conner. It wasn't that challenging getting there after all. I was joined by a few more bikers on board the ferry, but one guy dressed in shorts and Hawaii shirt, approached me very positively. 'How's it been, any problems on the way', simultaneous to thrusting his metal police badge in my direction. He was full of questions in a rather interrogating manner. He added he had a similar bike, albeit modified considerably to fit his short legs. When I asked his opinion about my surveillance observations, he was reticent to comment at first and then firmly added I had been suffering from cabin fever-road fever. His body language indicated he was uncomfortable and I had put him on the spot. I did think I was being almost seen off the premises. 'Where are you going now, why to La Conner and when are you crossing into Canada?' After my brief encounter on the ferry, my mind was working overtime-again and before I knew it I was pulling up in the exceptionally smart marina in the exceptionally exclusive marine town of La Conner. With expensive looking eateries, chique boutiques and many a million dollars bobbing on the water, it just stank of money and opulence. I found Craig on board his catamaran and after he asked me to remove my boots, I was invited on board. Remove my boots indeed! Over a mug of tea, we talked for an hour or more. A retired man in the autumn of his life, Craig talked about his family, his sailing trips and of course politics. As often I do with a fresh face, I asked Craig about my surveillance thing, my observations throughout the country and my recent encounters with the guy on the ferry. He was careful how he responded and simply said, it's possible, it's just possible in this country. Maybe I hadn't been over sensitive after all, just maybe I had been under surveillance? It was a pleasant afternoon in delightful weather and surroundings. The scene I discussed with Walter was set. Walter should be enjoying this type of lifestyle instead of continuing his labour of love renovating his Catskills estate. Craig agreed. Before I got too comfortable sitting on his millions, I headed off to the border town of Lynden in preparation for crossing into Canada the next morning. I could only find one motel in the small town. It was a rickety old affair run by an Asian gentleman. I couldn't swing a cat in my room, the water was cold, the towels stood up unsupported and the windows and doors all didn't fit anymore and creaked and groaned with every footfall. Needless to say, after refuelling body and bike, I slept like a log with Canada very much on my mind.

It was a deep sleep accompanied by a vivid dream that mentally unfolded with cinema graphic accuracy. My head was buzzing and my body aching. I was recounting the ride across the top of the country. I could hear the engine note of the bike in my subconscious as the kaleidoscope of roads, mountains, lakes and cities unfolded from the last 5000 miles or so. I could hear my voice in the dream. Maybe I was talking in my sleep? It had turned out to be a great ride across the top of the country. I completed the final section in the lower 48 pretty much as planned. The only real bad weather encountered was when leaving Maine. I recall the remnants of an active area of low pressure was still hanging around leading to some rain and low cloud. After crossing Lake Champlain and entering the impressive Adirondacks, the grey sky changed to blue and apart from the occasional thunderstorm, stayed with me pretty much for the rest of the month. Continuing west, I had the option to take a short cut into Canada, however, I elected to remain in the USA and followed the southern shores of Lakes Ontario and Erie. On the shores of Lake Ontario, the notable village of Sackets Harbour proved to be an enjoyable and hospitable stopover. Following the Sea Way Trail west, in complete contrast was the rather characterless city of Erie in North West Pennsylvania. When leaving Erie early on a Saturday morning, I was at the mercy of a collection of incredible thunderstorms all day. I was in a cone of protection and my path remained dry and calm all the way into Lansing. Someone was looking down on me that day. Leaving Michigan, I did take a short cut and crossed Lake Michigan on the high speed ferry from Muskegon into Milwaukee, Wisconsin. The enjoyable capital of Madison and the striking Wisconsin countryside gave way to the metropolitan sprawl of the twin cities of Minnesota. Thankfully they were the last major urban areas encountered on this section. Further west, the states got big again and entering the Dakotas, I really got a feel of open space and that big big sky. The sky appeared to wrap around the whole picture ahead. Next was Montana and with fun towns, open spaces and National Parks to die for, turned out to be an impressive state. I wasn't surprised. I want to live in Montana. My dream had decided it for me. Close behind in geographical spectacle were the gems of Yellowstone and the Grand Tetons in the North West corner of the Cowboy State. As if boasting similar geographical diversities, the rich lowlands, high desert and striking mountain ranges of Idaho came rolling quickly into my journey. Next and quite similar but with a coastline, Oregon also brags desert, mountains and the unmissable if not very eerie, Crater Lake. If that wasn't enough, I was even given the opportunity to touch base with the spirit of Howard Hughes and sit on the flight deck in the Spruce Goose. A quick jaunt up to Washington State concluded my 'across the top' sector and firmly putting 'the lower 48 in the bag'. So, I had managed to complete the lower 48, whilst remaining in the lower 48. That was good, that was a good statistic. I was happy with that. It had seemed a challenging prospect way back in February when I left Florida. Some barbed comments from onlookers and reminders of how big the USA is, had not deterred me in the slightest. I had successfully extinguished any journey demons quite early on and simply shuffled 'my box' along the route. My successful mind game had overcome the enormity of this solo trek which had got me from Key West in Florida all the way to this rickety old motel in Lyndon-Washington State and a mere 10 miles from the Canadian border. I awoke with a start at dawn from that very busy sleep. It could have been the morning chorus or a passing truck that returned consciousness and ended the journey in my dream. But I had completed that journey and it was no longer a dream. I had lived my American dream. Time to move on to number 49 and still 3000 miles of the dream to dream.

Part Eight – North for the Last Frontier

Lynden-Washington State to Juneau-Alaska

2199 miles

CANADA
USA
AK
Whitehorse
Watson Lake
YT
Skagway
Fort
Nelson
N
Haines
Juneau
BC
AB
AK
Dawson
Creek
PACIFIC
Edmonton
OCEAN
Prince
George
North for the Last Frontier
Calgary
Lynden WA to Juneau AK
Lillooet
Vancouver
Vancouver
Island
CANADA
Lynden
USA
150 miles
WA

DATE	START	FINISH	MILEAGE	CUMULATIVE	COMMENTS
20 Jul	Lynden WA	Lillooet BC	199	22374	1/99
21 Jul	Lillooet BC	Prince George BC	321	22695	99/97
22 Jul	Prince George BC	Dawson Creek BC	257	22952	97
23 Jul	Dawson Creek BC	Fort Nelson BC	286	23238	Alaskan Hwy
24 Jul	Fort Nelson BC	Watson lake YT	321	23559	Alaskan Hwy
25 Jul	Watson Lake YT	Whitehorse YT	279	23838	Alaskan Hwy
27 Jul	Whitehorse YT	Skagway AK	109	23947	S Klondyke Hwy
30 Jul	Auk Bay Ferry Terminal AK	**Juneau AK (49)**	16	23963	Glacier Highway Loop
July Total				**5198**	
1 Aug	Juneau AK	Juneau AK	61	24024	Glacier & local area

427

Chapter 72

Beautiful British Columbia

It would be easy to say 'see you back in the USA' and we can rejoin the journey in Alaska. But to miss out British Columbia and Yukon would be quite remiss considering the tremendous geography on the way. I got that tremendous geography on day 1 in Canada. The Canadian border post was completely deserted and free of any other traffic. I think my early arrival at the 49th parallel had taken the duty officer by surprise. She left the comfort of her office and greeted me into Canada with a wave of her arm and shouted, 'morning, stay 6 months if you like'. She must have seen my Union Flags on my jacket and bike. I had to remind her to at least have a look at my passport and take out the arrival docket thus declaring me clear of the USA for the moment. A quiet Highway 1 took me through a very sleepy Vancouver. At Horseshoe Bay, I picked up route 99 and things quickly got very rural. The coastal scenery around Lions Bay and Porteau was quite spectacular with steep wooded valleys and rocky gorges spilling down to the water edge. For a moment, it reminded me of the Big Sur back in California with the magnification turned up a few notches. Once clear of Whistler winter sports centre, I was suddenly completely out in a wooded and mountainous wilderness as I continued to climb towards the Lillooet and Chilcalin Ranges. These ranges form part of the Coastal Range and I guess all are component parts of the mighty Rockies that I would encounter again further north.

The bike was gobbling up the road with aplomb and I could almost detect an enjoyable snarl from the engine note as caressing the impressively sexy curves and climbs of route 99. It was something to savour up here and not to be rushed. I am not sure if I was on the same glass of wine, or had just opened another bottle. The province license plate motto of 'Beautiful British Columbia' has got it just about right. The geography is certainly pleasing to the eye and after only a few hours, memories of the USA were drifting away. Could I really say that after 6 months down there? This time I was definitely in a different country and not just a new state. I didn't want to rush this new bottle of wine and after just 200 miles, I made my first Canadian night stop in the former mining town of Lillooet. Set on one quite dusty main street, the town is equipped well with traveller's services and I easily found a motel. The locals call their town, 'British Columbia's best kept secret!!'. With a bit of history thrown in to a recreational paradise, I am sure they have some credence in their boast. Surrounded by unspoiled mountains, valleys and lakes, trekkers could go out for a days walk and return to the bar claiming they have trodden on virgin soil. I could easily believe that, the area was simply exuding that sort of remote and expansive feeling. After dinner and a walk through town, a strong breeze had got up and was filling a large national flag. The fresh red and white with that proud maple leaf was a fitting backdrop against the steep green wooded mountain sides. I was certainly in a different country now.

The next day I had the intention of getting well up into the province and had Prince George mentally book marked as a night stop. That was about 350 miles north and if the roads were a repeat performance of the day before, another rider's pleasure was in store. The weather was warm and partly cloudy with temperatures around 20 C. Temperatures back into degrees C in Canada and road distances in kilometres just added a few statistical confusions into the planning equations. Not far east of Lillooet I joined route 97, the Caribou Highway. With a few name changes on the way, 97 would take me the 1200 miles north to Whitehorse in Yukon and very close to the Alaskan border. I will continue to write in miles! Now I was in Canada, I no longer had any timescales to meet and could progress north with leisure. It was my intention to get up to

Whitehorse in a week or so and then drop down into Skagway to catch the ferry to Juneau. I had booked the ferry weeks back with the plan of jumping onto a new reservation if I didn't make it. In the meantime, most of British Columbia lay before me. In comparison to yesterday, the terrain flattened out considerably. I seemed to be riding on a huge plateau with just mile after mile after mile of fir trees. The road surface was excellent and overtaking logging trucks increased the difficulty level of my ride just a touch. Thinking about the sheer remoteness conjured up many idle thoughts. What if I broke down? What if I had a tyre puncture? What if I encountered bears on the roadside? What if I broke down and was sniffed out by a bear? That artist guy I had met in Yachats-Oregon had been surprised that I wasn't carrying some sort of weapon on this bit of the ride. I recall I dismissed his concern quite quickly and now I was in the thick of it, in the midst of a potentially dangerous territory with wildlife lurking, I was thinking I maybe should have taken his advice. If the worst come to the worst and I did have a roadside unscheduled stop, I would flag down a logging truck for help. I hope they were friendly types. As for cell phone coverage, forget it. After fuel at Williams Lake, the tranquil setting of McLeese Lake and the Oasis Café got my attention for a late breakfast. Jennifer the chatty waitress served me an excellent plateful of bacon, eggs, hash browns and a pile of toast. With hot black coffee, it hit the spot. A young wife of 22, Jennifer had been serving in the Oasis for 7 months, whilst her husband mined copper up the road in Gibraltar. She was not convinced she liked it and preferred a place with a bit more action. Other than the general store and a neighbourhood pub, that was about all in town. Looking across the lake and absorbing the incredible remoteness of this spot, I could really sympathize with her. Was this the place for a young couple? I guess they go where the money is and a mining job was not to be sneered at. A confident young lady and maybe with little opportunity for conversation we chatted as I ate. I mentioned my proposed destination of the day and she had yet to visit Prince George. That surprised me and with a population of around 80 000, is quite a bustling city and known as BC's northern capital. I had thought the shops and bars would perhaps attract Jennifer and her husband to reacquaint themselves with reality. Maybe they never got time off? After the vast and open province so far, arriving in the bustling city of Prince George later that day was quite a culture shock. It has all the trappings of any other city of that size, including high rise buildings. The original trappings from Prince George were from animals. It grew up as a fur trading post. Agriculture followed, then the city became an important rail and road junction and now the lumber industry and tourism dominate. The days planned distance had passed by quickly and I used Prince George simply as a pit stop. Motel, dinner, no exploration, no photos, simply a utility stop, with the intentions of making mile zero of the famous Alaska Highway the next day.

Prince George was buzzing first thing the next morning with commuters and logging trucks. It seems quite strange using the word 'commuter' up here. The roads were full and this is undoubtedly the employment and demographic melting pot of the northern bit of the province. A lot of the people going to work were at the wheel of huge logging trucks. Some were loaded some were empty. Without the colossal weight of several thick fir trees, the performance of these trucks changed from a struggling obese animal to a nimble athlete. I was being followed out of town by one of the latter. He was obviously heading for his next load and I think he was using me for a bit of early morning sport. Following me out of town through all the junctions and stop lights he matched me for speed and stuck closely to my tail. Once out of the city limits and in to the fir tree expanses once more, he was again right on my tail and held it there. I was making progress and he kept up close. I couldn't quite believe this, I am a riding an extremely powerful enduro motorcycle and was being chased to the point of being dangerous, by a logging truck! This was a re run of the Spielberg movie where the motorist gets tailed by the aggressive and spooky trucker. It felt strange and stopping at some construction lights gave me a break and time to think about how to shake this guy off when we got going. The stop light guy was dressed for the arctic and chirped that it had been below zero at dawn when he started and the morning was just starting to heat up so he could take off a couple of layers. He pointed to the truck behind and shouted, 'he'll be turning off soon to the lumber yard and you will go miles now without seeing much traffic until you get across the Rockies'. The truck driver was gunning his engine in anticipation of a green light and eager for movement. I heard the radio call to the stop light man calling the next batch of traffic through. He tapped me on the helmet and pointed to the road ahead. In one slick movement I shouted 'so long', and accelerated off into the clear road and saw nothing more of the once pursuing logger. That had made for an interesting 20 miles or so. Maybe they weren't a friendly bunch after all? The route continued with the backdrop of more stunning colours which were very soothing to an early morning eye. The deep blues of many lakes and dark greens of the millions of acres of fir trees, continued to fill my viewfinder. I was still on the high plateau and then suddenly the geography increased the tempo, when elevated and snaking parts of the road took on the Misinchinka and Hart Ranges, all part of the Rockies. I was crossing the spine of the Continental Divide again and after a couple of hours at altitude, descended rapidly into Chetwynd and Dawson Creek. For the last couple of hours or so, I had been feeling a 'thump thump' on the front of the bike and lower legs. I had dismissed these slightly annoying intrusions down to stones or debris from the road. This theory was a little weak considering the road surface was excellent and some of the best I had encountered throughout the continent. It wasn't until unloading the bike at the motel in Dawson Creek when I discovered the culprit or rather culprits. I had a collection of huge bugs all over the front of the bike that would have made an insectologist jump with delight. They were enormous creatures and looked like a locust crossed with a mosquito. It took an age to clean the beasties away and the remnants would have provided enough substance for a hearty stew.

Dawson Creek is the start point or mile zero of the famous Alaska or Alcan Highway. Much history of the construction is recorded in this interesting and quite energetic little town. Starting as an agricultural settlement on very fertile ground, the community rapidly grew into boomtown proportions at the commencement of road construction. It was a wartime project that was accomplished in astonishingly quick time. After the bombing of Pearl Harbour, the American movers and shakers suddenly decided a road was needed to provide transportation into Alaska. Construction started in March 1942 simultaneously at Dawson Creek in BC and Fairbanks Alaska. Up to 16 000 military engineers and civil contractors completed the highway in November the same year. Dawson Creek today is very much a traveller's stopover and the broad selection of motels, diners and museums, provides services for all tastes. Whilst photographing the mile zero high and impressive signpost, I was joined by a couple of guys from the towns visitors centre. They were involved in a local survey and enthusiastic to find out my reason for visit. I explained that it was quite simple and I would be using the Alaska Highway for the majority of its course north west bound. When I quizzed them, they were unable to confirm the expected road surface conditions along the way. 'Things change from year to year and winter's leaves its mark'. I suppose it was an unfair question considering I was expecting their knowledge to expand 1500 miles or so up into the Yukon and Alaska. My first experience of the highway was first thing the next morning heading out of town. It's route and my route heads north for Fort Nelson, before turning west for Watson Lake and crossing the Rockies again, this time for Whitehorse, the capital of the Yukon. Whitehorse was an important city on this sector, as after that followed Alaska and south into Juneau the capital. However, from Dawson Creek, I still had nearly a thousand miles to get to Whitehorse and a couple of night stops would be in order. I had heard several stories about road surface conditions and was mentally prepared for anything. So far so good and with long straight sections and sweeping curves over undulating terrain, all back dropped by scenery to die for, riding conditions were absolutely delightful. At mile 143 on the highway, Pink Mountain was the first small service area, providing eating, drinking and most important, fuel facilities, that I came across. I met some bikers here who were returning from the North West. They commented that the section of the highway between Destruction Bay and Tok had suffered considerably from last winter's perma frost. Progress for them had not been rapid, where surface damage, gravel and road construction had required caution. Good information, but these guys were riding HDs which didn't strike me as being the best machine for up here. Towns and service areas are few and far between on the highway and bikes like these HDs, with a relatively short range would have to pay close attention to fuel management. Not a problem with the 8 gallon capacity of the mighty GS, yielding 350 miles range if you are gentle. Another service encountered at these pit stops, were very basic airstrips adjacent to the road. If you took away the orange runway markers from some of them, the land would not be recognizable as an aircraft landing area. Some are extremely close to the highway, where the approach must be rather precarious considering the surrounding steep terrain, not to mention the rapidly changing weather. It must be seat of the pants flying. I had already seen a bright yellow Cessna with huge over size tyres, hanging on my shoulder and looking to be making an approach to the road ahead. At the last moment he veered off to a landing strip of sorts a short distance ahead. So far the road surface had been very good with only some short gravel areas and a few sections under construction. Stationary at the head of the line of traffic at one work area, I was joined by a Greyhound bus. The driver took the initiative to disembark and proceeded to chain smoke, whilst we exchanged traveller's notes of interest. He only had 8 passengers on board and out of Grande Prairie, Alberta, he was also en route Fort Nelson. A friendly chap with thick glasses and heavily nicotine stained fingers, we continued to chat and he recommended a motel in Fort Nelson. That was good advice and may prove to save some time on arrival. The stop at the road construction turned out to be over 30 minutes and a crowd of frustrated drivers quickly gathered around my bike. When we eventually got the nod from the stop guy to make ready to move, it was like the start of the 'whacky races' as one and all sprinted back to their vehicles, quickly starting up and gunning engines in readiness to move. In my exuberance to move off however, my acceleration was a touch more enthusiastic than usual and an opposite direction Police Station Wagon went into a frenzy of multi coloured flashing lights and waving arms. Blast! I didn't notice what my speed was, but if stopped, I may blame confusion between kph and mph for my alacrity. Thankfully the Patrol did not u turn and follow as I had previously experienced in Louisiana way back. Ironically, at the same time to this minor brush with the Canadian law, the Greyhound was close in pursuit and attempting an overtake. The posse of vehicles had a repeat performance of roadside social intercourse at the next road construction area. Thankfully the wait time was a lot shorter and as pulling way and attempting to overtake a very slow sweeper vehicle, I very nearly got run off the road. He did not want to be passed and swerved into my path, causing me to do hit the brakes hard. Thank God for ABS. No spill, but I was furious with this guy and his unnecessary manoeuvre. Once in the clear and pulling passed, I shouted a few choice words his way before returning to the spectacular vistas which provided instant chill out from that brief period of road rage. The Greyhound and the truck following saw it all and were both heavy with horns and lights when passing the wayward sweeper. The Greyhound was in an incredible rush and I just wonder if he had someone waiting for him in Fort Nelson. I was making excellent progress, whilst remaining alert for wandering animals. The Greyhound didn't have that concern and sprinted past me at a great rate of knots en route his drop off, dinner and slumber, prior to returning south east to Alberta at mid-night. By the time I had arrived in Fort Nelson, he was parked up and no where to be seen. I did however beat the truck driver into town that was in our gaggle. He joined me at the fuel station and commented in harsh but amusing tones about the Patrol Car, the excessive and unnecessary road construction, not forgetting the extremely errant sweeper driver. I cannot recall his destination, but as quickly as he had arrived, he had refuelled, lit a couple of cigarettes and was back on the road. Out of the dust from the departing truck, a bike pulled up loaded down with camping equipment. He had just returned from a trip up to the infamous Prudoe Bay. That's about as far north as you can get and the roads are about as challenging as you can get. Heading back down country for Washington State, he looked absolutely shattered. The most joined up I got out of him was that Anchorage wasn't impressive and avoid it if you can. That didn't sound good, that was journeys end. Well what of Fort Nelson? Mile 300 on the Highway-but I had clocked 286, so 14 miles had escaped some where. It's a BC northern community thriving on gas and lumber processing. My impression so far was that BC is dominated by the Alaska Highway, forests, mountains, wilderness and the oil, and gas industry. Towns like Fort Nelson are dotted around here and there providing services for the locals and the industrial workforce. I did a circuit of the place and there were plenty of accommodation options of varying standard from hotel to motel. I went for the Greyhound driver's recommendation and checked into the new looking motel on the main street. It was a good choice and with gentle persuasion the attractive desk clerk went deeper and deeper into her concessions and gave me the discount of my journey. I shall return to Fort Nelson. She was an extremely attractive and charismatic lady and, engaging my age guessing competition for a bit of sport, I thought she was about 28. She was a Grandmother of 43 and was still excited after marrying her man at the weekend. It was her second or third marriage and her spouse, even so soon after the event was hard at work. He was in a truck somewhere on the Alaska Highway. Across the dusty main road, fine food and ale in a vibrant diner soothed my weary bones after my first day on the Alaska Highway. The place was rocking with a mixture of gas workers, lumber truck drivers and locals out on the prowl. For early in the week, there was a party atmosphere with a lot of dollars flying around.

I had heard an awful lot about the wildlife up in this part of the world and so far, I had not experienced any close encounters. Was that the kiss of death? I am sure I was about to have another day in heavenly countryside, albeit it was starting to feel very remote as I got further north. Temperatures were gradually falling and the air no longer had that summer fragrance. Today turned out to be the day for wildlife. First it was large groups of Stone Mountain sheep that were out and about, quite nonchantally crossing the road with no care about the traffic. Next it was Elk, Caribou and Moose that caught my eye. Mile 422 at Toad River Services proved to be an excellent brunch stop. Other riders had the same idea and I met both Canadians and American riders over coffee. Some were heading north and some heading south for the USA. One of the 60 population of the tiny settlement, the lady in the joint fuel, shop and store, mentioned it was almost impossible not to observe wildlife around this area and I should be on alert for buffalo and bears further on. One of the bikers concurred and had been dodging a huge herd of buffalo grazing and foraging on the roadside a few miles back. I left Toad River with buffalo very much on my mind and a little after ten minutes back in the seat, the traffic ahead was stationary and at strange angles all over the road. The wildlife 'intelligence' report I had received was very much still valid and an enormous herd of these huge beasts, complete with cows and calves, were all over the place. It was a case of picking my way through them with great caution. They were not at all deterred by cars or photographers and were close enough for me to smell their grassy breath. Photography was a precarious affair whilst remaining astride the bike. An inquisitive bull advanced for a close look, as snorting and sniffing and I gently pulled away before he got any closer than a metre. One gentle push from his enormous girth would have sent me earthwards with a clatter and that was a risk I wasn't hanging around for. Later I spotted a black bear feeding on a deer carcass and a couple of Grizzly's sunbathing. Canadian Province number 2 on the trek soon got me into Yukon and the gateway town of Watson Lake. Another linear highway town, but with loads of amenities. Motels, supermarket, chalets, restaurants and a few shops scattered around the dusty lanes. The Northern Lights Space and Science Centre was closed, however, a walk around quite an incredible collection of road signs in the 'Signpost Forest', made up for any sight seeing deficiencies. An immense collection that I had seen nothing to compare. The collection was started by a homesick GI whilst working on the highway in 1942. He erected a sign stating the distance to his home town and the collection since grew and grew. The colourful collection is mainly from the USA, but I did see a few European chunks of metal, paint faded from years of severe winters. I checked into a brightly coloured roadside hotel. With a yellow and white paint scheme, it stood out for miles and looked an ideal central spot. My timing was perfect as within 10 minutes of my arrival a hell of a cacophony from a dozen or so HDs, signalled the arrival of quite a gathering of potential guests. They already had a reservation and the bikes were joined by a support truck. A support truck!

The highway, albeit carving a snaking route, was predominately in a westerly direction as leaving Watson Lake. After a brief dip back into BC, I became established back in the Yukon around the lakes of Teslin. It was a bright start to the day, which quickly deteriorated in light then heavy rain. Whilst refuelling at Teslin, I exchanged a few words with a couple of old boys on HDs. They were starting a circuit of camping and riding around Alaska and were just not looking forward to striking camp tonight in this rain. They were real bikers. After I mentioned my plans, they talked themselves into a motel stay instead. Whilst working out how to use an unusually complicated fuel pump that would not operate with plastic, cash or manually, thankfully a local guy came to my rescue and hit the buttons in the required sequence. We got talking and he was revelling in his new business project. It was a collection of tasteful chalets, done out with all the mod cons, specifically designed and to be marketed for the biker. I think the marketing and advertising would be very important however to get the required occupancy rate to keep afloat. The rain was quite amazing and the first serious precipitation I had experienced since crossing Lake Placid in New York State, 6 weeks and 7000 miles back. I had been lucky. The downpour did nothing to dispel my spirits in the consistently delightful scenery and after the odd shiver, I rolled in the Province capital of Whitehorse shortly after lunch. It is Mile 918 on the Alaska Highway and since crossing the Canadian border, 1663 miles had got me north of British Columbia and into the capital of Yukon. Whitehorse with a population of 25 000 or so is by far the largest and busiest city in the province. It proved to be an interesting spot for a couple of days with a smattering of Klondike History, busy bars and excellent local restaurants. I stayed in the High Country Inn which was a stones throw away from the town centre and amenities. With a 30 foot high metal mounted policeman in the garden, a collection of historic vehicles scattered around and nearby giant wall murals depicting Yukon life, the place had a great atmosphere. Not forgetting the world famous 'Frantic Follies' Vauderville Revue saucy dance show, which apparently has satisfied over one million customers! You must visit Whitehorse in Yukon Territory! Very local and atmospheric was the rather flimsy looking Klondike Rib and Salmon Restaurant. The menu and collection of local memorabilia inside took away any architectural concerns of the outside. Reasonably priced fayre including the delightfully deep orange flesh of local salmon, succulent Buffalo and Elk steaks, accounted for 2 dinners and one lunch during my stay in town. The wait for a table each time was worth it and standing in line in readiness for one sitting, an

English accent caught my attention. It was that of Barry Smedley and I just knew he wasn't a tourist. No, along with his Canadian partner Corinne, they live split geographical lives between Skagway Alaska and San Diego California. Skagway was next and Barry would prove to be an excellent contact in just a couple of days. I was quite excited but rather apprehensive about entering Alaska and state 49 the next day. Whilst fussing over my bike the night prior to departure back at the High Country Inn, a group of HDs joined me and set about unloading. We exchanged a few comments, but I detected something was just not right with these guys. When a couple of them headed to the hotel reception, the remaining guys told me the tale. It was the condition of the Highway that had led to their trouble and literally downfall. Between Destruction Bay and Tok was apparently like a battlefield with construction. I had already had a sniff of that information. Whilst ploughing through the mud, a couple of them had experienced a collision and the lady of the group was ejected from her pillion seat and was now carrying a broken arm. A couple of the machines were carrying much battle damage. They had a bit of tension in the group and were heading home, a long way home, all the way to New York City. Their advice about the road conditions was well received, however, this posse were on huge HDs, with a couple of them towing bespoke trailers. Hardly the rig for this neck of the woods. I kept my thoughts to myself as they admired the high and robust looking GS, that I am sure would revel in such terrain in a week or so.

Chapter 73

Back in the USA

The world had an extremely autumnal, verging on a wintry feel, leaving Whitehorse and Canada. It was only a hundred miles on the South Klondike Highway to my destination of Skagway. That short distance was a huge relief from the unseasonably cold conditions and my thermals may not have coped with a longer ride. Clearing Whitehorse and pointing in a southerly direction, the frequently talked about scenic highway, was completely shrouded in low stratus bashing into the hidden terrain. In short time, I was shivering uncontrollably and my gloved hands had become blocks of ice with little function over the bikes controls. I was hanging on! Progressing south, the visibility reduced and the wind increased considerably. Leaving Canada, the USA border was staggered some considerable distance ahead and I entered a long stretch of 'no mans land'. The morning's weather was rather apt for this chunk of wilderness. A little later on the huge 'Welcome to Alaska' sign was a mere dark shadow against the gloom and not worthy of a photo stop. The road continued to curve and twist through the murk and eventually, at the summit of White Pass, began a gentle descent into the USA. As if projecting a welcoming hand back into the USA, I broke through the base of the cloud and began to make out the real world and the sheer immensity of the surrounding mountains. An occasional shaft of sunlight was piercing the cloud and glinting off vertical waterfalls draining out of the heavens and accelerating down the cliffs and canyons. At the US customs Post, I was processed by a non smiling and stern looking official, who spent an age looking at his computer whilst leafing through my passport. Just what was he reading? Was he merely ticking the box, or were there comments about me in the electronic ether? Who knows-will I ever know. If I was denied entry after getting this far, what would I do? With no smiles and a firm request for the minimal re-entry charge, my passport was eventually returned complete with souvenir Skagway stamp, but most important, another 6 months granted with Uncle Sam. Maybe the guy was just doing his job slowly and efficiently, it was Sunday after all and at least I had not been detained like the mob of Latinos that were nervously corralled in the waiting area. After that reasonably stressful 15 minutes, I continued the descent into the surreal town of Skagway. By the time I had checked into a central motel, life had returned to my chilled body, blood was flowing again, extremities returned to the owner and I set about exploration of this new town.

Skagway? It's a small city with significant historical and geographical background. Sitting in Alaska's south east inside passage, Skagway played a key role in the dramatic Klondike Gold Rush of 1897. Thousands of fortune seekers poured through the towns busy streets heading north for the gold fields in the Dawson City area of Yukon and beyond. It became the gateway to the Klondike and a better port than nearby Dyea. At the peak of the Gold Rush, Skagway became a wild and lawless place, ridden with crime and prostitution. Breweries, brothels and saloon bars were numerous. After the Gold Rush, Skagway served as a port and a railhead. Life suddenly became relatively sedate. The next influx of people was during and after the hectic years of World War 2. During this period, thousands of troops were stationed locally whilst constructing parts of the Alaska Highway. Today a boom and bust tag is still appropriate. Boom in the summer and bust in the winter. Although the railway was a main industry for nearly 100 years, it closed as a fulltime operation in 1982. Today it operates in the summer months only, serving the hoards of tourists on day trips. The main type of tourist are day trippers. They arrive in the port on cruise ships from Seattle and other ports down south, sometimes as many as 4 liners a day. Passengers are disgorged into the board walked city and spend the day and many dollars browsing the shops that line Broadway. Some shops are tasteful, the majority are tacky. Trains, coaches, buses, shuttles and even horse drawn carriages meet the dollar waving tourist to transport them around and beyond, as part of their brief Alaskan experience. Thankfully they rejoin their vessel at the end of the day, returning the place to the locals. I came to Skagway to catch a ferry south and felt quite awkward surrounded by the throbbing masses. With two days and three nights until my sailing, I did however quickly adapt and was able to stand back and distance myself completely from the crowds and search out a few sanctuaries of solace. I am sure the summer influx of visitors is excellent for local trading. The tourists keep Skagway afloat and on the map so to speak. Tourist companies and shopkeepers work hard and make the most of the short earning period. But the majority of the businesses are run by out of town folk, who eject themselves with alacrity at the first sign of winter biting. That's when the cruise ships stop coming. The population then drops from around 3000 down to less than 600. Seasonal workers from tour companies, shops, hotels and bars and the like, all retreat to warmer climes and probably other jobs. Broadway gets boarded up and only the odd bar and shop remains open. Nevertheless, if you do take time to peer through the veil of modern exploitation, thankfully there is significant history in the nooks and crannies to satisfy the discerning traveller. However, the buried in the Gold Rush cemetery may turn in their graves if they knew how Skagway operated today. Remarkably, there is no hamburger joint of global renown in the town-yet. If there was, I am sure they would turn in their graves!

As much as I have offered critique of this vibrant little town that I shall put in the Sedona-Arizona and Jackson Hole-Wyoming league, the streets provided a haven of interesting characters to meet and engage. I targeted the locals for idle chat. There was Steven Hites for starters. Smartly turned out in derby suit and bowler hat, Steven meets tourist buses and attracts the motley and excited customers into his smart gift shop and Excelsior Café. If that wasn't enough, he acts as local host and singer on board the liners. His winter retreat is a scenic railway in St Kitts. Supported by an enthusiastic team, this guy has certainly got his life and businesses well lubricated. The arrival of a loaded tourist coach brought our enjoyable chat abruptly to an end, as Stephen greeted another bus full of greenback waving visitors. He threw a cd my way of his singing recordings. A tasteful Skagway souvenir from a guy with a great broadcasting voice and interesting accent. He had tones pleasing to the ear, almost similar to the Motel manager I had met organizing toast and waffles in his breakfast restaurant back in Golden Colorado. Then there were the girls in the Red Onion Saloon. The site of one of the many former brothels, the Red Onion offers not only bar and restaurant facilities, but also Brothel Museum Tours at a mere $5 for 15 minutes! The waitresses are dressed in period gowns, revealing deep cleavages and tread the wooden boarded floor in clip clopping high heeled shoes. It was whilst escaping to one of the town's real pieces of history that I was reacquainted with Barry Smedley that I met back in Whitehorse. Strolling slightly out of town on my second day, a walk to the Gold Rush Cemetery brought into focus the original function of the area. In a quiet and moody backwater, many a grave stone, is the evidence of former times. There was Duncan Mcfadden, died a young man of 44 on June 6th 1898 just after the Gold Rush, then Frank H Reid who survived to an age of 54 and gave his life for the honour of Skagway, next many more including Eggert Emil, Hasel Achison and Mrs. Minnie Rauke but to mention a few. Scattered around the hilly burial ground, are several graves marked 'unknown'. If the dead could talk I am sure this collection would make interesting conversation. From the town's noble men to crooks, money launderers to simple working folk, prostitutes to labourers, this small area is the final resting place for many that were entangled in local life at the crest of Skagway's history. A blast of a loud horn and the screeching of brakes from Barry's tour bus, quickly returned me to the twenty first century. He was in his office of the day and we reconvened in the evening. I was invited to Barry and Corinne's rather rustic but extremely cosy fixed trailer. Barry the Brit at 71, had survived high pressure business roles, divorce and illness and now was at peace in a different lifestyle. Resident in the USA for several decades and now a tour bus driver, Barry spends his summers in the local area feeding off the tourists falling off the cruise ships, whilst his wife Corinne, a 61 year old Canadian, works in a craft shop on Broadway. They leave their Alaskan home to the ice and snow in the winter and escape to sunnier vistas of the Pacific Ocean and California. It was a curry and red wine evening that started off sedately and accelerated into a frenzy of dialogue. Although not overtly a religious type, Barry maintains believe, faith, love and even a miracle approach to his existence. This mantra had got him through a lot of testing parts of his life. His words reminded me of the quote from 'the Last Word' that introduces this book. Suddenly unprovoked, Barry went for the jugular over his views of America and Americans. I was surprised by his outspoken comments, which quite categorically stated that the USA had peaked as a super power in the 1980s. That badge was no longer valid. "After the Second World War, the USA has always been at war and is still waving its mighty military stick across the world. This was the start of the rot and the start of global unpopularity. Why should they do this and why should they be allowed to do this?" Curry finished and now concentrating on the wine, Barry continued on a political theme. "It isn't the opulent USA of the past and does everyone know of the nation's debts? The average American, especially politicians, have absolutely no knowledge of global cultures and blunder around wrapped in the Stars and Stripes. Prospective politicians should spend a year travelling the world, after which their knowledge would develop to a level so they would be aware how their actions and decisions effect their constituents". This was quite bold dialogue, but Barry had been in the USA for over thirty years and his perception and views may be credible. Corinne mainly remained quiet, restricting her participation to the nod of head and the occasional 'yes, that's right'. When it was my turn, I asked Barry what were the typical traits of an American and he didn't hold back. "Arrogance, I want-I want, and by the way, gas prices govern the populations lives. The nation has always been used to cheap fuel and not at all accustomed to the continual hike in prices this year. Life revolves around the price at the pump". That was true for sure and throughout my journey, prices had consistently risen towards that heady $5 a gallon price that was unquestionably likely. It was only a matter of time. Finishing the wine, Barry concluded, 'America is not used to adversity, 9/11 was the first time that the nation had been under attack and they were just not used to it. Americans are parochial and certainly not big travellers. USA is a new country, only 200 years old really and should think hard outside the box how to develop and improve their global standing". Wow, interesting comments and what's more, interesting comments from a Brit living on the inside. Maybe it was the wine. It was dark and raining hard as I left Barry and Corinne's trailer and headed back into town. At the start of the boardwalk on Broadway, I literally stumbled across a locals bar. I took refuge from the rain and reflected over an Alaskan ale on the evenings events.

During my Skagway stay, the cloud never really left the steep mountains and the fjord like harbour remained cocooned in grey skies with few blue bits. I had contemplated an aerial photo trip, but the extortionate price for an hour's flight and the lack of airport navigational aids persuaded I kept my feet on a terra firma. That was disappointing and the enthusiastic airport staff assured me that they always were able to maintain 'visual flight rules' and relied upon GPS like kit on board to avoid the lofty rocky slopes. I wasn't persuaded and opted for the much cheaper White Pass rail trip, that wasn't that sedate and certainly not for the faint hearted. The powerful diesels haul carriages, hopefully full of non vertigo types, up a snaking route to an elevation a little short of 3000 feet. The booking clerk told me it is one of the steepest railway lines in the world and you will get a modern day feel of that famous Gold Rush period. She wasn't wrong and seated in the last carriage, whilst craning my head out of the window, I was frequently able to see the straining trio of locomotives and the remainder of the train, snaking around bends and crossing high scaffolding like bridges, on the way towards the summit. It must have been a hard life back in 1897 and 1898 at the peak of the Gold Rush. This is not friendly terrain and an incredible feat of engineering to build this railway back then. Occasionally, just occasionally, a few patches of blue sky provided a fine back drop against the snow capped Twin Dewey Peaks, Ab Mountain and Mount Clifford. Whilst disembarking the White Pass train back at sea level, I recognized a Lady in an old black and white photograph. "The Queen visits the North-Queen Elizabeth visited Whitehorse Yukon in 1959 and rode in

White Pass and Yukon Route passenger coach #256-Lake LeBarge" I had ridden in the Royal coach! 1959 was a damn fine year for me as well. On my final evening in town, I found an excellent fish restaurant down by the port. It was close to the ocean liners, but free of the hustle and bustle of trippers. With tall windows offering unrestricted views, I was able to look over the steep hills and the start of the Alaska Marine Highway that would take me south to my penultimate state capital city the next day.

Chapter 74

91 Miles to Ride

I was number one in line to board the Merchant Vessel Malaspina, early in the morning and eager to progress to what was really my journey objective. Juneau would be my 49th state capital connected on 2 wheels, leaving the 50th for Mr Boeing to arrange. Malaspina's engines were rumbling and throbbing in anticipation and the busy crew of handlers soon marshalled the couple of lines of traffic on board. One of the deck crew made a fuss of me and ensured my bike was on its centre stand, chocked and lashed down, before I went in search of breakfast. We were under way on time and soon leaving the small port of Skagway and the giant cruise ships behind. It's quite a long way down to Juneau with an expected sail time of five hours, with an intermediate stop at Haines. It was warm, humid and overcast down the finger like fjord of Taiya Inlet. Out of Haines and once established on Chilkoot inlet, the channel widened considerably and the early morning sun was just starting to burn off the gloom. Half way down the Alaska Marine Highway as the route is called, most of the cloud had lifted, revealing the steep glaciated slopes. The scenes resembled Scandinavia. The water ahead was absolutely calm and Malaspina's path created the first marine disturbance of the day. As if by arrangement, Hump Back whales were surfacing ahead, almost leading the way down to Juneau. It was a memorable journey and once through Favorite Channel and turning the corner into Auke Bay, Juneau came into view. The State Rangers tourist commentary finished as we berthed and in quick time multiple engine noise disturbed the tranquillity of the morning, as the ferry unloaded. After 16 miles on the Glacier Highway Loop from the ferry terminal and past the airport, I arrived in the compact downtown of Juneau. So, I had made it into my 49th state capital and how did I feel? I wasn't punching the air, but simply going through my well practiced arrival procedures. A long time ago, a travelling friend had said that the journey is always more interesting than arriving at final destination. I shared some feelings with that remark and was far more comfortable on the move and planning things, rather than journeys end or in a static position. I did of course have a couple of journey add-ons to play out, including the ride up to Anchorage and across the Pacific to Hawaii. So even though this was all I could do on the road to tick the 'capitals visited' box, I still hadn't fully completed the full journey. That and that alone livened up my relatively sombre feeling of anti-climax as I unloaded and moved into the very comfortable Silverbow Inn in central Juneau. The Silverbow had all the characteristics of a typical Brit B&B including an adjoining café offering free drinks and snacks to guests. Along with a comfortable breakfast room and library of books and tourist this and that, it was a fitting choice for my 49th capital digs.

I am sure a lot of the global population are not aware that little old Juneau is the capital of the mighty Alaska. They will assume it is the burgeoning and still growing big brother of Anchorage. Many Americans I had met throughout my journey in their own country had never heard of Juneau and also assume the capital of Alaska is Anchorage. That would be a very fair assumption, but like a lot of the state capitals, quite a bit of history has the answers. When the territories capital was moved from Sitka to Juneau in 1906, it was by far the largest city with Fairbanks and Anchorage well behind. But it was gold! 'There's gold in them there hills' that had a huge impact on the growth of Juneau. Gold was discovered in a local creek, leading to the development of the Alaska-Juneau mine, which continued operation until 1944. The city was named after one of the original gold miners-Joe Juneau-so it's all Joe's fault. Additionally, the ideal marine position of Joe's place was deemed to be a great stopping off place for prospectors and travellers heading up state. At the time, Anchorage was extremely disconnected and over a thousand miles away. Juneau remained the territory's largest city through the inter war years, however as Anchorage grew and technologies developed, there has been several unsuccessful attempts to move the capital. The territory of Alaska entered the Union as the 49th state in 1959. Statistics and coincidences now confirmed. I had arrived in my 49th journey state, which was the 49th to join the USA, aged 49!

Juneau sits at sea level and is surrounded by steep mountains and ice fields. For the majority of my stay, low cloud prevented any sightings of Mount Juneau towering above at over 3400 feet. Drizzle from dangling low cloud soaked the cities steep streets and hung over the whole area. The city cable car vanished into the mists at about 200 feet, leaving limited views of steep forested slopes below. The city centre is extremely compact and navigable on foot with ease. To complete my state capital pilgrimage, my priority was to drop by the State Capitol, which was literally around the corner from the Silverbow. Architecturally it is known as an Art Deco block with classical elements. Apparently, earlier enthusiastic plans to design and build a new Capitol Building have been put on ice for the moment. I just couldn't imagine a USA regular dome and cupola Capitol Building in this city. I think the present building goes with the image of this unique city in this extremely unique state. I joined a tour around the building and recall clearly the emphasis on the dialogue was very much on the abundant natural resources and the sheer enormity of Alaska. The chatty guide reliably informed us that if the outline of the state, which includes the arcing Aleutian Islands, if superimposed over the lower 48, bits of Alaska would touch the east and west coasts. She showed disbelieving members of the group, a small map proving the point. However, I wanted to check this geographical boast out for myself and later that day, did some research. The bragging rights turned out to be justified. But you have to park Alaska very carefully over the lower 48 to achieve the coast to coast stretch. So, if you put the straightedge of the eastern part of the state on the western edge of Lake Michigan, with the northern coastline towns of Barrow and Prudoe Bay nudging towards the Canadian border, Alaska would sag way down south covering a lot of states. The south east inside passage where I was, would reach Florida and the Atlantic Ocean and the curling Aleutian Islands would say hello to Texas, New Mexico, Arizona and get their feet wet in the Californian Pacific Ocean. Alaska's giant proportions are further confirmed when you consider a flight from Barrow to Juneau is 1100 miles, which is the same as taking a flight from Orlando, Florida to NYC. For Alaskans, size matters! Impressive geographical statistics which reminded me that I was very much in quite an isolated corner of the immense state. Alaska was originally nicknamed 'Sewards Folly', Mr Seward bought the then territory on behalf of the US Senate from the Russia Empire for a paltry sum of two cents per acre in 1867. A shrewd purchase by Mr Seward and by no means a folly today. Before leaving the Capitol, I did make a request to have a brief meeting with the State Governor, Sarah Palin. Her coverage on many news channels was increasing, where she portrays a friendly and charismatic persona. I am sure she would share a few words with a Brit who had ridden the USA. Alas, albeit her staff mentioned she would have been enthusiastic to meet me, Mrs. Palin was out of town on business.

Juneau is a stopping off place for the cruise ships which didn't surprise me. However, unlike Skagway, a couple of liners in town didn't dwarf the place, even though their presence was still evident. As well as liners plying Gastineau Channel, many a float plane operate on the water transporting tourists here and there. Juneau was a float plane hotbed of activity for many decades, as this type of transportation was quickly identified as the most efficient to get around this part of Alaska and beyond. From the large, airy and atmospheric Hangar restaurant, I was able to look out on the water and watch the activity of several turbine Otters in operation. The low cloud base and heavy rain did nothing to deter their function and their activity was non stop. Over lunch in the Hangar one day, I got talking to Greg Fort, who reliably informed me it takes a lot to keep the float planes on the water and this type of weather is typical for the Juneau area. It's the wet and dank south east, with significant rainfall every month. Temperatures rarely get above 70F in the summer. Greg continued, 'the float planes can normally maintain visual flight rules'. How could they do that with the cloud down below 500 for much of the time and still get to the glaciers for the boisterous passengers to take photographs? I had guessed Greg was from the aviation world and he turned out to be an Alaskan Airlines 737 Captain. Juneau was a regular stop for him, as was the Hangar Restaurant for lunch. We had aviation and biking in common and Greg's two wheels was a HD Fat Boy. Although all but over, he was slightly envious of my journey and commented he much preferred the freedom and independence of a long road trip rather than sitting on an electronic flight deck. Greg related the character and characters he had experienced over the years with Alaskan Airlines, had accounted for an interesting part of his flying life. This freedom and independence theme was cropping up quite frequently during conversation with Americans. Sheryl in the Sportsman Barbershop on Seward Street certainly shared that concept. She had been in the barbershop for over 25 years and had had enough of the dismal weather up here. She was on the brink of selling up and heading south to warmer weather. Somewhere with 4 seasons and a bit of sunshine. It was still raining outside. The streets were slippery and the locals and cruise line tourists were wrapped up in waterproofs with umbrellas unfurled. I could see her point indeed.

I had heard a few comments from travellers and bikers, that Juneau has the highest number of bikers per capita than anywhere else in the USA. Being landlocked, it seems an odd place to find so many motorcycle owners. However, a bit of research did confirm this boasting statistic and in 2006, there were 1025 registered bikers in the town alone. With only 91 miles of road to ride and barely 3 months of good riding weather, I am sure bikers of Juneau have to be damn hard-core types. Undoubtedly that goes with the territory up here. On my last day in town, the sun was shining giving the once stranded and gloomy looking place, a much fresher and appealing complexion. It was the day to go and find these 91 miles. A ride out to the impressive Mendenhall Glacier was the priority and being so close to thousands of tons of snow and ice in the middle of the summer was a surreal experience. Further, where else can you find a huge glacier so close to a city? It was a mere 15 minutes from downtown Juneau and aptly originally named Sitaantaagu-The Glacier behind the Town. In line with global warming trends, Mendenhall is receding, although experts predict that increased snowfalls caused by warm air, high up in the ice fields, may stabilise the overall melt. Whilst viewing the incredible ice monster, float planes frequently passed overhead, routing towards the extensive ice fields beyond my line of sight. At least today the tourists had the contrast of blue sky to add to their glacial experience. Road options were running out and I had already seen a sign for 'End of Road 24 miles'. Returning into town, I crossed the channel via the 10th Street Bridge on to Douglas Island, in an attempt to find more asphalt. It was reasonably limited, however, I did find an isolated road which provided more spectacular viewing of Mendenhall Glacier. Back at the Silverbow, I noticed I had only managed 61 miles. 30 miles had escaped somewhere.

I had completed the main objective of my journey by reaching Juneau the capital of Alaska. 49 States-49 State Capitals-172 days-23 963 miles-555.615 gallons of fuel-3 services-3 sets of tyres-1 headlamp bulb replaced. Journey's end really I guess. However, although a beautiful setting when there's no low cloud and rain and, quite a busy little place, it's still quite isolated. Juneau is landlocked and only connected by ferry and air. So you arrive in Alaska's capital by boat, plane or birth. My decision was to hit the road for another thousand miles and finish riding in Anchorage. First it was back on the Alaska Marine Highway and north up the fjord to Haines.

Part Nine – Onwards to Anchorage

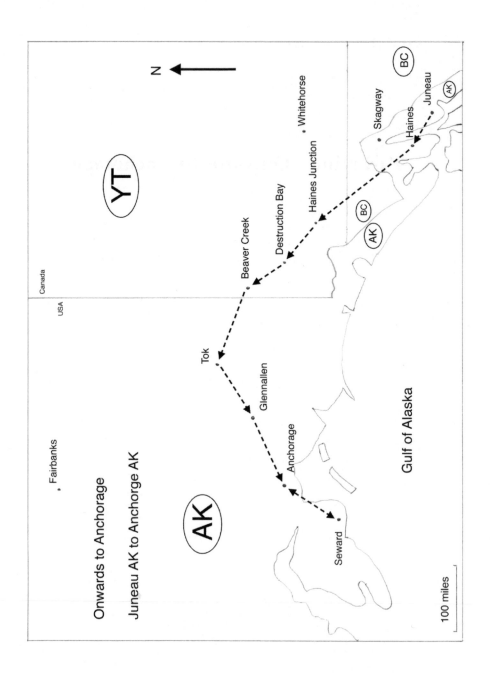

Onwards to Anchorage

Juneau AK to Anchorge AK

DATE	START	FINISH	MILEAGE	CUMULATIVE	COMMENTS
2 Aug	Juneau AK	Auk Bay Ferry Terminal AK	27	24051	City & local area
2 Aug	Haines Ferry Terminal AK	Haines AK	16	24067	Via Mud Bay Road
3 Aug	Haines AK	Haines AK	68	24135	Local scenic roads & State Parks
4 Aug	Haines AK	Beaver Creek YT	332	24467	Haines Hwy & Alaska Highway
5 Aug	Beaver Creek YT	Tok AK	112	24579	Alaska Highway
5 Aug	Tok AK	Tok AK	10	24589	City & Local
6 Aug	Tok AK	Anchorage AK	326	24915	Glenn Hwy
7 Aug	Anchorage AK	Anchorage AK	48	24963	City & Local
8 Aug	Anchorage AK	Anchorage AK	23	24986	City & Local
9 Aug	Anchorage AK	Seward AK	125	25111	Scenic Routes
9 Aug	Seward AK	Hope AK	72	25183	Scenic Routes
9 Aug	Hope AK	Anchorage AK	87	25270	Scenic Routes
11 Aug	Anchorage AK	Anchorage AK	11	25281	Into storage at Classic Motion

455

Chapter 75

Trail Towns

It was back on the Alaska Marine Highway for the 4 hour ferry journey north through the passages of Lynn Canal and the Chilkoot Inlet, to the isolated town of Haines. It was a moody journey down the narrow fjords with cloud hanging over the mountains. It was a very grey late afternoon with not a hint of blue sky, as Malaspina gently transferred us into a tranquil Alaskan early evening. The occasional sighting of a glacier studded into the steep slopes and waterfalls falling out of the clouds and tumbling down towards the depths, provided some photographic opportunities. The occasional splash from a hump back whale, in the calm water ahead of Malaspina, ignited some excitement amongst the passengers. The whales perhaps invigorated into increased surface activity by the rumble of Malaspina's engines, provided an impromptu escort north towards Haines. The atmosphere from an excited group of passengers made up for the grey weather. Everyone on board seemed in good form in anticipation of rejoining the mainland and the onward connection of the road infrastructure. I was befriended by a couple from Juneau. He was a retired fireman and now tour coach driver. Along with his wife, they were heading north into Alaska in search of relatives. Then there was Jim Gillette, his partner and dog, who had most of their worldly possessions in a huge vehicle. It was a conversion and a cross between a truck and a trailer. As well as living quarters, it contained bikes, jet skis as well as an assortment of other traveller's paraphernalia. Also a retired fireman, Jim had run a BMW bike dealers way back in the 1970s. Eccentric and enthusiastic about life and travels, Jim wanted to buy my bike on the spot! I laughed at his suggestion during our vibrant chatter on the deck, after which the cool of the approaching evening and an intriguing smell from the restaurant, forced me down a deck level. I was first in line at the restaurant counter and the aromas had now ascended to a delicious standard as the Asian chef proudly produced a chunky and colourful seafood curry. Saturated with huge prawns and pieces of salmon in a deep orange sauce, accompanied by light fluffy rice, all that was missing was a cool beer, as the Alaskan scenery slipped by. My culinary choice had set a trend and the majority of diners emerged from the cash register with plates piled high with the seafood curry. A trio of guys with the physique of NFL football players, sitting opposite, made quick work of the feast. The Malaspina's kitchen had done well. It was nearly dark as I disembarked at the ferry terminal and headed down Lutak Road towards the compact town centre of Haines. I had phoned ahead for a motel and was assured of a room, even though I was a relatively late arrival. For the second time in this journey, my GPS got confused and led me down Mud Bay Road and slightly out of town. I soon got lost on narrow roads and ended up asking directions from a local. With the bike still running, I knocked on the door of a tiny cabin and was greeted by a rather surprised looking young couple who were watching TV. I had overshot town, apparently I was not the first and signage was not good around here. Re-orientated I located the motel in ten minutes or so and was greeted by Dawn the stand-in manager. She had wandered where I had got to, as she had seen the ferry cruise down the inlet half an hour before. I shared my navigational blunders over a few laughs, as I was shown to a huge room. Dawn must have been telepathic and as passing on my thanks for waiting up, she mentioned that being a Saturday night, the main bar in town would be open for a good while yet. That was excellent news, it was already 1030 pm and a night cap was certainly in order. Rather similar to a Brit pub, the bar was still quite busy. Not pulsating or throbbing, but ticking over nicely with locals. One bar tender was on duty, serving ale and preparing food in a blur of coordinated and obviously well practiced activity. Luckily I arrived before a busy period and had a large glass of Alaskan ale in my mitt in quick time. The 3 giant guys I had seen on the ferry, had obviously not got lost on arrival and were already tucking into pizza. They must have been hungry to consider more food after that curry. We soon got talking and they turned out to be Christian Church representatives attending a mission in the area. They were all interested in my journey, my beliefs and my faith. The conversation did start to get a bit heavy and it was 2.30 am when we left the bar. I had enjoyed my spiritual evening with Chris Woolley from Ohio and Joe Wega from Pittsburgh, Pennsylvania and the third guy whose name escaped my notes. They did have a football connection after all, however, I declined their offer to participate in a game that had been arranged for them the next morning. That may have been just too much.

Haines is everything that an outdoors person could dream for. Submerged in pristine beauty, surrounded by abundant wildlife and endless opportunities for outdoor adventure. It sounds like a tourist headline, but actually those words are very realistic. I was persuaded to stay another day and night and not rush this glass of wine! I was ever conscious that the new bottle opened in British Columbia was quickly running out. Thankfully not inundated with tourists like Skagway, Haines turned out to be an interesting place. Walking around town the next day, I bumped into the couple with the large camper I had met on the ferry. They also had excitement after disembarking the night before. They had decided to do a bit of exploring prior to calling it a day. Whilst manoeuvring their lumbering machine down a narrow road, they had ended up in a river. The kind actions of a passing local in a heavy duty winch equipped truck, had saved their watery dilemma, which could have been a lot worse. Jim suggested I go and have a look at the river where they had had their mishap, but quickly cautioned me about Grizzly's. This caution was confirmed by the lady in the visitor's office, who seriously suggested I didn't go down to that river at all. Grizzly Bears were out and about in the lakes and rivers close to town at this time of the year. They are gorging on salmon prior to their winter snooze. She warned me to be on the lookout for these giant creatures, who now even challenge wading fisherman for their catch. With some trepidation, I rode around to the Lutak Inlet and found the river which was heavily populated with fisherman only. Camera at the ready just in case, on this occasion I didn't see a single bear. Just as well, maybe it was an omen, on such a narrow road and on a bike, if confronted by a Grizzly on the way to the river, I would have been extremely vulnerable. All I saw were plenty of yellow warning signs, 'YOU ARE ENTERING BEAR TERRITORY'-'DO NOT LEAVE FOOD UNATTENDED-UNATTENDED ITEMS SUBJECT TO IMPOUND AND $50 FINE'.

Later in the day, I became acquainted with my next door neighbours back at the motel. We chatted on the veranda, exchanging traveller's tales. They turned out to be a military family on the move from Elmsdorf Airbase Alaska to Langley-Virginia. That was some hike, although, I revelled in our conversation and could relate to these great distances with recent experience up my sleeve. The mum of the family was a serving Officer in the Air Force and she was accompanied by her Meatloaf look a like pony tailed husband, and son and daughter. I was getting closer and closer to the bad areas of the Alaska Highway, which this family had passed through only the day before. Apparently it was bad, but passable with no problems on the GS. They had quite a laugh when I mentioned the HD groups I had met en route, who had all been cursing the condition of the Alaska Highway at the top end. This family were amongst the nicest people I had met in the USA, very open and very considerate. They expressed their concerns on the economic situation in the country and would a new Government really rescue the situation? The military had mixed views about Democratic leadership, which was pretty much on the cards now as Barack Obama's popularity continued to sweep the nation. That was an interesting point of view. I had met several military veterans around the states, but this was my first opportunity to engage with a serving Officer. We all dined together and the generosity of this family continued when they refused to accept my contribution to the tab.

Haines was the sort of place I could have dropped anchor and enjoyed an extended stay. It was such a refreshing contrast to Skagway, although I am sure if the cruise liners stopped here, the streets would adapt for the tourists. The Haines Highway took me North West and very quickly back into Canada. In comparison to the chatty lady Canadian customs officer I had met when entering Canada 2 weeks ago, this one was surly and offered no smile. After I had turned off the bikes engine, her questioning was short and sharp and verging on being rude. I played the game, but even so, I was still very surprised with her heavy verbal attitude. I did get the impression that the car ahead, whose processing had taken an age, had tried to give her a hard time. Whatever, I wasn't impressed with my reception back into Canada. This customs post is so isolated, that a small community of cabins provides domestic facilities. In hind sight, it must be a bitch of an assignment. If the staff don't enjoy the isolated location and read good books, there is a chance they may go mad. Anyway, I was back into Canada, British Columbia briefly and then Yukon and in quick time climbed into low cloud and very cool temperatures. Haines Junction was next and very much a junction town it is. It stands on the intersection of the Haines Highway and the Alaskan Highway and I had intended a night stop here. However, it was only lunchtime and I had that urge to move on. The place was reasonably active with tourists but the small town was not bursting. The visitors centre confirmed there was not really a lot to keep me here. I quizzed an American family about the place and they said that if I thought Haines Junction was a one horse town, don't be surprised when I hit an even quieter Beaver Creek. They were crouched down looking at the map of my journey on the bikes panniers and by the looks of it giving their kids a quick geography lesson. The parents had a mixed look of disbelief and envy and it was obvious they had not seen anything like the extent of their country as me. I am extremely fortunate and will not forget that. After refuelling I decided to rejoin the Alaska Highway and continue to Beaver Creek. It would be another small trail town, with the usual amenities I am sure, but further progress towards journeys end. My route to Juneau had taken me off the Alaska Highway at Whitehorse and I rejoined the famous road at Haines Junction and continued North West. As if greeting me back onto the highway, the gloom lifted, revealing stunning snow capped mountain ranges and just beyond the tiny settlement of Silver City, the turquoise coloured water of Kluane

Lake. Over lunch at a well equipped diner in Destruction Bay, I was able to over look the dramatic lake and surrounding terrain. Nearby Burwash Landing and Destruction Bay are 2 of Yukon's smallest communities so the waitress informed me. There's not a lot here, which I immediately agreed with. But why the name Destruction Bay? Straight in with the answer, she continued that this small place has a short history and was established as a centre for construction and maintenance on the Alaska Highway. Rocks and materials from the local area were utilized and blasts from quarrying had christened the place. Another opinion stressed it was the wind that blew down structures built during the construction that gave the name. Shortly after lunch, I encountered a long section of road construction and was held up at red lights for quite some time. The stop light lady was full of conversation and related a bear story from yesterday. A Grizzly mother and 2 cubs had sauntered close past her station en route the lake, whilst her huge dog continued to sleep. I was about to ask her if the gargantuan mut had a function, but on this occasion, he or she was not alert to the potential dangers of Mrs Grizzly and family. The stop lady continued, that it's only seriously dangerous if you get between bear and cubs. Then it could be mayhem and potentially terminal. Other than that, they are more concerned about eating and sleeping. During our chat, the pilot vehicle arrived, driven by another lady, complete with another huge canine onboard. They obviously take this bear thing serious up here, but would any big dog be an adversary to a rampant grizzly? I think not. Maybe a barking distraction only, giving a few extra seconds to organise an escape? Once through the construction, the remainder of the ride to Beaver Creek was a mixture of asphalt, some gravel and quite a few frost heaves. It was my first experience of frost heaves that I had heard so much about. It's the melting and freezing perma frosts that cause the damage, resulting in an almost rollercoaster road surface, as well as cracks, potholes and frequent gravel areas. I encountered this rollercoaster and it made for an exhilarating ride all the way into Beaver Creek. It was as if a giant had got hold of the road and flicked it out of position. The road had not fallen to the ground neat and straight in its original position, but ended up in peaks, curves and even broken sections. That's how it was on the highway. It wasn't quite seat of the pants stuff, although some caution was required. The most westerly settlement in Canada, Beaver Creek is primarily a border post and service area on the Alaska Highway. My first view of the town reminded me of the comments the American family had made back in Haines Junction. However, after 332 miles since leaving Haines, this place would do for the evening. I am sure if I peeled back the skin a bit, something of interest would be revealed. It's a linear community stretched down the highway and when I pulled into town, a very dusty highway. The temperatures had risen nicely to the mid 70s, which was better than the chill of the morning when passing through the clouds on the elevated Haines Highway. One or 2 motels, cabins and even one hotel are set off from the highway. I chose a rustic looking place, oozing with character. The lobby multi tasked as a gift shop, food store and restaurant. The friendly owner checked me in and pointed to a cabin around the back. Before leaving, she shouted, 'you may get a ticket for the show tonight if you are quick'. Show?, A show in this dusty small place? I found my cabin around the back and chuckled at its weather beaten appearance, with peeling paint and weeds sprouting here and there. It was a bit close to some woods for comfort and I hoped that I would have no furry 4 legged visitors during my stay. The double roomed set up, proved to be an excellent choice, providing a comfortable and peaceful refuge after a long day in the saddle. The strange feeling of journey completion was really maturing now. It was a mixture of euphoria and anti-climax. The next day I would be back in the USA in another small town called Tok, leaving a left turn off the Alaska Highway and but a few hundred miles down to Anchorage. The bike had been fantastic and I would soon be saying goodbye to a great and reliable friend, that had quite simply become a very dominant part of my life. Putting those thoughts away for the moment, I just had to find out about this show. It turned out to be in the large hotel just down the road. An amusing musical story of Yukon life led by a professional cast, has been held in Beaver Creek for many a season. The small town is on the coach route for long range tourists and every performance is a sell out. I got the last ticket and enjoyed dinner and entertainment in a most unique setting. After the show, a selection of the audience crammed into the small bar and provided easy pickings for good conversation. Many, including a couple from Wisconsin that pinned me to the bar, had cruised up to Skagway and enjoyed the tourist rampage there. It was still daylight at midnight in Beaver Creek. Slightly confusing.

My slumber was not disturbed by any nocturnal assailant and after bidding farewell to the very friendly motel staff the next morning, I was back on the highway and very quickly back in the USA. This border guy was the chatty type and wanted to talk and talk and find out all about my trip. It was quite amusing when he said don't rush things, see as much as you can. I had to explain that after nearly 25 000 miles, it was nearly the end of the road. 50 miles later, I encountered the construction that I heard so much about. It was over 50 miles of rubble, mud, thick mud, gravel and pooled water. The majority of the construction was centred around bridge renewal and snaking diversions and re routes were required, guided by a plethora of pilot vehicles. Many of the stop-light guys and gals were offering apologies for the conditions. The bike was in its element over the challenging surfaces, though a little caution was required. I could now sympathise with the HD crews I had met along the trail. This was GS territory! It was only a 100 miles to Tok and my arrival coincided with heavy rain, which aptly signalled the end of my travelling day. A motel that I had been recommended was already full, however, I was installed into a more than acceptable alternative in quick time and pondered the final leg of the journey south into Anchorage the next day. Tok is another linear type place set on the roadside and grew up as a camp during the construction and maintenance of the highway. So much money was spent on the settlement, that it got the nickname of 'Million Dollar Camp'. There are many versions of the origins of the strange name of this little town. Was 'Tok' taken from the Athabascan word for 'peaceful crossing', that could fit I guess, or was it derived from connections to wartime 'Tokyo Camp', maybe, or simply named after some ones dog? Who knows, but today the town is bursting with facilities for the traveller. Motels a plenty, campsites, a well stocked supermarket, not forgetting an airstrip extremely adjacent to the road. Over dinner, I got talking to a local who had quite a pessimistic outlook. It was quite unusual meeting an unenthusiastic American, but his comments were reasonably justified and appropriate. He was the owner of a cabin complex and of course mentioned I should have stayed in his establishment. We talked of the highway and of hardships in the area. Many service areas have closed down through lack of business. That explains quite a few extensive and good looking places I had passed, that were boarded up, with access roads chained. He mentioned that a fuel delivery costs thousands of dollars which had to be paid for upfront. Some places just do not get the turn over to justify such forward costs. I had noticed that fuel and provisions were more expensive up here. I guess it's the price of getting things here that has to be factored into the economic equation for survivability. It's a hard life and even the resort hotels close around September. It was quite a sobering chat with Tok man, who after a couple of slugs of whisky, bade farewell and drifted back to his cabins. As a traveller at this time of the year, the winter hardships just never appear in focus.

Chapter 76

Glenn Highway into Anchorage

In an attempt to find some storage facilities for the bike in Anchorage, I had made several contacts down there. Tim Manwaring was one of them and although he couldn't offer any storage, he suggested I make him my first port of call when arriving in town. Tim's address was the last I punched into the GPS for this journey. Any local trips out of Anchorage would be a bonus. I couldn't get lost, it was 330 miles in a straight line on the Glenn Highway and I could simply sit back and take in the scenery. It was still raining when I left Tok and remained that way until west of Glennallen. A couple of things did stick out in my memory about the small town of Glennallen. Firstly, I had lunch in a great diner, second, I encountered my first $5 gallon of fuel. It was $5.069 and I uplifted 3.081 gallons. More statistics, but these weren't lies and way back in Santa Barbara, California when I was stung for my first $4 gallon, I did predict I would see a $5 gallon somewhere along my trail. Out of Glennallen, the rain cleared and revealed blue sky and tremendous views of the Chugach Mountain Range and several glaciers to the south. Many peaks including Mount Sergeant Robinson and Mount Marcus Baker stood out, providing a great backdrop. Progressing west and climbing, I came across a red light and more road construction, this time through a mountain pass. I was well rehearsed to deal with these interruptions and it was engine off, dismount, helmet off and chat to the stop guy whilst waiting for the pilot truck. This one was no different and it would be at least 20 minutes I was reliably informed. Coincidently, I was number one in the line, which had happened with uncanny frequency. Very soon an assortment of trucks and bigger trucks pulled up behind, forming a lot of traffic heading Anchorage way. Whilst taking in the view and giving Tim a quick progress report on my cell phone, I was joined by one and then 2 quite rough looking characters from a large truck. They talked like cowboys and were dressed like cowboys, including sweat stained Stetsons, tattooed forearms and both had huge hunting knifes strapped to their belts. They were full of questions and were eyeing my bike with interest, which they insisted in calling a 'motor scooter'. I had last heard that back in Mississippi and this dodgy looking duo were from Texas. Motor scooter must be the a southern term for a motorcycle. They thrust their business cards my way which revealed functions of 'Frontier Justice' and 'Construction and Tree Service'. Looking at them, I could believe the latter, but there was no way that one of these guys was a legal advocate. It's surprising what folks put on a calling card and the guy that was doing most of the talking was trying to convince me that he owned the largest ranch in Texas. What would the owner of the largest ranch in Texas be doing in Alaska driving a beat up truck? There is just a slight possibility that these 2 were up to no good. As our conversation continued, the occupants of the vehicle behind, got out and leant on the front of their truck with arms folded and took all this in. I got the impression they were watching over me, but what surprised me, was that both were wearing FBI T shirts. Could they be? No, that would be a touch overt, I am sure the FBI would operate a little more discreetly than that-wouldn't they? They were probably looking at the construction ahead and pondering the remaining miles into Anchorage. Anyway, it was nice to see them looking on, as who knows what the Texans were after. The cowboys suggested a meeting in town to have a closer look at my bike. I declined and the arrival of the pilot car diffused the situation nicely. I accelerated off through the uneven surface, gravel and rubble of the construction area and never saw them again. Interesting experience, thankfully I was surrounded by lots of people.

The remaining distance into Anchorage passed quickly and before I knew it, I was weaving through busy city traffic and following the arrows to Tim's address. Arriving in a tidy and respectable estate, I spotted Tim's house and he was outside polishing his Porsche. The garage was open, revealing the crammed contents, which included a couple of motorbikes, winter sports equipment, garden kit, clothes and you name it, it was in there. This garage was not for a car. Tim had finished work early to meet me, which was nice and we chatted over a drink in the garden. I didn't realise his intentions, but this initial meeting was to check me over and after half an hour or so, when I was asking him for motel advice, he sharply said, 'forget the motel, you can stay here for as long as you like'. I must have passed the test and not exhibited any undesirable character traits, unlike the Texans I had met a couple of hours back. 'We have a bedroom and bathroom downstairs, wifi and the works, you can use this as your base as you wrap up your trip, find storage for the bike and book your flights to Hawaii and England'. Wow-how about that! That would save me lots of dollars and I accepted this very kind offer with no thought. All I said was 'have you mentioned this to your wife?' He replied, 'don't worry, Elinda is at work, she won't mind, we will drop by and say hello when you have sorted yourself out'. What a way to end the trip, with this fantastic hospitality. Tim's priority was to get the bike in the garage, which I insisted was not necessary, but he did. Before I had time to unload and unpack, his next action was to hook me up to the internet. This guy knew the priorities of a traveller and I was particularly impressed so far. After I had 'checked in' and turned from fatigued and dirty biker, into a guy ready for a Porsche, it was off into city. After dropping by to see Elinda, dinner followed in a popular aviation themed bar, after which Tim insisted in taking me on a scenic ride down the Turnagain Arm inlet to the ski resort of Girdwood. I was normally in bed well before the time of this tour and after a reasonably long day in the seat, fending off the Texans and this busy induction into the Anchorage area, I was absolutely shattered.

The next couple of days were busy as I made en route arrangements. Bike storage, flight to Hawaii and last but not least flight back to England, all had to be arranged. I rode quite a few miles around the compact but busy Anchorage. With a population of well over a quarter of a million, it is now easily the states' largest city. I couldn't understand what the biker I had met early on the Alaska Highway was on about. He had said avoid Anchorage if you can. What was he on? It looked a great place. Ok there are touristy bits, but that is one of the main economic deliverables. Additionally, natural resources and a large military presence keep the economy bubbling. Aviation is quite a big hitter and Ted Stevens Anchorage International Airport is one of the world's busiest cargo terminals. The traffic is strongly linked to Anchorage's particularly useful Great Circle location. I dropped by the airport and the nearby float plane base which boasts as the world's busiest. It was quite unique watching lines of float planes land and take off, with heavy jets operating not that far away. After a quick visit to an aviation museum located at the float plane base, I was able to ride around the perimeter of the lake complex which was also a taxiway. 'Yer, no problems, just avoid any aircraft', was the advice and off I went. Later I commented to a pilot fussing over his Twin Otter, that a lot of old and unused floaters were dotted around the site. 'It's a money and occupancy thing, there's a long waiting list for a berth and the rules are if you keep them occupied, you're using them'. Obviously float plane berths are at a premium here and loads of pilots keep hold of them for decades and even pass them through the family from time to time. Float plane operation is a huge way of life in Alaska and in certain isolated places, are a families primary method of transportation.

It was now early August and I was experiencing a typical cool Alaska summer. I think temperatures may have staggered up to an acceptable level for short sleeves on the odd day, but the majority of the time an extra layer of clothes was necessary. Late June and July is the summer. I did have a spare day and took off down Turnagain Arm Inlet, witnessed a surging tidal bore rush in, crossed Moose Pass and made lunch in Seward. I had to visit Seward, after all, Mr William H. Seward bought Alaska from the Russians and I was in the territory of 'Sewards Folly'. It was only 125 miles, but it rained all the way there and back. But my trip to Seward was not in vain, as I sampled the states highly reputed halibut over a leisurely lunch in the Marina Restaurant. Moose Pass was still in cloud on the way back and finally, I trekked out to the tiny community of Hope on the southern shores of Turnabout, just hoping the grey would turn to blue. It didn't but the sun had been shining all day in Anchorage!

I had successfully found storage for the bike and Classic Motion in Anchorage, with purpose built facilities would look after the beast for the winter. I had checked out their premises, which were full of cars, trucks and bikes of various shapes and sizes. It looked like this was the end of the road for a lot of travellers and this storage facility was the ideal place. The day before I dropped the bike off, it got the first major wash and clean of the journey. Other than lights and licence plate and the odd very quick hose down, I had not got serious with water or sponge. It turned out to be quite a task and there was quite probably muck and grime from all over the 49 states down there somewhere. Quite a thought. It was a Sunday and I was doing a typical Sunday chore. Opposite from Tim's house, I could see at least 2 or 3 other residents doing the same thing. Half way through this therapeutic ritual, with my mind far far away, maybe in California or Montana, a police squad car screeched to a halt at the bottom of the drive. The Officer lowered the window, leaned across and urgently shouted, 'watch it there's a bear and 2 cubs coming your way'. I replied without thinking, 'a bear on the prowl, I'll get my camera'. The officer froze for a noticeable few seconds, lowered his sunglasses half way down his nose and uttered, 'you aren't from these parts are you, forget the camera, get indoors, or the bear may get you'. With that he was off to the next resident with the wildlife bulletin. Elinda had heard our exchange and as rushing inside, I confirmed the news. Naively without heeding the officer's advice, I did get my camera, but by the time I had returned to the street, the bear trio had moved back into the woods. Afterwards, I exchanged a few energetic words with Elinda as she was getting ready for work. 'No, this is no normal part of the world, a volcano is erupting in the Aleutian Chain sending ash towards the mainland and seriously effecting aviation, snow is forecast in the next month or so and dangerous wildlife is common close to the front door'. I had to laugh, but Anchorage versus the bear or rather the bear versus Anchorage is a common thing. Later that evening, there were 3 bear stories on the evening news. A black bear had seriously mauled a jogger, a trash eating bear was shot earlier in the day outside a downtown apartment and a bear and cubs were spotted walking through a residential area. The latter was my near bear experience and I am rather glad I didn't make the news.

The next morning I rode the bike for the final time on this journey. It was a mere 11 miles from Tim's house to Classic Motion in central Anchorage. I had previously done the paperwork and with battery disconnected and stabilizer put in the fuel system, the beast was quickly ready for deep storage. It was quite an emotional farewell which Joni the joint owner of CM, found particularly amusing. The bike had served me very well and other than routine services and new tyres, all that I had to replace was a lamp bulb. It had been an amazing 25 281 miles and almost tearful on departure, I gave the front of the beast a huge hug, shrugged off my emotions and made off from the premises quickly. I had that volcanic eruption on my mind. Hawaii bound in the evening, would that ash still be up in the air routes?

A maritime feel to Annapolis MD

Bike, truck and dome, Harrisburg PA

Amish farm with buggy – Leola PA

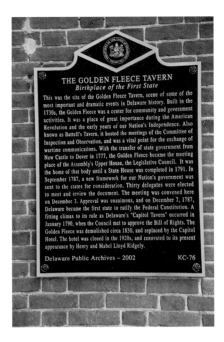

The Golden Fleece Tavern-scene of action-first state – Dover DE

Trenton NJ

Phoenicia NY-deep in the Catskills

Not a Swiss chateau in Albany – but NY state Capitol Building

Hartford CT

Floral dome in delightful Providence RI

Boston, MA

A bold statement from General Dix-Concord NH

Vietnam memorial-simple but effective-Augusta ME

Montpelier VT – America in miniature

Lowe's Store – White Mountains area NH

Lansing MI – not a sole in sight downtown on a very hot Sunday

Joe's Gizzard City Restaurant – Potterville MI – a Sunday lunch with attitude

478

Dusk shades – Madison WI – a beautiful city and Capitol Building

Nick's Restaurant Madison WI – The place to eat!

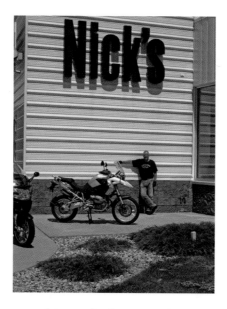

My personal BMW dealers – 'Nick's BMW' De Pere WI

Golden Blue-stunning contrasts – St Paul Capitol views-MN

A city from a city! Minneapolis from St Paul – 10 minutes on the bike

Mad Mary's steak house – a real cowboy experience – good vittals and excellent ale – Pierre SD

Bismarck ND – one of the country's few non-dome Capitol Buildings

The 'hi-line' dissects the guts of Malta MT – you don't hear 'em until they are on ya

'we don't make many sales these days' Malta MT

The early riser gets the best views – Glacier National Park MT

Sun rise colours and the rugged relief of Glacier National Park – MT

July snow fields – Glacier National Park MT

Volcano remnants – Glacier National Park MT

'Big Medicine' a rare white bison – Helena MT

Yellowstone WY eruption

Teton reflections WY

Teton summer colours WY

Enduro motorcycle and rugged mountains – awesome photographic combination! Tetons WY

Craters of the Moon National Park ID

Boise ID-friendly, compact and most unique geographical location

Crater Lake OR – eerie and foreboding deep blue depths

Return to the Pacific Ocean – Yachats OR

Salem OR – Capitol pool reflections

Olympia WA

Mount Rainier WA

*Looking through America: pasture, hills and mountains –
Mount Rainier area WA*

Start of the Alaska Highway – Dawson Creek BC

Main Street action – Skagway AK

Alaska mountains near Skagway AK

Juneau bound – whale escort

Heading for Juneau AK– early morning blues

Heading for Juneau – glacier in sight

Glacier close up – Juneau AK

Fjord like – Juneau AK

Daylight at midnight in Beaver Creek – Yukon Territory

The best fish and chips in North America at the Marina Restaurant – Seward AK

Bears a plenty up north BC, YT & AK

Busiest in the world so they say – Anchorage float plane base –
remarkably close to international airport and downtown

1959 was a damn fine year for me and Hawaii!

Number 50 and a full house – Hawaii state Capitol Building –
Honolulu HI

The surf board gives it away – Waikiki beach – Honolulu HI

No mistaking what this car does, but getting a speeding ticket may be challenging – Honolulu HI

And finally a hire BMW 650 ticked my final box – NSG is a BMW rider in all the 50 states of the USA – Honolulu HI

Surfing the USA! – Waikiki Beach HI

*'Valley of the Rocks' – Monument Valley UT – AZ State Line –
West is Best!!*

Colours of America – Sedona AZ

Towering summer storm clouds & the immense waters of the Great Lakes
– Lake Erie NY

Big Sky – Big Flag – The USA!!

Part Ten – Aloha State

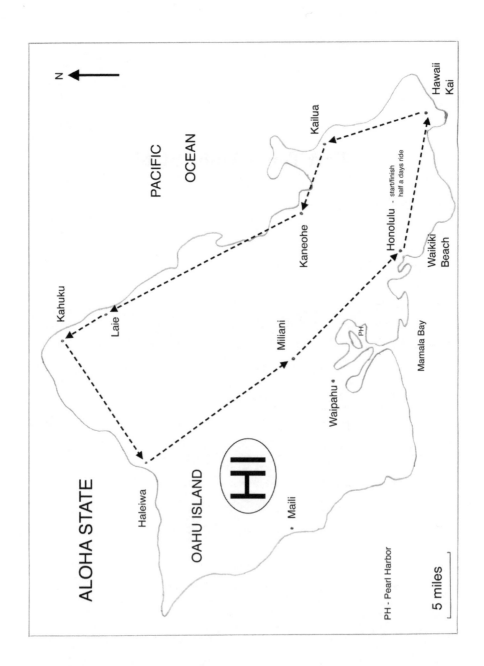

Chapter 77

Not all were strangers

As if providing a final challenge, a last reminder of the aggressive, dynamic and frequently unsympathetic properties of Mother Nature I had so frequently experienced, I had one more thing to contend with which was completely out of my hands. Not the weather this time, but an erupting volcano in the Aleutian Chain was venting ash at a less than friendly velocity up to 45 000 feet. Mount Kasatochi was the culprit and it's surprising what an impact on modern lives, that a volcano on an island only a couple of miles across, can inflict. Moreover this little hot mouthed baby is miles out down the Aleutian Arc and not far from the Russian Bear. Volcanic ash had made its way up into the jet stream and had been drifting east across the Gulf of Alaska for the last couple of days. Flights in and out of Anchorage had been delayed considerably and yesterday, all night flights had been completely cancelled. An early arrival at the airport was on the cards in an attempt to jump onto an earlier flight. The airport was busy but not mayhem as it had been the last couple of days with stranded multi-stated passengers camped out. With an intermediate flight outbound, Alaskan Airlines very kindly put me on the next flight to Seattle, which was 3 hours earlier than booked. That should get me going still in daylight which was what I wanted. Seattle airport terminal and an uncomfortable seat added to the multitude of locations I had rested my bones throughout this journey. As if by pressing a button, the early morning tidal wave of passengers arriving at the gates was my alarm call. One of the tidal wave looked vaguely familiar, however, travelling fatigue and dreaming of Hawaii, dismissed any serious mental research. The flight to Honolulu was nearly six hours. That's quite a hike when you consider I wasn't changing countries. The Pacific is a big pond and covers about one third of the earth. When I saw that familiar looking guy on the plane, it was who I thought it was after all. What an absolute coincidence and what were the statistical odds of bumping into an old colleague on the same flight? Hard enough in Europe or even England, but after doing 25 500 miles on a bike through the USA over nearly 7 months, who would have put money on meeting a known person on a flight from Seattle to Honolulu? What was the statistical probability of this meeting?

Chapter 78

The 50th

Although I did not want to rush my Hawaii experience, I had listed my brief objectives for my visit. They were to kiss the surface of the 50th State and my 50th visited on this journey, kick the tyres of a BMW hire bike and caress the asphalt of O'ahu Island, keeping rubber side down of course. Alas I couldn't do a 'Pope' thing at the airport and kneel down and kiss the tarmac. Jet way equipped, all and sundry, yawning and struggling with baggage after the 6 hour flight, were transferred directly into an oppressively busy terminal. To keep it simple, I had decided to stay close to the airport and still have easy access to the city centre. Hence the beach resort of Waikiki was a good base for a few nights, leaving a short bus ride into the capital city of Honolulu. For non Hawaiian specialist, it may be worth a quick look at the geography over here. When most folk think of Hawaii, including myself, do you get past one island and the city of Honolulu? There's a lot more out there and the archipelago lying around 2000 miles south west of mainland USA, comprises of 8 main islands. In decreasing size they are, Hawaii-The Big Island, Maui-The Valley Island, O'ahu-The Gathering Place, Kaua'i-The Garden Isle, Molok'i-The Friendly Isle, Lana'i-The Pineapple Island, Ni'ihau-The Forbidden Isle and finally Kaho'olawe-The Target Isle. I gave myself quite a geography lesson en-route and exploring the chain in extent would take another 6 months. The attractions in this tropical paradise vary from commercial beach resorts, to quiet romantic and deliciously beautiful isolated hideaways, to active snow capped volcanoes. For this visit alas, I was staying on the third largest island, the most populated and the most commercial. I am sure I could bear it for a few days and concentrate on the job in hand and maybe return to the paradise areas at a later date. Waikiki indeed is the commercial, expensive, smart in some areas and very tacky in others, resort town. As expected the place was a blend of tourist shops, boutiques, bars, restaurants, clubs, with hookers patrolling the evening streets. There is the famous Waikiki Beach itself, which does reduce the overall bruising impact of the bustling place just a little. However, most days it was full of scorched and burnt Orientals, loud tourists and wanabee surfers of varying standard. However, I must not lose sight of the fact that I had arrived in my 50th state. I didn't track down any true Hawaiian locals on my first night amongst the raptures of bars and restaurants. Most were holiday makers from the mainland including a rocket scientist from NASA and the personal assistant to a well known computer anti-virus company, whom I sat between at a glitzy bar grill. I didn't quite need an advance on my mortgage for a steak and beer, but these were not Waffle House prices. The attractive and busty PA was with her muscular 8 foot tall black partner, who spent the evening telling me how to pronounce aluminium. I interpreted his vocabulary was just a touch limited or maybe tainted by the booze, so my conversation gravitated towards the rocket scientist. I had never met a rocket scientist. This young man had been sent to Hawaii to de-stress after a taxing period working on the Orion spacecraft and launch platform.

I had secured the important bit. Bike hire in a couple of days. That would leave a bit of free time to do the historical bits downtown. There is actually a lot more history to Hawaii than Pearl Harbour and famous surfers, if you take the time to dig just a bit. A visit to the Iolani Palace will set the scene. It is an extremely impressive building and somewhat overshadows the present day State Capitol. The latter, completed in 1969 is known as a flat topped international style pavilion which is set in a shallow reflecting pool.

It was a BMW 650GS that was my 2 wheeled mode of transport that was the final piece in the jigsaw. Slightly underpowered and sounding like a frustrated sewing machine, in comparison to the big brother 1200 cc beast that had been my steed for the last 6 months, it was nevertheless pleasing to get astride a bike. It was BMW which was the main thing and as it turned out, the only one available for hire on the island. Fate had turned a kind hand and I was able to tick that final box of riding a BMW in every US state. Thank you. Just as refreshing was the euphoria of getting out of the Waikiki melting pot of traffic and people, in search of the real Hawaii. I hadn't done any serious planning for this jaunt which turned out to be a 130 miles anti clockwise circuit of the island. Once clear of Honolulu and established on the coastal road, early morning showers quickly cleared, revealing unlimited views of steep cliffs and the morning surf crashing onto the almost deserted beaches. North of Kaneohe, the island gets much much better and a beach retreat in or close by Kahaluu, Kaaawa or Hauula could be appealing. The fuel tank of this bike is miniscule and whilst refuelling at Laie, I got my first sighting and communication with real Hawaiians. They were girls in their early twenties serving in the fuel station and café. Unfortunately, they were reluctant to engage in any conversation other than niceties when dispatching my change. I desperately wanted to question a local and get comments on the state of the nation and the state of Hawaii. It could wait. Over lunch in Kawela Bay at the top of the island, I did meet someone who was not backward at coming forward. Graham McDonald from Australia, along with his English wife, were also taking in the island for a couple of days, prior to heading off elsewhere in the Pacific. It was still hard to comprehend I was on American territory in the middle of the Pacific Ocean, with Indonesia and Australia in easy reach to the south west. So close to that part of the world, naturally the Hawaiian chain is a popular stomping ground for the Aussies, as well as Japanese and Koreans. After Kawela, this little ride around the island was quickly running out. At Haleiwa, it was a left turn down the middle of the island, passing muddy pineapple plantations and quickly the rural tranquillity switched to an 'interstate' type highway. Yes a busy highway, for the final run into the metropolis. The highway was 'H1' and with H2, H3 and H201 completing the set around the island, a map isn't really required even for the most geographically challenged biker. All that remained was a few photographs with the bike back at the dealers, which really drew a line under this adventure and now I had a feeling of completion. The real journeys end was upon me.

Lunch and a walk around the bustling Honolulu China town didn't provide any Hawaiian interview opportunities. However, not all the market vendors were Chinese. I engaged with Marilyn, who had the most strange accented English and sold the best bananas around. Marilyn turned out to be from the tiny island group of the Republic of Palau, way past Guam and close to the Philippines. Palau got its independence in the early nineties and must be one of the youngest, if not smallest nations. Palau enjoys an association with the USA, however, on reflection, I am rather glad it is not the 51st state. A trek another couple of thousand miles south west from Hawaii, may just have been a journey too far. I cornered my 'real' Hawaiian back in the hotel and was extremely interested in his comments and views about being American. Although he was a young man and had been born an American, family generations before him still felt strongly about what was on their passport today. They were striving to achieve some sort of recognition to being from Hawaiian heritage and not the mainland USA. Independence of course would be marvellous and that's what a lot of the 'die hards' dream for. But that would be in an ideal world and today with the gargantuan American infrastructure around the place, from tourist resorts to an assortment of military bases, that would never happen. The islands are well and truly entrenched into America. Nothing will change in my life time, as much as a select band of 'original stock' and token activists mutter in the shadows about independence. It wouldn't be affordable for starters. I kept my views to myself and didn't share them with my rather open interviewee. Let's face it, if you roll out the map and look at the global picture before you, Hawaii is an extremely strategic location to be under the auspices of the USA. Including the acquisition of Alaska, the Americans have gathered some useful territories over the years.

Kasatochi had exhausted eruptions over the last couple of days, leaving flight paths clear of ash. That allowed an uninterrupted and comfortable direct flight back into a cool and cloudy Anchorage. All that remained was some fond farewells to my hosts, leaving Europe very much on my mind. Journeys end.

Part Eleven – … and Finally

Chapter 79

... and what about these strangers?

'They are over paid, over sexed and over here'. Wasn't that the tag that was attached to the American airmen when they moved into many an English village as their Air Force joined the Second World War? But wasn't this the start point of when Europeans really got to know the modern American? After the war and as the 50s and 60s unfolded, America became the land of opportunity. Everything was big, big cars, big roads, big homes, big fridges and big food. Fuel was cheap and a complacency undoubtedly set in. A complacency of 'we want' and 'we get'. Isn't that about right? So, to some of the global population, Americans got the personality identities of being brash, garish, rude, ignorant, arrogant and greedy. Yes, greedy, we want we get. Some say that they are a blinkered race. I even had adverse comments from a Brit who has lived in the USA since the 1970s. His descriptive vocabulary had not mellowed throughout his 30 years immersion in the country. I remember his words well, where his descriptives peaked with arrogant and parochial. But are all these barbed comments really fair? Aren't they from geographically challenged Europeans, who have never seen the Atlantic Ocean, never mind having set foot in the USA? They probably formulate their short sighted opinions after seeing a group of loud Americans in a tour group in their home patch. I agree, groups of American tourists can be over powering, but do their characteristics represent the nation? Should we or I, use the words friendly, kind, open and helpful. Having given the 50 states a close inspection over the last 7 months, I think I have a rational complexion of this mighty country and burgeoning population. Albeit I sometimes hear the usual comments thrown around from Brits and Europeans, they are typically from people who have never dangled their passport into the pot pourri of the USA. I do agree, some American invitational exuberance, can place them in almost unachievable scenarios. 'Drop by, you can have the world and I will provide it for you'. Thankfully the majority of American invitations I received came to enjoyable fruition. Particularly noteworthy was the chance meeting with Jim Trovato in Stone Mountain, Georgia, after which a proliferation of en route connections materialised. It's good to talk. I agree, my extensive journey and mode of transport may have generated a bit more interest from the locals, but if I was from China travelling on a push bike, or an extrovert student pushing a fridge through the 50 states, I am sure I would have been treated in the same cordial manner.

And what about this accent thing? I had been identified frequently as an Australian. It was good fun at first, but quickly wore thin, especially with plenty of national identity evidence around person and bike. Alas, some folk didn't even recognise the Union Flag! Many didn't check where I was from, but simply assumed I was Australian. 'He doesn't sound American, so he must be from Australia!' It would have been nice for them to say, 'a ha, he's not from America so he must be from Britain'. I am afraid not and at times I felt like unfolding a large map and giving the occasional en-route roadside geography lesson. But whilst accepting that Americans are not good with accents, having thought long and hard, I failed to come up with an answer to explain why the majority of the population didn't recognise my very Brit tones. So maybe, just maybe, if Americans don't recognise a stranger's accent, they become confused and instantly assume Australia has invaded. But can we ever mistake an American for anyone else?

Throughout my journey, I was convinced I was under surveillance from time to time. Even though I have an extremely credible background and a ten year visa, I frequently had unusual occurrences providing supporting evidence to my assumption. What is my foundation for this? Well, we all know that America is paranoid about home security, especially after the appalling attacks on New York's Twin Towers-9/11. Since then the world of travel and screening of travellers in and out of the USA has changed from casual to severe. I recall my visa processing in London was formal and efficient, but I was asked many questions about the trip, it was "why why why, why are you doing this. I want to know why you can take a year off work and isn't your trip simply dangerous and unachievable? I remember the interview very well. I reminded the interviewer that crossing a street in London is dangerous, especially with all those buses around. Anything can be dangerous in life if you are not careful. Maybe he was a little envious, but his final words of, 'visa approved, best of luck because you damn well need it', were a little harsh. Who knows where my paper work went next and who, what, where got alerted about my expedition. But with rational analysis, I could understand suspicions. Who takes a year off work and takes a US capital city journey? What is this guy doing? Is he gathering any information, is he gathering any intelligence, could there be a chain of security embellishments about to happen throughout the USA? Especially in a Presidential Election year. I had been accused of suffering from 'cabin fever' by a few folk. I am in my own world and that's when the mind can work over time with little logical and rational thought. But no, I always kept an open mind and was always out of my cabin in fresh air. My personality prevents such introvert characteristics and every day I was talking to strangers. Rest assured USA, that my intentions were completely honourable and all that I was gathering were photographs and statistics to satisfy an ambition I set earlier in life.

My journey coincided with the Presidential Election. This was not planned, but made for an interesting sub-theme whilst connecting the capitals. I did feel I got to know the main characters of the political show. Their smiles, their nuances and the repeated words that filled their speeches on a daily basis. Down to basics, it was the real live people, the real simple working population that it was such a pleasure to meet. They made this journey so enjoyable. It wasn't just a motorcycle journey, it was a demographic and geographical extravaganza, through a country rich with opportunities to explore these two themes. My real people experiences were an extremely rich cocktail that maintained a vibrant fizz to the end of the glass. I recall meeting that young single Mother in a diner in rural Mississippi. She was striving to make ends meet, earning I am sure the minimum wage and admitted to having never left her state. But it was her honesty and a friendly smile that said a thousand words. Then there was the veteran Marine pilot I met in an Amarillo bar. He openly recounted when he was shot up badly by an enemy missile which spoiled his day and ended his flying career so abruptly in the 60s. I shouldn't forget the teacher in the small Indiana town I passed through on the way to Indianapolis. She was very candid about having and keeping a good job in the unstable economic period. To the non critical eye, the local area was a rich agricultural land, awash with expensive looking ranches and vehicles out the front. The teacher firmly identified this may be a façade to the traveller and only the minority have the luxury of land and farm. The majority of the local population were struggling, on the poverty line and even classed as poor. Can you believe that, poor people in America? I could go on and on, but the same underlying theme always surfaced with the many Americans I met throughout the 50 states. They are all striving to achieve freedom and independence. Most acknowledge that the USA may not be the superpower of decades past. Most want a stable economy and the ability to put food on the table, keep their job and plan their next holiday.

If you take the time to peer through the vast veneer of the USA, which I certainly had and did, I think those hostile adjectives I used to describe Americans at the beginning of this chapter, should be erased. The nation's population has mellowed and matured. Yes some can still be described as parochial and internationally lacking, but garish, brash, rude, ignorant, arrogant and greedy may now be unfair. Can't we say that about any population? Maybe it's the sheer volume of people in the USA that has encouraged such sweeping descriptives. 'A nice country, shame about the people', is I think considerably unfair. My detailed analysis of the strangers I met, mainly revealed a friendly, kind, hospitable and helpful population. They are great innovators, problem solvers and entrepreneurs. After all, we mustn't forget the average American is very fond of the average Brit.

Chapter 80

Becoming a '50 Stater'

This is the chapter I have been looking forward to putting down in print. Many many times whilst in the seat on many a road, I would ponder the final words of this gargantuan journey. Well, the time is now here. The football game is over and I have won.

So where do I start to sum up my geographical experiences of the United States of America? Becoming a *'fifty stater'* means so much to me. My choice of bike was spot on and the reliable German machine was undoubtedly a healthy contribution to successful completion. It just kept on going and going. As reported so often, even though my carefully researched route progressed north through the continent in layers, coinciding with the seasons unfolding to my benefit, the weather was always my main challenge and threat. From twister to gales to torrential rain, from super cool temperatures and ice, to scorching and sizzling conditions, you name it, I saw it, experienced it and luckily endured it. But how did I endure it? It was easy and I used modern tools. GPS and laptop. Simple. My modern electronics were my support team. Overall, I was a little surprised about the poor condition of the roads, but quickly got used to them and having the right bike for the job, helped my cause. The roads are certainly not all smooth as silk with mile after mile of pristine asphalt as we may see from the movies. No, ruts, bumps and a plethora of seasonal construction, are always out there to catch the unprepared. It's a big country to maintain and the weather must have a huge impact on the condition of the road surfaces. Not forgetting the masses of traffic surging north, south, east and west on the comprehensive network of interstates, highways, beltways and urban circulars. Not all roads were bad and I encountered a lot of fantastic surfaces here and there. Americans get quite sentimental about some of their roads. Some get notoriety and go down in history. Route 66 comes immediately to mind and I particularly enjoyed riding a section around Amarillo in Texas. It was known as the 'Mother of all Roads', alas it is no longer categorized as a modern highway and exists only in portions here and there marked with historical brown signs. Then the Pacific Coast Highway! Just reading those 3 words conjures up all sorts of images. It does for me anyways, although I have had the pleasure of riding those sweeping, climbing and descending delicious curves, flanked by the deep blues of the crashing Pacific on one side and the dark green afforested valleys on the other. And how about the 'Going to the Sun Highway', that transports you through Glacial National Park in North West Montana? Ohh Montana and this park were like heaven, I was in a different world, on a different planet and riding that highway was a high point. I could go on and wax lyrical about similar asphalt treats along the way. The Interstate is also held in high motorist repute from place to place. 'You can do it in a one shot on I-80' 'Are you using I-70 that way?' The advice and comments were continuous. Purpose designed and built to get the traveller across the country and into urban nerve centres, I did actually enjoy using the Interstate from time to time. If I needed to get somewhere quickly, it was the obvious choice. If I needed to avoid bad weather and flooding on country roads, the interstate would do it. The interstate served its part in getting me through the journey. As the journey matured, and although I purposely avoided them, sometimes, I had no option and an Interstate got me somewhere quickly and efficiently and maybe ahead of pursuing inclement weather. I recall 2 chunks of Interstate that stick in my mind. I-40 west of Amarillo and I-80 east from Salt Lake City are particularly memorable carving through impressive geography.

As I used them to navigate my way west, east, north and south through the nation, what about the state capital cities? To give them a top fifty ranking maybe difficult and could be unfair. I saw some on good days and some on bad days. Some were swamped in bad weather, some out of season and some absolutely delightful. So where do I start? I thought a top five would be a good idea. So my top 5 are Raleigh-North Carolina, Cheyenne-Wyoming, Madison-Wisconsin, Boise-Idaho and Juneau-Alaska. Why isn't Austin-Texas in there, what about Nashville? You must have missed Boston. No, I didn't miss any of the 50 and had a few general rules that I used for my capital city barometer. Since it gets so many accolades as being a cool place, Austin was closed the few days I was there. I thought I would get that in quickly. As for the burgeoning urban centres that are state capitals, I dismissed them straight away in the contest. So that takes out the Phoenix's, Boston's Nashville's and similar. I preferred the smaller capitals which always had more character. Raleigh, because it was the first capital of that description that I encountered. Compact, cosy and friendly and close to the Smoky Mountains, the North Carolina capital was an enjoyable spot. Cheyenne because it was rustic, unpretentious and extremely welcoming after a 500 mile ride from Salt Lake City. I hit the university capital of Madison in mid summer and was bowled over by the striking Capitol Building on the hill, with bar and restaurant outfitted roads spoking off in many directions. It was also the unique setting of the Wisconsin capital on the elevated isthmus, which added to the enjoyable 2 day cocktail. Then Boise, another friendly and unassuming capital with a great cosmopolitan feel. It was perhaps the mystic of this little place on the edge of the high desert in the physically diverse state of Idaho that capped it all. Finally, Juneau, yes little old Juneau of Alaska, way down in the states inside passage. Juneau was number 49 on my trail and hence actually getting there and 'ticking off' the final ride into a state capital, helped choose this place. The unique marine setting and nearby mountains and huge glaciers undoubtedly promoted this capital into my USA premier league. That's my top 5, however, every capital was different and interesting. Even Jackson Mississippi had its moments! As for my favourite state, west is best!

The journey was both cerebral and physical. It was like managing a huge game of risk, simultaneous to climbing Mount Everest. From the many hours planning in the evenings, to the many long and weary days on USA hardtop, it was the Mother of all road trips! What is for sure, after I have had time to reflect and draw breath, I am always on this journey. I am always on the road in the USA. A day never goes by, when I am not reliving the excellent, good, bad and ugly of the USA. From coast to coast, from urban monster to city to town, from National Park to towering mountain ranges to the wide open windy Great Plains and hot arid high desert, there is so much to remember from the kaleidoscopic geography of the United States of America. As a grand finale and a recap, here is one final sentence, one final statement from my geographical experience whilst Talking to Strangers, a motorcycle ride through the fifty states of the United States of America. Take a deep breath and hang on tightly.....

Beginnings were in humid Florida, followed by cool runnings down the gulf coast into Louisiana and Huey Long's Capitol, then after Austin Texas came Mississippi, Alabama and laid back Georgia and prior to the Carolinas a coastal diversion to Savannah and Charleston were followed by Columbia and Raleigh and then the first big push west, west into the Smoky Mountains, the city of music in Tennessee and onwards to Arkansas, Oklahoma and then the land turned red in Amarillo and Santa Fe New Mexico was such a delight, next came red hot Arizona, followed by desert, mountains, forests and the glorious Pacific Coast of impressive California, tiny Carson City in Nevada only got a day, Vegas got 2 and then Utah turned out to be the best kept secret in the Union, a state packed with red rock surprises, then it was the big east through the guts of the country starting in the cowboy capital of Cheyenne Wyoming and accelerating across the Rockies through Colorado, descending into the Great Plains of Nebraska, prior to a pin ball run through the agricultural heartland states of Kansas, Iowa and Missouri, before forging east through Illinois, Indiana, the blue grass of Kentucky, are you keeping up, leading into Ohio, West Virginia and Virginia, not quite on the east coast and then into Maryland and a dash through Delaware after DC diversions, followed by Pennsylvania, New Jersey, New York, Connecticut, delightful Rhode Island and continuing north into Massachusetts via Cape Cod,

New Hampshire and then Maine lobster finished the north east after which west into Vermont I went and keeping south of the Great Lakes into Michigan, across 70 miles of water into Milwaukee Wisconsin and further west for the twin cities of Minnesota, are you still there, and on through the Dakotas and into Montana, ohhhhhhhh Montana what a heavenly place, followed by delightful Idaho, west is best for me, and finally Oregon and Washington State put the lower 48 in the bag, after which it was a long haul north through beautiful British Columbia and Yukon, a cruise down the Alaskan Marine Highway and into number 49, little old Juneau Alaska and if not enough, another ferry and another couple of thousand miles and journeys end in isolated Anchorage, leaving a long hop across the Pacific to the Aloha State, completing the 50 with a well earned cocktail in Honolulu, Hawaii and full stop, Amen, time to put the feet up with a cool beer and reflect.

So there you are, the United States of America in one sentence! I hope you were right there with me! After such a mammoth journey and so much of the tremendous geography in my view finder for over 6 months, just how does the USA figure in my international league? A difficult question. I am a global centurion. Through working, living, holidaying and week end hopping, I have visited over 100 countries. From the metropolitan monsters of London, Sydney, Sao Paulo and Mexico City, to all points of the European compass, to the sweaty jungles of Central America, to the isolated and chilled islands off the Scottish Coast and way down in the South Atlantic Ocean, not forgetting the scorched deserts of Namibia and Mongolia and the remote steppe of Kazakhstan, my passport has been around the worldwide block once or twice. The moon has so far evaded me. How on earth, yes very apt words, how on earth can I give the USA a rating? Albeit it's an 'in your face' type of country and you either love it or hate it, it seems to have everything a traveller desires. Well, I love it, so lets put it this way, the United States of America is not my favourite country, but it's in my top one !!

The End

Nick Gilroy
York
England
2 Jan 2013

Complete Bike Log

The Full Journey Log

State capital cities numbered and highlighted

DATE	START	FINISH	MILEAGE	CUMULATIVE	COMMENTS
2 Feb			15	-	Delivery Mileage
3 Feb	Fort Myers FL	Fort Myers FL	62	77	Familiarisation
5 Feb	Fort Myers FL	Key West FL	265	342	Run In
6 Feb	Key West FL	Key Largo FL	103	445	Run In
7 Feb	Key Largo FL	Fort Myers FL	172	617	Run In
8 Feb	Fort Myers FL	Fort Myers FL	10	627	**1st Service @ Gulf Coast Motorcycles-FM & test ride**
9 Feb	Fort Myers FL	Crystal River FL	201	828	Via Homosassa
10 Feb	Crystal River FL	**Tallahassee FL (1)**	164	992	
11 Feb	Tallahassee FL	Tallahassee FL	29	1021	Local City Ride
12 Feb	Tallahassee FL	Pensacola FL	192	1213	I-10
12 Feb	Pensacola FL	Pensacola FL	40	1253	Naval Aviation Museum at Pensacola NAS
13 Feb	Pensacola FL	**Baton Rouge LA (2)**	247	1500	I-10
15 Feb	Baton Rouge LA	Beaumont TX	190	1690	I-10
17 Feb	Beaumont TX	**Austin TX (3)**	247	1937	InterState + USA 290
19 Feb	Austin TX	Nacogdoches TX	247	2184	USA 79 & 7
20 Feb	Nacogdoches TX	**Jackson MS (4)**	355	2539	USA21/87/I-55

DATE	START	FINISH	MILEAGE	CUMULATIVE	COMMENTS
23 Feb	Jackson MS	**Montgomery AL (5)**	255	2794	I-20 & US80
24 Feb	Montgomery AL	Montgomery AL	30	2824	City & local-Day
24 Feb	Montgomery AL	Montgomery AL	8	2832	
25 Feb	Montgomery AL	Stone Mountain GA	174	3006	Stone Mountain for **Atlanta GA (6)**
25 Feb	Stone Mountain GA	Stone Mountain GA	5	3011	Local & Fuel
29 Feb	Stone Mountain GA	Savannah GA	260	3271	I-16
29 Feb	Savannah GA	Savannah GA	19	3290	Local
Feb Total				3290	
01 Mar	Savannah GA	Savannah GA	50	3340	Toynbee Island & rtn
02 Mar	Savannah GA	Charleston SC	119	3459	I-95/US17
05 Mar	Charleston SC	**Columbia SC (7)**	119	3578	Interstate
05 Mar	Columbia SC	Columbia SC	35	3613	Columbia City & local
06 Mar	Columbia SC	Concord NC	112	3725	Interstate network
06 Mar	Concord NC	Concord NC	11	3736	Local recce Speedway Blvd
07 Mar	Concord NC	**Raleigh NC (8)**	165	3901	I-85/I-40/US1
09 Mar	Raleigh NC	Summersfield NC	155	4056	US158
10 Mar	Summersfield NC	Summersfield NC	80	4136	Local & dog search
11 Mar	Summersfield NC	Asheville NC	174	4310	US158 & I-40
11 Mar	Asheville NC	Asheville NC	7	4317	
12 Mar	Ashville NC	**Nashville TN (9)**	319	4636	US19/US441/I-40
16 Mar	Nashville TN	**Little Rock AR (10)**	357	4993	I-40
20 Mar	Little Rock AR	**Oklahoma City OK (11)**	350	5343	I-40
22 Mar	Oklahoma City OK	Amarillo TX	250	5593	I-40
22 Mar	Amarillo TX	Amarillo TX	15	5608	Local & Route 66
24 Mar	Amarillo TX	Amarillo TX	130	5738	Palo Duro Canyon & local Amarillo
25 Mar	Amarillo TX	**Santa Fe NM (12)**	282	6020	I-40 & US 285
25 Mar	Santa Fe NM	Santa Fe NM	14	6034	Local City
27 Mar	Santa Fe NM	Farmington NM	224	6258	US 84/64
27 Mar	Farmington NM	Farmington NM	15	6273	Local City
28 Mar	Farmington NM	Sedona AZ	380	6653	US64/160/163/89
29 Mar	Sedona AZ	Sedona AZ	79	6732	Local area & Jerome
30 Mar	Sedona AZ	Chandler AZ	131	6863	I-17 & link road
31 Mar	Chandler AZ	Chandler AZ	97	6960	**Phoenix AZ (13)** & Chandler local area

DATE	START	FINISH	MILEAGE	CUMULATIVE	COMMENTS
March Total				**3670**	
1 April	Chandler AZ	Chandler AZ	12	6972	**Bike 6K service CHANDLER BMW & local**
2 April	Chandler AZ	Chandler AZ	17	6989	Chandler local
3 April	Chandler AZ	Chandler AZ	93	7082	Cave Creek & return
4 April	Chandler AZ	Chandler AZ	20	7102	Local & airfield
5 April	Chandler AZ	San Diego CA	353	7455	US237/I-8
6 April	San Diego CA	San Diego CA	33	7488	City & Beach local
7 April	San Diego CA	Santa Barbara CA	215	7703	I-5/PCH
8 April	Santa Barbara CA	Santa Barbara CA	38	7741	Mountains & local
9 April	Santa Barbara CA	Monterey CA	250	7991	Route 1 & The Big Sur
10 April	Monterey CA	Monterey CA	142	8133	Carmel Valley-Carmel/Monterey & local area
11 April	Monterey CA	Half Moon Bay CA	137	8270	Via Gilroy & Santa Cruz-via US 1
12 April	Half Moon Bay CA	Mill Valley CA	46	8316	Golden Gate Bridge
12 April	Mill Valley CA	Mill Valley CA	26	8342	Local & coastal route 1
13 April	Mill Valley CA	Mill Valley CA	39	8381	San Francisco & Golden Gate Bridge areas.
14 April	Mill Valley CA	Santa Rosa CA	46	8427	US101 north
15 April	Santa Rosa CA	**Sacramento CA (14)**	90	8517	Nappa Valley
16 April	Sacramento CA	Tahoe City CA	131	8648	US50 & 89
16 April	Tahoe City CA	Tahoe City	33	8681	Lake Tahoe scenic ride & local area.
17 April	Tahoe City CA	**Carson City NV (15)**	40	8721	US27 & 50
18 April	Carson City NV	Oakhurst CA	267	8988	US88 & Yosemite National Park
20 April	Oakhurst CA	Oakhurst CA	87	9075	Local south Yosemite area
21 April	Oakhurst CA	Lone Pine CA	320	9395	41/178/14/395
22 April	Lone Pine CA	Lone Pine CA	90	9485	Sierra Nevada area
23 April	Lone Pine CA	Las Vegas NV	220	9705	Via Death Valley
24 April	Las Vegas NV	Las Vegas NV	27	9732	**New tyres @ Las Vegas BMW**
25 April	Las Vegas NV	Mt Carmel UT	200	9932	I-15/ US9 & 89
27 April	Mt Carmel UT	Mt Carmel UT	127	10059	Zion NP & local canyon areas

DATE	START	FINISH	MILEAGE	CUMULATIVE	COMMENTS
28 April	Mt Carmel UT	Torrey UT	250	10309	Via Bryce & Capitol Reef NPs. Scenic route 12
29 April	Torrey UT	Torrey UT	98	10407	Capitol Reef NP & local area.
30 April	Torrey UT	**Salt Lake City UT (16)**	243	10650	us24/72/10/31/89 & I-15
April Total				**3690**	
2 May	Salt Lake City UT	Salt Lake City UT	60	10710	Alta & Snowbird Ski Resorts.
3 May	Salt Lake City UT	**Cheyenne WY (17)**	442	11152	I-80
4 May	Cheyenne WY	Cheyenne WY	20	11172	Local area
5 May	Cheyenne WY	Cheyenne WY	20	11192	Local area
6 May	Cheyenne WY	Estes Park CO	93	11285	I-25 & US34
6 May	Estes Park CO	Estes Park CO	46	11331	Rocky Mountain Park
7 May	Estes park CO	**Denver CO (18)**	61	11392	US36/92
7 May	Denver CO	Denver CO	30	11422	City & local
9 May	Denver CO	**Lincoln NE (19)**	501	11923	I-70/I-76/I-80
11 May	Lincoln NE	Lincoln NE	76	11999	SAC aerospace museum//Lincoln & local area
13 May	Lincoln NE	Omaha NE	45	12044	**12K service-BMW Omaha NE**
13 May	Omaha NE	Lincoln NE	45	12089	Rtn to Linc only
14 May	Lincoln NE	**Topeka KS (20)**	167	12256	US75
14 May	Topeka KS	Topeka KS	21	12277	Topeka local
15 May	Topeka KS	**Des Moines IA (21)**	271	12548	Kansas & Interstates
15 May	Des Moines IA	Des Moines IA	27	12575	City & local
16 May	Des Moines IA	**Jefferson City MO (22)**	283	12858	Scenic route 63
17 May	Jefferson City MO	Jefferson City MO	5	12863	City & Capitol
17 May	Jefferson City MO	St Charles MO	117	12980	Lewis & Clark trail route US94
17 May	St Charles MO	St Charles MO	12	12992	Historic town area
18 May	St Charles MO	St Charles MO	53	13045	St Louis-Gateway Arch & St Charles
19 May	St Charles MO	**Springfield IL (23)**	111	13156	I-55
19 May	Springfield IL	Springfield IL	13	13169	Local & City
20 May	Springfield IL	Springfield IL	23	13192	Local & City
21 May	Springfield IL	**Indianapolis IN (24)**	200	13392	Route 36

DATE	START	FINISH	MILEAGE	CUMULATIVE	COMMENTS
21 May	Indianapolis IN	Indianapolis IN	13	13405	Local & City
22 May	Indianapolis IN	Indianapolis IN	20	13425	Local & City
23 May	Indianapolis IN	**Frankfort KY (25)**	163	13588	US31/7/214
23 May	Frankfort KY	Frankfort KY	15	13603	Local & City
24 May	Frankfort KY	Aberdeen OH	108	13711	US460/68
25 May	Aberdeen OH	**Columbus OH (26)**	112	13823	US62
25 May	Columbus OH	Columbus OH	9	13832	Local & City
28 May	Columbus OH	**Charleston WV (27)**	165	13997	US23/35
29 May	Charleston WV	**Richmond VA (28)**	311	14308	I-64
30 May	Richmond VA	Richmond VA	7	14315	Local & City
31 May	Richmond VA	Laurel MD	138	14453	I-95
May Total				**3803**	
2 June	Laurel MD	**Annapolis MD (29)**	28	14481	32/I-97
2 June	Annapolis MD	Laurel MD	27	14508	I-97/32
3 June	Laurel MD	**Harrisburg PA (30)**	102	14610	I-95/695/I-93
3 June	Harrisburg PA	Leola PA	43	14653	30
3 June	Leola PA	Laurel PA	118	14771	30/I95/695
5 June	Laurel MD	**Dover DE (31)**	94	14865	301/302
5 June	Dover DE	Laurel MD	94	14959	302/301
6 June	Laurel MD	Chantilly VA	50	15009	Washington Beltway
6 June	Chantilly VA	Laurel MD	50	15059	Washington Beltway
8 June	Laurel MD	Hightstown NJ	164	15223	NJTP
8 June	Hightstown NJ	Belmar NJ	37	15260	33/ocean front drive
8 June	Belmar NJ	Hightstown	37	15297	33
9 June	Hightstown NJ	**Trenton NJ (32)**	21	15318	33
9 June	Trenton NJ	Hightstown NJ	21	15339	33
9 June	Hightstown NJ	Phoenicia NY	174	15513	206/I-287 & I-87
10 June	Phoenicia NY	**Albany NY (33)**	88	15601	28/42/23/I-87 Catskill drive
10 June	Albany NY	Albany NY	10	15611	Local & City
11 June	Albany NY	**Hartford CT (34)**	141	15752	I-90/I-91
11 June	Hartford CT	Hartford CT	20	15772	Local & City
12 June	Hartford CT	Newport RI	91	15863	134 rural route. Newport for access to **Providence (35)**
12 June	Newport RI	Newport RI	30	15893	Ocean drive, city & local

DATE	START	FINISH	MILEAGE	CUMULATIVE	COMMENTS
14 June	Newport RI	Provincetown MA	139	16032	Day on Cape Cod
14 June	Provincetown MA	Marlborough MA	139	16171	I-495
15 June	Marlborough MA	**Boston MA (36)**	43	16214	1-495 & MTP
15 June	Boston MA	Marlborough MA	42	16256	MTP & I-495
16 June	Marlborough MA	**Concord NH (37)**	79	16335	I-495/3
16 June	Concord NH	Concord NH	8	16343	Local & City
17 June	Concord NH	**Augusta ME (38)**	142	16485	202 rural route
17 June	Augusta ME	Augusta ME	11	16496	Local & City
18 June	Augusta ME	**Montpelier VT (39)**	202	16698	Scenic route 27 & 2
19 June	Montpelier VT	Sackets Harbor NY	219	16917	Lake Champlain Ferry/route 3 west
20 June	Sackets Harbour NY	Erie PA	315	17232	Lake Ontario & Erie- Shore Scenic Highway
21 Jun	Erie PA	**Lansing MI (40)**	330	17562	Multi Interstate
22 Jun	Lansing MI	Lansing MI	45	17607	Local & city & Potterville
23 Jun	Lansing MI	Muskegon MI	100	17707	To Ferry Port for Lake Michigan Lake crossing.
23 Jun	Milwaukee WI	Huntley IL	100	17807	Various highways
24 Jun	Huntley WI	**Madison WI (41)**	105	17912	County roads & Interstate
25 Jun	Madison WI	Appleton WI	105	18017	151
26 Jun	Appleton WI	De Pere WI	25	18042	**18K service & new tyres @ NICK's BMW De Pere WI**
26 Jun	De Pere WI	Appleton WI	25	18067	
27 Jun	Appleton WI	**St Paul MN (42)**	288	18355	Route 10
27 Jun	St Paul MN	Minneapolis MN	7	18362	University Blvd
28 Jun	Minneapolis MN	Minneapolis MN	1	18363	Fuel & Beer run-city
29 Jun	Minneapolis MN	**Pierre SD (43)**	402	18765	169/99/14
June Total				**4312**	
1 Jul	Pierre SD	**Bismarck ND (44)**	207	18972	83
2 Jul	Bismarck ND	Malta MT	419	19391	I-94/200S/200/24/ 2
3 Jul	Malta MT	St Mary MT	282	19676	2/89
4 Jul	St Mary MT	Missoula MT	210	19886	2/93 VIA Glacier National Park
5 Jul	Missoula MT	**Helena MT (45)**	114	20000	I-90 & 12
5 Jul	Helena MT	Helena MT	20	20020	City & Local
6 Jul	Helena MT	Gardiner MT	180	20200	12/89

DATE	START	FINISH	MILEAGE	CUMULATIVE	COMMENTS
6 Jul	Gardiner MT	Mammoth Hot Springs WY	7	20207	Yellowstone Visitors Centre & local area recce
6 Jul	Mammoth Hot Springs WY	Gardiner MT	7	20214	
7 Jul	Gardiner MT	Jackson Hole WY	165	20379	237/191/22 via Yellowstone & Teton Parks
8 Jul	Jackson Hole WY	**Boise ID (46)**	348	20727	22/33/31/26/20/I-84 Via Craters of the Moon NP
11 Jul	Boise ID	Chemult OR	374	21101	20
12 Jul	Chemult OR	Yachats OR	335	21436	Via Crater Lake NP &101 Oregon Pacific Highway
13 Jul	Yachats OR	**Salem OR (47)**	106	21542	101/22
13 Jul	Salem OR	McMinnville OR	27	21569	County roads
13 Jul	McMinnville OR	Salem OR	27	21596	County roads
15 Jul	Salem OR	**Olympia WA (48)**	168	21764	I-5
16 Jul	Olympia WA	Fife WA	33	21797	**Oil & Filter change & safety check @**
16 Jul	Fife WA	Olympia WA	33	21830	**South Side BMW Fife WA**
18 Jul	Olympia WA	Mt Rainier WA	71	21901	County Roads to
18 Jul	Mt Rainier WA	Olympia WA	71	21972	View Mt Rainier
19 Jul	Olympia WA	Lynden WA	203	22175	Scenic coastal ride
20 Jul	Lynden WA	Lillooet BC	199	22374	1/99
21 Jul	Lillooet BC	Prince George BC	321	22695	99/97
22 Jul	Prince George BC	Dawson Creek BC	257	22952	97
23 Jul	Dawson Creek BC	Fort Nelson BC	286	23238	Alaskan Hwy
24 Jul	Fort Nelson BC	Watson lake YT	321	23559	Alaskan Hwy
25 Jul	Watson Lake YT	Whitehorse YT	279	23838	Alaskan Hwy
27 Jul	Whitehorse YT	Skagway AK	109	23947	S Klondyke Hwy
30 Jul	Auk Bay Ferry Terminal AK	**Juneau AK (49)**	16	23963	Glacier Highway Loop
July Total				**5198**	
1 Aug	Juneau AK	Juneau AK	61	24024	Glacier & local area
2 Aug	Juneau AK	Auk Bay Ferry Terminal AK	27	24051	City & local area
2 Aug	Haines Ferry Terminal AK	Haines AK	16	24067	Via Mud Bay Road
3 Aug	Haines AK	Haines AK	68	24135	Local scenic roads & State Parks

DATE	START	FINISH	MILEAGE	CUMULATIVE	COMMENTS
4 Aug	Haines AK	Beaver Creek YT	332	24467	Haines Hwy & Alaska Highway
5 Aug	Beaver Creek YT	Tok AK	112	24579	Alaska Highway
5 Aug	Tok AK	Tok AK	10	24589	City & Local
6 Aug	Tok AK	Anchorage AK	326	24915	Glen Hwy
7 Aug	Anchorage AK	Anchorage AK	48	24963	City & Local
8 Aug	Anchorage AK	Anchorage AK	23	24986	City & Local
9 Aug	Anchorage AK	Seward AK	125	25111	Scenic Routes
9 Aug	Seward AK	Hope AK	72	25183	Scenic Routes
9 Aug	Hope AK	Anchorage AK	87	25270	Scenic Routes
11 Aug	Anchorage AK	Anchorage AK	11	25281	Into storage at Classic Motion

State Abbreviation &
Most Popular State Nickname

Alabama	AL	Heart of Dixie State
Alaska	AK	The Last Frontier
Arizona	AZ	Grand Canyon State
Arkansas	AR	Land of Opportunity
California	CA	The Golden State
Colorado	CO	Centennial State
Connecticut	CT	Constitution State
Delaware	DE	The First State
Florida	FL	Sunshine State
Georgia	GA	Peach State
Hawaii	HI	Aloha State
Idaho	ID	Gem State
Illinois	IL	Prairie State
Indiana	IN	Hoosier State
Iowa	IA	Hawkeye State
Kansas	KS	Sunflower State
Kentucky	KY	Bluegrass State
Louisiana	LA	Pelican State
Maine	ME	Pine Tree State
Maryland	MD	Old Line State
Massachusetts	MA	The Bay State
Michigan	MI	Wolverine State
Minnesota	MN	Gopher State

Mississippi	MS	Magnolia State
Missouri	MO	Show Me State
Montana	MT	Treasure State
Nebraska	NE	Cornhusker State
Nevada	NV	Silver State
New Hampshire	NH	Granite State
New Jersey	NJ	Garden State
New Mexico	NM	Land of Enchantment
New York	NY	The Empire State
North Carolina	NC	Tar Heel State
North Dakota	ND	Peace Garden State
Ohio	OH	Buckeye State
Oklahoma	OK	Sooner State
Oregon	OR	Beaver State
Pennsylvania	PA	Keystone State
Rhode Island	RI	Ocean State
South Carolina	SC	Palmetto State
South Dakota	SD	Mount Rushmore State
Tennessee	TN	Volunteer State
Texas	TX	Lone Star State
Utah	UT	Beehive State
Vermont	VT	Green Mountain State
Virginia	VA	The Old Dominion
Washington	WA	Evergreen State
West Virginia	WV	Mountain State
Wisconsin	WI	Badger State
Wyoming	WY	Equality State
British Columbia	BC	
Yukon	YT	

About the author

Nick Gilroy was born and grew up in the English Lake District. Perhaps being surrounded by this spectacular landscape, was the catalyst for him to discover and explore similar places around the world and he very soon developed a 'wanderlust' approach to life. Through a combination of work and leisure, he has subsequently visited and travelled in over 100 countries. Recent projects have included working and living in Central Asia, The Gulf Countries, North Africa and the Russian Federation. When not professionally globetrotting and planning future motorcycle journeys, Nick lives in the delightful Roman City of York in North England. This is Nick's first book.